RECONCEPTUALIZING DEVELOPMENT IN THE GLOBAL INFORMATION AGE

RECONCEPTUALIZING DEVELOPMENT IN THE GLOBAL INFORMATION AGE

Edited by
MANUEL CASTELLS
AND
PEKKA HIMANEN

OXFORD
UNIVERSITY PRESS

OXFORD
UNIVERSITY PRESS

Great Clarendon Street, Oxford, OX2 6DP,
United Kingdom

Oxford University Press is a department of the University of Oxford.
It furthers the University's objective of excellence in research, scholarship,
and education by publishing worldwide. Oxford is a registered trade mark of
Oxford University Press in the UK and in certain other countries

First Edition published in 2014
Impression: 1

Published in the United States of America by Oxford University Press
198 Madison Avenue, New York, NY 10016, United States of America

British Library Cataloguing in Publication Data
Data available

Library of Congress Control Number: 2014939578

ISBN 978–0–19–871608–2

Printed in Great Britain by
Clays Ltd, St Ives plc

Contents

Contents

Acknowledgements

This book is not only a joint project of its international research team but we have been fortunate to be able to rely on the support of yet a larger group of people. We are grateful to all of them for all the intellectual interactions as well as the very important practical assistance. So many people have contributed that it is impossible to list everyone individually. Therefore we want to thank you all collectively before expressing our special thanks to the following key groups related to the final production of this book.

First, we want to thank the collaborators that have managed the whole research project underlying this volume. Our gratitude goes to Clelia Garciasalas and Reanna Martinez from the Annenberg School of Communication, University of Southern California, and to Noelia Diaz Lopez, from the Internet Interdisciplinary Institute, Universitat Oberta de Catalunya.

Second, we want to acknowledge the institutional or financial support to this project from the following: Annenberg School of Communication, University of Southern California; the Internet Interdisciplinary Institute, Universitat Oberta de Catalunya; the School of Information, University of California, Berkeley; the Academy of Finland; the Finnish Innovation Fund Sitra; the Finnish Agency for Innovation Tekes; and the Finnish Prime Minister's Office.

Third, we want to express our gratitude to the people who have helped with the first editing phase of the book. Our special thanks here go to Melody Van Wanzeele for her copyediting work and to Kristian London, Owen Witesman, and David Hackston for translating parts of Chapters 3 and 10.

And, finally, we want to express our warmest thank you to the whole team at Oxford University Press. It has been a real pleasure to cooperate with all of you with the highest professional rigor and passion. We want to express our special recognition to our editor David Musson for all his expert guidance throughout the process of publication of this book. And we want to extend the same recognition to all the others included in his OUP team, including

Acknowledgements

but not limited to our book editor Emma Slaughter, assistant editor Clare Kennedy, the marketing manager Ellen Carey, and the foreign rights group of Jennifer Child and Catherine Johnson-Gilbert (as well as Emma Gier). This book has been a result of a truly global network production: so thank you all!

List of Figures

Chapter 2

Chapter 3

Chapter 4

List of Figures

Chapter 6

Chapter 7

Chapter 8

List of Figures

Chapter 9

Chapter 10

List of Tables

Chapter 3

Chapter 4

Chapter 5

Chapter 6

Chapter 8

List of Tables

Chapter 9

Chapter 10

List of Contributors

Manuel Castells is University Professor and the Wallis Annenberg Chair in Communication Technology and Society at the University of Southern California, Los Angeles. He is also Professor Emeritus of Sociology and of City and Regional Planning, University of California, Berkeley, as well as Director of Research in the Department of Sociology, and Fellow of St John's College, University of Cambridge. He has been Professor and Director of the Internet Interdisciplinary Institute, Open University of Catalonia, Barcelona. He was Distinguished Visiting Professor at the Massachusetts Institute of Technology (2004–9), and Distinguished Visiting Professor at the Oxford Internet Institute, University of Oxford (2009–11). He has published 26 books, including the trilogy *The Information Age: Economy, Society and Culture* (1996–2003) and *Communication Power* (2009). He was a founding board member of the European Research Council and also of the European Commission's Institute of Innovation and Technology. He holds 18 Honorary Doctorates from universities around the world. He received the 2011 Erasmus Medal from Academia Europaea, the 2012 Holberg Memorial Prize from the Parliament of Norway, and the 2013 Balzan Prize from the Balzan Foundation.

Pekka Himanen is Professor at Aalto University in Helsinki (2005–14) and currently a Visiting Scholar at the University of California, Berkeley. He is one of the best-known researchers on the Information Age, whose books have been translated into over twenty languages. After obtaining his PhD in Philosophy from the University of Helsinki at the age of 20, Himanen moved to carry out research first in England and then in California (Stanford University and the University of California, Berkeley). The best-known publication of this research is his book *The Hacker Ethic and the Spirit of the Information Age* (2001). With Manuel Castells, Himanen has also co-authored the influential book *The Information Society and the Welfare State* (2002), which has been discussed worldwide in leading academic and political circles.

List of Contributors

Himanen's work has been recognized with several awards, such as the World Economic Forum's respected Global Leader for Tomorrow Award in 2003, and his appointment by the WEF as a Young Global Leader in 2005. Himanen has advised leading global organizations and corporations, from the United Nations to Silicon Valley companies. He is also a co-founder of the Global Dignity initiative with Crown Prince Haakon of Norway and John Hope Bryant, a member of President Obama's advisory council on financial capability; an initiative that operates in over fifty countries throughout the world. The Global Dignity initiative includes Nobel laureates Professor Amartya Sen, Archbishop Emeritus Desmond Tutu, and President Martti Ahtisaari of Finland, as well as Sir Richard Branson and Ambassador Andrew Young as its Honorary Board members. Himanen has given invited keynote speeches in leading international forums, including a talk to the CEOs of the world's 60 biggest information technology companies, and the concluding speech of the World Economic Forum meeting, jointly with Desmond Tutu.

AnnaLee Saxenian is Dean and Professor at the UC Berkeley School of Information. She is the author of the acclaimed *Regional Advantage: Culture and Competition in Silicon Valley and Route 128* (1994), which explains the innovative dynamism of Silicon Valley through a comparison with its East Coast counterpart. She currently serves as Chair of the Advisory Board for the National Science Foundation's Directorate on Social, Behavioral, and Economic Science. Saxenian's book, *The New Argonauts: Regional Advantage in a Global Economy* (2006), examines how immigrant engineers from Silicon Valley have transferred technology and entrepreneurship to emerging regions in their home countries, from Taiwan and Israel to China and India. Saxenian's other publications include *Silicon Valley's New Immigrant Entrepreneurs* (1999) and *Local and Global Networks of Immigrant Professionals in Silicon Valley* (2002), along with dozens of articles in refereed and popular journals. She holds a PhD in Political Science from MIT, a master's in Regional Planning from UC Berkeley, and a BA in Economics from Williams College, Massachusetts.

You-tien Hsing is Pamela P. Fong Family Distinguished Chair in China Studies and Professor of Geography at University of California, Berkeley. She is the author of *The Great Urban Transformation: Politics of Land and Property in China* (2010) and *Making Capitalism in China: The Taiwan Connection*

(1998), and co-editor of *Reclaiming Chinese Society: The New Social Activism* (2010). She holds a PhD in City and Regional Planning from the University of California, Berkeley.

Nico Cloete has been the full-time Director of the Centre for Higher Education and Transformation in Cape Town since 1997. He is also Extraordinary Professor of Higher Education, University of Western Cape; Visiting Professor, Masters Programme in Higher Education, University of Oslo; Honorary Research Fellow, University of Cape Town; and is a Director of the Centre for Higher Education Trust and Collaborating Partner in the Centre of Excellence in Scientometrics and STI Policy, Stellenbosch University. He was actively involved in academic staff organization and was President of the University of Witwatersrand Staff Association (1991–2) and General Secretary of the Union of Democratic University Staff Associations of South Africa (1993–4). He was the research director for the Nelson Mandela-appointed National Commission on Higher Education (1995–6) and served on the South African Ministerial Advisory Council for Universities. He initiated the Higher Education Research and Advocacy Network in Africa (HERANA) in 2009 and is the coordinator of this network. He has published widely in psychology, sociology, and higher education policy. His latest books are *Higher Education and Economic Development in Africa* (2011), and *Shaping the Future of South Africa's Youth: Rethinking Post School Education and Skills Training* (2012).

Alison Gillwald is Executive Director of Research ICT Africa, an ICT policy and regulatory think tank based in Cape Town, South Africa, which hosts an Africa-wide research network. She is also adjunct professor at the Management of Infrastructure Reform and Regulation Programme at the University of Cape Town Graduate School of Business. She served on the founding Council of the South African Telecommunications Regulatory Authority (SATRA) and the first Independent Broadcasting Authority prior to that. She has chaired the national Digital Broadcasting Advisory Task Team and served on the African Communications Ministers' Expert Panel. She has advised and been commissioned by regional bodies, governments, regulators, and competitions commissions on the continent, and multilateral agencies, including the African Development Bank, infoDev, the Commonwealth Telecommunication Organisation, the International Telecommunications Union and ICANN. She is widely published in the areas of telecommunications and broadcasting policy and regulation, gender, and political economy.

Isidora Chacón is Professor at the Master of Library Science of the University of Costa Rica. She has also been a professor at the National University of Costa Rica. She has been Director of Research of the Ministry of Education in Costa Rica, as well as Professor of Methodology at the Judicial School of the Costa Rican Judiciary. She has also been a researcher and policy advisor on human development as part of various international research teams, including the United Nations Development Program. She holds a master's in Sociology from the National University of Costa Rica and a doctorate in Education from La Salle University, Costa Rica.

Fernando Calderón is currently Director of the Program of Innovation, Development, and Multiculturalism at the National University of San Martín, in Buenos Aires, Argentina. In 2012–13 he was Professor and Research Fellow in the College d'Études Mondiales, Maison de Sciences de l'Homme, in Paris; in the Academia de Humanismo Cristiano, Santiago de Chile; and in the PhD Program in Social Sciences at the University of Córdoba, Argentina. He has been a professor at the Facultad Latinoamericana de Ciencias Sociales (FLACSO) in several countries, and at the following universities: the Universities of San Andres in La Paz and San Simón in Cochabamba, Bolivia; the Universities of Chile, Valparaíso, and of Alberto Hurtado, Santiago, Chile; the Open University of Catalonia in Barcelona; and the Universities of Austin, Chicago, Berkeley, and Cornell, in the United States of America. He has also lectured at several universities in Latin America, as well as in countries around in the world. He was Executive Secretary of the Latin American Social Science Council (CLACSO), Social Policy Advisor at the Economic Commission for Latin America and the Caribbean (ECLAC), and Special Advisor on Human Development and Governance in the United Nations Development Program (UNDP). He was Coordinator and Senior Advisor in ten Human Development Reports in various countries in Latin America, Europe, and Africa, and at sub-regional and global levels. He was Coordinator of the Program of Political Analysis and Prospect for Latin America (PAPEP). He is the author of 23 books on democracy, social movements, culture, and development, and coordinator and editor of another 30 books about these topics. In 2000 and 2002, the Human Development Report in Bolivia, which he coordinated, received the Award for the best Human

Development Report in the world. In 2008 he received a prize from the University of Chile for his contribution to Sociology. He has also been distinguished with the title of Honorary Professor by the University of San Simón in Cochabamba, Bolivia. He holds a master's in Sociology from the University of Chile, and a doctorate in Sociology from the École des Hautes Études en Sciences Sociales, Paris.

Introduction

Manuel Castells and Pekka Himanen

Development, in our view, is the process by which people, individually and collectively, enhance their capacities to improve their lives according to their values and interests, thus claiming their dignity as human beings. From this perspective, development is the overarching purpose of personal strategies and institutional policies. The conditions in which development operates have significantly changed in the Global Information Age—our age—a historical period characterized by the technological revolution in information and communication, the rise of the networking form of social organization, and the global interdependence of economies and societies (Castells 2000; Castells ed. 2004). This volume aims to redefine the means and goals of development in this new context, while taking into consideration the contributions of other scholars, (e.g. Sen 1999; Wilson 2004; Heeks 2006; Avgerou 2010; Walsham 2013; ul-Haq 1999; Stiglitz et al. 2009).

The intention of the analysis presented here is threefold: first, to characterize the specific mode of development—informational development—which we consider to be the driver of the creation of material wealth in the twenty-first century; second, to reconceptualize human development as the fulfillment of human wellbeing in the multidimensionality of the human experience, ultimately affirming dignity as the supreme value of development; third, to probe the relationship between informational development and human development, starting from one assumption and one hypothesis.

Manuel Castells and Pekka Himanen

The assumption is that the increase of material wealth does not necessarily lead to greater wellbeing, let alone to human dignity. This is for two main reasons: because the redistribution of wealth is usually uneven due to the control of resources by economic, cultural, and political power elites; and because people's wellbeing, individually and collectively, may result from values and beliefs that are different or contradictory with the values guiding the generation of material resources. The hypothesis at the source of the intellectual project presented in this volume is that there can be a synergistic relationship between informational development and human development. Namely, the resources obtained by the process of informational development are critical for the sustainability of human development in all its dimensions, including environmental sustainability, equity, and liberty.

In return, human development may feed back into informational development, thus enhancing the productivity of the production process characteristic of this mode of development. This is because informational development ultimately results from the increasing capacity of humans to create and innovate while reducing negative externalities in the ecosystem and in the social system. This capacity is a function of the betterment of human life, both in its material condition (health, education, habitat, amenities of everyday life, environmental quality, cultural creation, communication potential), and in its ethical and political component, a key for social stability that enables the cumulative effects of development in people's livelihoods.

However, the potential synergistic relationship between informational development and human development, which we consider to be the key source of social progress in our time, is often undermined by social and institutional factors. The fulfillment of the promise of new, superior forms of development depends on institutional and social factors inherited from a history characterized by exploitation, oppression, and ecological destruction, as much as by human creativity and people's empowerment. This is why we have conducted our investigation in diverse contexts, selected to maximize the chance of obtaining empirical answers to these normative questions, according to a research design presented and explained in the first chapter of this volume. For instance, we have contrasted the diverse developmental paths of the two areas of the world that are typically considered to be among the most advanced expressions of informational development: Silicon Valley and Finland. We have also assessed the specific form of interaction between informationalism and human wellbeing under the conditions of a development model rooted in pacifism, by examining the developmental experience of the only country in the world that has abolished its armed forces, more than six decades ago: Costa Rica.

The richness of the empirical observation gathered in the case studies of this volume has provided a template for grounding theoretical discussions on the concept of development, as well as policy debates on development practice in the current stage of human evolution. Three chapters in this volume deal with this central question from a plurality of intellectual perspectives. Furthermore, all the case studies are informed by the analyses elaborated in the theoretical chapters. Indeed, this volume is not a collection of isolated case studies. It is the product of a cooperative research project, designed from its inception by a global network of researchers, and constantly modified by the interaction that took place during several meetings held in different cities (Helsinki, Barcelona, Los Angeles, and Berkeley) between 2011 and 2013. Nevertheless, while the research questions and the methodology of inquiry are largely common, the analytical answers are diverse, since we have retained the different approaches proposed by the authors in this book. This is because we do not believe in the possibility of a fully integrated theory at this stage of research. Rather, we have mapped out a terrain of cross-cultural research on one of the most fundamental questions of our time: how the potential of creativity and wellbeing unleashed by the informational revolution can be harnessed for the progress of humanity instead of becoming a factor in reinforcing the unsustainable, destructive process of development that characterizes much of our interdependent world. However, we do not believe that there is one policy or set of policies that could be applied to all societies. Therefore, the specific policy implications of our analysis have been considered in each one of the case studies presented in this volume. The key questions to be tackled to guide development toward human wellbeing are similar in different contexts, but the policy answers to these questions ought to be shaped by the characteristics of each society. This volume aims to identify these key questions, and reconceptualize the process of development in ways that could be used for appropriate policy design in specific contexts.

The volume is organized into three parts. In the first, we propose an analytical framework that has informed, in broad terms, the discussion presented in this book, within the plurality of its contributors' perspectives. We also explain the rationale behind the selection of the case studies. The second part includes the case studies in a sequence derived from our analytical framework. In the third part we attempt to reconceptualize development, taking into consideration what we have observed as well as some key contributions of the ongoing debate on the subject.

By raising these questions and grounding them in observation—including the discussion on the concept of "dignity as development"—we hope to contribute to a policy debate that should provide specific answers linked to the conditions of each society, answers which should be enacted by democratic institutions in a concerted global effort to save humankind while there is still time.

PART ONE

Analytical Framework

Models of Development in the Global Information Age: Constructing an Analytical Framework

Manuel Castells and Pekka Himanen

What is development?

Development, from our perspective, is the self-defined social process by which humans enhance their wellbeing and assert their dignity while creating the structural conditions for the sustainability of the process of development itself. Although the concept is ideologically loaded, in our strict definition it is not. The values that inform development goals can be very different; from economic growth calculated as accumulation of material wealth and measured by GDP or income, to holistic development, including the conservation of nature and the happiness of humans, or dignity as a comprehensive concept as proposed by our book.[1]

Dissatisfaction with traditional measures of development in terms of GDP growth led to the popularity of the concept of human development in contrast to economic development. However, human development itself is a black box, the content of which largely depends on the normative standing of social actors and institutions in different contexts. Furthermore, in the Global Information Age, we think development must be newly understood within the mode of informational development, as defined by Castells (2000, 2000–4), and by Castells and Himanen (2002). Although this conceptualization is not unanimously accepted in the field of development studies, we believe it is relevant when referring to a world characterized by a new socio-technical paradigm rooted in information and communication technologies. Indeed, as Geoff Walsham, one of the leading scholars in this field, writes: "A number of years ago, I had a paper rejected by a mainstream development studies journal without review, solely on the grounds that technology and development were not part of their remit. There are signs that this is changing" (Walsham 2013: 50). This **is** changing (Heeks 2006; Thompson 2008; Gurumurthy 2010; Lundvall et al., eds. 2009; Carnoy et al. 2013). We place ourselves within this stream of research that sees development as a result of the interaction between the economy, technology, society, and culture, in a complex set of relationships that we are trying to disentangle in ways that could be useful for tackling the issues that policy-makers find in the real world.

In fact, there is a wide diversity of development processes that refer to the quantitative and qualitative enhancement of different dimensions of the human experience. Yet, for the sake of simplicity, we will propose that there are two fundamental processes of development: increase in material wealth and increase in human wellbeing. Both categories may include very different content, and to some extent they overlap. However, by material wealth we mean the amount of resources generated in the production

---

[1] We do not in this volume engage in the presentation and discussion of all the different theories of development; this will allow us to focus on our specific contribution to this field of study. For broader theoretical debates in the development literature we refer to the thorough discussion by Jan Nederveen Pieterse (2009). See also Willis (2011); Brett (2009); Preston (1996); Rapley (2007). For a critical perspective see Rahnema (2013), and Rahnema and Bawtree, eds. (1997). Among the development theorists and policy experts Amartya Sen (1999) and Fernando Fajnzylber (1983, 1989) have been particularly influential in inspiring our thinking on development as presented in this volume.

process in which human labor works to extract a surplus of product in relation to the resources and labor invested in the process. By human well-being we mean the use of the resources generated in the production process to improve human quality of life according to the cultural values and personal preferences embedded in a given social organization. We also mean the establishment of institutional procedures and rules that maximize the capacity of humans to define autonomously the uses of the surplus generated in the production process. In terms of recent historical experience, a proxy for material wealth is economic growth, and a proxy for human wellbeing is the set of goods and services provided by the welfare state and other institutions and organizations, such as non-governmental organizations. A proxy for autonomy in the appropriation of the product refers to the empowerment of people and communities in the management of their wellbeing. In these three dimensions, information and communication technologies play a major role, as shown by a growing body of research (Wilson 2004; Fu, Pietrobelli, and Soete 2011; Foster and Heeks 2011: Fernandez-Ardevol et al. 2009; Castells 2009; Castells 2012; Sey et al. 2013).

The capacity to determine the uses of material wealth depends on the material conditions of livelihood, such as education, health, housing, transportation, environmental livability, cultural creativity, public safety, and the like, which in turn depend on the production of material wealth to sustain its creation and improvement. At the same time, the living conditions in a given society affect decisively the productivity of the process of production itself. The triangle of relationships between material production, human well-being, and socio-cultural organization is what lies at the core of the development process. Different value systems and different philosophical conceptions will place different emphases on each aspect of the development process, including the notion that the growth of human happiness and the conservation of nature could imply reduction rather than growth of material wealth (Schor 2010).

Nonetheless, this diversity of normative understanding of the development process does not affect the components of the web of interaction that lies at the source of the evolution of humankind. Furthermore, in the perspective of evolutionary theory, historical experience shows that humans have always striven to assure their control over natural forces, and over sources of wealth and power, including knowledge and technology; to survive the natural competition of the species and to get ahead in their competition with other humans (Mokyr 1990). It may well be that we are reaching a point of self-destruction in pursuing this one-dimensional logic of increasing material wealth and its corollary, military and knowledge power, as we destroy the ecological and social foundations of our existence (Nolan 2009). However, our analysis focuses on the experience of development as it is currently pursued on the planet, with the hope that understanding the mechanisms and options of development may facilitate the control of its undesirable consequences while there is still time to correct them.

Both in social sciences literature and in policy debates, the critical question in dealing with development nowadays is to examine the relationship between economic development (increase in material wealth), human development (improvement of human wellbeing), and institutional development (the empowerment of humans to act on their social organization) (Hirschman 1958; Sen 1999; Social Science Research Council 2012; Fajnzylber 1989; Ostrom 2005; Roberts 2010).

Economic development is largely determined by the combination of social and technical relationships of production. Social relationships of production refer to the social organization created by the holders of the means of production (ultimately embodied as capital in capitalist societies, and as state power in statist societies) to ensure their control over the production process, be it in finance, entertainment, or electronics. The technical relationships of production refer to the technological and managerial arrangements that induce the growth of productivity in the production process. In the Global Information Age, for the time being, social relationships of production are essentially capitalist, although in some societies (China, Vietnam, Cuba) there is a mix of a statist mode of production (control of production via control of the state) and a capitalist mode of production because of the dependence of statism on a globally networked, capitalist economy. The technical relationships of production have been deeply transformed as they have shifted from an industrial model of development (based on the new forms of generation and distribution of energy, and vertically controlled mass production as an organizational form) to a new socio-technical paradigm, represented by the informational mode of development.

Informational development

The concept of informational development refers to informationalism, a new form of socio-techno-economic organization that became fully constituted on a global scale in the early twenty-first century (Castells 2000, 2000–4).

Informationalism did not replace capitalism. In fact, it powered a new form of capitalism now prevalent everywhere: informational-financial capitalism (Castells 2000, 2000–4; Hutton and Giddens, eds. 2000; Cohen 2005; Stiglitz 2010; Lybeck 2011; Castells, Caraça, and Cardoso, eds. 2012).

The historical equivalent of informationalism was industrialism, which developed in both capitalist and non-capitalist versions. What characterizes informationalism is the widespread use of microelectronics-based digital information and communication technologies that allow the diffusion of networking forms of organization in all domains of economic and social life. It also powers information processing and digital communication, enabling the expansion of the knowledge base of the economy and of the information society. Information technologies allow for knowledge and information to be distributed and applied to all activities in any context, in a way similar to the transformation of production processes enabled by new technologies of energy generation and distribution during the two industrial revolutions. The concept of informationalism rejects technological determinism, while acknowledging the crucial role of technology embedded in social organization and culture. Networking is an essential component of informationalism; this is why the dominant social structure of our time can be characterized as a global network society (Castells 2000–4).

Networking, as the organizational transformation characterizing informationalism, induced unprecedented flexibility and efficiency in the processes of management, production, distribution, and exchange. This resulted in a substantial increase in productivity growth from the mid-1990s onward, signaling the rise of what was called "a new economy," (Castells 2001; Castells ed. 2004; Arthur 1994; Kelly 1998) until the structural crisis of 2008, derived from the self-destructive mechanisms of financial capitalism, halted productivity growth and job creation (Engelen et al. 2011). New technologies provided the infrastructure for global networks of communication and transportation. This, in turn, led to the formation of a global economy; that is, an economy with the technological, organizational, and institutional capacity to operate as a unit in real time on a global scale. These global networks did not include all people and territories in the world. In fact, only a minority of workers and managers were directly connected through these networks. However, all of the core activities in every economic dimension everywhere became connected in a global architecture of networks and nodes on whose performance the rest of the economy now depends.

Competitiveness of territories and firms became largely dependent on their ability to follow the rules of the informational economy: value-making

11

by transforming information into knowledge, and then applying knowledge to all the tasks to be executed on the basis of the technological and human capability embedded in the system. As industrialism (based on the energy revolution) determined a new geography of production and appropriation of wealth around the world, so did informationalism (based on the information and communication technologies revolution).

A substantial body of academic and technical literature provides evidence of the positive, synergistic relationship between informationalism, productivity, and competitiveness for countries, regions, and business firms (Castells 2005; Kleine 2013; Malecki 1997; Dosi et al. 1998; Ul-Haque and Bell 1998; Mowery and Rosenberg 1989; Kemerer 1998; Fajnzylber 1983, 1989). But this relationship only operates under two conditions: organizational change in the form of networking; and enhancement of the quality of human labor, itself dependent on education and quality of life. Economic development, in any of its various definitions, came to be associated with the ability to restructure economies, organizations, and institutions to support the informational mode of development. However, an equally important body of literature shows that wealth generation and human wellbeing cannot be equated, and that productivity growth and enhanced competitiveness do not necessarily lead to greater human wellbeing. In fact, in many instances, dynamic economic growth worsened the living conditions of large numbers of people as well as their natural environment (Nolan 2009; Schor 2010; Constantini and Mazzanti 2012; Genevy, Pachauri, and Tubiana 2013; Berek et al. 2011; Allen and Thomas, eds. 2000; Asmes and Gruden 2013). This is why a new approach to development policy was introduced long ago: human development as defined, for example, by the United Nations Development Program's Human Development Reports.

Human development

In our view, human development refers to a process of enhancement of the living conditions that make humans human in a given social context. Thus, it can be interpreted in a very broad way. It certainly includes what traditionally have been considered the components of the welfare state: health, education, public transportation, culture, and public insurance or subsidy in case of distress (unemployment, poverty, special needs in housing, transportation, social services, etc.). But it also should include the whole range of elements that constitute "quality of life," as determined by recent social research. These comprise job creation, work quality, and environmental sustainability, as the natural environment is a source of key dimensions of quality of life including health. Moreover, environmental sustainability is often considered to be an expression of inter-generational solidarity, thus it is a fundamental dimension of wellbeing for the human species at large. Wellbeing also encompasses other dimensions of human life such as personal security, the prevention of violence, the avoidance of war, and the protection of basic human rights such as personal dignity, privacy, communication rights, and protection against discrimination.

In the broadest sense, a holistic human development perspective leads to the feeling of happiness as the synthesis of human experience, as proposed in some innovative policies, such as Bhutan's Gross National Happiness Index (Adler Brown 2009), or in the recent works of a large network of researchers and activists proposing a strategy of de-growth, in which the goal of increasing GDP should be replaced by a strategy of multidimensional human enhancement (Schor 2010; Conill et al. 2013).

Indeed, there is a growing school of thought that considers happiness (defined in a number of ways, often controversial) as the core dimension of human development (Layard 2005). In fact, the "pursuit of happiness" has long been stated as an overarching goal of the human endeavor, a goal enshrined in the constitutions of some countries, including the United States. If this is the case, and if informationalism is the most dynamic, synergistic form of socio-economic organization in our time, **the central question in development policy nowadays, in all contexts, is the relationship between informational development and human wellbeing**.

In the traditional development paradigm, there was the implicit or explicit notion that wealth had to be produced before it could be redistributed. Thus, enhancing productivity and competitiveness in the global networked economy becomes the priority. As the argument goes, the more resources are generated, the more the benefits of economic growth will trickle down to the population at large by way of the market and/or the government. The problem is that the market does not usually play an adequate role as an equalizer but instead rewards the winners, except for some corrective mechanisms based on meritocracy. Furthermore, the dynamics of informational capitalism have led to a structural financial crisis, metamorphosed into a fiscal crisis, that is devastating many European economies, and is diminishing the prospects of economic growth in the US, particularly in terms of job creation and equity (see Engelen et al. 2011; Castells, Caraça, and Cardoso, eds. 2012). While most of the world is still growing, this growth is led by exports that are largely dependent on the conditions in the core economies. Besides, if the global financial crisis has still not spread in the newly industrialized economies, a new financial crisis at the core may destabilize the entire global system, based on networked interdependency.

Therefore, the role of government in creating the conditions for balanced informational development (including regulatory mechanisms, e.g. the Tobin tax or control of offshore banking), as well as in fostering social wellbeing, is paramount. Corrective and redistributive policies depend on the state. But then another major issue arises, namely that government bureaucracies in charge of human development often engage in the politics of redistribution. This means that they use the mechanisms of the welfare state to create the conditions for political patronage and clientelism as the basis for inducing the dependency of citizens vis-à-vis the state (Crouch 2013). This is the opposite of a developmental approach focusing on the modernization of the economy and the empowerment of society. The outcome of this separation between the logic of informationalism and the logic of welfarism is the formation, in most countries, of a small, highly dynamic, knowledge-producing and technologically advanced sector, under the dominion of the financial sector. This dynamic sector is connected to other similar sectors in a global network but excludes a significant segment of the economy and society in its own country, as shown e.g. in the chapter by Nico Cloete and Alison Gillwald on South Africa in this volume. This is, in fact, the structural basis for the growing inequality, polarization, and marginalization that characterize the situation in most countries in the world, despite high rates of growth in many areas of the planet in the last decade. And yet, it could be a meaningful link between informational development and human development that, if made explicit and articulated in policy terms, could generate synergistic effects leading to both higher productivity growth and greater human wellbeing. Why this is not the case in most countries has to be determined by empirical analysis specific to each context. We can, however, draw a few lessons from recent experiences of development in different areas of the world.

The living conditions of the population at large have been shown to improve in two ways. The first is through technological diffusion and spread of networking forms of organization by allowing new regions and countries to enter the global market in multiple industries. The second is by enabling widespread access to information and communication that is critical to produce, trade, and deliver social services, including education and health.

It is not just a question of producing advanced technologies, but especially of having the capacity to acquire and efficiently use new information and communication technologies. It is not only about innovating and selling Internet applications but also about developing Internet-based tourism, Internet-based high-value-added agriculture, technology-enhanced manufacturing, digital cultural products, etc. The World Economic Forum, in cooperation with Paris-based INSEAD, constructed a Networked Readiness Index that they show to correlate with the economic competitiveness of economies around the world (World Economic Forum, various years). Particularly significant are the positive effects of mobile communication on the efficiency of small producers and the social capacity of the poor in developing countries. Thus, a study on the impact of mobile communication in Latin America showed, on the basis of econometric analysis and ethnographic evidence, that the spread of mobile communication (which has reached roughly 80% penetration in the population at large) is positively correlated with economic growth and with the reduction of poverty, although it is neutral in relationship to inequality (Fernandez-Ardevol et al. 2008). A stream of research on the impacts of the diffusion of mobile communication in developing countries has shown the positive effects of networking technologies in improving the economic performance of small producers, the living conditions of the poor, and the social life of the population at large (Sey et al. 2013; Maurer 2012; Horst 2013; Sey 2011).

As for overall quality of life, in sharp contrast with media prejudice against the Internet, research by Michael Wilmott in Britain, analyzing 35,000 interviews from the University of Michigan's World Values Survey, has established a direct link between a happiness index and informationalism, using the frequency and intensity of Internet use as a proxy of informationalism. The more intense and frequent the use of the Internet by an individual, the higher the value of his/her score in the happiness index. The statistical relationship between diffusion of ICTs (information and communication technologies) and wellbeing holds also for countries as a whole (see the BCS Information Wellbeing Index Reports, May/July/September 2010).

This finding may be explained by two variables: sociability and empowerment. Happiness is linked to a dense network of social support. Happiness correlates with the feeling of autonomy and empowerment that people have in their lives (Koo 2013). The Internet, as we know from twenty years of empirical research (particularly from the USC Center for the Digital Future's World Internet Project), increases sociability both online and offline, as the two forms of sociability feed into each other. And the use of the Internet increases empowerment, as documented by another stream of research, including the survey research of Castells in Catalonia and the studies conducted by the Oxford Internet Institute, the Pew Institute, and the global studies by Gustavo Cardoso and his team (Castells et al. 2007; OII 2009; Rainie and Wellman 2012; Cardoso, forthcoming). According to Willmott, the feeling and practice of empowerment is particularly significant for dominated groups, particularly women and poor people. This is why the positive effects of the Internet on happiness are stronger in poor countries and among the weaker segments of the population. In sum: the Internet enhances sociability, freedom, and empowerment, and these conditions lead to a higher level of happiness—the subjective indicator of human wellbeing.

Furthermore, the diffusion of social networking on the Internet, amplified by the explosion of wireless communication (over two billion Internet users and over six billion mobile phone subscribers in the world in 2013) is at the source of the rise of mass self-communication—a key factor in the vitality of social movements and socio-political change nowadays (Castells 2009; 2012). Thus, informational development becomes a key factor in another essential dimension of human development, namely political development that is linked to the defense of democracy and to the affirmation of dignity (Howard 2011). Political development is defined as the enhanced capacity of people to rebel against injustice and enact social change—as the Arab revolutions, the "indignant" movements in Europe, the Occupy movements in the United States, and the social movements in Turkey and Brazil have shown between 2010 and 2014 (see Himanen 2012; Castells 2012).

Thus there is, potentially, a synergistic feedback loop between informational development and human development, increasing dignity in the broadest sense. This positive interactive effect, in some rare instances, is being sought for inclusion in government policies trying to promote both. The success story of Finland is the best example of the critical role of the state in steering, through public policy, both informational development and human development (see the chapter by Himanen in this volume). Development experiences in Singapore, Taiwan, Costa Rica, Chile (in part), and other countries provide rich observational material to support the concept that government policies that are aimed at connecting the two processes can induce a dynamic and redistributive model of informational-human development (cf. chapters in this volume by Isidora Chacón as well as by Manuel Castells and Fernando Calderón).

But we know of many cases (e.g. California) in which informational development is one-sided and operates in the absence of deliberate government policies to enhance human development. In the case of Silicon Valley, immigration and entrepreneurialism provide the necessary human resources for the innovation drive at the source of economic growth, as documented in the research by AnnaLee Saxenian since the 1980s (cf. her chapter on Silicon Valley in this volume).

In all cases, our studies show that the politics of development, rooted in social interests and power relationships, largely condition the strategies of informational and human development and their interaction.

The split between informational development and human development may lead to pathologies in the two processes.

On one hand, if capital accumulated in the dynamic sector of the economy is not recycled into the improvement of social conditions, including wages, it feeds the creation of virtual financial capital connected to real estate bubbles and financial creative destruction. Thus, to revisit the origin of the 2008 crisis in the US and Europe (which was not, in fact, a global crisis), in the US, paradoxically, the crisis coincided with the rise of the new economy, an economy defined by a substantial surge in productivity as the result of technological innovation, networking, and higher education levels in the workforce (see Castells et al., eds. 2012). Indeed, in the US, where the crisis first started, cumulative productivity growth reached almost 30% between 1998 and 2008. However, because of the absence of redistributive policies, real wages increased by only 2% over the decade. In fact, weekly earnings of college-educated workers fell by 6% between 2003 and 2008. And, yet, real estate prices soared during the 2000s. Lending institutions fed the frenzy by providing mortgages, ultimately backed by federal institutions, to the same workers whose wages were quasi-stagnant or diminishing. The hope was that productivity increases would ultimately catch up with wages as the benefits of growth would trickle down. This never happened because financial companies and realtors reaped the benefits of the productive economy, inducing an unsustainable bubble. The financial services industry's share of profits increased from 10% in the 1980s to 40% in 2007. The value of its shares increased from 6% to 23%, while the industry only accounts for 5% of private sector employment.

In short, the very real benefits of the new economy were appropriated in the securities market, and used to generate a much greater mass of virtual capital that multiplied its value through lending to a crowd of eager consumers/borrowers. The results are now well known. The possibility of financial collapse was spelled out in detail in a book, published in 2000, edited by Tony Giddens and Will Hutton, and co-authored by Manuel Castells, George

Soros, and Paul Volcker, among others, intentionally titled *On the Edge: Living in Global Capitalism* (Hutton and Giddens, eds. 2000).

On the other hand, proceeding with human development without engaging in full-scale informational transformation leads to the fiscal crisis of the state, because of unsustainable growth in public spending in relation to the productive base of the economy, as argued in the chapter by Castells, Chacón, and Himanen in this volume. As governments resort to massive borrowing, the dramatic increase in sovereign debt ultimately forces them into austerity policies, drastic cuts in social spending, and shrinking of public employment and public services (Engelen et al. 2011). The result is the rise of popular protests, social movements, nationalistic reactions, and sometimes populist, demagogic movements that destabilize societies and political systems, as recent developments in the European Union show (Crouch 2013).

Human development in contemporary culture includes environmental sustainability. The absence of a comprehensive public policy in the environmental realm leads to damaging environmental conditions. This is reflected in deteriorating public health and in an increased likelihood of man-made natural catastrophes. In contrast, when policies set up a direct link between informationalism and sustainability, they open up new markets in ecologically friendly production, including in the most traditional sector of agriculture, with knowledge-based, high-value-added organic produce contributing to balanced economic growth. The synergistic triangle between knowledge economy, human wellbeing, and environmental sustainability could contribute in significant ways to a new model of development capable of improving the quality of life in all its dimensions.

Yet, in most of the world the separation between informational development and human development continues to prevail, with negative effects for both processes. This split is particularly acute in the so-called emergent economies, including the BRIC countries (Brazil, Russia, India, China). The dynamic sectors in these countries, as well as in some of the Latin American, Asian, African, and Middle Eastern economies, are fully incorporated into the global networked economy working within the informational paradigm. However, the benefits of this growth are not only unevenly distributed, but also wastefully used—often to feed conspicuous consumption by the upper middle class, corruption of political elites, or extravagant bureaucratic or military expenses. Ultimately, the lack of human development spoils the promise of informationalism in the absence of a conscious public policy aimed at correcting the pitfalls of the markets and the abuses of bureaucrats. What this public policy could be has to be determined within the context of specific societies, although we will draw some lessons from our case studies in our concluding chapter.

Even the booming economy of China is finding the limits of an inhuman development approach in the recurrent social protests and violent rebellions of workers, peasants, and displaced urban residents. Cynicism and distrust have become pervasive in Chinese society leading to a fundamental moral crisis, as observed and argued by You-tien Hsing in this volume. Furthermore, when human development is disconnected from informational development, social policies are frequently used as mechanisms of paternalistic control and political patronage, as shown in Nico Cloete and Alison Gillwald's chapter on South Africa in this volume. This blocks the positive feedback loop between quality of life and informational productivity.

Cultural identity and development

A critical factor that conditions the processes of both informational and human development is cultural identity (see Castells 2000–4; Castells and Himanen 2002; Himanen 2012). If collective identity (being national, ethnic, or otherwise) defines the boundaries of the society engaging in a development process, both human and informational, the linkage between both processes will be tighter. This is because identity implies an effort toward building social cohesion between those sharing the identity (e.g. Finns). Thus, as argued above, investment in human development is a collective good in a national–cultural community. As a result, informational development is supported by homegrown human resources and benefits from public policies aiming to favor the national interest through informational development. In turn, informationalism creates the economic basis for social policies that enhance national identity by reinforcing social cohesion in a given society.

On the other hand, if informationalism is dependent primarily on entrepreneurialism, with little support from government, as is the case in California, it leads to individual identities: project identities that do not refer primarily to a community or to the wellbeing of the community but to the accomplishment of the innovators, and to the wellbeing of individuals and their families in the process of wealth creation and technological innovation. As a result, individual strategies, corporate strategies, and public policies are independent dimensions of a process that ultimately decouples informational development and human development.

For any given society, the critical matter would be how to integrate the three dimensions: informational, human/collective, and human/personal. This largely depends on the internalization of the collective identity perspective in the individual identity perspective. At the two extremes are Finland (strong national identity that provides the basis for social cohesion and human development that leads to informational development) and Silicon Valley (individual identity that leads to informational development as a way to personal development). The more a society is split between the receivers of human development goods and the innovators who create wealth, the more informationalism develops in specific segments of the economy while human development is constructed in the realm of public policy.

Each type of identity has its own potentially negative effects on the synergistic interaction between informationalism and human development.

The more collective identity (e.g. national identity) becomes exclusionary vis-à-vis the outside world, the more the feedback from human development to informationalism becomes limited to those humans included in the community. The result is a depletion of talent and a potential withering of the sources of innovation; for instance diminishing the contribution of immigration as a source of talent and entrepreneurship. A second result is the decoupling of informationalism and the boundaries of the national community as the enterprises thriving on informationalism expand by extending their global networks rather than deepening their national roots, as was the case of Nokia in Finland.

The more individual identity prevails, the more informationalism depends on entrepreneurialism that tends to seek personal development rather than commit to the human development of the territorial community. It follows a deterioration of the living conditions of the community at large, in spite of the personal improvement of the innovators. Private wealth of a minority contrasts with poverty of public goods and services for a large segment of the population, ultimately creating islands of prosperity that will face increasing difficulties in the absence of proper public services (schools, healthcare, basic urban facilities, environmental degradation).

A crisis of informationalism in a given context may lead to a crisis of human development as economic resources run out. A crisis of human development undermines the quality of labor at the source of the knowledge and innovation economy. This is a key dilemma in Europe's challenge of building a revamped, informational welfare state (see the chapter by Castells, Chacón, and Himanen in this volume).

The potential effects of these interrelated crises are also mediated by the type of identity prevailing in each kind of development model. When collective identity (e.g. national identity) is dominant, the economic crisis may lead to xenophobia and isolationism. When identity is primarily individual, the crisis may lead to sharper competition and eventually to migration toward greener pastures. When identity is split in terms of social inequality between the innovators and the recipients of social benefits from the welfare state, individual identity opposes collective identity, disassociating informationalism from human development, thus fragmenting society.

In analytical terms, without considering the interplay between culture, informational development, and human development, it would be difficult to understand the trends that underlie the overall process of development in a given society, and in the global network society. Ultimately, the cultural link is decisive for whether the more holistic goal of everyone's opportunity to lead a dignified life is fulfilled or not (see the concluding chapter by Himanen). Dignity as the goal of development refers to everyone's opportunity to fulfill his or her unique human worth in life. And, in our Global Information Age, this requires a positive relationship between informational and human development—joined together by a sustainable cultural link.

Models of development: a typology behind our case studies

There is a diversity of development models currently operating in the global economy. We do not understand models as normative constructs that should guide development strategies. Rather, we use the term "models" in the tradition of social sciences: to mean a schematic representation of a set of practices and institutions that characterize a particular path of development, derived from the observation of the development process.

To investigate development in its social and institutional diversity, we have constructed an analytical typology of development models, and have then proceeded to the empirical analysis of different cases that epitomize the various combinations of economic development and human development. Thus our typology results from the crossing of two main axes of coordinates:

Intensity of informational development
Intensity of orientation toward human development

The typology puts emphasis on the characteristics that define each of the models, and so in reality most countries mix several of these characteristics— they are not "pure" representations of a given type. Yet, by examining cases in which certain features appear to be more salient, we can understand the different sets of relationships between informational development and human development in diverse institutional and cultural environments.

For our empirical study, we have selected countries in different regions of the world and at different levels of economic and human development. They are deemed to be somewhat illustrative of the different types that result from the crossing of our two main analytical axes. The empirical justification of each of these characterizations can be found in the specific case studies that are presented in this volume. For the sake of clarity of our overall argument, we make explicit here the rationale of our research design, leading to the selection of the case studies that structure this volume.

We have differentiated three levels of informational development: high, medium, and low. For each one of these levels we have differentiated three levels of human development: high, medium, and low. We emphasize the fact that levels of human development can only be differentiated within each level of informational development, because the availability of resources for human development vastly differs according to the potential of wealth generation associated with the intensity of informationalism. For the characterization of our typology we have considered as an indicator for human development the level of coverage of human needs by governments, in the traditional terms of the welfare state. This does not preclude a revision of this narrow conception of human development, which will be critically discussed in other chapters of this volume. Here we use the extent of the intervention of the welfare state in a given context as a simple indicator of the emphasis on human development in each one of the cases under study.

Thus, for countries, areas, or regions with a high level of informationalism, we have identified three cases with different levels of policy orientation toward human development relative to each other: Finland, with a high level of human development; the European Union as a whole, with a medium level of human development; and Silicon Valley, with a low level of public support for human development.

For countries with a medium level of informationalism we have considered three cases with different levels of human development: Costa Rica, with a high level relative to other countries in Latin America; Chile, with a medium level relative to Costa Rica; and China, with a low level relative to the two Latin American countries. In considering Costa Rica as a case of high-level human development, we have included in our criteria the pacifist model. Costa Rica was selected because it has an additional and unique feature: it is a development model largely based on pacifism as an institutional feature, as it is the only country in the world without armed forces, a characteristic that frees resources for social goods and services and strengthens institutional stability. In fact, the absence of war-making capability can be considered to denote a high level of human wellbeing, since the culture of peace is a fundamental dimension of human happiness and dignity.

Finally, we have analyzed a country, South Africa, with a low level of informationalism, relative to Europe and Silicon Valley, and with a low level of human development relative to Costa Rica, Chile, or even China. This characterization is in spite of the fact that some economic activities, government institutions, and small segments of the population in South Africa are fully informational. However, as shown in the chapter on South Africa in this volume, the levels of both informational development and human development in the country as a whole are relatively low vis-à-vis the other countries and regions in our study, particularly when compared with the potential existing within the country.

The usefulness of this typology lies in the fact that it allows us to analyze the interplay between informationalism and human development at different levels and in a variety of social, cultural, and institutional contexts. However, we are not conducting a direct comparative analysis between these different areas, because the situations are so different that they cannot be compared in rigorous terms. Rather, we are proceeding with cross-cultural analysis, using the diversity of contexts to study the interaction between human and informational development in a variety of social systems.

Some remarks are necessary to interpret this typology of case studies. It is simply a heuristic tool to organize thinking about development models in our world. It emphasizes that the critical connection is the relationship between informational development and human development. It takes into consideration the institutional variation of these models. It does not refer to the complexity of a whole country, and in one case we do not observe a country but a region (Silicon Valley). But in all cases we investigate the features that define the dynamism of each type of development, the outcome in terms of human development, and the conditions under which synergy is induced or not between informational economic growth and human wellbeing. Countries are not models: many aspects of these societies are left out of our analysis, an analysis that is focused on what is essential in the development process. Yet, in our view, models are not purely theoretical constructs. They exist in reality, and we extract them from our observation and identify the components that lead to diverse economic and social outcomes. In reality, industrialism and informationalism mix in most cases. For instance, China has embarked on a gigantic project of technological modernization: it is the world's largest producer of computers, and the country with the highest absolute number of Internet users and mobile phone subscribers. Nonetheless, the predominant logic of its economic development model is still largely based on industrialist logic: growth as a function of the amount of investment of labor, capital, and raw materials in the production process. Similarly, Costa Rica and Chile have a strategy for increasing their informational potential, and some sectors in South Africa (e.g. the financial sector) are fully informationalized. Yet, we emphasize the dominance of the underlying model in each case to find an analytical relationship between processes of informational development and human development.

Furthermore, as mentioned above, the use of the term "model" does not have a normative implication in our analysis. To say that Finland is informational and ranks high in human development is not to purport the Finnish model as the most desirable. Indeed, the case study of Finland reveals failures in this model that could stall the development process in the absence of a necessary institutional and cultural adjustment. Among other things, the slowing down of technological innovation in Finland, the deep crisis of Nokia, and the disruptive effects of an extreme version of national identity in sectors of the Finnish society show that the processes of development we have identified may have different futures depending on the social and organizational dynamics of their practice, to be identified in each specific context. In addition, the experience of any country cannot be directly replicated in very different institutional, cultural, and technological conditions. But the developmental logic of each model yields lessons about how to expand informationalism, how to enhance human wellbeing, and how to further a synergistic interaction between the two faces of the development process.

Thus, the intellectual project of this volume is not to present a collection of case studies, however interesting they may be. Instead it is to provide a grounded analysis of the diversity and multidimensionality of the process of development in our age, the Global Information Age. This is why, after proceeding with the case studies following the analytical framework we have presented here, we will conclude with an effort to rethink the meaning of human development. We will suggest some holistic development strategies derived from the lessons learned in our cross-cultural, analytical journey, with the concept of "dignity as development" and with a "Dignity Index" as an accompanying first proxy for its operationalization (see Himanen's concluding chapter).

PART TWO

Case Studies

Chapter 2

The Silicon Valley Model: Economic Dynamism, Social Exclusion

AnnaLee Saxenian

Introduction

Silicon Valley is not only the birthplace of the information technology revolution; it also remains the world's leading model of informational economic development. The region's record of information technology-based entrepreneurship and innovation has been acclaimed, and imitated, for decades. By the turn of the century, the region's entrepreneurial ecosystem had spread across the entire San Francisco Bay Area, generating new wealth and continually recycling it into innovative new ventures. The region continues to attract world-class talent and incubate successful start-ups—with a handful in each generation growing into corporate giants like Apple and Google—at the same time as new centers of technology entrepreneurship have emerged around the US and in other parts of the world, from Finland and Israel to China and India. For some observers these economies pose a challenge to Silicon Valley's leadership. This chapter argues that the region's problems are closer to home: Silicon Valley is threatened less by foreign competition than by decades of neglect of the collective social and human development that underpins its economic success. As the region emerges from the current economic crisis, the failure to invest in the local infrastructure, aggressive cuts to funding of public education and other government services, and the rising cost of living contribute to an increasingly unequal society. The San Francisco Bay Area still offers an enviable quality of life for individuals who can pay the high and rising costs of housing, education, and other services. Those who cannot will be increasingly marginalized.

Setting the stage

The agricultural Santa Clara Valley offered a beautiful landscape, a Mediterranean climate, and a low cost of living to newcomers in the post-WWII decades. Silicon Valley's technology pioneers had little difficulty attracting their peers to this increasingly resource-rich environment—an environment that was enriched with national, state, and local investments. Federal funding during the Cold War promoted ongoing technological advances in the region's universities and research labs (O'Mara 2005). The state of California invested in high-quality infrastructure and developed leading-edge public services—including its acclaimed Master Plan for higher education (Douglass 2000). Housing in the formerly agricultural valley was cheap compared to the rest of the country, and local governments provided good schools and livable communities. This allowed the region's technology firms to attract top engineering talent from the rest of the country by the tens, and even hundreds, of thousands. Yet few of the region's pioneers recognized the central role of the public sector in their growth. Most embraced the mistrust of the government common in the West at the time—and attributed their own successes, and the economic dynamism of the region, to entrepreneurial genius (Saxenian 1994).

By the late 1970s San Jose was the fastest-growing urban area in the nation and residents were already worried about rising housing costs, crowded freeways, and environmental degradation (Saxenian 1983; cf. Rogers 1984). These early signs of the costs of unplanned growth were easy to overlook, however, amid the breakneck pace and invigorating process of inventing a new world, and the associated wealth generation. It was easy for newcomers to take the high level of public goods and services in Silicon Valley for granted; to see them as naturally occurring like the beauty of the coastline and the balmy weather. And because the region's growth was neither anticipated, nor "planned," it was common at the time to attribute the success of Silicon Valley to the absence of state involvement— a worldview that was consistent with then-dominant beliefs in the power of an unfettered market.

The 1992 report *An Economy at Risk* by a group of Silicon Valley business and civic leaders called attention to the deterioration of the region's economic infrastructure and quality of life in the face of intensifying global competition. The report marked the mobilization of a private–public partnership: Joint Venture: Silicon Valley Network (JV:SV), that was organized to confront these issues of shared concern (SRI International 1992). In more than two decades of existence, however, JV:SV has failed to deliver on its goals because it lacks the political authority or resources to address the deeper challenges facing the community.

Nor are elected public officials at the local level well positioned to take on these issues. Political authority is fragmented across more than a hundred city and town governments and nine counties in the San Francisco Bay Area. The region's local governments are highly differentiated and frequently act in their own narrow interests (for example, to restrict or curtail the growth of housing, or to stand in the way of new infrastructure developments), while county governments have almost no independent authority. There are also numerous special-interest agencies, each dedicated to a single purpose— such as transportation, air and water quality, shoreline conservation, and long-term land use planning. Locally elected officials oversee these agencies (in part to protect local government interests) and the limited authority they have is often contested. As a result, there is no mechanism for addressing collective problems at the regional level ranging from transportation congestion and rising housing prices to the deterioration of education and air quality (Terplan 2013).

The state-level agencies that oversee education, transportation and housing, environmental protection, health and human services, and workforce development are constrained by a highly dysfunctional political process. The California constitution allows direct participation of the electorate in decision making through initiative, referendum, recalls, and ratifications. Since many voter initiatives take the form of constitutional amendments, the constitution, at 110 pages, is the world's third-longest (after the state of Alabama, and India). The state's voters have repeatedly used the initiative process to create financial obligations without regard for the sources of the funding. At the same time, in 1978 the well-known voter-backed initiative, Proposition 13 (officially named the People's Initiative to Limit Property Taxation), placed strict limits on property tax rates, undermining the tax base for cities and localities. Prop. 13 also amended the constitution to require a super-majority (two-thirds of the votes) for any tax increases (Citrin ed. 2009). This made it increasingly difficult to balance the state budget without growing cuts to public programs. The problem was compounded by legislative grid-lock because, until recently, the constitution also required a supermajority to pass the state budget. (In 2010 the constitution was changed to require a simple majority vote to pass the 2010 budget as a result of Proposition 25.)

The economic downturn in 2007 revealed the structural problems in the state's political economy. While the immediate cause of the multi-billion-dollar state deficit was falling tax revenues (due to falling housing values and incomes)—and compounded by high and rising obligations for state employee salaries and benefits—the constitution made it impossible to address the deficit except with major cuts to budgets for core services. This disproportionately affected the public education system, which accounts for half of the state budget, with the deepest cuts going to K-12 education and the community colleges, followed by the University of California and the California State Universities. California's public schools, ranked as among the best schools nationwide in the 1960s, had already fallen to 48th in surveys of student achievement prior to the recession. Many observers attribute this to the effects of Proposition 13.

Local governments, equally hard hit by the recession, were also forced to delay or further cut infrastructure investments and reduce service levels for core activities like police and fire protection. The cities also competed for job growth that brings tax revenues (sales tax and commercial property taxes) rather than building new houses. As a result, while the region added 1.1 million housing units between 1950 and 1980, or some 40,000 per year, growth slowed to 24,000 units per year between 1980 and 2000. Moreover, the location of the new homes has been far from locations with the strongest job growth, these having resisted new housing development. The bridges, tunnels, roads, and mass transit systems in the Bay Area are aging and often inefficient. The Metropolitan Transportation Commission (MTC) projects funding shortfalls for regional infrastructure of close to $50 billion in the next 25 years, with no obvious solutions. It remains to be seen whether Silicon Valley, and the Bay Area, have the will and capacity to innovate politically, as they have technologically, to find new ways to revitalize the public institutions and infrastructure that undergird their prosperity. In what follows I summarize the dynamics of the Silicon Valley economy, and then detail the challenges that the region faces as it emerges from the current economic downturn.

Entrepreneurship-led growth

In the post-WWII era Silicon Valley's entrepreneurs pioneered not only powerful new information and communication technologies, but also a decentralized and adaptive model of regional growth. Many regions around the world today contribute to the development and diffusion of new information technology, but Silicon Valley remains a technological leader—as recurrent boom-and-bust cycles facilitate waves of entrepreneurial experimentation, followed by periods of consolidation and redeployment. The deepening capabilities of the agglomeration of technical and engineering talent, research and educational institutions, and financiers and other professional service providers offer an unparalleled base of skill and resources. The intermingling social and professional networks that result from high rates of turnover in turn support speedy and flexible recombination of resources, insuring the resilience that allows the regional economy to defy repeated predictions of its demise.

The sustained dynamism of Silicon Valley confirms that entrepreneurship is primarily a social and institutional, rather than individual, process. The successful spin-offs from the region's established companies in the 1950s and '60s and the practice of sharing resources openly contributed to a regional culture that supported rapid collective learning across firm and industry boundaries. The financial successes of the region's semiconductor start-ups not only validated entrepreneurship as a desirable (and potentially lucrative) career path, but also contributed to the belief that technological innovation was more likely to come from start-ups and small firms than from more established companies. Local engineers increasingly aspired to become entrepreneurs, not corporate executives, and the region became home to a growing network of entrepreneurial role models and mentors. This base of entrepreneurial experience and know-how—the failures as well as the successes—in turn contributed to the success of subsequent generations of Silicon Valley start-ups (Saxenian 1994).

The institutions that support entrepreneurship-led growth emerged in Silicon Valley in the 1970s and '80s, long before they became common elsewhere. They included: a sophisticated venture capital industry; a wide range of professional service firms (law, banking, real estate, research, design, etc.) specialized in the needs of technology businesses; a legal system that supported the high rates of mobility between firms (by refusing to enforce non-compete contracts); a well-developed educational system including top research universities as well as community colleges that provided up-to-date technical training; and a diverse range of professional and technical organizations that supported open exchange and joint learning about current technical and business challenges. Over time, the region has also become home to a dense concentration of sophisticated customers and suppliers that push new start-ups to learn and iterate quickly. Of course Silicon Valley also benefits from a national economy with well-functioning capital markets, the rule of law, intellectual property rights, and other institutions (e.g. bankruptcy law) that support entrepreneurial success. Policymakers seeking to replicate the Silicon Valley model in very different contexts often overlook the importance of these national institutions. (See also Bresnahan, Gambardella, and Saxenian 2001.)

The Silicon Valley ecosystem continues to support an unusually high rate of entrepreneurship and entrepreneurial churn. In each year between 1995 and 2012, between 10,000 and 25,000 new enterprises were started. In the same period, between 5,000 and 15,000 enterprises were closed. Moreover, the location of start-ups has changed. In the early 1990s, the majority of start-up activity was concentrated in the South Bay (between Palo Alto and San Jose), but by 2010 the rate of start-ups had risen and they were commonplace throughout the entire Bay Area. The city of San Francisco, for example, historically seen as far from Silicon Valley is now among the most desirable locations for entrepreneurial businesses.

While historically financing a new business required access to inherited wealth or government support, the Silicon Valley model of venture capital allows teams with good ideas to raise money to support new products, processes, and services, and to share the risks as well as the benefits of those investments. Over the past decade, Bay Area start-ups regularly received 30 to 40% of all US venture capital investments and 20% of total global venture investments. In 2011 this amounted to investments of $11 billion in 1,077 deals. (Bay Area Council Economic Institute 2012.) Angel investors contributed another $50 million to very early stage start-ups (and likely far more, since angel funding is not well documented). The region benefits from a virtuous cycle as angel and venture capital investments support the experimentation, innovation, and wealth creation which in turn support subsequent cycles of angel and venture capital activity. Moreover, the high rate of failure (only one in 20 start-ups succeed) among venture-funded start-ups supports both individual and collective learning in the region, insuring that the average quality of start-ups improves over the long term.

This is not to suggest that the region is home to small- and medium-sized firms alone. A handful of the start-ups in every technology generation grow to become global leaders in a particular sector. However, the high level of churn ensures regular turnover in the ranks of the region's top companies over time. In the 1980s the four largest companies in Silicon Valley were Hewlett Packard (HP), Intel, National Semiconductor, and Memorex. In 2002, the top four included Cisco and Sun, neither of which existed two decades earlier, along with HP and Intel. Eight of the top 20 companies in 1982 were no longer in existence in 2002. Conversely, five of the top 20 in 2002 had not yet been started in 1982. By 2010, Apple had joined the top four and companies like Google and eBay were in the top ten for the first time. Today's corporate giants also include Pixar, Genentech, Facebook, LinkedIn, Yelp, Twitter, and Zynga. New generations of companies sometimes eclipse and sometimes coexist with the former leaders. Others are acquired or go out of business, releasing new cohorts of experienced workers and managers into the local labor market.

Innovation as recombination

Innovation in Silicon Valley is the result of the deepening specialization of the capabilities of local firms, on one hand, and the recombination of these specialized capabilities, often in unanticipated ways, on the other. Specialization ensures focus and excellence, and reintegration supports experimentation and innovation. Discussions of innovation assume, often implicitly, that there are fixed technology trajectories for firms, regions, and nations to follow. This leads policymakers to focus resources on particular technologies or industry sectors: biotechnology, nanotechnology, and so forth. This approach is informed largely by the economic successes of late-industrializing nations like Japan and Korea. By mobilizing policy support and investment to transfer technology for established industries like steel and autos, these nations were able to "catch up" to the technology frontier. Their cost and scale advantages, along with incremental but cumulatively significant improvements, in turn allowed them to become successful global competitors.

That era is gone. Globalization and the information technology revolution mean that technical knowledge, both explicit and tacit, diffuses far more quickly than in the past. While some locations might gain temporary competitive advantage based on first mover status or low production costs, these will not provide enduring advantages. While breakthroughs can happen anywhere, they can also be quickly imitated. The Silicon Valley experience over the past four decades suggests that successful innovation requires recombination of changing capacities, rather than mastery of any fixed subset of capabilities.

Vertical specialization (or fragmentation) has been evident since the region's early years. The social division of labor (the division of labor between firms, not within a firm) becomes increasingly complex as individual entrepreneurs explore new vertical niches, and as new combinations of specialized components, products, and services create entirely new and specialized sub-sectors. The semiconductor industry is instructive. In the 1970s, specialized equipment makers began to spin off from the vertically integrated semiconductor device manufacturers (IDMs). Soon there were hundreds of firms specializing in different aspects of equipment making. By focusing on just a single type of equipment or input into the manufacturing process, these specialist firms were able to make more progress than would have been possible in a firm that was trying to create both equipment and manufacturing inputs. Later the stand-alone manufacturing foundry (or fab) emerged in Taiwan, allowing the separation of chip design from manufacturing. This created new generations of specialized independent chip designers who could experiment with novel capabilities and designs because they weren't burdened with the costs and operational challenges of a foundry. By focusing on narrower and narrower slices of the process, each was able to innovate in their own area, and by collaborating with other specialists they learned jointly and, in some cases, defined entirely new products and markets. This process also allowed specialists to find customers and partners outside of their traditional arena: chip designers who initially served only the large chip makers started to design chips for telecommunications, and then consumer electronics and personal computers, and eventually even car makers, mobile device makers, and so forth. The semiconductor industry thus grew from fewer than a dozen companies in the 1970s to thousands of independent producers worldwide in the 2000s. The process of specialization and recombination accelerated the pace of innovation in Silicon Valley, giving the region's firms a decisive advantage over their more highly integrated competitors located in other parts of the nation and the world (Saxenian 2006).

Today the Silicon Valley ecosystem supports multiple experiments with differing solutions to a problem. This may appear wasteful, but it ensures the pursuit of a wide range of technical alternatives and the selection of the best through competition. In recent decades, computing has been redefined as firms compete by improving or recombining components (microprocessors, specialized ICs, displays, power supplies, etc.), by shrinking components and/or devices, and by adding new features such as cameras or radio communication. Apple's iPod, iPhone, and iPad represent further recombination, and close integration of hardware and software with distinctive new designs and services. The latest generation of web applications—web browsers, search engines, social networking—likewise all combine similar components (BITS), including programming languages, protocols, standards, software libraries, productivity tools, etc. (Varian 2010).

This pattern of innovation through recombination continues to blur the boundaries between sectors (PC, laptop, tablet, mobile devices; computation, communication, entertainment, etc.). In a world in which these boundaries are becoming indistinct, the most valuable skill is the capacity to recombine changing capacities, rather than to master any fixed subset. This means that the evolution of technologies and industries is not knowable in advance. It also explains the difficulties that Nokia has faced in recent years. While Nokia was focused on optimization of large-scale production of its phones, firms like Apple and Google were integrating computing, telephony, the Internet, and entertainment on mobile devices in new ways.

Silicon Valley technology evolution

Figure 2.1 shows the evolution of Silicon Valley technology and illustrates the changing focus of innovation and competition in the region, as well as rising productivity. The shifting industry focus—from defense and IC production in the 1960s and '70s, to computer hardware and software in the '80s, and finally to more information-based activities with the Internet and the cloud in recent decades—has been associated with growing value added

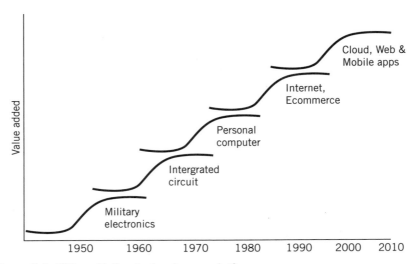

Figure 2.1 Silicon Valley technology evolution

per employee. Activities that are initially pioneered in the region such as chip assembly and manufacturing, computer manufacturing and assembly, and software services typically become standardized and relocated to lower-cost locations—leaving only the highest-value-added activities in the high-cost region. While in retrospect we can characterize the region's dominant products and technologies in each decade, even the most prescient observers are unable to predict future waves of innovation.

The productivity of the Silicon Valley workforce has been higher than the rest of the US for several decades, and in recent years it has also been growing at a higher rate than other regions. In 2010 productivity was $147,000 per employee, well above the US level of $105,000 per employee, and higher than peer regions such as Seattle ($124,009) and Boston ($119,000). Average wages have increased significantly faster than in the rest of the country as well. In 1981 Bay Area wages were on average 16% higher than the US as a whole; by 2010 they were 52% higher. This difference is reflected in incomes, with a median household income in the Bay Area of $82,500 in 2010— 37% higher than statewide and 41% higher than the national median (Bay Area Council Economic Institute 2012; Collaborative Economics 2013).

The most striking measure of the region's innovative capacity is its disproportionately high and growing share of US patent registrations (see Figure 2.2). In 1990, Silicon Valley accounted for about 4% of total US patent

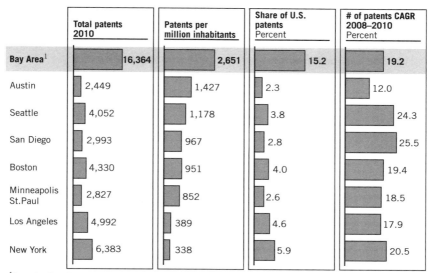

	Total patents 2010	Patents per million inhabitants	Share of U.S. patents Percent	# of patents CAGR 2008–2010 Percent
Bay Area[1]	16,364	2,651	15.2	19.2
Austin	2,449	1,427	2.3	12.0
Seattle	4,052	1,178	3.8	24.3
San Diego	2,993	967	2.8	25.5
Boston	4,330	951	4.0	19.4
Minneapolis St.Paul	2,827	852	2.6	18.5
Los Angeles	4,992	389	4.6	17.9
New York	6,383	338	5.9	20.5

[1]Data for San Francisco and San Jose MSAs

Figure 2.2 The Bay Area compared with its peer regions in terms of patents granted

Source: Bay Area Council Economic Institute, 2012a, Exhibit 9

registrations and one-quarter of California's. By 2011 the region accounted for 15% of US patents and half of California's. The Bay Area registered 2,651 patents per million inhabitants in 2010, more than double second-place Austin with 1,427 (Seattle had 1,178; Boston, 951; and New York, 338). With only 2.3% of the nation's population, the Bay Area generates 15.2% of all US patents—a number that has grown 20% annually in recent years. (Collaborative Economics 2013; Bay Area Economic Council Institute 2012a, b, c).

The industrial and occupational profiles of the Silicon Valley economy continue to evolve as well. The driving force of the regional economy in the 1980s and '90s was the development of computer hardware and software; today the region's economic core is in professional, scientific, and technical service industries as well as information services (Internet). Comparative data show that the region is heavily specialized, compared to the rest of the US, in three innovation-led sectors—information, computer and electronic manufacturing, and professional and scientific services. These sectors make up approximately 30% of the regional economy (compared to 15% of

Industries	2005			2010		
	Percent of Bay Area real GDP	Percent difference from U.S. share[1]		Percent of Bay Area real GDP	Percent difference from U.S. share[1]	
100% =	$395 billion			$419 billion		
Construction	4.5	−0.4		3.0	−0.3	
Education	1.0	0		0.9	0	
Health services	5.2	−1.4		5.6	−1.6	
Financial services	22.4		1.8	20.2	−1.4	
Information	6.9		2.2	8.2		3.0
Leisure & hospitality	3.7	−0.1		3.3	−0.1	
Computer & electronic product manufacturing	5.7		4.2	9.2		6.9
Other manufacturing	8.9	−2.0		9.1	−0.4	
Professional, scientific and technical services	11.1		4.2	12.0		4.7
Wholesale trade	4.6	−1.2		4.9	−1.4	
Retail trade	6.1	−0.5		5.4	−0.9	

[1]Positive figure indicates that the Bay Area has a greater degree of its GDP concentrated in the industry than does the U.S. overall

Figure 2.3 The Bay Area's increasing specialization compared to the US as a whole in computer manufacturing, information, and professional services

Source: Bay Area Economic Institute, 2012a, Exhibit 4

the US economy as a whole), but they account for 100% of its growth since 2005 (see Figure 2.3).

As firms in the region pursue increasingly higher-value-added activities, they require an increasingly well-educated work force. Today, the occupations that are most heavily represented in the region are in computing and mathematics, and in architecture and engineering (these occupations are three times as concentrated in the Bay Area as they are in the US economy as a whole). Management and business and financial operations occupations are also 50% more concentrated in the region than in the nation. Not surprisingly, this is reflected in relatively high education levels. By 2010, 46% of workers in the Bay Area possessed a bachelor's or more advanced degree, compared to 28% nationwide. Not only does this make the Bay Area one of the nation's best-educated metropolitan areas, but its advantage has been growing. The proportion of workers with at least a bachelor's degree grew from 36% to 46% between 1990 and 2010 (Bay Area Economic Institute Council 2012a).

The globalization of labor markets

Silicon Valley's research and innovation ecosystem has attracted the "best and the brightest" from elsewhere in the US, and increasingly from abroad, for over half a century. The region today boasts a diverse and deep base of skills and know-how, reflected by levels of educational attainment that surpass all but one peer city in the US (Boston). The region's workforce grew during the 1970s and '80s by attracting native-born engineers and scientists from all over the United States. Since 1990, Silicon Valley firms have grown primarily by attracting US-educated, foreign-born engineers into the region. In 1970, only 15% of the region's science and engineering workforce was foreign-born, mainly from Canada and Europe. By 2000, this had grown to 53% of the skilled workforce, and by 2011, 64% of the region's scientists and engineers were foreign-born (while a majority are from China and India, they come from all over the world). Today the net new growth of the region's highly educated workforce is overwhelmingly due to the rise of the foreign-born population. The high majority of these immigrants hold graduate degrees in the science, technology, engineering, and mathematics fields (STEM), as well as in business management. They have been at least as entrepreneurial as their native-born counterparts and have contributed to technological innovation as well as to the creation of significant numbers of new jobs and wealth for the regional economy (Saxenian 1999). Moreover, the diversity that results from the mixture of talented immigrants from all over the world also contributes to the creativity of local businesses.

While poor countries like India and Taiwan initially complained about the loss of their most talented scientists and engineers to the US, the falling costs of communications and travel have resulted in a process that looks more like "brain circulation" than "brain drain." Foreign-born engineers travel regularly between the US and their home countries, and have seeded new centers of technology and entrepreneurship in formerly developing regions (Saxenian 2006). As a result, even the smallest firms are now part of global value chains and have operations and partnerships around the world. The global supply chain for the iPad is a good example. While product design, architecture, and software remain in the US, the firm gets flash memory from Samsung (Korea) and Toshiba (Japan), LCD displays from LG (Korea) and Innolux (Taiwan), final assembly by HonHai (Taiwan), and touch screen displays from Wintek and Sintek Photonics (both in Taiwan).

Globalization has been a double-edged sword for Silicon Valley. It has sustained the local talent base, and opened up new markets and new sources of low-cost skill and talent, while providing access to new collaborators. The Bay Area is now the fourth-largest exporting region in the US, and its proximity to and strong trading relationship with fast-growing Asian economies should support the long-term expansion of trade (Bay Area Council Economic Institute 2012a). The region's largest export partners, in declining order, are Taiwan, Japan, Singapore, Hong Kong, South Korea, and China. However, these countries are aggressively investing in domestic research and educational institutions and infrastructure—and actively recruiting domestic talent back home. While the threat of a "reverse" brain drain is often overstated in the media, the reality is that Silicon Valley increasingly competes with growing regions in Asia and Europe for its most important resource—talent—as well as for technological and market leadership.

The health of the Silicon Valley economy depends on it continuing to attract world-class professionals, entrepreneurs, and their families from around the world. Yet the region is now one of the highest-cost metropolitan areas in the US. Home prices in the region are the third-highest in the country (behind New York and Honolulu) and they are increasing faster than other urban areas. The federal government has put restrictive caps on the visas that allow employers to recruit highly skilled foreign-born workers. And many of the features that attracted top talent to the region in the past— open space, high-quality education, modern infrastructure, and efficient services such as police, hospitals, and community and social programs— are being undermined by ongoing cuts associated with the budget crisis. A report summarizing a Silicon Valley Leadership Group CEO survey (2013) concludes:

A deteriorating state infrastructure in areas ranging from public education to public transportation has added to the difficulties of recruiting the best workforce, finding them housing and educating their children to be tomorrow's world-class workforce.

Stagnant employment and growing inequality

The Silicon Valley economy began to recover from the recession in 2010 and shows the typical signs of a renewed cycle of dynamic growth: start-up activity, tight labor markets, and rising wages and rents. Employment growth in the Bay Area outpaced both the state and the nation between 2010 and 2012, even though the public sector, where substantial numbers of jobs were lost, has not recovered. Nevertheless, employment in the region is still below its previous 2000 high point, and unemployment remains stubbornly high at 7%. In other words, the productivity of the private sector in the region continues to rise along with GDP per capita, but it has not been associated with employment growth.

The stagnation of employment has been accompanied by growing income disparities, paralleling other large US urban areas. The lack of higher education is now a significant hindrance in the Bay Area economy. While median incomes rose for residents with graduate or professional degrees between 2007 and 2011, incomes for those with less than a bachelor's degree have fallen substantially. The region's Hispanic and African American residents, whose educational attainment is low, were disproportionately affected. Only 23% of Hispanics and 12% of African Americans have a bachelor's degree or higher, compared to over 50% of Asian and white residents. Incomes for Hispanics and African Americans fell 5 and 18%, respectively, in this short four-year period. Today, the median income for residents with graduate degrees is five times higher than for residents without a degree (Collaborative Economics 2013).

The "missing middle" of the income distribution is now more pronounced in Silicon Valley than the rest of the nation. Incomes and jobs for the region's most highly educated workers are rising steadily, while incomes for low-skilled workers are not (although they remain well-compensated relative to their counterparts outside of the Bay Area). Meanwhile, opportunities for workers in the middle-income range have diminished over time. Median household income in the region was just over $76,000 in 2010. At that time there were more workers in low-income households with median household incomes below $38,000 than there were in moderate-income households with median incomes between $36,000 and $61,000 (Bay Area Council Economic Institute 2012b).

The region's low- and middle-income workers are concentrated in four low-wage industries: retail trade, healthcare and social assistance, accommodation and food services, and manufacturing, with particularly high concentrations in the first two. A majority of these workers are in occupations such as administrative support, sales, and food preparation and services. Not surprisingly, relative to the overall population, low-income households are close to twice as likely to be African American and 50% more likely to be Hispanic than they are to be white or the other races that the census measures (Asian or Pacific Islander or Native American). They are more likely to be young (a majority are under 36 years old) and have lower educational attainment. While 87% of high school students in the region graduated in 2011, only 23% of African American and Hispanic students met the entrance requirements for the University of California or the California State University systems, compared to 72% of Asians and 55% of whites.

Income distribution has worsened in the region for a decade and a half. Between 1980 and 1995, the Gini coefficient (a measure of inequality, with 1.0 as maximal inequality) for the Bay Area was 0.48, below that of both California (0.49) and the US (0.495). However, inequality rose sharply in the mid-1990s and continued to rise for the next 15 years. By 2012 the Gini coefficient for the Bay Area (0.525) had surpassed both state (0.522) and national (0.508) levels. For comparison, the Gini coefficient for Denmark, after taxes and transfers, is approximately 0.25, while that of South Africa is closer to 0.70 (Bay Area Economic Council Institute 2012).

Rising housing prices create a growing burden for the region's low- and middle-income communities. While low-income communities have long been concentrated in the region's historic urban core—San Francisco, Oakland, and Richmond—they are now getting squeezed out of San Francisco as technology start-ups increasingly locate there. Rents are also at an all-time high in the region, and 46% of the region's renters devote more than 35% of their income to rent. Increasingly, the region's low- and middle-income households are being forced to live in suburban locations distant from their workplaces, with longer than average commutes. Researchers predict that these commutes will worsen as the shift of work from traditional transit-based job centers to auto-centric office parks in higher-income areas potentially makes these commutes to lower-skill jobs unaffordable to workers with limited education.

It is easy to see how the low- and middle-income communities in the region are particularly disadvantaged by the high housing costs, the poorly maintained and congested roads and highways, the low quality of the education system, and the state disinvestment in higher education. However, these are also significant problems for the technology employers in the region who are experiencing shortages of skilled workers, and who will need to continue to attract them from outside of the region.

Residence in segregated, high-income communities allows many households to avoid the worst effects of budget cuts and ensures access to good schools and well-maintained roads and parks, as well as to high-quality healthcare and urban services. However there is no way to privately address the problems of the regional transportation infrastructure. The core of the transit system is located in the cities, which have a declining share of employment, job growth being sprawling and decentralized. Less than half of all jobs in the region are currently accessible by public rail, bus, or light rail system. Not surprisingly, public transit now accounts for less than 11% of all commutes.

Privatization is one option. Silicon Valley companies, for example, often provide food, exercise equipment, and other services for their workforces. A handful of technology firms have recently created what has been described as "an alternate transportation network of private buses—fully equipped with WiFi—that threads daily through San Francisco, picking up workers at unmarked bus stops," taking employees via commuter lanes to their campuses in the South Bay, thus allowing them to avoid the overcrowded freeways and inadequate mass transit in the region. As of August 2012, there were six different companies providing bus services for their employees. Google alone runs about 150 trips daily all over the city. One report estimates that these buses transport about one-third of the number of passengers daily of the public alternative, Caltrain (Stamen Design 2012). However, this is not a solution that most of the region's start-ups or less-wealthy firms could pursue.

Demographic trends suggest the limits of this strategy. In the next two decades the current workforce will be retiring (including primarily highly educated baby boomers) and the Asian and Hispanic populations will make up a growing share of the regional population. Some 60% of all employment opportunities in the region between 2010 and 2020 will come from job replacements (refilling existing jobs) rather than newly created jobs. These jobs will likely require workers with higher skill and education levels than in earlier generations. Where will these workers come from, when local employers are already complaining about skills shortages? Most likely employers will hire a mix of both local workers and outsiders—as in the past. In the first case they will need to provide the region's younger generation with high-quality education or training and ensure access to affordable housing, transit, and public services. In the second, they will need to ensure the region can continue to attract the talented workers and their families away from other regions which offer lower-cost housing, good schools, great universities, world-class infrastructure, and a clean environment. In short, continued economic development will require solutions to the political and social problems that have undermined the quality of the education, infrastructure, housing, and quality of life in the region.

What next?

The San Francisco Bay Area remains a thriving center of technological innovation. An economic system that began in Palo Alto and San Jose has now spread to encompass not only San Francisco and the East Bay, but the whole nine-county region. However, the public investments in infrastructure and services that were essential in supporting the creation and early growth of this economic system have been neglected. The challenges facing the region's education and transportation systems, its housing and infrastructure, as well as the environment will require political and social innovation. The nature of the problems is well recognized by local political leaders, business groups, planners, and activists. Each of these groups has documented some or all of the challenges.

The top priorities of the Silicon Valley Leadership Group (a public policy business trade association based in San Jose) include education, energy, the environment, health, housing and land use, transportation, and community—the issues that "affect the economic health and quality of life in Silicon Valley." The Bay Area Council, a business public policy association with roots in San Francisco, has established the Bay Area Council Economic Institute (BACEI), a public–private partnership of business, government, labor, and higher education committed to insuring the "economic vitality and competitiveness" of the region. The Institute publishes frequent reports on the state of the regional economy and related issues such as competitiveness, trade, infrastructure, and science and technology."The Bay Area—A Regional Economic Assessment" (BACEI 2012) provides exhaustive documentation of the sources and nature of the region's economic growth as well as the impediments and challenges facing the region.

The Bay Area "Joint Policy Committee" was created in the 1990s to coordinate the planning efforts of four existing regional agencies: the Association of Bay Area Governments (ABAG), the Bay Area Air Quality Management District (BAAQMD), the Bay Conservation and Development Commission (BCDC), and the Metropolitan Transportation Commission (MTC). Their board members and executive staff meet regularly under the auspices of the Joint Policy Committee to talk about issues of shared concern such as regional economic development, climate change, energy, and the environment. However the group has no authority to mandate change or prohibit anything. For example, MTC oversees the Bay Area transit system, but the "system" consists of 27 separate agencies that are fragmented across multiple jurisdictions and do not coordinate their services, resulting in inefficient duplication and unnecessary complexity that undoubtedly reduces transit use in the region.

In 2008 the California Senate passed Senate Bill 375, which mandates that all metropolitan regions in the state complete a "Sustainable Communities Strategy," an integrated long-range transportation plan and linked land use and housing component that supports a growing economy, expands housing and transit options, and reduces the pollution caused by car and light truck greenhouse gas emissions. This led to the formation in 2010 of OneBayArea by the four regional agencies. Their tag line is "Preserving the Bay Area's Quality of Life through collaborative planning." In early 2013 the group released a draft of "Plan Bay Area" and they are soliciting input through town halls and hearings across the region. They plan to adopt the plan in June 2013, and to update it every four years as dictated by Senate Bill 375. This is evidence of greater collaboration between the agencies, particularly ABAG and MTC. However, it makes no changes to the existing governance of the single-purpose regional agencies and, critically, it has no authority to require local governments to alter land use to comply with regional goals.

The Joint Venture: Silicon Valley Network, the public–private partnership created in Silicon Valley in 1993 in response to fears about the region's loss of competitiveness has grown and evolved with changing leadership. However, its focus remains on bringing together leaders from business, government, labor, academia, and the community to "provide analysis and action on issues affecting our region's economy and quality of life." JV:SV publishes an annual *Silicon Valley Index*, which provides data at the regional (rather than the state or local) level. This allows for comparison, between a variety of areas, of the region's performance over time, with detailed indicators for each of the following: people, economy, society, place, and governance. JV: SV, more than the other groups, is a distinct organizational form (compared to traditional business associations and public agencies), and as such can often be quite innovative in its thinking—but it also has no legitimacy or authority to accomplish change. It may be best understood as a public policy think tank that focuses on the regional, rather than the city, state, or national level.

There are two dominant proposals for the political transformations needed to restore the balance of human and economic development in Silicon Valley: one envisions the creation of a stronger framework for governance at the regional level; the other involves reform of the state and local governments to make them more responsive and effective. They are not incompatible, but the locus of change is different, and some issues may be better addressed by one plan than the other. For example, reform of the state and local governments may not effectively overcome the problems created by the fiscal inequities between cities that result in a range of different service levels and competition for sales and commercial property taxes. On the other hand, the reform of regional governance will do nothing to address the problems that stem from the dysfunction of the state and its constitution.

Several efforts to create regional government or stronger regional authorities in the Bay Area failed in the 1990s. As a result, the region remains dependent on the existing single purpose agencies and lacks a way to balance different goals and integrate planning of land use, transportation, and environmental and natural resource protection across the region's many diverse cities and towns. Rather than trying to create a single powerful regional government, the new approaches seek to take lessons from other regions that have alternative forms of governance. The following ideas are drawn from a Special Analysis in the 2013 *Silicon Valley Index* (produced by JV:SV and the Silicon Valley Community Foundation). One approach is to focus employment growth in the region near transit in existing downtowns and employment areas—following the experience of Washington, D.C. Another direction, taken by Portland, Oregon, involves greater planning of land use in order to ensure that sufficient housing is built near employment centers. An elected body, Metro, oversees long-range regional planning and maintains an urban growth boundary. It is backed by strong state law and can require localities to adopt zoning that meets the region's plan.

The seven-county Twin Cities region (Minneapolis and St Paul) has, since 1975, shared a portion of local tax revenues between jurisdictions. All of the municipalities in the region contribute 40% of the growth of the commercial and industrial tax base to a regional pool that is then redistributed based on population and the existing tax base. This tax sharing reduces the zero sum competition between jurisdictions for commercial and industrial development by ensuring that all share in the fiscal benefits of this growth. This is part of a comprehensive regional agency that also operates the region's bus system, collects and treats wastewater, manages regional parks, and conducts comprehensive long-range planning.

Another goal might be to bring transit operators in the region into a single organization. In Seattle an agency, Sound Transit, which was formed by an agreement between the three Seattle area counties with authorization by the Washington state government, plans and manages all regional rail and bus services, while each county still runs its own local bus services. The Bay Area could also follow Portland, Toronto, and New York, all of which have created a single regional transit operator, with a merger of BART and Caltrain along with the regional buses across the Bay. This would dramatically improve the user experience by coordinating the visual identity, scheduling, fare structure, and customer service operations. It would also make it easier for the organization to seek sales tax funding.

Finally there are models of preparing the region for rising sea levels due to climate change. Four counties in southeast Florida (representing 30% of the state's population) have formed a compact to collaborate in establishing a climate change action plan. The Southeast Florida Regional Climate Change Compact authorizes the development of strategies to coordinate regional preparation for and adaptation to a changing environment, using regional mapping of the projected sea level rise. This allows them to prepare for sea level rises by planning a land use approach to potential flood areas and by identifying a way to pay for the shoreline infrastructure. All of these approaches to regional governance would require institutional change at the regional level. The alternative approach would focus on reform of existing institutions.

One of the most visible responses to the economic crisis was the formation in 2008 of **California Forward**—a nonpartisan, nonprofit organization "working to bring government closer to the people and move the state in the right direction—forward." The organization works with local communities, which they see as the best equipped to solve their own problems, and on emphasizing the link between many of the problems that threaten the future and the state government, which they characterize as "ineffective, unresponsive, and unable to fix itself." Their mission is "to work with Californians to help create a 'smart' government—one that's small enough to listen, big enough to tackle real problems, smart enough to spend our money wisely in good times and bad, and honest enough to be held accountable for results." In particular, they are intent on restructuring the relationship between state and local governments so that they work better together for everyone.

Five major California foundations—the California Endowment; the Evelyn and Walter Haas, Jr. Fund; the William and Flora Hewlett Foundation; the James Irvine Foundation; and the David and Lucile Packard Foundation—came together to create California Forward. It is a bipartisan group and its leadership is drawn from a diverse group of business, labor, faith, and community organizations from all over the state. Its early reform efforts focused on: (1) stabilizing the state fiscal situation through budget reform; (2) changing political incentives with redistricting and a top two primary system; and (3) restructuring state and local government to drive innovation and results.

The group has also initiated a statewide conversation on reform called **"Speak Up CA"** which is designed to mobilize citizens across the state to learn more and to help shape its reform proposals. Their long-term vision involves continuous improvement in the performance of education, transportation, and health and human services, along with the creation of a sound governance system that will allow the state to shift resources from prisons back to universities. They believe that efficiencies and innovation in regulation will allow businesses to pay higher wages while still remaining competitive, and that growing middle-income jobs will reduce demand for public services and increase tax revenue. In the words of the California Forward website:

To achieve this vision, Californians need to rethink how leaders are selected and guided, how they make key fiscal and policy decisions, and how government agencies organize cooperative efforts around shared goals. This vision will require more Californians to be more meaningfully involved, as consumers of public services, as taxpayers, as voters, as neighbors, as citizens.

Their priorities include:

- making the state's fiscal process far-sighted—focusing beyond the next budget cycle and the next election cycle to the next generation—by evolving the revenue system to create stable support that reflects the changing economy, aligning authority over fiscal decisions with responsibility for delivering services, and focusing on results to create accountability and restore public trust
- aligning state, regional, and local efforts to effectively respond to public imperatives by encouraging partnerships of local and state agencies and private organizations to break down the walls of bureaucracy and share resources and authority to address economic, social, and environmental needs
- working to make the democratic process and elected officials more responsive to the public interest and the will of the people—by giving citizens more control over the political process and ensuring elected officials are motivated and empowered to respond to the needs and priorities of all Californians

- working to make the political discourse more reflective of the state's diversity so that the public process is more open and fair, more representative of and more responsive to the lives and views of the people

It is too early to judge whether California Forward will succeed in its bottom-up efforts at institutional and social innovation. The group garnered important early successes. For example, it was a strong supporter of Proposition 11 in 2008, which mandated the creation of the California Citizens Redistricting Commission charged with redrawing California's Senate, Assembly, Board of Equalization, and Congressional districts based on information from the 2010 census. Previously, the districts had been drawn by the legislature itself, insuring that 99% of incumbents were regularly re-elected and none of the 120 seats had changed hands in recent elections.

Many more successes will be required to ensure the dynamism of California in coming decades.

Chapter 3

Reconstructing the Finnish Model 2.0: Building a Sustainable Development Model?

Pekka Himanen

Introduction

In my book with Manuel Castells, *The Information Society and the Welfare State: The Finnish Model* (2002), we argued that the Finnish model showed that it is possible to have a competitive development model that is based on forming a virtuous circle between informational and human development—or, to put it in other terms, between a competitive innovation-based economy and an inclusive welfare state.

This was against the (still) widespread idea that the only way to be competitive in the global network society is by following the Silicon Valley model, despite its downsides in human development.

Yet, Finland has been able to become a competitive innovation-based economy, being the home of the telecommunications company Nokia and the Linux operating system that runs much of the Internet, as well as combining this with a welfare state that is among the world's most inclusive in terms of human development.

We also paid attention to the Finnish experience because it is an example of a relatively poor country's very rapid development into one of the world's most competitive economies and inclusive welfare societies in just a few decades. Even as late as the beginning of the 1950s, over 50% of the Finnish working population was in agriculture and forestry. And as late as the end of the nineteenth century, 6% of the population had died of hunger (during the so-called hunger years of 1866–7). The Finnish model showed that through systematic policy-making, significant development results could be reached, even in a relatively short time period. This was another universally important lesson for the thinking of other countries' development models.

Now, a little over ten years later, we are in a new situation in which all development models are faced with new, very big challenges. And by this, a reference is made not only to the "Great Recession" (the name I prefer to use for the global economic crisis that started in 2008, which served as a dead-end for the preceding models; see our work on this crisis in Castells et al. 2012, including Himanen 2012). The biggest challenge is the broader project of reconstructing a sustainable development model that can answer the deeper and even grander challenges, ranging from sustainable economy to sustainable wellbeing and sustainable environment. Therefore, it is analytically a very important moment for reassessing the Finnish model and its ability to represent or reconstruct a sustainable development model.

Reassessing the state of the Finnish model

Let us start by first making a big-picture assessment of the general state of the Finnish model, based on empirical data. At this biggest-picture level, the core of the Finnish model—the virtuous circle between its economy and the welfare state—still continues. The main elements remain the same. First, in terms of the economy:

- Finland continues to be one of the most competitive economies (ranked as the third most competitive by the World Economic Forum in 2012, above the US, which is ranked seventh).

- Finland continues to be ranked as one of the most innovative economies (both in terms of having one of the highest levels of research and development investment in the world, almost 4% of the GDP, and having one of the highest levels of income from patents and royalty fees per capita; in both of these areas, Finland ranks above the US).
- Finland's GDP per capita of $49,350 USD is more than that of the US and the biggest EU economies of Germany, France, and the UK.
- Finally, in the context of the current Great Recession and the consequent public financial crisis, Finland remains one of the few countries that still has the highest credit rating of AAA from all the main agencies: Standard & Poor's, Fitch, and Moody's (something that the US and most European countries no longer have).

At the same time, the main elements of the welfare state continue as before, including:

- Free, public, and high-quality education for all, from primary school to the universities (with Finnish students ranking the highest in the OECD PISA student performance comparisons).
- Mostly free, public, and high-quality healthcare that covers everyone, as well as strong social security for unemployment, retirement, etc.
- Inclusiveness of development, in which the levels of poverty, income inequity, and gender inequality are among the lowest in the world.
- Special features such as a free, public childcare as a subjective right for all, run by university-level educated teachers.

Table 3.1 provides some of the key data for putting the economic and wellbeing dimensions in numbers.

But in our 2002 book, we listed some challenges for the sustainability of the Finnish model. The picture was definitely not all rosy then—nor is it now.

So what follows here is an analytical reassessment of where the Finnish model currently stands on these key dimensions of a sustainable development model: informational development, human development, and the cultural link between these. Or, in other words, how Finland has been able to answer to the big challenges of sustainable economy, sustainable wellbeing, and their sustainable cultural link. Ultimately, what is under discussion is what it would take to reconstruct the Finnish model to also meet the new challenges in a sustainable way.

Table 3.1 A comparison of selected economic and wellbeing indicators

	Finland	USA	China	Chile	S. Africa
Economy					
Competitiveness (GCI)	5.55	5.47	4.83	4.65	4.37
Innovation (patents per capita)	277.1	137.9	6.5	3.8	6.8
GDP per capita (US$)	49,350	48,387	5,414	14,278	8,066
Wellbeing					
Income inequality (Gini)	26.9	40.8	41.5	52.1	57.8
Gender Inequality Index (0 = most equal)	0.075	0.256	0.213	0.346	0.462
Student performance (PISA score)	544	496	577*	439	N.A.

Sources: World Economic Forum (2012); World Bank (2013); UNDP (2013); OECD (2009).
Note: China's PISA score is for Shanghai only.

Of course, this discussion is analytically important for all other countries thinking about their sustainable development models as they move forward.

The chapter will be divided into three parts: (1) Informational development: sustainable economy; (2) Human development: sustainable wellbeing society; and (3) cultural development: sustainable cultural link.

Informational development: sustainable economy

Let us start with informational development, which is directly linked to the sustainability of economy in the context of the global network society. Here the basic elements of the Finnish informational economy remain strong, as already shown by some key figures above. Particularly, the foundation of informational development—the R&D investment—remains among the highest in the world. The Finnish R&D investment was already 3.4% of GDP, or twice the average of the advanced economies, at the time of our 2002 book, and it has actually increased even further since. Figure 3.1 demonstrates this development.

However, in spite of this high, continued level of input into innovation, the output is actually declining in a way that is linked to two of the key

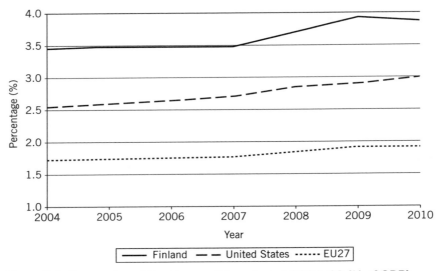

Figure 3.1 Research and Development Investment 2004–10 (% of GDP)
Source: Main Science and Technology Indicators, OECD Science, Technology and R&D Statistic.

challenges for the future of the Finnish model that we listed in our 2002 book. These two factors are: the need to expand the informational innovation economy beyond Nokia, and the need for a culture of renewing creativity ("the hacker ethic," as analyzed by Himanen in 2001).

The struggles of Nokia showcase both challenges, so let us take a look at the company's development. It will provide us with important general analytical observations and lessons.

The case of Nokia

The following figures on the development of Nokia's market value and revenues tell the dramatic story of how Nokia's value has dropped from its highest, over 200 billion euros in 2000, to a little less than 10 billion euros in the late summer of 2013 (see Figure 3.2). (At the beginning of September 2013 Nokia finally made significant corporate restructuring, which will be described later.) During this period, Nokia lost 80% of its market value: the price of its market share had dropped from its peak of about 30 euros to just above 2 euros.

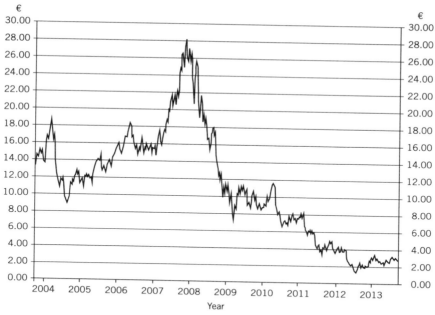

Figure 3.2 Development of Nokia's market value for 2003–13 (value of one share in euros)

Source: Taloussanomat (2013).

Figure 3.3 shows the same development in terms of the changes in Nokia's revenues since its renewal from a conglomerate to a mobile communications company in 1992 (with the new leadership of Jorma Ollila, who took the reins when Nokia was nearing bankruptcy).

As can be seen from Figure 3.3, there are several important turning points in Nokia's development. The first part of the growth under Ollila's leadership was related to the introduction of the new digital mobile communications technology for both the networks and the phones (the GSM), which began around 1992 but started to spread rapidly from the mid-1990s. Then, at the turn of the millennium, there was a dip because of the so-called "technology bubble," which was due to a combination of overheated markets and some public regulatory mistakes (as described shortly).

However, Nokia continued to grow strongly through the rest of Ollila's leadership—that is, until 2006. Since then there has been a continuous decline. This cannot be said to be due solely to an unsuccessful change of leadership to the former CFO, Olli-Pekka Kallasvuo, for 2006–10 (the period in which he was CEO before getting fired).

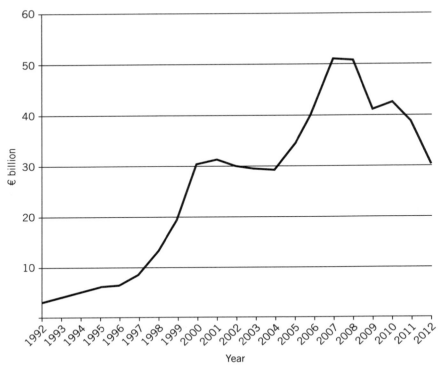

Figure 3.3 Development of Nokia's revenues, 1992–2012 (billion euros)
Source: Nokia's annual reports for 1992–2012.

Likewise, since 2010, the collapse of Nokia can hardly be said to be solely the responsibility of the new CEO Stephen Elop, who was hired from Microsoft, although clearly major mistakes were made, such as the decision to discard Nokia's own operating systems and shift to the Windows ecosystem. Right after becoming the CEO, Elop announced that Nokia's current operating system was like a "burning oil platform" and that Nokia would end its development and introduce new phones based on Windows in two years. An industry analyst has called the consequences of this event "the Elop effect," a reference to two well-known management research literature terms: the "Osborne effect" and the "Ratner effect." The first refers to damaging current business by simply announcing a new product at the wrong time, however good it may be; the latter refers to the fact that if the CEO of a company claims its products are bad, people will agree, even if they are actually relatively good. So when a CEO announces that a company's current products are bad and says that good ones are coming much later, people stop buying the current product and the company becomes devalued, even if its current product line would have been relatively good—and even if the future product would be *really* good. This is what has been called the "Elop effect" (see Ahonen 2011).

However, a deeper analysis must go beyond the individuals leading a company. What Nokia really missed were two larger matters that were happening in its technological business environment: first, the launch of Apple's iPhone; and second, major public regulatory misjudgment.

The first deeper matter is a longer-term lesson from the brief history of IT: you have to open up your platform enough for others to join you in its innovation. In fact, though Apple invented the personal computer and introduced it to the world, it originally lost to its competitor, the IBM–Microsoft PC, because Apple had a closed architecture that prevented others from developing applications for its system, whereas the PC environment was based on an open architecture in which any enthusiastic, innovative person could start creating new applications: this is, for example, how the PC became both entertainment equipment (computer gaming) and a business productivity tool (through the Lotus 1-2-3 spreadsheet program developed by Mitch Kapor) (cf. Himanen 2001b on "The Brief History of Computer Hackerism"). However, despite the advice of many leading experts to open its environment, Nokia's culture could not see that doing so would be in its broader self-interest.

What has happened since 2007 is truly paradoxical. Apple—the company known for having the highest degree of closedness—surprised everyone by launching its iPhone with an open environment, for which anyone can develop apps. Then, later, Samsung followed suit by choosing the Google Android operating system, which is built on Linux, the open-source operating system created by the Finnish Linus Torvalds!

Because of its history, Nokia has a very deeply rooted engineering mindset. It has always emphasized the advanced technical features of its products—and often, in objective comparisons, they have truly been more advanced than those of their competitors. However, this led to Nokia's failure to see how the ICT business had changed to become more and more about content and the design of access to that content (still, for a long time after the launch of the iPhone, Nokia continued to send the message that it was in the technology business, not in the content business, and that these are separate).

The second, deeper matter is that a major public regulatory mistake was made in the heated years of the "technology bubble." In effect, these public policy decisions in Finland and in Europe took the competitive advantage away from the only IT field where Europe was leading in the competition with America. This refers to how the move from mobile phones to the mobile Internet was hampered by the Finnish and European decisions to sell the "air" used for this communication (3G) for unprecedented prices of billions of euros. For example, in the case of Finland, this nearly led to the bankruptcy of the leading teleoperator, Sonera (now part of TeliaSonera), at the turn of the millennium.

Table 3.2 links changes in Nokia's development to these deeper contexts.

Finally, in September 2013, Nokia announced that it would sell its unprofitable mobile phones business unit to Microsoft and focus on its money-making mobile networks business, which was also part of its telecommunications roots (Nokia also kept its location technology as well as its extensive patents portfolio for licensing). It remains to be seen whether there will be other elements to the new strategy, and how it will work.

However, it must finally be emphasized that ICT is by its nature a business of very rapid changes, where quick turns for both the negative and positive are possible. Apple itself was almost bankrupt before it renewed itself and started its new rise. And Nokia's own history tells the same story that rising from near collapse is possible. Time will tell.

The most important level here, however, is the analytical one: The interest here is not in one single company. The real analytical interest lies in the question of the ability of the economy to both keep its culture of renewing creativity and expand this kind of innovation-based informational development more generally. This is the universal challenge of sustainable economy in the context of the global network society.

Expansion of the informational innovation-based economy?

It is, therefore, important to evaluate the empirical experience of Finland in this regard. In fact, the same is true for Finland as for any other country: the struggles of a single company would not be so important if the informational innovation economy was expanding around this industry, and even leveraging the momentum it has created.

So what is the actual situation in the Finnish case? First, it must be observed that new things have been developing after Nokia. The best-known example in the ICT field is the area of mobile gaming, including companies like Rovio who are behind the best-selling game *Angry Birds*

Table 3.2 Nokia's development from 1992 to 2012, with key context

	Nokia's internal developments	Technological and public environment
1992	Jorma Ollila becomes the CEO and refocuses on mobile communications	Public R&D support for GSM. Teleoperator deregulation
1993		
1994	Nokia launches its hit phone 2110	Experts on the government's information society council advise applying ICT to renew welfare services (health, etc.)
1995		
1996	Nokia launches the first, very technical, "smartphone," called Communicator	
1997		
1998	Nokia becomes the world's biggest mobile phone producer	
1999		
2000	Nokia's market value peaks	Public decision to sell the 'air' for mobile Internet 3G removes the European competitive advantage
2001		
2002	Nokia launches its first 3G phone	Experts like Torvalds, Kapor, and Himanen emphasize that openness is needed for others to join in creating apps

(*continued*)

Table 3.2 Continued

	Nokia's internal developments	Technological and public environment
2003		
2004	Ollila chooses to join the board of forestry company UPM as its Vice-Chair	Experts like Joi Ito emphasize the significance of design in the future of the ICT business
2005		
2006	Olli-Pekka Kallasvuo is made the new CEO	
2007	Nokia Networks merges with Siemens	Apple launches iPhone
2008	Nokia says that iPhone is marginal—Nokia has the biggest market share	Experts like Sabel and Saxenian warn that without leadership at the cutting edge mobile phones become commodities
2009		
2010	Stephen Elop is made the new CEO	
2011	Elop announces the "burning platform memo" and allies with Microsoft	Against expert advice, Nokia discards its leading Symbian OS and discontinues its development of a new open-source MeeGo OS
2012	Nokia struggles the whole year to sell its old products before the new ones arrive	Samsung's Android leads the overall market share, followed by Apple whose market value is the world's biggest; Nokia's value is shrinking

Source: author, using data of Nokia's internal developments from Taloussanomat, and of mobile phone market shares from IDC (in 2011 it already rejected a purchase offer of 1.5 billion euros) and Super-cell, behind the game hit *The Clash of Clans* (in 2013 the company sold its 51% share for 1.1 billion euros).

Also, some former Nokia engineers have started new companies that might have future growth potential. As an example, when Nokia decided to ally with Microsoft Windows in the IT ecosystems competition, some of the people who were leading the development of Nokia's new operating system called MeeGo left to form their own company, Jolla, that uses it as its platform (MeeGo is a Linux-based open-source system).

However, Table 3.3 of the ten biggest ICT companies in Finland shows that in terms of current revenues, employment, and overall significance to the Finnish economy, Nokia has not yet been followed by new major ICT start-up growth stories, if we evaluate the currently existing situation only through the normal hard economic criteria:

All of the companies on this list are basically the same as they were in 2002; Nokia is still by far the biggest (even after its restructuring). It is then followed by the leading teleoperators. Tieto remains the only IT software company on this list. The multinational companies offer the same IT services in Finland as they do in other countries. The only recent start-up company that has reached the Top ten as a new entry is 3 Step IT, which provides

Table 3.3 Top ten Finnish ICT companies based on revenues in 2012

Company	Revenues (€M)	Employees	Operations
1. Nokia	38,659	134,171	Mobile communications
2. Tieto	1,828	18,098	IT services
3. Telia-Sonera Finland	1,619	4,303	Teleoperator
4. Elisa	1,530	3,757	Teleoperator
5. Also Nordic Holding	953	716	Wholesales
6. Dna	728	1,008	Teleoperator
7. Hewlett-Packard	477	681	IT equipment and services
8. Fujitsu Finland	444	2,868	IT equipment and services
9. Logica Finland	431	3,242	IT services
10. 3 Step IT	392	214	IT services

Source: Tivi 250.

services for IT equipment management. What has disappeared from the list is the Finnish electronic manufacturer services network—now largely gone.

Still, the struggles of Nokia and the low level of major new ICT entrepreneurialism does not mean that nothing else is happening: in fact, the struggles of Nokia have led to a less-expected positive expansion of informational economy through former Nokia top executives, who have left and taken their experience of running a global innovation-based company and applied it to new sectors of the economy. At the moment, the most striking example is Kone, which is run by Matti Alahuhta, the same executive who was responsible for the strongest growth years of Nokia mobile phones. Under his leadership, the market value of Kone has experienced very high growth and is now in fact already more valuable than Nokia (15 billion euros, which means that even if Nokia remains Finland's biggest company in terms of revenues, it is no longer number one in market value). Kone is not directly in the ICT business; it is a more general technology company (of elevators and escalators) that is expanding the experiences of informational innovation-based growth to the wider economy.

Other former leaders of Nokia have started to lead companies in other sectors of the economy, ranging from technology to forestry and even mining. It is, in fact, this wider expansion of the informational development model that will be most critical for the overall future of Finland's sustainable economy—not just that there are new and specifically ICT-related start-ups and growth stories, though this is naturally also needed. In order to build a sustainable economy on solid ground, Finland needs both: a thriving ICT sector as well as the expansion of informational economic development throughout the whole economy. At the moment, the Finnish ICT sector's productivity matches Silicon Valley's; however, on the level of the overall productivity of the economy, Finland's productivity is 77% of the level of the United States (OECD 2012; based on the figures for GDP output per work hour input).

However, the positive news here is that recent economic studies show that there is a significant and relatively easily applicable way of increasing the overall productivity of the Finnish economy. This links to a Finnish paradox: Finland has been one of the world's leaders in producing new ICT for others, yet it does not apply this itself to reform its own economy!

According to the EU KLEMS productivity studies, starting from the mid-1990s, US ICT investments have corresponded to a 1.0 percentage point productivity growth and in Sweden to 0.7 percentage points in the corporate sector. In Finland the figure is 0.5 percentage points (cf. EU KLEMS 2011).

This suggests that in Finland the productivity potential of ICT remains underutilized and has not fully spread to other industries besides ICT production itself. One could therefore postulate that the systematic application of ICT across different fields of the economy has the potential to yield at least that additional 0.5 percentage points of further growth. This would be an extremely significant stimulus in creating a future of sustainable economy instead of the projected slowing growth of the Finnish economy over the coming years of aging population.

In fact, Finland is suffering from the old paradox of "the shoemaker's children going barefoot." Productivity growth in Finland has come overwhelmingly from ICT production, but outside the ICT sector itself, the application of ICT has fallen well below its potential. A study carried out by the Ministry of Transport and Communications in conjunction with the Research Institute of the Finnish Economy Confederation ETLA entitled "The Internet in Finland" (LVM 2010) shows that if ICT production is included when calculating the influence of the Internet on GDP, Finland ranks first in comparison to the United States and select European nations. But if ICT production is ignored, then Finland places last in the influence of the Internet on GDP. So, the "Finnish paradox," as a new form of the well-known "Solow paradox," can be summarized in this way: Finland produces Internet technology, which it exports but does not use itself! The use of Internet technology in service delivery is an especially underutilized opportunity.

If the utilization of ICT could be combined successfully with simultaneous reform of management and work culture through organizations—that is, the combination of the three types of productivity growth-inducing innovation, i.e. technological innovation, organizational culture innovation, and product/service innovation—then even under moderate estimates this would represent a possible source of that additional 0.5 percentage points of GDP growth for the Finnish economy that it is behind the US in this regard. Of course, on the practical level, such a reform should be linked to a broader program of productive wellbeing, combining informational development with the innovative reform of organizational culture, important from the perspective of full potential productivity growth. In order to succeed, this sort of information society program would have to be adopted as a strategic plank of the government program, with labor market organizations committed to strategic cooperation in support of sustainable growth in Finland.

Among this larger informational renewal, it would be good to keep in mind Finland's actual biggest ICT success story, which is not Nokia, but something else: the Linux open-source operating system, created by the 21-year-old

Finnish student Linus Torvalds, which runs half of the entire Internet and half of all the world's mobile phones—over half the technological infrastructure of the entire Information Age! (See Netcraft 2013 for Internet server shares and IDC 2013 for mobile phone OS shares: the market-leading Google Android operating system is a Linux variant.) In fact, many everyday devices that most people don't even think of as having operating systems run on Linux: from TVs to video recorders to game consoles and even digital pianos or gas pumps (not to mention that 90% of the world's fastest supercomputers, used to calculate the most complicated scientific problems or your weather forecast for tomorrow, use Linux). As a free and open operating system, Linux has quite unlimited possibilities for new applications that go beyond the economic.

Human development: the wellbeing society of the Information Age

The second major challenge that the Finnish model is currently facing in a new way is the challenge of sustainable wellbeing, or the question: How can the industrial welfare state be renewed into an informational welfare society 2.0—or the wellbeing society of the Information Age?

The application of the just-described informational development to the public sector itself, in addition to the private sector where it has already shown significant productivity gains, will be one key element. But it is not the only one. (Cf. also the approach of Timo Hämäläinen on a "sustainable wellbeing society;" 2013.)

Let us start again with a big-picture identification of what are the current biggest new challenges to sustainable wellbeing—or, in other words, to the old welfare state.

The three new challenges of the Information Age

In the Information Age—understood as the new socio-economic structure that Castells describes in his trilogy *The Information Age: Economy, Society, and Culture* (1st edn. 1996–98, 2nd edn. 2000–4), the important point being that informational development combines with significant socio-economic changes—the welfare state of the industrial era faces the following three big, new challenges, with which it is historically unaccustomed to dealing (which is not to say that the old tasks of the welfare state are disappearing; the following come in addition to them):

BOX 1

1. **Lifestyle challenges**

- *Aging*: a lifestyle in which people are having fewer children and living longer
- *Physical wellbeing*: a lifestyle in which there are mutually exacerbating obesity and lack of physical activity
- *Psychological wellbeing*: a lifestyle involving challenges to psychological wellbeing, such as depression, work-related stress, etc.

2. **Economic challenges**

- *The sustainability deficit of the welfare state*: a shift in the maintenance ratio—in other words, fewer workers are supporting a larger population of the elderly
- *Economic austerity*: the overall prospects for scant economic growth in Europe
- *Ecological sustainability*: the limits of ecologically sustainable growth, which can intensify material scarcity

3. **Informational challenges**

- *Information technology*: exploiting information technology, including biotechnologies
- *Organizational culture*: new forms of organizing, including management and work culture
- *Innovation-based productivity growth*: growth in productivity achieved through a combination of the above

---

Lifestyle challenges

Let us detail these challenges in the order of their magnitude. To begin with, challenges related to wellbeing are increasingly linked to lifestyle (see Giddens and Himanen 2006). Challenges in aging derive from a lifestyle in which people have fewer children and are able to live significantly longer lives than before. Infectious diseases have been replaced by physical and psychological lifestyle-related factors, such as diabetes and the cardiovascular diseases linked to obesity and lack of physical activity. Challenges to psychological wellbeing have risen to the fore, ranging from various forms of illbeing (such as depression and work-related stress) to deeper expectations of a life of not only illbeing eradication, but of actual promotion of wellbeing, in work and other arenas of life.

These developments are ultimately global (currently for most of the developed countries, but also, increasingly, for the developing ones). Life expectancy has more than doubled since 1900, when it was 35 years: people now live twice as long as they did a century ago. According to an analysis by the future work group of the World Economic Forum, one-fifth of the world's population is already overweight, and in terms of psychological wellbeing, depression will rise to become the world's second-most-common illness by 2030—more common than, for instance, cardiovascular disease or cancer (World Economic Forum 2007; see WHO 2008 projections for 2030).

Returning to the nineteenth-century antecedents of the welfare state helps to illustrate the difference between the welfare state of the industrial era and the welfare society of the Information Age. When von Bismarck, in order to guarantee the cooperation of workers as industrialism made its breakthrough, created the first forms of old-age pensions, catastrophic insurance, and healthcare in Germany, through a social contract struck between companies and the workforce, the average life expectancy was only about 40 years, and the greatest causes of illness and mortality were infectious diseases (on the prehistory of the welfare state, see for example Hennock 2007). In Finland as well, the first steps toward the welfare state were taken in the nineteenth century, in the form of civil servant pensions. The retirement age was lowered from 70 to 65 in 1826, and then to 63 in 1866, which remained the going age all the way up until the 1990s, with the expected length of a worker's career also the same 35 years for the whole period. Of course, in nineteenth-century Finland, the average life expectancy was also 35 years, so few were able to take advantage of this pension age in practice.

Economic challenges

The second major challenge being faced in the welfare state is economic sustainability. This is keenly crystallized in the enormous sustainability deficit in the funding of the welfare state and poses a new challenge for the welfare systems of developed nations, especially in Europe. In these countries, the welfare states proper of the industrial era developed during the boom-time conditions of post-World War II expansion. Building and funding the welfare state was made possible in part by the high birth rate of the baby-boom generation and its subsequent entry into the workforce. As the population ages, a fundamental shift will take place in the maintenance ratio for elderly care.

Again, returning to the past can concretely illustrate this shift. In 1950, every third person in Finland was under the age of 15, and only one in fifteen was over the age of 65. By 2030, on the other hand, every fourth Finn will be over the age of 65, and only one in six will be under the age of 15. A transition is underway, from the "Finland of the young" of the 1950s through the current "Finland of the middle-aged" to the "Finland of pensioners"—and, correspondingly, from the "Europe of the young" through the "Europe of the middle-aged" to the "Europe of the pensioners." A radical change in maintenance ratio is consequently happening, so whereas in the Finland of 1950 there were ten people of working age for every individual over the age of 65, and now there are four, in 2030 there will be only two people of working age funding the wellbeing of each individual over the age of 65. This change is taking place across Europe, but Finland will face it first.

This shift will create challenges for the funding base on which the welfare state is built, particularly when exacerbated by a decrease in career length compared to continuously growing life expectancy. In the case of Finland, time in the workforce has remained, on average, the same projected 35 years as was the case in the late 1800s and when the pension system was established in the 1960s. When the Finnish welfare state proper and its pension system were being built in the 1960s, life expectancy was ten years lower than it is today. The "compact" that gave rise to the emergence of the welfare state was, then, that an individual's time in the workforce would be 50% of their anticipated life expectancy. Nowadays the life expectancy of Finns is 80 years, meaning the proportion of overall life span spent in the workforce is less than 45%—and when, by 2030, life expectancy rises to 85, then, based on the same assumptions, time in the workforce would only be approximately 40% of overall life span.

This poses a challenge for the sustainability of the welfare state, culminating specifically in the sustainability deficit in its funding. One essential aspect of this problem is that it is structural, meaning that even good economic growth alone cannot solve it. And yet this set of circumstances worsens Europe's already slow overall prospects for economic growth, which if realized would mean increasing scarcity of material resources. In the end, it also intertwines with the most fundamental challenge to sustainability, namely the overall ecological sustainability of the marriage of the industrial economy and the welfare state. Exceeding the limits of ecological sustainability would mean increasingly severe scarcity of material resources. In terms of logical consequences, this leads us in the same direction, albeit from a different perspective, as lifestyle-based challenges to psychological wellbeing: in other words, in the new sustainable welfare society, we also need investments at the "immaterial" level; at the level of holistic wellbeing. Indeed, the fact of the matter is that even if material resources were utterly limitless in terms of economic or ecological sustainability, this would still not guarantee sustainable wellbeing in the most inclusive sense of the term, which in addition to physical dimensions must also encompass promotion of non-material wellbeing.

Informational challenges

The third challenge is the question of what an informational welfare society—a welfare society in the Information Age—might look like (cf. the chapter in this book by Castells, Chacon, and Himanen). The welfare state emerged as defined by the structures of the industrial era, ranging from technology to organization and its cultures of leadership and work. Informational development means a major transformation in our technological foundation; one brought about by information technologies, which, to use the term inclusively, embraces biotechnologies as well. Their exploitation is just beginning in the welfare society. Another fundamental aspect of the rise of new technology is the fact that it simultaneously dismantles the hierarchical, system-centered structures of the industrial era. This makes new types of organizing possible, and posits an operating culture in which people, not the system, are at the center. At the same time, information technology facilitates a major innovation-based increase in productivity in which welfare services can be realized more effectively and efficiently than before. This culture inherently involves people, as the users of services, in service development. Through its operating culture, informationalist development also indicates a path toward something new, by placing the focus on people.

Taken together, all of these developments jointly guide us forward from the welfare state of the industrial era to a new kind of welfare society: they place individuals as subjects and the advancement of each individual's comprehensively sustainable wellbeing at center stage.

Ultimately the challenge goes even deeper, to the question of the ultimate goals of the welfare state, which must be redefined for the Information Age (this relates to the core idea in this book of some deeper and more holistic goals for development—the idea of "dignity as development;" see especially Chapter 10 by Himanen).

The ethical values and goals of the welfare state

The welfare state of the industrial era did not originally emerge as a philosophical enterprise, but as a political one (see for instance Fraser 2009). Since then, its foundation has certainly taken various philosophical formulations, with John Rawls's *A Theory of Justice* (1971) perhaps one of the most influential. According to Rawls's theory, a just society must be designed so that one does not know what status one will hold within it—as if from behind a "veil of ignorance." A just society is one where people can agree on its guiding principles without knowing what their status—social, economic, or otherwise—will be. Extrapolating from this basis, the principle of equal opportunity, for example, is inherent to a just society.

Three major principles stand at the heart of the original ethics and social philosophy of the welfare state:

1. The aim of the welfare state is to create equal opportunities for all, independent of the arbitrary circumstances (social, economic, or other) of one's birth. This is because it is just.
2. The aim of the welfare state is to grant everyone equal protection against the vagaries of life. This is because it is just.
3. The aim of the welfare state is to include everyone as a member of society in benefitting its advances. This is because it is just.

From the ethical perspective, then, the foundation of the welfare state is the precept of fairness. In line with these principles, the objective of the welfare state is to advance the wellbeing of all. On a concrete level, this means guaranteeing health, education, a decent living, a sound environment, etc., for all.

Historical development of the welfare state 1.0

Practically speaking, the notion of a welfare state emerged within the context of the Great Depression and World War II (see for example Fraser 2009). In England, William Beveridge led the commission that drafted the 1942 industrial-era welfare-state program Social Insurance and Allied Services, also known as the "Beveridge Report" (Beveridge 1942). The report established the goal of removing "five giants on the road to reconstruction: want, disease, ignorance, squalor, idleness." The first of these was a reference to social security, the second to healthcare, the third to education, the fourth to housing, and the fifth to employment. Beveridge's platform thus took US president Franklin D. Roosevelt's formulation of the freedoms for which the Allies had fought (the 1941 State of the Union address) a step further.

The term "welfare state" itself was coined by archbishop William Temple, who used it in his 1941 book *Citizen and Churchmen*. In his bestseller from the following year, *Christianity and the Social Order*, he presented a more thorough rationale for this concept, grounded in Christian ethics, arguing how the welfare state was consistent with the precepts of Christian social justice.

In England, the post-war Labour cabinet led by prime minister Clement Attlee during the period 1945–51 began to carry out the proposed welfare policies. There was consensus in England on the welfare state, all the way up until the radical reforms of Margaret Thatcher's cabinet.

On a global level, the UN Declaration of Human Rights covenant on economic, social, and cultural rights is, for all practical purposes, an expression of the idea of the welfare state, even though it does not include the term itself (UN 1948).

In Finland, the formation of the welfare state into a national enterprise was given a powerful boost by Pekka Kuusi's 1961 work *Social Policy for the Sixties* (Kuusi 1961; for more on his role, see Tuomioja 1996). Like Beveridge, Kuusi did not use the expression "welfare state" himself. For Kuusi, the core issue was equalization-targeted income redistribution, which was to be seen not only as an expense but, on the contrary, an investment in the social conditions necessary for economic growth. Naturally, the Finnish model of the welfare state was also powerfully influenced by the "Nordic model" carried out in neighboring countries (Esping-Andersen 1990).

Welfare state 1.0 was, then, industrial society's response to the lacks or deprivations that had grown increasingly acute from the combined effects of the Great Depression and World War II. The welfare state became an expanded New Deal, as Roosevelt's compact for pulling together to survive the Great Depression was known. Now, in the presence of the current Great Recession, we are casting about for a new "social compact." What we need now is a vision of a post-Beveridge—or, in Finland's case, a post-Kuusi—welfare state program.

What could be the components of this updated welfare society—"welfare society 2.0?" Before we continue, it is important to stress that this updated welfare society must continue to realize the ethical values and aims of the original welfare state. The welfare state 1.0 has had an enormously positive impact in terms of decreasing poverty, illness, ignorance, and misery—and these welfare services and the types of taxation that guarantee equal opportunities, protection, and inclusion in a manner experienced as just must continue to exist in order to eradicate these problems. We are not yet finished with the job of eradicating deprivation; on the contrary, new challenges in terms of poverty and inequality have since arisen and must be answered.

Indeed, we can only take steps toward a welfare society 2.0 from the foundation of the welfare state 1.0. At the same time, we must broaden our perspective, both in addressing the new challenges to welfare described above, as well as going even further in terms of ethics and aims. From this wider perspective, welfare and the economy eventually come together in a picture of much bigger scale than in Beveridge's or Kuusi's day. It is not only a matter of income redistribution, although that is one part of it. The core of the link between wellbeing and the economy lies in increasing investments in education and universities, including support of research and development, in addition to traditional healthcare and other welfare services. This will produce highly trained experts and innovators to carry economic success forward—and economic success, for its part, makes it possible to continue funding welfare services and redistributing income in an equalizing fashion. The key issue is, actually, the sparking of precisely this sort of positive cycle between wellbeing and the economy, rather than a vicious cycle—and ultimately the formation of a positive cycle of sustainable wellbeing, a sustainable economy, and ecological sustainability as opposed to a vicious cycle.

From the welfare state to the wellbeing society: five new giants

As we move forward from the foundation offered by the industrial welfare state 1.0 toward the welfare state 2.0 of the Information Age—what can be called the wellbeing society—we must also delve into the eventual objective of the latter. Because the industrial welfare state emerged to eradicate want and lack, in other words, various forms of deprivation, despite all its positive achievements it has not gone far enough in meeting its ultimate aim: advancing the wellbeing of all. It is vital to recognize that, just as the lack of disease is not the same thing as health, the lack of misery is not same thing as wellbeing—not to mention happiness, used here as a name for the highest state of wellbeing.

On a philosophical level, there are five new giants on the path to a wellbeing society. In objectives, they all contribute to not only eradicating deprivation but also the necessary aim of promoting wellbeing proper.

Positive vs. negative

The first giant new step that must be taken is a shift from the negatively framed conception of the welfare state, defined by the eradication of (physical) deprivation, to a positively framed conception of the wellbeing society, defined by the ultimate goal of advancing wellbeing.

As a matter of fact, if we generalize, the industrial welfare state has been more of an "illbeing removal state" due to this negative definition of wellbeing. For instance, the healthcare system is more aptly an "illness care system" than a real system for promoting health, if we use the criteria set in the best-known definition of health, that of the World Health Organization: "health is a state of complete physical, mental, and social wellbeing and not merely the absence of disease or infirmity" (1946).

In a similar way, non-deprivation is not the same thing as wellbeing. Wellbeing is not the same as the lack of lack—and, therefore, the highest aim of the welfare society cannot be "the lack of lack!"

We can compare this to recent academic research on wellbeing and happiness in the new field of positive psychology. Its famous manifesto in 2002 began with Martin Seligman's statement: "For the last half century psychology has been consumed with a single topic only—mental illness." This is the first sentence in Seligman's work *Authentic Happiness*, and refers to an earlier observation by Abraham Maslow, the founder of humanist psychology: "The science of psychology has been far more successful on the negative than on the positive side; it has revealed to us much about man's shortcomings, his illnesses, his sins, but little about his potentialities, his virtues, his achievable aspirations, or his psychological height. It is as if psychology had voluntarily restricted itself to only half its rightful jurisdiction, and that the darker, meaner half." (Maslow 1954. For research results on wellbeing in positive psychology, see such seminal works as Seligman 2002 and 2011, Layard 2005, Gilbert 2006, Lyubomirsky 2008, Fredrickson 2009, and Kahneman 2011.)

In the same vein, we can proclaim a manifesto for the wellbeing society: "For the last 50 years, the welfare state has concentrated on one thing only: reducing illbeing. In the upcoming 50 years, we must concentrate on how we can actually promote wellbeing."

Proactive vs. reactive

Another giant step that needs to be taken as part of this renewal is transitioning from a reactive welfare state to a proactive wellbeing society. The industrial welfare state reacted to issues only when they had already developed into problems. If we generalize, we could claim that the welfare state has been good at dealing with problems that, in the wellbeing society, would not even be allowed to develop.

A fellow researcher aptly expressed the reactive nature of the existing welfare state with the metaphor of a man saying to his friend: "I have some really good advice for you once your wife leaves you." His friend replies: "I'd much rather hear your advice on how I can keep my wife from leaving me in the first place!"

This describes another way in which the industrial welfare state has been an "illness care system;" in other words, it reacted only once an illness had been allowed to progress. But genuine promotion of health would mean proactively pursuing those courses of action in which obesity (the single greatest cause of physical illnesses in wealthy nations) is not allowed to develop into a problem, or people are not left alone to gradually succumb to depression (the leading cause of sick leave and permanent disability in wealthy nations).

Indeed, if we take a critical look, what we've ended up with has not been a healthcare system but a system concerned specifically with treating illnesses, not sustaining health. We must transition from an illness care system to a healthcare system proper. And this need will grow increasingly acute, because as noted in the above description of the new challenges to wellbeing, these challenges are increasingly lifestyle-related at both the physical (for instance, eating, drinking, exercise or lack thereof) and psychological (for instance, mental illness) levels.

Subject vs. object

The third giant step that must be taken is moving from treating people as objects of the welfare state to seeing them as subjects of the wellbeing society. In other words, this is a change from the system-centered welfare state of the industrial era to the human-centered wellbeing society of the Information Age.

At times, users of the industrial welfare state feel that the system does not exist for them, but that they exist for the system. It is not unusual for individuals to experience welfare services treating them not as clients to be served, but as objects who should be grateful for favors received from the system. The key to distinguishing between a service and a favor is recognizing that "you are not doing me a favor, you are serving me" and "I am the reason you have a job." The difference is the same as that described by the statements "hospitals exist for doctors" versus "hospitals exist for patients."

In this context, a paradox of welfare services emerges, which can be crystallized in the expression "treated but hurt." Welfare services always consist of social interaction. However, the recent research on wellbeing cited earlier indicates that quality of interaction is one of the greatest factors affecting one's experience of wellbeing. This is why it is crucial that the operating culture of welfare services be organized in such a way that these interactions promote wellbeing, or at least do nothing to detract from it. The wellbeing society treats people as subjects rather than objects.

Taking this a step further still would mean involving people as subjects in the development of wellbeing services; in other words, taking advantage of the general logic of the aforementioned informationalist development: bring in users, as the source of many of the best ideas and solutions, to participate in service development, since they're the ones for whom the services exist. This is a new innovation model that has already spread to all other spheres of life, and it could, if systematically carried out, offer significant potential for developing a wellbeing society of the Information Age.

This approach has an additional important aspect: it's not just a question of the wellbeing society treating people as subjects; it's also a question of people treating themselves as subjects of their wellbeing. Even though the notion of the welfare state entails the concept of the state being responsible for these services, normal adult humans are also always responsible for caring for their own wellbeing and that of their loved ones. Caring cannot be outsourced to the state as a task for which it is solely responsible, just as we cannot ultimately outsource our lives to be lived by anyone else. Nor can we simply subcontract health from society. We cannot outsource accountability for our health; we also need to carry responsibility for it, for instance in terms of physical lifestyle choices. In the end, the wellbeing society is not something located somehow mystically outside of us; a wellbeing society emerges from everyone playing their part to contribute to wellbeing.

Holistic vs. partial

The fourth necessary giant step is a shift from a partial approach to wellbeing to approaching it holistically. This is a step similar to the distinction between a reactive welfare state and a proactive wellbeing society. Now we need to insert an important addendum from another perspective. In the industrial welfare state, we reacted to problems already caused by some other segment of the "welfare society." The task of the industrial welfare state is to try and correct issues that have been allowed to develop into problems in another part of the system, such as working life. To generalize, the welfare services offered in the welfare state 1.0 are the part of society that tries to treat the illbeing that prevails elsewhere in that same society.

The holistic approach of the wellbeing society means the systematic advancement of wellbeing in, for instance, the education system, culture of leadership and work, etc. We know from the cited research on wellbeing that three classic factors promoting wellbeing are:

- autonomy: freedom, agency, empowerment
- social relations: the quality of social relationships and the experience of belonging to a community
- meaningful activity: work, play, etc.

These three basic factors must now be very systematically disseminated to all cultures of learning, work, etc. Ultimately, genuine wellbeing in life can only be promoted holistically. This touches particularly powerfully on the largest new wellbeing challenge: mental health. Whereas a partial approach worked relatively well in removing the physical deprivations of the industrial welfare state, the psychological wellbeing now included in the aims of the wellbeing society of the Information Age cannot be achieved in any other way than through the holistic approach outlined here. Unless psychological wellbeing is pursued, we will run into a paradox in which the result is a welfare state full of people who are not faring well! This paradox can be seen in the current figures on psychological illnesses.

State vs. society

The fifth giant step that we must take is a shift from the welfare state to a more inclusive wellbeing society. Before elaborating any further, it must be stressed here that this does not mean reducing the state's obligations with regard to any of its welfare responsibilities. As a matter of fact, the concept of the wellbeing society activates the state to act more broadly for wellbeing than before, by, for instance, promoting psychological wellbeing in the spheres of education and work.

At this juncture, it is critical to be conceptually very precise. In the concept of the welfare state, the mission of the state is seen as responsibility for ensuring the fair realization of equal opportunity, protection, and inclusion for all, according to the ethics described. This task is assigned to the state, because even though it does not do a perfect job of carrying it out, the state is, as the only democratically controlled party representing the interests of all, the best alternative. The state's legitimacy to collect taxes is also centrally tied to this responsibility for providing wellbeing: we pay taxes in the expectation that the state will take responsibility for ensuring the realization of equal opportunities, protection, and inclusion.

In this regard, the mission of the state is viewed in exactly the same way in the concept of the wellbeing society of the Information Age. In the wellbeing society, the state is held even more accountable for carrying out this task.

It is useful to explicate this conception carefully here: the aforementioned notion of the welfare state means that the state is responsible for realizing welfare services. But this does not mean that the state must also realize all of these services itself. It may well realize the majority of them, but in addition, innovations from companies and NGOs can contribute to their realization. Responsibility for realization of services means responsibility for their organization—in other words, funding and quality. But citizens benefit from better services and greater selection. The balance between these two is a political choice faced by every society. In the sense described above, the industrial welfare state has been a nationally unifying project, earning commitment across party lines. In contrast, the issue of execution level is a pragmatic and political one that reflects the various political parties' lines of demarcation. It is critical to note that these are two distinct issues.

Nevertheless, regardless of the specific extent to which companies and NGOs, for instance, participate in the provision of the welfare services according to the principle described earlier, society also needs the active contributions of these companies and NGOs. It is important that we have wellbeing entrepreneurship, where someone who has developed a new and better way of doing things—for instance, a higher-quality, more humane form of living for the elderly—starts disseminating it and expanding its acceptance in practice. And the fact that participation arising from self-initiative flourishes in a wellbeing society is also an intrinsic value.

In fact, without in any way detracting from the responsibilities of the state, the wellbeing society of the Information Age encourages active and voluntary participation in citizen association activities; for instance, helping elderly people who live alone, or joining inclusive sports clubs. These direct forms of caring promote societal wellbeing that combines social relationships and community belonging, the free choice of using one's own gifts, and engaging in meaningful activity. And this brings wellbeing not only to those "helped" but also to the person participating, in the best sense of the principle of "giving is getting."

The initiative of the public sector can create a welfare state, but it does not yet create a full wellbeing society, which is the objective proposed by the concept of the wellbeing society of the Information Age.

The renewal of the welfare society in practice

On the practical level, to meet the above three major new challenges of the welfare society that are linked to lifestyle, economy, and technology—and in order to achieve its deeper goals in the Information Age—the following three

---

BOX 2

1. Lifestyle challenges

- Psychological illbeing factors have become the leading reason for early retirement. On average the Finns retire at the age of 60, which is several years below the official retirement age that ranges from between 63 and 68 years (ETK 2012).
- 3/4 of Finns experience that "the work culture is currently so stressing and pressing that this is leading to the burnouts" (EVA 2013).
- The economic cost of early work retirements giving mental health reasons as a clinical diagnosis is 10 billion euros per year through lost work output, which is equal to 1/5 of the Finnish government's annual budget (Finnish Institute of Occupational Health 2010).
- More broadly calculated, the economic cost of early retirements due to non-wellbeing in working life is 25 billion euros a year through lost output, which is almost 1/2 of the government's annual budget (cf. the calculations made by the cited FIOH researchers for the Ministry of Employment and Economy: Ahonen, Hussi, Pirinen 2010).

(continued)

BOX 2 **(CONTINUED)**

2. Economic challenges

- The dependency ratio between workers and pensioners for whom they provide has radically changed since the establishment of the industrial welfare state: now it is 4:1, and with current trends it will be 2:1 in 2030 (Statistics Finland 2012).
- As the dependency ratio keeps changing, the sustainability deficit of the welfare state keeps growing. Based on estimates of the EU Commission and the Ministry of Finance, the sustainability deficit is roughly 5% of the GDP, or 10 billion euros.
- The average length of a working career continues to remain 35 years as the expected lifetime continues to grow faster even than expected (VNK 2011 and Statistics Finland).
- In the early-1990s depression, the employment rate dropped from the pre-depression level of 75% and has since then remained at a little under 70% (Statistics Finland 2012).

3. Informational challenges

- According to analyses by the VTV and the Ministry of Finance, the informationalization of the Finnish welfare state has so far not advanced significantly; instead, it's been characterized by the following problems (VTV 2012 and VM 2010):
- Slow progress: as an example, the national electronic patient data and e-prescription systems were already a part of the national information society vision in 1994 and its follow-up strategies prepared by specific ministries, but they are still not in use (cf. VM 1994 and STM 1995).
- Productivity growth has been marginal because the adoption of ICT has not succeeded.
- There has been a problem with the leadership needed for this type of broader renewal.

---

issues are decisive for the case of Finland (Box 2). They are all simultaneously examples of moving from the top-down welfare state to a wellbeing society that includes the whole society—with people at its center—in much more holistically participatory ways.

They are linked to the following empirical picture of the current Finnish situation and what is the best available empirical knowledge about the

---

BOX 3 **THE EFFECT OF DIFFERENT FACTORS ON THE PUBLIC ECONOMY'S SUSTAINABILITY DEFICIT**

- General productivity growth of 1.25% would decrease the deficit by 1%
- Productivity growth in the welfare service provision by 0.25% would decrease the deficit by 1%
- The lengthening of working careers by one year would decrease the deficit by 1%
- A rise in the employment rate of 2% would decrease the deficit by 1%
- An increase in immigration by 10,000 persons per year would decrease the deficit by 1%

Source: Ministry of Finance STM SOME model (2012).

---

measures that would in practice have the biggest effect in answering to the current model's sustainability deficit.

Box 3 gives the figures that the Ministry of Finance has provided for this research into the factors that would have the biggest effect on the above challenges (using its mathematical model, called SOME).

Putting the empirical facts presented together, there are clearly three big policy-making areas that play a key role for creating the basis of sustainable wellbeing—or "the wellbeing society of the Information Age":

The first is productivity. The potential of general productivity growth in the private sector has been addressed here. But here, the most direct way of making a difference is to increase the productivity of the welfare state itself. So, first, there would need to be the kind of informational renewal of the structures of the industrial welfare state that has been referred to and is described in more detail in Chapter 4 on the "welfare state 2.0." In this model, the Finnish model would be upgraded one step further. It has already been based on the idea that the welfare state is not just a cost, that is funded by a competitive economy; the point of the virtuous circle is that the welfare state is an investment that provides highly skilled people with the good health and security necessary to continue the success of the economy. But this would take it even one step further: it would mean that the informationally renewed welfare state would provide the sustainability for the whole virtuous circle between the competitive economy and informational human development. It would in a way shift the thinking about which one is the "ultimate basis" of the other, in this modern version of the "chicken-and-egg" circle.

Second, a new deal must be found between work and wellbeing. The ratio of those working and those receiving welfare has to be maintained at a sustainable level. Here, of course, one crucial question and part of the solution is the ratio of the productivity of work to the productivity of providing the wellbeing. However, this alone will not be sufficient if enough people choose not to work and instead retire early as a result of burning out or other forms of mental illbeing in their working life—that is, if an equivalent of at least 1/5 of the government's budget is lost this way every year. What would be needed is some kind of a program of "productive wellbeing" that would renew the management and working culture to combine both innovation-based productivity and wellbeing. And, in fact, in the end these are linked: people who feel well can sustain their productive innovativeness, which again generates wellbeing. Similarly, this would mean a shift in the thinking on the relationships between productive innovation and wellbeing.

The third empirical observation is that a more open immigration policy could also help greatly to maintain the sustainability of wellbeing. So, contrary to the idea of "immigrants coming into our country and taking our wellbeing," the immigrants are actually crucial to generating wellbeing for ourselves—yet another shift of thinking between the relationship of the factors. This, of course, does not happen only because of the number of workers increasing and, therefore, the dependency ratio becoming more sustainable, but also because of the effects that such openness has for the general culture of creativity, as documented for example by AnnaLee Saxenian's work in her chapter of this volume (see also her book *The New Argonauts* on its role in innovation in the Silicon Valley global network).

In all of this, ultimately, it becomes clear that what is finally being talked about is not only a structural but also a cultural change. The wellbeing society of the Information Age is a different culture of doing things to the industrial welfare state (it is in a way also applying the "hacker ethic" to wellbeing issues, as already suggested by Himanen in 2001).

Culture: the culture of creativity

This leads us to the final key component in the question of reconstructing a sustainable development model in the Information Age: its cultural dimension.

There are three key cultural dimensions that are especially important in this context (cf. Himanen's 2001 book *The Hacker Ethic* as an analysis on the elements of the culture of creativity of the Information Age). The first one is a culture of "creative entrepreneurialism," understanding "entrepreneurialism" here broadly as a name for any form of active fulfillment of one's potential, whether in business or something else.

It has already been mentioned several times here that the shift to a full form of informational development is ultimately also cultural—and how it is this cultural level that has been hindering the renewal needed for both a sustainable economy and sustainable wellbeing.

In fact, ultimately, some of the biggest challenges for the future of Finland's ability to reconstruct a sustainable growth model are related to some mental features of its culture of creativity.

Let us start by evaluating the empirical reality of a culture of creative entrepreneurialism, using the empirical data on business entrepreneurship and attitudes toward it as an example. The first observation here is that Finland has a very low level of start-up entrepreneurialism: for example, whereas in the US the start-up entrepreneurship rate of people between the ages of 18 and 64 is 13%, it is less than half of this in Finland (6%, as measured by the Global Entrepreneurship Measure 2012). In fact, Finland's figure is among the lowest of all advanced economies.

Studies on values and attitudes give light to the cultural background of this phenomenon. The Finnish Business and Policy Forum EVA has conducted an annual survey on Finnish attitudes and values for the past three decades and these studies clearly show that, on the cultural level, entrepreneurialism is discouraged. According to the most recent survey by EVA, one in two Finns think that "only a crazy person" chooses to become an entrepreneur in Finland (EVA 2013). This is related to two factors that are like different sides of the same coin.

First, entrepreneurial failure is seen as a personal failure, in a cultural context that can be described as "a culture of shame." This is very different from the American ideas of "you can fail without being a failure," "you can make a mistake without being a mistake," or "falling forward." Therefore, it is also very different from the Silicon Valley idea that failures are actually also merits: failures show that you've tried and yet you've not given up—in the spirit of there ultimately being no big difference between failing or succeeding, as they are both forms of learning ("this doesn't work;" "this works"). (In the EVA study, 56% cite "the culture of risk-avoiding" as one of the top weaknesses of Finnish competitiveness.)

Second, this relates to the idea that no one should succeed more than others, or what can be described as "a culture of envy"—a distorted form of the idea of equality. In fact, the answers to different attitude surveys by the Finns, including the one by EVA referred to, could be summed up in this way: in Finnish culture, the only thing that is even less accepted than failing is to actually succeed! The strength of this attitude is evident in the most recent EVA study, in which 75% of respondents said that a more positive attitude would be required toward entrepreneurialism for people to choose it. Currently, the social price of both failing and succeeding is too high. If this attitude toward the culture of creativity continues, as a distorted interpretation of what equality as a societal value implies, it will be one of the major obstacles for the entire sustainability of the Finnish model in its future attempt to creatively renew its economy, attain wellbeing, and have a flourishing cultural life. (It is not an unimportant observation that a key group of the most talented Finns, from Linus Torvalds to leading artists and scientists, have chosen to move elsewhere—for example, to the United States and the United Kingdom.)

The second major key challenge relates to the openness that the culture of creativity requires. In fact, as we argued in Chapter 1 on the analytical framework, cultural identity is a key mediator for a longer-term virtuous or vicious circle between sustainable informational and human development—or, to put it in different words, for a virtuous or vicious circle between a sustainable dynamic economy and a sustainable welfare society.

For the reasons mentioned in Chapter 1, a strong collective identity can be a strength in many ways: it can be a strong basis for linking economic development to human development through an all-inclusive welfare society that at the same time legitimizes the whole development model. The existence of such a strong Finnish cultural identity is also reflected in the EVA study: 72% of the respondents think that "it is a good fortune and privilege to be a Finn." This strong cultural collective identity could be a particular strength if it could consider all people living in the country to be "Finns" as much as anyone who happened to be born in the country: in this case, Finland could combine a strong collective cultural identity with an openness to immigrants.

However, the empirical data shows that Finland remains one of the most closed countries in terms of immigration. In fact, it has one of the lowest levels of foreign-born population in the whole world—and especially among the advanced economies: 4.2%, compared to the United States (three times that level, at 13.5%), the United Kingdom (11.2%), or its neighbor Sweden

(14.1%); not to mention the levels of immigration in Silicon Valley that Saxenian cites in Chapter 2 of this book.

The surveys on Finnish values show a culture behind this, in which attitudes remain very closed toward others. In fact, there is a big contradiction: based on what is known of the needs of the future sustainability of the Finnish economy and wellbeing, increased immigration would be one key required element. As cited here, for example, the Minister of Finance has shown by calculations that an increase of immigration by just 10,000 per year would mean a 1% reduction in the welfare society's sustainability deficit.

Still, even knowing this—and even if there continues to be very strong support for the welfare state (80% agree that even if the welfare state means higher taxes, they would continue to support it)—52% of respondents to the same poll by EVA reject immigration as even a potential tool for economic revival (only 6% gave their full support for increasing immigration as an option). In fact, even knowing the economic realities, still only 32% are ready to agree with the statement that "the threatening aging and decrease of the Finnish population require easing immigration to Finland." Finally, in the same study, one in two people rationalized that "the Finnish reserved attitude towards foreigners is simply wise caution, not ignorance or racism" (EVA 2013).

Empirical data is the best way to get a real picture of a loaded cultural matter such as whether an increasing culture of closedness is a real trend or not. Since we wrote our original book on the Finnish model (Castells and Himanen 2002), the biggest political change has been the rise of the True Finns party, which received 19.0% of the vote in the most recent parliamentary election in 2011 and became the third-biggest party.

A profile of these voters has already been presented in our joint book on the global economic crisis (2012). To sum it up briefly here, the core reason for the rise of the True Finns has been its strong nationalist opposition to all forms of openness—whether it is immigration, the European Union, or the euro—as representatives of the global network society (see Himanen 2012; cf. also Rahkonen 2012 for the statistical data). The True Finns are a Finnish version of the rising ultranationalism that runs on a populist premise without offering solutions to the serious and acute challenges.

Figure 3.4 shows especially clearly how the True Finns have grown from being a completely marginal party outside parliament in 2005 to a new and permanent member of the three biggest parties, under the conditions of the global economic crisis. Its strongest rise took place under the conditions of

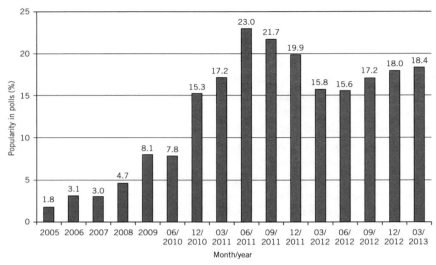

Figure 3.4 Support for the True Finns in the polls between 2005 and 2013
Source: Political party support polls by YLE and Taloustutkimus (2004–13).
Note: the parliamentary elections were held in 2007 and 2011.

the Great Recession that started in the US in the fall of 2008 and which hit Europe especially hard when it developed into a public fiscal crisis that required Finland to participate in the eurozone bailout packages for Greece and Portugal (especially in 2011 when the popularity of the party peaked as the biggest party in the polls shortly after the elections; since then, only a very minor margin has kept it from becoming the biggest party).

Ultimately, a pro-European Union, pro-euro coalition was able to form the government. However, the closed attitudes of the True Finns influence all politics toward openness for foreigners. In practice, immigration has disappeared, even as an option, from the Finnish discussion, so the True Finns have also impacted on the other parties' courage to stand for openness—not to mention that, in the landslide election victory of 2011, the True Finns even influenced the European Union's political mindset, by putting the whole European bailout package for Portugal at risk. Since then, there has been a continuously declining trend in solidarity between European countries.

This brings us to the third key element in the culture of creativity: the first being creative entrepreneurialism (understanding "entrepreneurialism" here broadly as a name for any form of active fulfillment of one's potential, whether in business, arts, or something else); the second, openness to others (the culture of enriching interaction); and finally, thirdly, trust. (One can also compare this list to Himanen's 2001 analysis on the elements of the "hacker ethic" as the culture of creativity of the Information Age.)

In this third dimension comes also the more hopeful part of the cultural level of the Finnish model in its potential to reconstruct a renewed sustainable development model to meet the big new challenges. Trust is one of the biggest assets of the entire Finnish model in which, first of all, the virtuous circle between a competitive economy and an all-inclusive welfare state means that everyone can feel that they have more or less the same opportunities in life, from education to health, and can trust in the strong social security safety net, given life's unpredictable situations, such as unemployment or retirement.

Secondly, this trust is further maintained and increased by the development model's way of including everyone as beneficiaries of the development, which is evident in the fact that Finland still has some of the lowest levels of poverty, income inequity, and gender inequality in the world.

In fact, this cultural strength of high trust in the Finnish model is reflected strongly in all international comparisons related to trust, from the UN and Gallup world studies on the trust in society's institutions (such as the government), to the measures of trust in other people. For example, roughly 60% of Finns report that they trust others in their society, whereas the same figure for the European Union in general and the United States is about 35% (UNDP 2013).

So perhaps this foundational element of trust could provide a new basis also for openness to others and a culture of creative entrepreneurialism. If it could, then we could imagine a new round of thriving innovation-based informational growth in the economy as well as a flourishing culture of pioneering innovation of "the wellbeing society of the Information Age." So, instead of showing the world the technological project of being "the number-one information society in the world," it would be showing the way to a new "wellbeing society of the Information Age," with the opportunity for everyone to lead a dignified life as its ultimate development goal. Then, this could become the new Finnish collective cultural identity project (to use Castellsian terms): building the new wellbeing society of the Information Age as an example that combines sustainable economy, sustainable wellbeing, and their sustainable culture—in a way in which being a "Finn" would mean participating in this project, regardless of one's birthplace.

It goes without saying that such a project will not be easy. But it should also go without saying that without the ability to recreate the cultural level of the development model, instead of a future of flourishing there could be a fate of withering. Finland has one of the best starting points, to be the first to succeed in reconstructing a sustainable development model as an example for the rest of world. Therefore, it is both analytically and politically valuable for all to observe the Finnish experience. Ultimately, how this model develops will very crucially be decided based on which culture the country chooses: will it be the culture of creativity, with innovation, openness, and trust? Or will Finland give in to the opposite?

Chapter 4

Toward the Welfare State 2.0? The Crisis and Renewal of the European Welfare State

Manuel Castells, Isidora Chacón, and Pekka Himanen

Introduction: Information technology, networking, and the welfare state, in the context of the fiscal crisis

Since 2008 Europe has suffered a major financial crisis with significant consequences in the global financial markets and in the world economy, including the United States and the newly industrialized countries. At the heart of this financial crisis there is a fiscal crisis that has led to a crisis of sovereign debt. And at the core of this fiscal crisis there is the crisis of the sustainability of the welfare state that has been a distinctive feature of European societies in the last half-century (Pestieau 2006). The European Union is being brought into tighter fiscal and financial integration to overcome the potential risk of the dissolution of the euro. A new European Treaty has furthered the integration in terms of fiscal policy and common banking regulation, paving the way for increased coordination of macroeconomic policies.

However, regardless of the success or failure of this risky project, any constitutional document will be just a piece of paper unless a reform of the public sector, with the welfare state at its center, is undertaken. And information and communication technologies, together with organizational transformation and a proper use of better-educated human resources, are a key component of this reform of the welfare state.

This is not an exclusive European problem, albeit it is in Europe where the need of the transformation of the welfare state is more acutely felt because of the scope and size of the European welfare states and the critical role these public institutions and policies play in ensuring social cohesion.

The welfare state (basically health, education, social security, including pensions, and a variety of government services and transfers) is becoming unsustainable in the medium term in the current context of fiscal crisis in most EU countries. This is because of its skyrocketing costs, particularly in health and pensions, under the conditions of an aging population (Hay and Wincott 2012). Such a trend will place governments and citizens on a collision course, with unpredictable consequences, unless there is a transformation of the model of relationships between economic growth and the public sector, with the formation of a virtuous circle of positive feedback between the two processes, along the lines that Castells and Himanen analyzed in their book on the Finnish Model of the Information Society (Castells and Himanen 2002).

Indeed, in terms of the economy at large, the financing of the pension system and other key components of the welfare state is not dependent only on a demographic calculation: active workers over dependent population. Rather, it is a function of the ratio of the productivity of workers over the cost of sustaining the dependents, both in numbers and cost of services. If productivity increases substantially per employed worker it could support a much larger number of dependents. But there is another productivity effect to be investigated in this ratio: productivity gains in the denominator of the ratio, specifically productivity gains in the government sector and in the public services sector at large that would reduce the actual costs of services. While we know the difficulty of measuring productivity in services and in public services in particular, there are measures of efficiency that could be used as a proxy.

We know that the technological transformation of ICT under the right conditions of **organizational networking, improved human resources,** and **managerial innovation** has been a major factor in the productivity surge associated with what we used to call the new economy, particularly in the US and Scandinavia. Over the period 1995–2004 in the EU, ICT drove half of all productivity gains, mainly through efficiency gains in the ICT sector and investment in ICT. Later evidence shows that in 2004–7, before the financial crisis hit, Europe entered into a second phase of ICT impact, delivering productivity gains in the economy at large. ICT industry accounts for about 5% of European GDP and for 25% of total business R&D. Over half of European employees now use computers at work, and 80% of these computers have access to the Web. According to the World Internet Project in 2010, the majority of the population of all countries surveyed reported that going online at work improved performance or productivity (except in Sweden, where only 39% reported gains). Econometric analysis of the aggregate production function of European economies indicates that a 10% increase in ICT capital is associated with 0.23% growth in firm productivity—well above what theory suggests should be the impact of capital investment (0.16%).

Although productivity statistics on the impact of ICT in the public sector are not available, we can safely hypothesize that there is an extraordinary reserve of productivity and efficiency in the public sector because almost all the work in this sector is based on processing information and setting up communication. Higher productivity in the sector means providing more services with fewer workers. Greater efficiency means reducing costs and improving quality. Thus, in a long period of fiscal crisis, rather than cutting the delivery of public services, so reducing living standards and potentially triggering social unrest, a reformed welfare state could provide more and better services at a lower cost. ICT, and related organizational innovations, could play a major role in this strategy. The new frontier of expansion of the Internet and of networking technologies seems to be primarily in public administration, health, and education. And so, can we think of the emergence of an informational welfare state? Yes and no. It all depends on the proper articulation between technological transformation, organizational transformation, and management of the social process of reforming the welfare state. Indeed, from productivity analysis in the business sector we know that what are called "unmeasured, complementary assets" may play a big role in determining the overall impact of ICT. Thus, the key issue for research and analysis is to identify these mysterious complementary assets. In this chapter we suggest some tentative hypotheses.

At this point we must be specific, sector by sector, highlighting the main ideas, and referring to selected documentation for the empirical evidence on which this analysis is based. We will present an overview of developments in e-governance, e-health, and e-learning, all part of the public sector, being legally public or private. By public services sector we mean a sector that is not being driven primarily by profit-seeking strategies, although some segments of the sector (e.g. for-profit hospitals or schools) may escape this definition. Even in these cases, however, the profits come largely from hidden government subsidizations for the operating costs of private health or private education. The figures included throughout this chapter illustrate selected empirical evidence in support of our analysis.

The digital state: from e-government to e-governance

Over the past decade European governments have invested billions of euros in rolling out e-government procedures and e-government infrastructure. There are two dimensions to this effort. First, e-government, meaning the transformation of government bureaucracies into computerized, networked systems, both internally and in relation to other governmental units. Second, e-governance, the relationship between governments, citizens, and business. There has been considerable progress of full online availability of e-governance services in Europe, although more for business and less for citizens (Figure 4.1).

Although still lagging, the e-networking of business and public administrations in most EU countries has introduced network technologies on a massive scale. In terms of network sophistication (mainly broadband and interactivity potential), the EU is in the fourth tier for transactional e-services out of five tiers defined internationally. e-government 3.0 is looming on the horizon, merging government communication, business applications, and social media platforms with the semantic web in order to deliver personalized services. The projection (by Gartner Research) is that the percentage of public web pages with some kind of semantic markup is approaching 70%.

However, for the time being, e-government in the EU is behind on its promise. Figure 4.2 shows that in most countries the diffusion of Internet use in society at large is way ahead of the uses of e-government services, and

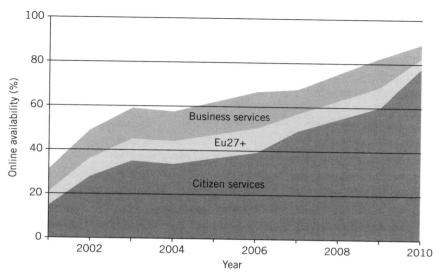

Figure 4.1 European full online availability of e-governance services for businesses and citizens, 2001–9

Source: "Digitizing Public Services in Europe: Putting Ambition into Action," 9th Benchmark Measurement, European Commission, Directorate General for Information Society and Media, 2010.

Table 4.1 provides information on how the Internet has been used to interact with public authorities. Figure 4.3 shows the limited use of e-government services and the concentration of these services in mere information retrieval with limited interactivity.

It appears that governments have focused on certain areas of citizen interaction that are of the governments' interest. Success stories can be found in a few key sectors. In Spain, the Tax Agency prepares the tax returns of all citizens, and sends them electronically in most cases for verification and signature only; this has dramatically improved tax collection and limited fraud. Also in Spain, there is growing use of the electronic ID card to access a web of integrated public services. In France, a portal called mon.service-public.fr is a user-customized and highly secured (via identification) single access point to all the public services available online, some of which are entirely transactional. A personal account enables users to keep track and know the status of all their interactions with the public administration. Also in France, the e-procurement platform Marchés Publics makes it possible to

93

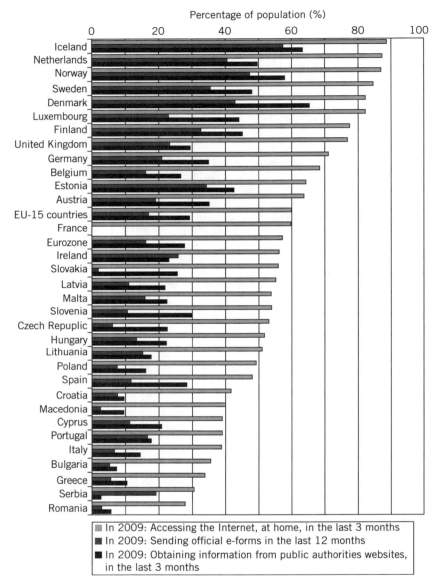

Percentage of population (%)

■ In 2009: Accessing the Internet, at home, in the last 3 months
■ In 2009: Sending official e-forms in the last 12 months
■ In 2009: Obtaining information from public authorities websites, in the last 3 months

Figure 4.2 Internet access, use of e-forms, and use of government websites, Europe, 2009

Source: eGov: From Option to Obligation, Deloitte Touche Tohmatsu Limited, based on data from Eurostat, 2010.

Table 4.1 Use of the Internet for various kinds of interaction with public authorities in the last 3 and 12 months, as a % of Internet users

Values as % of people which used the Internet in the last 3 months	2008	2009	2010
I have used the Internet, in the last 3 months, for obtaining information from public authorities websites	41.3	42.2	40.7
I have used the Internet, in the last 3 months, for downloading official forms	25.8	26.8	25.9
I have used the Internet, in the last 3 months, for sending filled forms	19.0	19.5	19.3
I have used the Internet, in the last 3 months, for interaction with public authorities	45.8	46.2	45.8
Values as % of people which used the Internet in the last 12 months	**2008**	**2009**	**2010**
I have used the Internet, in the last 12 months, for obtaining information from public authorities web sites	49.9	51.2	52.5
I have used the Internet, in the last 12 months, for downloading official forms	34.4	36.1	37.4
I have used the Internet, in the last 12 months, for sending filled forms	25.3	26.3	29.4
I have used the Internet, in the last 12 months, for interaction with public authorities	54.0	55.8	57.9

Source: Eurostat, Community Surveys on ICT use in Households and by Individuals.

regulate the bidding process by requiring bidders to submit their applications and tender by electronic means only (following in the wake of Chile Compra, one of the first and most successful experiences in the world in terms of transparent, web-based public market transactions). The electronic social insurance card Vitale is being widely used in France. Sweden, according to the UN e-government survey, is the world leader in terms of e-government readiness, on the basis of a different model, a network of web portals dedicated to specific themes. The Baltic countries are well positioned in e-government use and innovation.

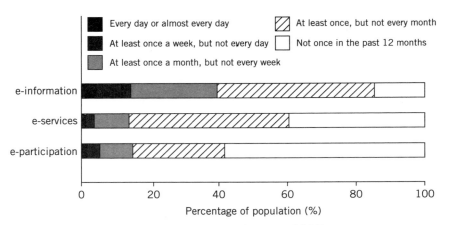

Figure 4.3 European use of e-government by type, 2008

Source: Study on User Satisfaction and Impact in EU27, European Commission Director General for Information Society and Media, 2008.

However, in general terms, there are key unsolved issues linked to difficulties in transforming internally government agencies in a networked administration. Let us be specific about the issues and the problems involving a networked administration.

A networked administration is an organization based entirely on networks. Networks between departments, within departments, between different levels; national, European, local, regional. These shared networks require access to common databases and horizontal relationships between units while maintaining information accessible to everyone and real-time interactivity; this allows hierarchical controls to keep working.

This networking implies that databases are inter-operable and accessible. This is the essence of the whole system. More specifically, networked administration requires inter-operable software programs, open for the development of customized applications. Here, open-source software is the project. But common standards are required to make different open-source procedures compatible. It also requires new rules for administrative relationships that have to become horizontal.

This new, networked administration can only be managed on the basis of Internet and computer networks. But this is the easy part. The key is the micro-powers game within the bureaucracies, as we will argue below. Transparency of the administration and citizen participation is dependent upon a number of technical and organizational conditions, such as connecting Internet and intranets, and legal access to stored information by using friendly communication procedures. Every administrative action needs to have an accessible electronic record. Online interactivity between databases and citizens, and between citizens and every service and unit of the administration, should be the norm. Multimodality of communication is essential, and could include not only mobile phone but also digital IPTV as an access point. These are standard conditions for a transparent and networked e-administration. However, a number of obstacles have been detected in international experience to implement a networked administration. The main obstacles are as follows.

First of all, some technology providers dictate solutions that are not always the most adequate. Yet, bureaucrats do not want problems, so they contract with technology providers that have brand name and packaged supply solutions. To prevent this bureaucratic logic in the building of the networked administration, public agencies' administrations need to develop an autonomous technological capacity to evaluate and decide. Open-source could facilitate the issue, but the problem lies in the difficult interoperability and standards. Sometimes, the ideological preference for open-source solutions creates a backlash among practitioners who prefer user-friendly technologies in off-the-shelf programs. The issue is the need to develop a robust system in an in-house technological unit, adapted to the characteristics of each service. Then inter-operability with other systems must be included in the technological solution. Indeed, open-source software must be able to interact with proprietary software. Ultimately the issue is the need for an autonomous technological policy from the administration, and the means to carry it out.

Second, the hierarchical structure implicit in most bureaucracies contradicts the networking logic. Computer networks, because they are pervasive and have electronic records, tend to eliminate areas of uncertainty. In his classic analysis of organizational dynamics in bureaucracies, Michel Crozier showed that micro-powers in the organization appear in areas of relative autonomy that offer managers bargaining power over the interpretation of formal rules of the bureaucracy. Informationalization of the rules and instructions, with an electronic record for each process, considerably reduces autonomy. Therefore, low-level managers have a vested interest in blocking the informationalization of the organization, and often succeed in slowing down the process or even making it so costly that it comes to be reversed.

Third, the transparency associated with computerized information systems creates problems for the private uses of public administration, and ultimately makes corruption more difficult. Thus, we witness resistance to transparency from the hidden interests nested in many areas of the public administration.

Manuel Castells, Isidora Chacón, and Pekka Himanen

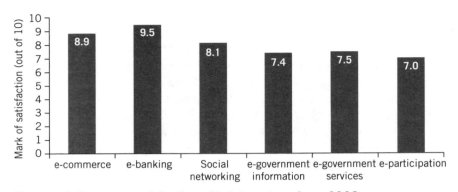

Figure 4.4 European satisfaction with Internet services, 2008
Source: Study on User Satisfaction and Impact in EU27, European Commission Dir General for Information Society and Media, 2008.

Fourth, efficiency and participation are not the same. Articulating both in the logic of the network is not easy. In fact, the lack of interest in real participation from governments leads to very limited use of participatory procedures. e-participation ranks the lowest in terms of citizen satisfaction with Internet services (Figure 4.4).

Fifth, labor needs an adaptation to the networking process, both in its operating capacity in technology, and in the uses of its autonomy of decision-making. The transformation of the organizational process may call into question workers' rights, and the working status quo, particularly in a union-ized public sector. Thus, negotiation with labor unions is a most critical issue for technological and organizational change. Productivity and flexibility can be achieved in exchange for improvement in wages, working conditions, and training programs.

Sixth, and importantly, there is often a lack of interest and knowledge from the organizational leaders in changing the status quo. And without determined leadership at the top, there is little chance of true organizational change.

In fact, the challenge of transforming public administration comes from the fact that two opposing principles have to be reconciled: bureaucracies give priority to security and reliability; innovation implies risk. The ability to combine security and risk conditions the emergence of a very strange, yet decisive, organizational species: the innovative bureaucracy. What inter-national experience shows is that the decisive factor for networking admin-istration and public sector services is the articulation between cultural change, organizational change, and technological change. And for this, leadership is required, supported by the participation of workers and users in a negotiated process of innovation by trial and error.

In the European context, the shift from the bureaucratic state (best exemplified by the Napoleonic construction in France or Spain) to the networked state is a major cultural and institutional change, prompted and implemented, but not caused, by Internet-based technologies. Ultimately, informationalization of the administration requires the reform of the state. It requires transforming the logic of the state from the state as a political machine to administration as a managerial machine, or, in other words, from the administration of people to the management of matters, and from political domination to service delivery. Because of the magnitude of the change, in fact, the process is contradictory, slow, and often stalled.

The promise of e-health: a technological utopia?

The health system represents in all countries a substantial share of GDP and employment. It also provides our most needed service: the maintenance of our bodies and minds.

It is also the privileged space of the biological revolution, and it is based on scientific and technological innovation. Technology is at the heart of health care. Moreover, the health system is entirely dependent on processing information.

Yet, while technology is paramount in advanced medical care, the penetration of Internet and ICTs in the management of the health system and in the interaction with patients and people at large is still well below the possibilities of transformation.

In the EU in 2010, 92% of hospitals were connected to broadband but 52% had bandwidth below 50 Mbps. Yet, electronic data exchanges outside the hospital with other providers were still not common: 54% of acute care hospitals do not have electronic exchange of clinical care information; 57% did not exchange laboratory results; and 57% did not exchange medication lists. Only 5% of hospitals had any kind of electronic exchange of clinical care information with health-care providers in other EU countries. Moreover, the use of a wireless infrastructure was very limited, and only 35% had a unified infrastructure able to support specific applications. More importantly, the vast majority of applications in computerized systems were used for routine bureaucratic tasks (Source: European Commission 2009f).

Manuel Castells, Isidora Chacón, and Pekka Himanen

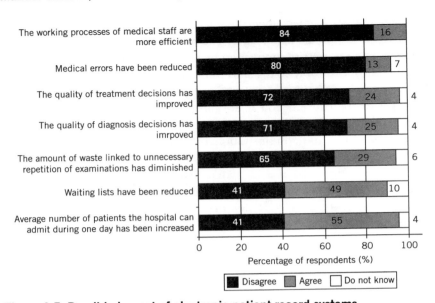

Figure 4.5 Possible impact of electronic patient record systems
Source: eHealth Benchmarking III, European Commission Directorate General for Information Society and Media, 2009.

The limited diffusion of ICTs in hospitals is not surprising when observing the response of medical personnel to potential benefits (Figure 4.5). Accordingly, 95% of the patients do not have online access to their records.

In e-health, the key transformation is not to introduce ICT or telemedicine, but to redesign the whole system, on the basis of Internet and intranets, as a network of networks; networks that condition the functioning of the whole process: networks between health providers and patients via health information webs; networks from patients to patients, the self organization of the patients both in associations and informal networks; networks between insurance systems and service providers; hospital intra-networks; inter-hospital networks; networks between primary care units and specialized hospitals; connection from emergency care units to other emergency care units and to the broader service provider; and home health-care networking with the parent health-care provider. In the perspective of preventive medicine and public health institutions, it is essential to foster inter-networking and networking with the population at large (interactivity of the network, in contrast to one-way dissemination of information).

Furthermore, for the proper management of the health system as a whole, the networking between providers, patients, and paying systems—either public health administration or private insurance companies—is essential.

Ultimately, the patient is the key node in the system, and all information is processed around them. But the focus on patients requires: a) connecting the whole network via a shared clinical history, accessible from all points in the system; b) individualizing information through a health card in the pocket of every citizen; and c) connecting the health system and the drug delivery system by computerizing the networks and making the health-care provider pay by a pharmacy card in the hands of each patient.

This system is in the process of implementation in various degrees in different countries, but finds extraordinary obstacles in its way.

Why is there such a resistance? We can provide some tentative answers on the basis of a major study directed by Manuel Castells on the transformation of the health-care system in Catalonia between 2003 and 2007.

While the Catalan context is specific, in fact, during the period studied, the Catalan government was engaged in a very ambitious program of reform in the management of the health-care system. The results of such an effort were mixed, due to a number of obstacles that were identified in the research project, which we summarize here (Castells et al. 2007): a) professionals felt that organizing their activity by electronic networking could jeopardize their autonomy (particularly vis-à-vis insurance companies and public health administration); b) patients feared loss of privacy and consequences for the control of their lives; c) systems were deployed for cost-reduction purposes, not for quality or service; d) the segmentation of the system became more difficult, which challenges the micro-powers of medical bosses in their departments; e) the autonomy of patients using the Internet challenges the power of the expert. Consequently, "voodoo medicine" gets its day by spreading non-professional advice and misguided information over the Internet; f) health workers lost autonomy and needed retraining; g) the process of health care becomes hyper-specialized and dominated by technology. Hospitals become the center of the health-care system, with the consequent loss of the generalist physicians and the demise of a holistic vision of health care. This is not only a matter of growing scientific specialization, but also the result of the need to predefine every action in the health system in order to quantify, budget, review, and be paid for each action. Routinization of procedures leads to standardization of health care. The patient is no longer a case in themselves; h) patient communities formed as web networks are under-utilized, and yet when they emerge, researchers have observed a positive effect on their health (Grau 2011).

Therefore, vested interests in health organizations condition the networking of health care in ways that induce a system that, rather than patient-centered (the ideology) or doctor-centered (traditional medicine), becomes health management-centered.

Yet, because of cost problems, the informationalization of the health-care system is expanding rapidly, particularly in large hospitals, although intranets and SAP networks are more important than Internet and external networks with both providers and patients. This leads to increasing use of standard protocols and reduced autonomy of medical professionals. For instance, nurses have been largely transformed into executants of protocols. Thus, health reform is both a technological and organizational process, and requires the integration of professionals in a new approach to medical care.

Re-learning to learn: e-learning in practice

Of course the Internet, and not only the computers, is potentially a key medium to transform teaching and learning. This is the technological basis for the shift from transmission of knowledge to learning to learn because information is on the Internet. A study by USC researchers Martin Hilbert and Priscila Lopez published in *Science* in May 2011 calculated that of all information existing on the planet in 2007, about 97% was digitized and most of it was potentially accessible over the Internet (Hilbert and Lopez 2011). Since the information is available over the Internet, the key skill for people to acquire is the mental and educational capability to decide which information is needed for a given task, how to find it, and how to recombine it. Furthermore, the key learning practice is a lifelong learning strategy that requires high-quality distance education.

Equipment is not a problem. In Europe, in 2009, at least 75% of 15-year-old students were studying in schools where they shared one computer with no more than four classmates, and at least 50% of students were in schools where there was one computer for every two students. Some type of computer equipment is available in nearly all primary schools. However, interestingly, though the technology with the most positive impact is the interactive whiteboard (53% of users report positive impact), it is only used by 12% of the respondents. Furthermore, m-learning is considered to be the educational technology of the future, both for the administrations' relationships to the students, and for learning processes themselves: who wants a laptop when most kids have, and know how to use, a computer that is called a "smartphone?" And yet, it is used by less than 10% of the respondents (teachers) in their classrooms.

On average in Europe, if both desktop and laptop/tablet use, whether connected to the Internet or not, are aggregated, there are 14 per 100 students at grade 4, 19 at grade 8, 21 at grade 11 (general), and 31 at grade 11 (vocational). Of these computers, almost all are Internet-connected (there is less than one non-Internet-connected PC per 100 students at all levels). In the EU, there are from 5 to 12 students per online desktop computer: 8 per 100 students at grade 4, 13 at grade 8, 14 at grade 11 (general), and 21 for every 100 grade-11 vocational students. The older the student, the more online computers are available. Laptops (including tablets, netbooks, and mini-notebooks) are becoming pervasive in Europe's schools, almost all of which are Internet-connected at every level. At grade 4, benchmark changes since 2006 as regards computers per 100 pupils show an increase in the numbers of such computers per 100 students from 9.5 (EU25+2 average) to 14.7. Benchmark changes since 2006 as regards computers per 100 pupils at grade 8 show an increase in the numbers of such computers per 100 students from 10.9 (EU25+2 average) to 17.8. And at grade 11 (general), benchmark changes since 2006 as regards computers per 100 pupils show an increase in the numbers of such computers per 100 students from 12.7 (EU25+2 average) to 20.6. Benchmark changes since 2006 as regards computers per 100 grade-11 (vocational) pupils show an increase in the numbers of such computers per 100 students from 15.8 (EU25+2 average) to 29.5 (Source: European Commission, 2012a).

However, what research shows in various contexts is a limited use of the Internet integrated into the actual learning process. It is either used in a specialized class, or homework, but is not often a part of the classroom activity. And very often computers and mobile phones are forbidden in the classroom, allegedly because they distract students, in spite of the widespread and dynamic practice of multitasking. We do not have conclusive evidence on the effects of the Internet on the learning process, but overall there seems to be a positive correlation between the use of the Internet and academic achievement. Some studies report problems with focus and memorization in an Internet learning environment, but others emphasize that using the Internet enhances the recombination capacity that is generally acknowledged as being at the source of innovation and creativity.

In fact, data show that many more students use computers for information retrieval, a generalized practice (Sources: Indicators on ICTs in Primary and Secondary Education, European Commission Directorate General Education and Culture, 2009; Digital Competences in the Digital Agenda, Digital Agenda Scoreboard, European Commission, 2012a).

Some arguments explaining the lack of integration of Internet-based learning in the classroom are related to teachers' resistance because they are losing power in the classroom due to their lack of familiarity with the system. This may be so. But this is not because they do not know how to use the Internet. In a study on a representative sample of Catalan schools in 2005 (Momino and Sigales et al. 2007), 100% of schools reported Internet connectivity, but the Internet was used in the classroom, on average, only two hours per month. However, teachers at home used the Internet 12 hours per week and students at home used it 10 hours per week. Three-quarters of the children connected to the Internet to do their classwork, but only 4% of those connecting to the Internet did so from school.

Thus, the issue is not the familiarity of the teachers or students with the Internet but the inability of the school system to connect them in the classroom because of arcane organizational procedures and regulations. The education system has not been retooled for the information society. Among the often-cited reasons for this conservatism is the ideology of rejecting the Internet to preserve what teachers traditionally know how to do. Of course there are some old studies showing that computers have no effect on scholarly achievement, but a) these studies are about computers, not the Internet, and b) if there is no transformation of the school, they actually become a tool of chaos and discrimination (fast learners learn faster, slow learners regress in comparison). In addition, because this is a cultural gap, this relates also to the parents' education and reproduces inequality. The school should then be the center of the Internet in the public interest, but corporatism and lack of new pedagogy in the schools slow down the transformation. Yet, there is an increasing trend of students' collaboration, the key use of networking technologies. The key trend is introducing the practice of collaboration by using the Internet, as shown in Figures 4.6–4.15.

In practice, the growing gap between the digital culture of the students and the traditional literacy of the teachers is cited as one of the major factors for the drop-out rate of 30% in secondary school observed in some European countries (including France, Italy, and Spain).

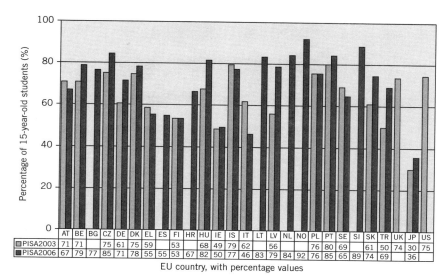

	AT	BE	BG	CZ	DE	DK	EL	ES	FI	HR	HU	IE	IS	IT	LT	LV	NL	NO	PL	PT	SE	SI	SK	TR	UK	JP	US
□ PISA2003	71	71		75	61	75	59		53		68	49	79	62		56			76	80	69		61	50	74	30	75
■ PISA2006	67	79	77	85	71	78	55	55	53	67	82	50	77	46	83	79	84	92	76	85	65	89	74	69		36	

EU country, with percentage values

Figure 4.6 Percentage of 15-year-old students using computers for collaboration, 2003 and 2006

Source: Indicators on ICTs in Primary and Secondary Education, European Commission Directorate General Education and Culture, 2009.

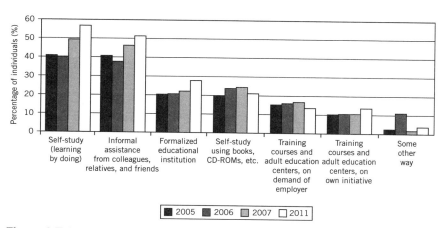

Figure 4.7 Ways of obtaining Internet and computer skills (% of individuals, 2005–11)

Source: Digital Competences in the Digital Agenda, Digital Agenda Scoreboard, European Commission, 2012.

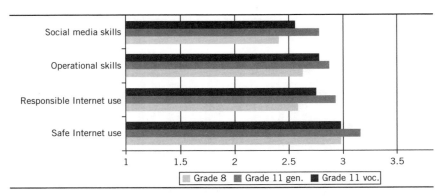

Figure 4.8 Students' confidence in their ICT skills (mean score of students; EU level)

Source: Digital Competences in the Digital Agenda, Digital Agenda Scoreboard, European Commission, 2012.

Percentage of students who agreed or strongly agreed with the following statements

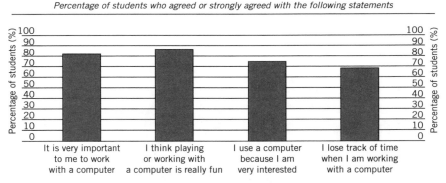

Figure 4.9 Percentage of students who reported positive attitudes toward computers (OECD average = 28)

Source: 2009 Results: Students Online, Digital Technologies and Performance, PISA, OECD 2011.

The bewilderment of the university system in the digital age

In most universities there is already a blended system in practice (a mixture of virtual interaction and classroom interaction), as professors and students interact more online than face to face, and students largely rely on resources

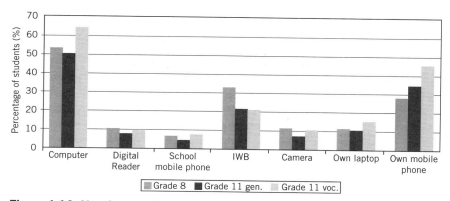

Figure 4.10 Use for learning purposes during lessons, at least once a week (Grades 8 and 11; EU level)

Source: Digital Competences in the Digital Agenda, Digital Agenda Scoreboard, European Commission, 2012.

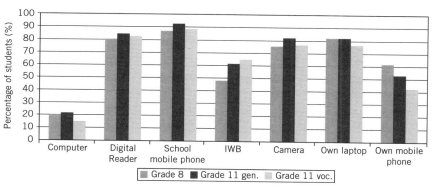

Figure 4.11 Use for learning purposes during lessons, never or almost never (Grades 8 and 11; EU level)

Source: Digital Competences in the Digital Agenda, Digital Agenda Scoreboard, European Commission, 2012.

found and shared on the Internet. But this is in fact a system that has grown on an ad hoc basis, and usually it is student-driven.

Fully virtual, 100% Internet-based universities are still an exception, although there is a growing trend in this direction. The Open University of Catalonia (UOC) has been a successful trendsetter, after its establishment as early as 1995 as a fully web-based public university, with over 60,000

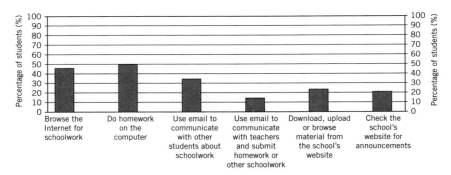

Figure 4.12 Percentage of students who reported that they did the following activities at home for schoolwork at least once a week (OECD average = 29)

Source: 2009 Results: Students Online, Digital Technologies and Performance, PISA, OECD 2011.

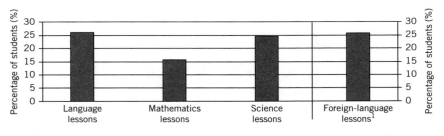

1. OECD average for computer use during classroom lessons in a typical school week, not adjusted for the number of students who do not have any lessons in the subject each week.

Figure 4.13 Percentage of students who reported that they use a computer during regular classroom lessons at least sometime during a typical week (OECD average = 29)

Source: 2009 Results: Students Online, Digital Technologies and Performance, PISA, OECD 2011.

students in 2012. The Open University of the United Kingdom and The Open University in the Netherlands are now largely web-based, although they still maintain some traditional forms of distance learning. Most distance universities mix Internet with different communication technologies, including video and videoconferencing. These distance universities are the fundamental institutions for lifelong learning, the new frontier of higher education. In

understood in the totality of the human condition, and the policies for its betterment should be coordinated and complementary. This approach would maximize the quality of life resulting from the policies, while eliminating redundancy and contradiction between different agencies and their action. Once the holistic concept is fully analyzed and applied to policy design, networking, with the help of ICTs, could provide the organizational platform for the holistic welfare state.

This is the welfare state that we call the welfare state 2.0, adapted to and created by the informational model of development.

However, given the institutional and cultural obstacles we have identified in this chapter, this vision of a new welfare state would require a fundamental reform of the institutions and policies of the currently existing welfare state (Bonoli and Natali 2012; Ferrera 2008). For such a reform to be socially and politically feasible, it would be necessary, in each country engaging in the fulfilment of this vision, to establish a social compact between all social actors and political institutions, in a similar process to the one that led historically to the constitution of the industrial welfare state.

Chapter 5

Development as Culture: Human Development and Information Development in China

You-tien Hsing

Introduction

Human development, as defined in Chapter 1 of this book, is "a process of enhancement of the living conditions that make humans human in a given social context." Pekka Himanen defines the goal of development as "the culture of dignity." Following this direction, I consider human development as the culture of development that is as much about recognition as about redistribution. Information development, which connects information technologies with social transformation, interacts with human development and shapes the process and results of development in a given time and place. In this paper I will discuss China's human development and its relationship with information development in the past thirty years. I focus on the dilemma between China's impressive Internet expansion, an unquestionable sign of information development and the hope for democratization for many China watchers, and the predicament in human development characterized by a prevalent culture of institutional and interpersonal distrust. I argue that the intense distrusting relationship within the citizenry and between the state and society, both online and offline, has slowed down the insecure state's undertaking of substantial reforms, and prevented the wary citizens from organizing transformative networks.

I have divided this chapter into four parts. I begin with China's developmentalism since the 1980s, characterized by the persistent party state dominance and fortified by the coalition of the political and economic elite. Then I move on to China's human development, focusing on the current social predicament of the commodification of justice and rights, as well as the cultural crisis of distrust under the Chinese model of developmentalism. In the third section I outline China's Internet culture against the backdrop of its information development on a platform for wide-ranged users and activities. In the concluding section I suggest that the cynical culture offline has aggravated the misinformation and deception online. The success of China's information development is more salient on the economic front than the sociocultural front, consistent with the Chinese model of developmentalism.

China's developmentalism

While the model of the developmental state has been applied to the case of post-Mao China, the long-term trajectory of China's development has been very different from other East Asian developmental states like Taiwan and South Korea. One of the most visible distinctions is that while Taiwan and South Korea developed multi-party democracy and an active civil society in the post-developmental state era, the Chinese Communist Party state continued, and even reinforced, its grip over the society after waves of marketization and socioeconomic diversification in the past three decades. Indeed the CCP, the largest communist party in the world with an 80 million-strong membership, is far from being a contention-free organization. Yet the very fact that it continued to grow and attract the talented and ambitious graduates from top universities to join its ranks thirty years into the market reform needs to be explained. How has the CCP regime managed to get this far?

The durability and expansion of CCP power needs to be analyzed in the context of Chinese developmentalism in the past three decades. China's developmentalism, characterized by continued state intervention and direct participation in the rapidly expanding market, has been evolving along the following axis:

First, the trend of fiscal decentralization and the increase of local state autonomy since the 1980s. Instead of wholesale privatization, China's reforms featured the emergence of the local state as a motor of market expansion, and the subsequent reconfiguration of the fiscal relationship between the central and local states.

Between the 1980s and early 1990s, ownership and managerial authority of many SOEs (state-owned enterprises) was transferred from the central ministries to local governments, linking local state budgets with the profitability of these former SOEs, now owned and managed by local government entities. The revenue sharing scheme between the central and local was 20 to 80%, one of the most decentralized revenue sharing ratios in the world.

Along with the fiscal autonomy of the local state was the fiscal liability: local governments had to take on much greater fiscal responsibility for overhead, social welfare, and capital investment. As a result, local state leaders, whose promotions depended on local GDP growth, became highly motivated to search for new sources of revenue and GDP boosters. They were engaged directly and indirectly in profit-making enterprises, especially property development and land lease sales. Because of the increasing significance of the local state in the process of economic expansion, Jean Oi (1992) has termed it "local state corporatism."[1]

The single-party polity allows the CCP to decentralize its resource control down the party hierarchy to local governments without having to worry about competition from other political parties at the local level. The local state continued to enjoy administrative authorities and the fiscal autonomy to conduct business and keep the extra budgetary revenue in local coffers. This makes the Chinese experience different from the East European transition economies of the 1990s, in which the multiparty political system makes decentralization a less plausible option for the central government leaders.

But the "local state," like the state in general, is not a homogeneous entity. The last three decades witnessed a shift in the level of the local state that had played the leading role in China's economic expansion. In the 1980s and

---

[1] Oi, Jean C. (1992). "Fiscal Reform and the Economic Foundations of Local State Corporatism in China," *World Politics*, Vol. 45, No. 1, pp. 99–126.

early 1990s, during the era of high-level decentralization, rural, lower-level government at the township and village levels took the lead in rural industrialization and market expansion. By the mid-1990s, the motor of growth had shifted to the urban-based municipal government that consolidated its authority over the rural hinterland and took the lead in urban expansion at the expense of the rural sector.

Second, the trend of recentralization since the mid-1990s. The rise of the local state is far from a lineal process. As a response to the overly decentralized economy of the 1980s, central government has strived to recentralize control over the economy since the mid-1990s. Under the new fiscal regime, local governments' share of revenue decreased from 80% to 45% of the national total, while its expenditure remained at the level of 70% of the national total.[2] In addition to much-increased central revenues, the central government also embarked on restructuring the SOEs, aiming to consolidate state assets, with the principle of "keeping the big fish and letting go of the small shrimps." Smaller SOEs were merged into hand-picked large SOEs, and oligopolistic or monopolistic central-state-owned corporate groups were formed. The consolidation campaign covered a wide range of strategic sectors, including finance, hydropower, logistics, petroleum, petrochemical, steel, shipbuilding, telecommunications, media, precious metal, defense, aerospace, food, infrastructure construction and real estate, tobacco, etc. The result of this attempt to recentralize the economy was not a simple sway back to the centralized planned economy. Rather, the new political economy since the late 1990s has been marked by competition, negotiation, and alliance building between different levels of the state in resource and financial control.

Third, blurred boundaries and cross-sectoral coalitions between the state and non-state sectors. Under the principle of "keeping the big fish and letting go of the small shrimps" in SOE restructuring, the small shrimps were privatized through merger or manager buyout. This sector has consequently created a very complex ownership structure and elaborated business networks within and across different sectors and industries, making it impossible to draw a definite line between the "state" and the "private." The result of this is that medium and small-scale businesses

---

[2] Zhou, Feizhou (2006). "Ten Years of Tax Reforms: The System and its Impact (*fenshuizhi shinian: zhidu jiqi yingxiang*)," *Chinese Social Sciences* (*zhongguo shehui kexue*), No. 5, pp. 110–15.

continue to exist, with high birth and mortality rates due to the highly unstable financial conditions.

The continued dominance of the CCP regime over this rapidly expanding and diversifying economy is made possible by the integration of the interests of the political and economic elite at different levels. While the CCP state maintains a clear control over the economy, such control is decentralized within the party-state structure, shared by different segments and levels of the party-state.[3]

The key actors in China's statist economy are what I have called the bureaucratic entrepreneurs and entrepreneurial bureaucrats. By entrepreneurial bureaucrats I refer to current government officials whose primary responsibility is to run businesses directly, such as CEOs of national-level state-owned enterprises, directors of special development zones, or heads of government-owned investment firms. By bureaucratic entrepreneurs I refer to business owners, CEOs, and top-level managers of corporations that have strong connections with or backgrounds in state institutions, including firms fully or partially financed by government or party organizations, public utility and service agencies, and military units that have been restructured into shareholding companies. The difference between the bureaucratic entrepreneurs and entrepreneurial bureaucrats lies in the level of their connection with the state. They can be further divided into three tiers.

I have discussed elsewhere the detail of this model.[4] Here I will briefly outline the three tiers of political and economic elite. The top-tiered political-economic elite, the entrepreneurial bureaucrats, represented by the CEOs of national-level state owned enterprises, are an extension of the party state. They are ranked in the same bureaucratic hierarchy as government and party officials. Most of the CEOs of top-tier SOEs have long and extended experiences in the party, government, or military systems. Veteran CEOs of

---

[3] Andrew Nathan and David Shambaugh used the terms "resilient authoritarianism" and "adaptive authoritarianism" to explain the durability of CCP power, based on elite cohesion. While the theses are challenged by other students of Chinese politics for their inability to deal with rising contentious politics since the 2000s, the concept remains a useful starting point to explain the CCP's organizational strategies. Nathan, Andrew (2003). "Authoritarian Resilience," Journal of Democracy 14 (1): 6–17. Shambaugh, David (2008). *China's Communist Party: Atrophy and Adaptation*. Berkeley and Los Angeles: University of California Press.

[4] For details of the bureaucratic entrepreneurs and entrepreneurial bureaucrats, see Hsing, You-tien (2012). "No Crisis in China? The Rise of China's Social Crisis," in Manuel Castells et al. (eds), *Aftermath: The Culture of the Economic Crisis*. Oxford, UK: Oxford University Press. pp. 251–77.

top-tier SOEs are often appointed as provincial governors or party secretaries, and vice versa.[5] Top-tiered SOEs and their CEOs bear the prestige, expectation, and political mandates that few lower-level, local state-owned enterprises or private firms could match. The mid-tiered elite is composed of both entrepreneurial bureaucrats and bureaucratic entrepreneurs associated with major urban governments of leading metropolitan centers like Beijing, Shanghai, Chongqing, Guangzhou, Chengdu, and Nanjing, etc. This group controls more than half of the national GDP and more than 80% of the employment. They are the predominant regional force in China's new territorial order, and have often dealt with central–local contention, especially over the issue of land development and financial regulation in the late 2000s.

The third tier of bureaucratic entrepreneurs is made of lower-level elites with two types of background. One is those who have originated from the rural private sector and who are then recruited into the lower-ranking party state system at the village, township, or county level. The second type follows an opposite direction. These are local officials who leave the state sector positions and start businesses on their own. But often their connections with the state sector continue to play an important role. Because they are relatively further from the core of the state, the third-tiered elites are more like bureaucratic entrepreneurs than entrepreneurial bureaucrats.

What these bureaucratic entrepreneurs and entrepreneurial bureaucrats have in common is that, as the major actors in the market, they have a strong affiliation with state bureaucracy. The level of their affiliation with the state has a direct implication on their competitive position in the market, influencing their access to information, finance, and other key resources like land and energy at highly subsidized prices, and the level of their monopoly.

The CCP state's dominance of the economy is consolidated through the integration of the political and economic elite at these different levels.

---

[5] Yang, Ruilong; Wang, Yuan; and Nie, Huihua (2013). "Mechanism of Bureaucrats' Promotion: Evidence from National-level State-owned Enterprises, (*zhunguanyuan dejinshen jizhi: laizi yangqide zhengju*)," *World of Management* (*guanli shijie*), No 3. In the campaign for scientific management of SOEs, the State-Owned Assets Commission started to recruit high-level managers of the SOEs from outside of the existing state bureaucracy from 2004. But according to a survey, only 30% of the new recruits were still in their positions by 2009. And the majority of those who stayed on had a background in the state sector. [Zhou, limin, Xiao Liang (2010). *yangqi quanqiu haixuan zaiqihang wangjie kongjiang liucun buzu 30%*, (Central Level SOE Management Recruitment Started Again, Less than 30% of the Previous Recruitment Stayed)] <http://finance.sina.com/bg/chinamkt/sinacn/20100702/181789396.html>.

Resource control is concentrated in the hands of the CCP state, but decentralized within the immense party-state apparatus, and shared (not necessarily in an even manner) amongst a large hierarchically organized elite. This statist economy, marked by the dynamic structure of concentration and decentralization, is the foundation of China's continued economic expansion. Its primary goal is to sustain the power of the CCP. This power structure has certainly not been contention free, and fierce competition among various segments of the party-state is well known. The hierarchically organized and internally decentralized resources and power sharing scheme has proved to be effective for the most part in holding the party together at the time of globalization and market expansion.

In addition to the 80 million party members, the total number of state employees comprises another 60–70 million,[6] excluding the military and police force. The number of state employees has doubled in the last ten years, and continued to grow despite the calls for slimming the size of the state. This 140–150 million-strong party-state membership is not just about the size of the state sector payroll, but also the state sector employees' privileged access to public goods like better schools and health care that could not be attained by money alone. While the political-economic elite class of varied scale and scope might not manifest consistency and cohesion, they do form a coalition based on shared interests and belief in the necessity of maintaining the power of the CCP. The hierarchically organized and internally decentralized resources sharing scheme has proved to be effective for the most part in holding the party-state together at the time of globalization and market expansion.

Human development

The other side of the concentration of power and money within the party-state system is growing social disparity. China's Gini coefficient rose from 0.25 in 1984 to the alarming 0.491 by 2008, before dropping to 0.474 in

---

[6] Yang, Jisheng (2011). "Analysis of Social Class of Contemporary China (*dongdai zhongguo shehui jieceng fenxi*)," Jiangxi gaoxiao publisher; Xiong, Jianfeng. (2013). "Survey of the Scale of the Government Payroll (*zhongguo caizheng gongyang guimo diaocha*)," *Phoenix Weekly*, No 10, April 22, 2013, <http://big5.xinhuanet.com/gate/big5/forum. home.news.cn/thread/123108644/1.html>.

2012, still one of the highest in the world.[7] If calculated by the distribution of property assets instead of income (income is skewed because of continued welfare subsidies to privileged groups and unreported income), the figure would have risen to 0.661 for 2008. The rural–urban income gap was about 1:4 by 2006, if we take into account the welfare benefits available only to urban residents.[8]

Contentious politics is also on the rise. In 1993 there were about 8,000 reported cases of "public order disturbance," including protests, demonstrations, picketing, and group petitioning. The number rose to 90,000–100,000 in 2007, with more than 4 million participants.[9] The Ministry of Public Security released statistics of "mass incidents" showing increases of popular protests from 10,000 cases in 1993 to 60,000 in 2003, and then to 180,000 in 2010.[10]

The causes of the conflicts could be excessive fines and punishment of family planning violators, land grabs with inadequate compensation and forced removal of residents, or confiscation of the property of street vendors in the campaign to clean and modernize the city. Yu Jian Rong, a social scientist at the Chinese Academy of Social Sciences, suggested that about 70–80% of the cases since the early-2000s were land-related, triggered by under-compensation of land appropriation, inadequate relocation arrangement, and forced demolition and relocation. My own research showed that between 1990 and 2009, farmland conversion and inner-city redevelopment have displaced no less than 75 million rural and urban residents. The number could easily double if we include repeated displacements as the cities have expanded outward in several waves over the past two decades. The number of protests increased as destruction of homes and communities accelerated.[11]

The Chinese government has been taking systematic action to vent the heat since the early 1990s. The Administrative Litigation Law was

[7] Official Gini coefficient: 0.479 (2003), 0.473 (2004), 0.485 (2005), 0.487 (2006), 0.484 (2007), 0.491 (2008), 0.490 (2009), 0.481 (2010), 0.477 (2011), 0.474 (2012); <http://news.backchina.com/viewnews-228772-big5.html>.

[8] Li, Pei-lin et al. (2008). *Social Harmony and Stability in China Today* (*zhongguo shehui hexie wending baogao*), Beijing: Social Science Press. pp. 32–3 & pp. 66–7.

[9] Yu, Jianrong (2009). "The Bottom Line of Social Stability (*shouzhu shehui wending de dixian*)," lecture at the Association of Attorney in Beijing, Dec 26, 2009. <http://hkwalker.net/v3/archives/3139>.

[10] Lee, Ching Kwan and Zhang, Yong Hong (2013). "The Power of Instability: Unraveling the Microfoundations of Bargained Authoritarianism in China," *American Journal of Sociology*, 118(6): 1–34.

[11] For more detailed analysis, see Hsing, You-tien (2010). *The Great Urban Transformation: Politics of Land and Property in China*. Oxford: Oxford University Press.

implemented in 1990, which allowed citizens to sue the government. In addition, all levels of government set up specifically designated agencies to deal with people who would write to local leaders or visit their offices in person to voice grievances and lodge complaints. But peasants' and inner-city residents' experiences of seeking justice through the legal and bureaucratic systems were largely disappointing, and often antagonizing.[12] People who chose to take the administrative route to voice grievances were also met with bureaucracy that was more inclined to stop the protestors or retaliate than to resolve conflicts. Consequently, as Lianjiang Li has found, petitioning has an ironic effect of weakening peasants' trust in central government's capacity as well as its commitment to protect citizens' rights (Li 2008: 210).[13] Many municipal and district courts, which were under local governments' jurisdiction, would not accept cases related to highly explosive issues such as one-child policy violation, land grabs, demolition, and involuntary relocation imposed by the local government.

Disillusioned, some people turned cynical, while others became perpetual visitors to government offices at higher levels to lodge complaints.[14] Some turned radical.

By the late 2000s, to deal with the mounting social conflicts that were not resolved by the legal institutions and existing bureaucratic routines, the Chinese government instituted a new regime of "social stabilization." Local leading officials' performance evaluations and chances of promotion were strictly conditioned by whether there were any reported cases of broadly defined "disturbances of social order." Just one such case would be sufficient to terminate an official's career. Consequently, social stabilization began to take top priority in local governments' daily operation. Specific offices of "Social Stability Maintenance" were set up at all levels of local government. Long and comprehensive checklists of conflicts that could threaten social stability were sent to different departments of the government. The threats

---

[12] See Note 11. Also Lee, Ching Kwan (2007). *Against the Law: Labor Protests in China's Rustbelt.* Berkeley: University of California Press.

[13] Li, Lianjiang (2008). "Political Trust and Petitioning in the Chinese Countryside," *Comparative Politics*, Vol. 40, No. 2 (2008), pp. 209–26.

[14] Once people start to make trouble, or are seen as troublemakers or leaders of outbreaks, they have taken a path of no return. Once people take part in a riot, they are blacklisted by local governments and seen as a stability threat. They are constantly harassed and watched by the government, and many can no longer lead a normal life or even keep their jobs. In this process, these people found more reasons to lodge complaints to the higher-level government, and continued their protests. As a result, they turn into long-term "troublemakers" for the regime of stability maintenance.

included demolition conflicts, youth unemployment, counterfeits, media reporting, veterans' employment, natural disasters, ethnic and religious conflicts, ecological destruction, enterprise restructuring, food and drug safety, infrastructure and ecological construction projects that entailed relocation, etc. Various social sectors were mobilized to help maintain social stability, including middle and high school students. Students were encouraged to report on signs of social instability, such as excessive fees, electricity safety, food safety, students bringing knives to schools, unsafe building, traffic problems around the campus, political thoughts of teachers, etc.[15] During the politically sensitive time of the Annual People's Congress meeting and CCP national meeting, blacklisted "troublemakers" were put under surveillance 24/7. The government also mobilized "volunteers" to patrol communities and commercial streets to help the government maintain social stability. The high-security regime to preserve stability has added a tremendous workload and financial burden on local governments, and built a new platform of state–society interaction.

The predicament of human development in China, against the backdrop of income disparity, social contestations, and the state's effort to maintain its legitimacy, is anchored at the grassroots level when the citizens clash with lower-level state agents during protests, or interact with the state agents during the process of bargaining and negotiation under the regime of stability maintenance.[16]

While violent protests with incidents of deaths and serious injuries continued to take place, in most cases inner city residents and farmers have chosen to bargain with government officials at the moment of conflict, especially since the late 2000s. The interaction between citizens and grassroots state representatives can be dissected along the following logic: (1) the citizens are generally aware of the political and economic disparity, and such awareness is usually accompanied by their (2) cynicism about individuals' incapability to make any difference to change the disparity; hence (3) many citizens resort to negotiation and bargaining with state managers for a

---

[15] For example, see a report on a high school in Fujian province responding to the provincial Bureau of Education to start the campaign of preventing instability at schools: <www.zanczx.com/ReadNews.asp?NewsID=716>.

[16] For a useful report on the party cadres' discussion of social stability maintenance, see Yuting, Han (2011), "A class in the Chinese Communist Party Academy" (*dangxiao yike*) *The Economic Observer*, 2011-11-26, <http://www.eeo.com.cn/2011/1126/216587.shtml>. For an insightful and thorough analysis of the regime of stability maintenance and its implication in the relationship between the state and society, see Lee, Ching Kwan and Zhang, Yong Hong (2013).

pragmatic resolution at the moment when immediate distributional contention occurs, while (4) interpersonal and institutional trust quickly deteriorates in the individualized games of bargaining with government officials.

Social stability maintenance is not simply yet another bureaucratic routine but a political campaign that demands results. To keep their jobs, which are still some of the best career options around, officials have tried both carrots and sticks in their negotiations with protestors.

Few government officials would apply violence right from the beginning, as the political cost could be high. They would first send officials to individual homes to try to negotiate with the residents and persuade the non-compliant. At the moment of forced demolition and relocation, to prevent an escalation of conflict and facilitate the smooth process of demolition, local governments would begin deploying hundreds of employees from various government agencies, including schoolteachers, to accompany demolition crews to the sites to demonstrate the government's authority. Hired private security guards, paramilitaries, armed police officers in armored vehicles, and even helicopters were deployed as a show of force, to be available in case of confrontations. For local cadres, carrying out hugely unpopular policies like family planning or demolition and forced relocation could be as tense as mini-warfare. And wars are expensive, financially and politically. From time to time, thugs were hired to attack stubborn relocation holdouts physically. On some occasions, enraged villagers would attack demolition crews and clash with the security force. Desperate villagers would prepare homemade explosives for self-defense. Physical injury and deaths could happen to either side. Protracted confrontation threatened to interrupt the demolition process and slow down the debt-financed construction projects, and caused negative publicity and poor performance evaluation for local leaders. Under the regime of "social stabilization," such confrontation could cost them their jobs.

To prevent the conflicts from escalating or spreading, and under pressure from central government to avoid physical confrontation, local officials used monetary compensation to quieten down the stubborn and shrewd protestors. Since 2008, an increasing number of municipalities, districts, and counties have set up a special "Judicial Supplementary Fund," or more directly, "Social Stability Maintenance Funds" to pay off those who threaten to create negative PR for the leaders. Under the centralized local authority, top leaders would mobilize all resources to combat such incidents of instability. The scale of the stability maintenance campaign was conditioned by political priority. The goal was a quick solution and restoration of social order, aided by violence or cash—or both.

With either approach, conflicts were resolved only on extra-legal platforms. For most of the aggrieved people disillusioned with the judicial and bureaucratic system, the cash compensation was often the best possible result for their struggle to seek justice. Through time, people also learned that the size of the compensation was conditioned by the scale and scope of the trouble they made for local leading officials. The more troublemaking and greater threat to "social stability," the more cash—regardless of whether the government action or people's reaction was within the realm of legality or justice.

The most fundamental issue here, however, is not just the setback to the rule of law or the swollen state budget of public security (which exceeded the national defense budget in 2011). What this regime of social stability maintenance has brought is the commodification of citizens' perception of justice and rights. For the aggrieved and the unjustly treated, either in the case of farmers facing industrial pollution or land appropriation, or of migrant workers facing illegal dismissal and under-compensated work-induced injury, the aggrieved citizens measure the success of their justice-seeking by the size of their cash compensation. Constrained in their struggle by limited political space, cash became the goal and the measure of justice. Meanwhile, the government's retreat to governance by a combination of violence and cash has weakened the legitimacy of the state, and officials have lost the trust of citizens. Based on their ethnography of grassroots governments in Beijing and Shenzhen, Ching Kwan Lee and Yong Hong Zhang (2013) used "bureaucratic absorption" to explain the bargaining process between the state and society, and aptly called it "bargained authoritarianism."

The state has been relying on economic expansion to maintain its legitimacy and consolidate its grip over society under conditions of increasing social disparities and contestations. The regime of stability maintenance has been the CCP state's answer to the question of authoritarian resilience since the late 2000s, fortified by the commodification of citizenship rights.

One of the most immediate consequences of the commodification of citizenship rights and state bargaining is a profound sense of distrust among all players in the game. As citizens negotiate for material and cash compensation in the face of injustice, government officials often respond with trickeries and deceptive tactics to weaken the bargaining power and divide the interests of the protestors. In return, citizens grow increasingly suspicious and develop counter tactics when dealing with one another and with the officials for better compensation packages. The multi-dimensional distrust between individual citizens and between citizens and government officials did not start in the 2000s, of course. Throughout the struggles of numerous political campaigns and the Cultural Revolution of Mao's era, in which family members and long-term friends, neighbors, co-workers, and colleagues were forced to denounce one another in public meetings and personal interactions, society had been left with ingrained suspicion. The wounds had hardly had a chance to heal and only grew larger after the 1990s, when the competition for resources in both the political and economic arena intensified, and social division deepened. Ironically, the culture of distrust and sense of insecurity produces a distressed but manageable society, and prevents the social predicament from turning into a political crisis for the CCP regime.

China's human development in the new millennium, therefore, is characterized by increasing income disparity, social contention, commodification of justice and rights, and the distrustful relationship among citizens and between the citizen and the state.

Such a predicament is more of a cultural than a social crisis: it is a cultural crisis precisely because it does not automatically generate social or political crises. It is from such a predicament of human development and cultural crisis that I will turn to the question of information development in China.

Information development

The Internet has been at the forefront of information expansionism in China. Growth in the number of users since 1995, when the Internet first became commercially available, has been exponential. By the end of 2012, China had 564 million Internet users and 181 million bloggers, with a penetration rate of 42%, a 3.8% increase from the year before. The Sinophone Internet is now the world's largest cyber community (CNNIC 2013).

Many Western observers maintained an optimistic view of the power of the Internet, especially in the first few years of the Internet boom. Pulitzer Prize-winning columnist Nicholas Kristof (2005) had predicted that the rapidly expanding Chinese blogosphere would represent a political threat to the Chinese Communist Party's power. Kristof began his article entitled "Death by a Thousand Blogs" with the statement that "the Chinese Communist Party survived a brutal civil war with the Nationalists, battles with American forces in Korea and massive pro-democracy demonstrations at

Tiananmen Square. But now it may finally have met its match—the Internet."[17]

But such optimism has not been sustained by the fact that the Chinese Internet has been expanding alongside the increasingly powerful apparatus of state censorship over cyberspace. The state has been investing in increasingly sophisticated surveillance technologies to detect, filter, and delete content, using the infamous programs of the so-called Great Firewall and Golden Shield. More than 20,000 Internet police have been recruited over the past ten years, and propaganda workers and in-house monitors at thousands of websites hired. The hugely popular and rapidly growing micro-blog Sina weibo, started in 2009, has in fact employed more than 4,000 censors.[18] The state at all levels installs surveillance systems over cyberspace to monitor citizens. A more recent controversy over the cyber power of the Chinese state focused on the People's Liberation Army-sponsored, large-scale, well-organized, and persistent cyber hacking against international businesses and government organizations, and the US and Chinese governments have been accusing one another of state-sponsored hacking.[19] Information and communication technologies could indeed help fortify and keep the authoritarian regime resilient online and offline.

How do we comprehend these two seemingly contradictory pictures about China's information development without falling into the trap of a simple dichotomy between the optimistic anticipation of a "blog revolution" and the pessimistic submission to the omnipotent party-state and its censorship? Perhaps the first step to take is to examine what Chinese netizens do online and if their online activities are threatening the CCP regime. According to CNNIC's recent surveys, while micro-blogging grew the fastest between 2009 and 2011, the leading uses of the Internet in China have been instant messaging (80.9%), search (79.4%), news (71.5%), online video (63.4%) and online gaming (63.2%) (see Table 5.1).

Netizens go online for a wide range of purposes: to get news of various kinds, to play games and watch movies, to shop, to chat, and to get advice on

[17] Kristof, Nicholas (2005). "Death by a Thousand Blogs," *New York Times*, May 24, 2005.
[18] See special report on China and the Internet, "The Giant Cage," *The Economist*, April 6–12, 2013.
[19] The Mandiant Report (2013). "APT 1: Exposing one of China's Cyber Espionage Units," (<www.mandiant.com>). For analysis of the controversy, see <www.nbcnews. com/technology/technolog/mandiant-goes-viral-after-china-hacking-report-1C8513891>.

Table 5.1 Selected Most Frequently Used Services (12/2009–12/2011)

Services	2009		2010			2011		
	Number of users (million)	Penetration (%)	Number of users (million)	Penetration (%)	Growth	Number of users (million)	Penetration (%)	Growth
News	307.69	80.1	353.04	77.2	14.7	366.87	71.5	3.9
Search Engine	281.34	73.3	374.53	81.9	33.1	407.40	79.4	8.8
Instant messaging	272.33	70.9	352.58	77.1	29.5	415.10	80.9	17.7
Online gaming	264.54	68.9	304.10	66.5	15.0	324.28	63.2	6.6
Online video	240.44	62.6	283.98	62.1	18.1	325.31	63.4	14.6
Blogging	221.40	57.7	294.50	64.4	33.0	318.64	62.1	8.2
Email	217.97	56.8	249.69	54.6	14.6	245.77	47.9	−1.6
SNS	175.87	45.8	235.05	51.4	33.7	244.24	47.6	3.9
Internet literature	162.61	42.3	194.81	42.6	19.8	202.67	39.5	4.0
Forum/BBS	117.01	30.5	148.17	32.4	26.6	144.69	28.2	−2.3
Micro-blogging	—	—	63.11	13.8	—	248.88	48.7	296.0

Source: Han, 2012: 8.

investments and relationships. Similarly to the US, entertainment, sports, relationship, and investment-related sites dominate China's largest weblog portals. However, infotainment is not all there is to Chinese cyberspace. Rongbin Han (2012) maintained that social issues are also widely discussed on Internet forums like Tianya.cn, the largest online forum in China, which claims almost 70 million registered users with over one million of them simultaneously online during active periods throughout the day. The rapidly growing personal micro-blogs, in which the host has discretion over the topic and audience, have become important sites of public forum.[20] The young and hip writer Han Han, who is also a professional car racer, is widely popular for his bold sociocultural critiques. His Sina blog site boasted 592 million hits and 1.2 million followers between the end of 2006 and June 2013. Han Han's record was matched by popular psychologist Su Qin's 553 million hits. Yao Chen, a TV actress, had 47 million fans on her site. The popular writer, actress, and psychologist's huge following was nevertheless dwarfed by the financial investment guru Xu Xiaoming, whose blog has attracted 2.1 billion hits over the last seven years.[21] Survey data also shows that the desire to communicate does not have to be externally mobilized. Young Chinese bloggers, like others around the globe, were motivated by the desire to "record one's own feelings/emotions" (64%) and "express one's opinions" (37%) (Leibold 2011: 1026).[22] In short, there have been great variations in Chinese netizens' online activities. While not all of the online participation was politically motivated, the political implication of the online community still deserves further investigation.

Based on two years of online and offline ethnography, Rongbin Han (2012)[23] provided an in-depth analysis of the political implications of China's

---

[20] Han, Rongbin (2012a). *Challenging the Regime, Defending the Regime: Contesting Cyberspace in China*, unpublished dissertation. Department of Political Science, UC Berkeley.

[21] Xu Xiaoming: <http://blog.sina.com.cn/u/1300871220>; Su Qin: <http://745843844.qzone.qq.com/>; Han Han: <http://blog.sina.com.cn/twocold>; Yao Chen <http://www.weibo.com/yaochen>. Accessed on June 7, 2013.

[22] Leibold, James (2011). "Blogging Alone: China, the Internet, and the Democratic Illusion?" *Journal of Asian Studies*, 70(4): 1023–41. Leibold quoted Yangzi, Sima and Pugsley, Peter (2010). "The Rise of a 'Me Culture' in Postsocialist China: Youth Individualism and Identity Creation in the Chinese Blogosphere." *International Communications Gazette*, 72(3): 287–306; Wallis, Cara (2011). "New Media Practices in China: Youth Patterns, Processes, and Politics." *International Journal of Communication*, 5: 406–36.

[23] Han, Rongbin (2012b). *Power of the Internet and Its Limitations: Understanding Online Expression in Chinese Cyberspace*, unpublished PhD dissertation, Department of Political Science, UC Berkeley.

Internet. His research demonstrated that **both** the state censors **and** the online communities are fragmented in various ways. The censorship regime is highly fragmented among various government agencies. This is partly because of the usual rifts and territorialism between bureaucratic units. More importantly, local governments use the surveillance system not just to uphold the party line and suppress freedom of speech for the sake of it, but also to employ the local censorship regime to keep local scandals local and avoid unwanted attention from supervisory government offices. Information manipulation by local state agents to "hide the harvest" is hardly news in any time or place, particularly for large countries like China. Information censorship technologies could help advance the cause of hiding the harvest and dirty laundry. In other words, while Internet censorship technologies are tools of information control, they could be used to weaken the coherence of state power.

The online communities were not more coherent than the state censorship regime. It is well known that the Chinese propaganda agency has recruited a large number of online commentators to steer online conversations in politically correct directions and to attack the incorrect ones. These hired commentators were known as the "Fifty Cent Party" because they were said to be paid fifty cents RMB, about eight cents USD, per post. A more intriguing part of the story is the emergence of what Han called the "voluntary Fifty Cent Party." Han argued that the highly diversified online communities have created discourse competition among netizen groups, including those nationalistic "regime defenders" who launched attacks on critics of the Communist Party state. These "voluntary Fifty Cent Party" extremists often used language and tactics that were even more aggressive than those of the hired guns.

To complicate the picture further and beyond the dichotomy of politically progressive and regressive online activisms, Han probed the dynamics of "pop activism" online. He described the blurred boundary between political messages and popular entertainment in pop activism: "... pop activism is entertaining and popular in the cybersphere and it relies heavily on creative and artful use of rhetorical techniques like comedy and satire. It consumes political topics and often targets political actors, particularly the censorship organs of the party-state."[24]

---

[24] Han, Rongbin (2012).

So politics is entertaining and entertainment can be political. China's "Internet galaxy," to borrow Manuel Castells' term, is composed of a wide spectrum of actors and activities that can be both political and apolitical, progressive and regressive. And the politics of the Internet is not restricted by the political agenda of dominance and autonomy. While many Western observers were obsessed with the political question concerning Internet censorship and freedom of speech in China, the economics of the telecommunication industry and market has been undeservingly overlooked. The success of China's information development, if not found on the human development front, is found in its impressive commercial expansion.

While three-quarters of China's netizens, about 420 million, logged on through their mobile phones, China produced 1.18 billion mobile phones, 67.5% of the world's total, worth 81 billion USD in 2012. The sale of mobiles and other ICT electronics brought China-based manufacturers 8.5 trillion RMB ($1.3 trillion USD).[25]

Compared to ICT equipment production, the value-added service (VAS) sector in China's ICT has been more profitable, yet much more concentrated. It is in the hands of three giant broadband and mobile service firms: China Unicom, China Mobile, and China Telecom. All of them are state-owned. Despite multiple rounds of industrial restructuring since the early 2000s, under pressure from the WTO to break state firm oligopolies, the VAS industry continued to be heavily concentrated. Two out of the three giants formed the nationwide duopolies in the mobile and Internet access service sectors, and each of the big three enjoyed regional near-monopolies in the fixed line market. Below the three giants, there were five operators in Internet backbone services, and a fringe of many small dial-up or broadband non-nationwide providers.[26]

e-Commerce is another rapidly expanding field. Given the large number of people using the Internet to shop, play games, search, watch videos, and connect via social media, Internet business in China today is far bigger than it is in any other country. The number of online shopping transactions in China

[25] ICT annual statistics 2012, <http://www.miit.gov.cn/n11293472/n11293832/n11294132/n12858387/15173031.html>.ICT import-export statistics 2012, <http://www.miit.gov.cn/n11293472/n11293832/n11294132/n12858462/15136598.htm>. Gartner, "Gartner Says Worldwide Mobile Phone Sales Declined 1.7 Percent in 2012," <http://www.gartner.com/newsroom/id/2335616>, Table 2. Worldwide mobile phone sales to end users totaled 1.75 billion units in 2012.
[26] Liu, Zhong and Whalley, Jason (2011). "Anti-competitive Behaviors in Managed Competition: The Case of China's Telecommunications Industry," *Communications of the Association for Information System*, Vol 28 Article 36, pp. 611–28.

was expected to surpass the US (Amazon.com and eBay combined) in 2013. In 2012, China had more than 200 million online shoppers who spent $200 billion, ten times more than they did in 2008. The market is dominated by Taobao, which is responsible for about 60% of the parcels delivered by couriers in China. The search engine Baidu (with market capitalization of 30 billion USD), the online gaming company Shanda and platform Tencent, and online video platforms Yuoku and Tudou (with market capitalization of 2.8 billion USD), are all among the most profitable companies in China. While these firms are a result of private entrepreneurship, they have nevertheless benefitted from the state policy of protecting domestic Internet platforms for their "presumed, and often proven" political reliability, as *The Economist* put it.[27]

A less visible, but nevertheless sizeable segment of the Internet economy is the large and diverse industry of Internet monitoring and censorship. *The Economist* estimated that the central government has invested 160 million USD in the so-called Great Firewall to block foreign websites since the late 1990s. Golden Shield, a system used for domestic surveillance and filtering, was estimated to have cost 1.6 billion USD. More than 100 Chinese companies are offering no less than 125 surveillance products to local governments. University faculty members were commissioned to develop Internet surveillance programs. Again, surveillance systems could be used for various purposes by various users. Black market Internet companies, for example, can take advantage of their connection with local government agencies to sell illegal services to individuals, including officials, and to delete negative reports about themselves from websites.[28] In total, information consumption contributed about 9% of the total national GDP in 2013, with a projected annual growth rate of 20% between 2013 and 2015.[29]

In short, the political side of information development in China is an expansion of communication without a definite indication of broadened political space for the citizens. In the meantime, it has been a successful commercial operation for the information industry. Consistent with the

---

[27] "A Giant Cage: Special report on China and the Internet," *The Economist,* April 6, 2013.

[28] *The Economist,* April 6, 2013.

[29] Yang, Chunli (2013). "The Contribution of Information Consumption to GDP (xinxi xiaofei dui jingjinzengzhanglu gongxian youduoda)," 8-20-2013. *Eastern Morning News (dongfang zaobao),* <http://epaper.dfdaily.com/dfzb/html/2013-08/20/content_806701.htm#>. Zou, Weiguo (2013). "The Policy Behind Information Consumption (xinxi xiaofei beihoude jingji shizheng luxiantu)," <http://finance.people.com.cn/n/2013/0815/c1004-22569316.html>.

analysis in the first half of this chapter, the large state-owned enterprises have been the biggest winners in the expanded and state-controlled market of the Internet and mobile telecommunication, as well as other related industries and services.

China's Internet culture and culture of development

Sales of services to delete negative web reports and the black market trade of fake followers to boost popularity of starlets or bloggers were among the flourishing Internet businesses in China. Such Internet frauds are only the tip of the iceberg. Deception comes in varied forms and levels on the Internet. James Leibold (2011) elaborated on the worldwide potential for fraudulence in Internet culture: " . . . while the Internet has dramatically increased people's access to information, it also threatens to undermine the accuracy and meaning of much of this knowledge." China is no exception. Examples of Internet rumors, misinformation, and deception abounded in the 2000s. In the wake of the 2003 SARS epidemic, online rumors suggested that the virus was a biological weapon invented by Taiwan and the United States to destroy China, while stores ran out of vinegar once it was suggested as the only antidote to the infection (Leibold 2011, Chiu 2003).[30]

One of the best-known examples of deception and forgery in China's Internet culture concerns a tiger. The South China tiger, *Panthera tigris amoyensis*, has not been seen in the wild since 1980. But in October 2007, a farmer in the northwestern Chinese province of Shaanxi claimed he had risked his life to shoot 30-plus digital photographs of a South China tiger in the wild. The Provincial Forestry Bureau immediately verified the authenticity of the farmer's snapshots. They rushed to hold a press conference to announce the "rediscovery" of the extinct tiger under their jurisdiction, with the hope that it would boost the fame of the place, get state recognition and funding to establish a protection zone for the tiger like the Giant Panda conservancy in Sichuan, and promote the local tourist industry. However, the photographs were soon questioned. Netizens doubted the pictures and claimed they were fake. Urged by the public and wildlife experts, the national Forestry Ministry formed an investigation team to visit the site on

---

[30] Chiu, Lisa (2003). "Outbreak of Rumors Has China Reeling," *SFGate.com* (7 May) <http://articles.sfgate.com/2003-05-07/news/17493093_1_sars-cases-beijing-mayor-meng-xuenong-sars-epidemic>.

October 24, but their report has remained unpublicized. By early 2008, the Shaanxi provincial government reprimanded the forestry bureau for violating official regulations, but it also held a press conference to support Zhou's "discovery" without further evidence. The Forestry Bureau subsequently issued a public letter apologizing for publicizing the photos, though it refrained from commenting on their authenticity.

What is intriguing about this case is that the embarrassing scandal did not stop others from trying their luck with the same hoax. Only one month after the farce of the "paper tiger" in Shaanxi subsided, another scandal involving a fake South China tiger was exposed. This time, the one who committed the forgery was a journalist with a county TV station in Hunan province, another poor and desperate region. The journalist announced that he had "unintentionally videotaped" a suspected South China tiger in the mountainous area of Hunan province. Again, local officials immediately jumped on it and supported the journalist's claims. High-level provincial and municipal officials organized an inspection tour to the site where the tiger was allegedly videotaped. They concluded that the journalist's videotape was factual. But just four days later, the provincial forestry bureau announced that the big cat in the film was in fact a Siberian tiger borrowed from a circus from another province, which happened to be on a performance tour in Hunan. The journalist was subsequently blamed for making the forgery to enhance his own fame and commercial interests.[31] There is no further information about whether the officials who supported the forgery or the journalist were punished.

While the cases of the South China tiger forgeries were eventually clarified, many other forgeries have remained on the Internet. One immediate consequence of these scandals is that information on the Internet is considered increasingly unreliable. Online anonymity protects individuals while also creating space for frauds. Leibold (2011) cited one Chinese blogger's statement: "On the Internet, even [when] you provide facts about yourself, people won't believe it. They think that you make them up. So it doesn't matter whether you provide real or fake information because nobody trusts the information on the Internet."[32] In the same article, Leibold also cited a survey showing that those who thought the Internet was reliable decreased

---

[31] Zhong, Wu (2008). "'Paper Tiger' Tales Shred Credibility," *Asia Times*, April 3, 2008. <http://www.atimes.com/atimes/China/JD03Ad01.html>.

[32] Leibold (2011); cited in Xun, Liu (2010). "Online Posting Anxiety: Impacts of Blogging," *Chinese Journal of Communication*, 3(2): 202–22.

from 52% to 26% between 2003 and 2007, while those who thought it was unreliable more than doubled, from 9% to 22%. A 2009 survey of bloggers found that nearly half thought either most or some of the information on blogs was untrustworthy.

Online vigilantism, the so-called "human flesh search engines" (*renrou sousuo yingqing*) of China's cyberspace, is yet another regressive form of Internet culture. "Human flesh search engines" can be a powerful form of digital activism to expose scandals, but very often they bring "invasion of privacy, exposing and publicly humiliating, harassing, and consequently silencing those who hold different views" (Leibold 2011: 1032).

Deception and online vigilantism is inseparable from the offline cultural crisis that I outlined in the previous section on human development. In my research on home demolition and relocation of inner-city residents and land grabs in rural areas, trickery was an essential part of the strategies of expansionist local officials and their developer allies.[33] Compensation cash was promised but the delivery was often delayed and reduced. Those holding out against relocation were "invited" to the demolition office to talk about compensation packages only to find their homes razed to the ground upon their return. Villagers were told that the relocation housing would be ready for them with their names on the title documents, upon their signing of the demolition and relocation agreement. But only after they signed the agreement, left their homes, and moved to the relocation housing did they realize that they now owed rent and management fees to the developers and they did not have the title to the relocation housing units. As residents learned from other relocatees' experiences, they came up with counter-tactics to combat the officials' subterfuge. Some invented "ghost family members" to maximize the compensation package that is calculated on the basis of the size of the household. Others brought a can of gasoline to the demolition office to make self-immolation threats. While these tactics and counter-tactics are not always successful, they happen frequently and regularly enough that both sides learn to take these games into account when dealing with one another. On one occasion when one dissatisfied holdout threatened the demolition official with a can of gasoline for self-immolation, the official thought he was bluffing and told him to go ahead. To show his determination and to save face, the holdout soaked himself with gasoline and set himself alight. As a result, the dead man's family received more compensation cash for their

---

[33] Hsing, You-tien. (2010).

demolished house. Again, justice was measured by cash, and trust was replaced by mind games.

The culture of distrust is reinforced by and reflected in the regressive digital culture described by Leibold. The new technologies that enable fast-paced, widely spread flows of messages excite, but also exhaust and disillusion the users quickly. The culture of suspicion, in turn, comes back to haunt online activism. In Han's (2012) observation, Chinese netizens have been extremely anxious about each other's "true" identities and motivations in their online communication. Indeed netizens could be successful in discrediting the CCP regime by exposing the state's manipulation and distortion of public opinions online, as demonstrated by the Southern Weekend incident in January 2013, in which tens of thousands of netizens gathered to protest against the replacement of a poignant New Year's editorial on political reform with a piece of party propaganda.[34] Yet online protestors are equally suspicious of alternative political views. As the regime challengers practice pop activism and mock the official lines, they are also ready to question the intentions and competence of democratic activists. Take the two best-known leaders of the 1989 Tiananmen student movement as an example: Chai Ling was blamed for risking other students' lives for her personal ambition, and Wang Dan was accused of betraying China's national interests by receiving funds from the US and Taiwan's pro-independent DPP administration (Han 2012). The online platforms, therefore, worked to silence as much as to facilitate public forums. Han further suggested that such suspicion and anxiety over each other's identity and motivation has led to isolated online communities with highly guarded access, instead of more inclusive networks in cyberspace.

As a result, in a deeply divided society with increasingly violent protests, it is not surprising to find opinions that demand greater, rather than less state intervention to maintain social stability. Nearly 84% of survey respondents thought that content on the Internet should be controlled, with 83% identifying violence, 65% malicious speculation, and nearly 30% online chatting as being in need of control, while 85% looked to the government to censor this content. Between 2003 and 2007, there was an over-50% decline in those who thought that Internet empowers the people.[35]

The large number of netizens and the availability of digital infrastructure are elements of the developmental program to modernize China. For sure,

---

[34] <http://china.dwnews.com/news/2013-01-06/59062697.html>.
[35] Leibold (2011), p. 1033, quoting Guo (2007).

the Internet provides a sea-changing platform for building public forums under an authoritarian regime.[36] While netizens get online to engage in a very wide spectrum of activities that could be political or apolitical, progressive or regressive, many do participate actively in the public forum of cyberspace. Meanwhile, cyberspace is inseparable from social space, despite its image as a placeless space. Chinese netizens are embedded in a cultural crisis, featuring commodification of justice and waning of trust at all levels. While anxiety about misinformation is an integral part of the Internet culture at large, the offline culture of distrustfulness and cynicism can only aggravate the online culture. The question here is not just the effectiveness of the state censorship and the apparatus of "social stability maintenance," or the liberating effect of online communication. What is also at work is the cultural crisis of distrust that prevents the wary and anxious citizens from building expandable and transformative social networks online and offline, and the insecure and defensive state from taking more meaningful steps on political reform. To use the framework of Manuel Castells' (2012) recent book, *Networks of Outrage and Hope*,[37] it is this cultural crisis in contemporary Chinese society, among other factors, that has prevented the outrage in social protests from transforming into a strong sense of hopefulness, which is an essential ingredient of sustainable and transformative social movements. When one loses the sense of hope, one is also too disillusioned to imagine.

---

[36] Yang, Guobin (2009). *The Power of the Internet in China: Citizen Activism Online*. New York: Columbia University Press.

[37] Castells, Manuel (2012). *Networks of Outrage and Hope: Social Movements in the Internet Age*. Cambridge: Polity.

Chapter 6

South African Informational Development and Human Development: Rights vs. Capabilities

Nico Cloete and Alison Gillwald

Restoring dignity

This chapter will analyze informational and human development in South Africa. In the case of informational development, the structural basis for this growth in many countries has been the expansion of a highly dynamic, knowledge-producing, technologically advanced sector that is connected to other similar sectors in a global network while excluding a significant segment of its own economy and population (Castells and Cloete 2011). This is the case in South Africa. In relation to human development, South African apartheid was on one hand about inequality, in terms of access to and participation in the economy. But, on the other hand, exclusion under apartheid was also about discriminatory laws that affected the legal rights of black people. Before elaborating on economic disparities and inequalities, with ICT and higher education as particular lenses, we wish to start with the struggle for rights. Human rights formed not only the scaffolding for economic exclusion, but affected something equally fundamental: dignity.

The year 2012 marked the 100th anniversary of the African National Congress (ANC) as well as their 18th year at the helm of the post-apartheid South African state. As part of the centenary celebrations and in recognition of the foundation laid by the 1955 Freedom Charter for the Constitution and Bill of Rights, the party celebrated Human Rights Day under the theme: "Working together to promote unity in diversity and human dignity for all" (GCIS 2012). Dignity clearly underpins those demands in the Freedom Charter that go beyond the legal rights of equality and citizenship, and which address the rights to opportunity, education, land, jobs, and security; to sharing the country's wealth. As the Freedom Charter declares, the restoration of dignity to those "robbed of their birthright to land, liberty and peace by a form of government founded on injustice and inequality" is captured in the founding provisions of the Constitution, which refer to the establishment of a sovereign democratic state based on "human dignity, the achievement of equality and the advancement of human rights and freedoms" (RSA 1996). Clause 10 of the South African Bill of Rights tells us: "everyone has inherent dignity and the right to have their dignity respected and protected" (RSA 1996).

These references are of course not novel. References to dignity are found in the Preamble to the Charter of the United Nations and the Universal Declaration of Human Rights, and in the constitutions and resolutions of numerous other international rights bodies. What made them so extraordinary in South Africa is that, after decades of struggle against apartheid and two years of consultation and consensus-building thereafter, they no longer merely represent an international or domestic rallying call for humanity, but a progressive constitutional triumph over one of the most malevolent institutionalized systems of indignity, racism, and repression known to humanity.

What makes these evocations particularly poignant at this historical juncture is that, after nearly two decades of liberation, for the vast numbers of citizens that remain unemployed, the children without access to text books or still learning in mud classrooms, child-headed households as a result of their parents' inability to access life-sustaining health care, together with those who eke out an existence on social and welfare grants in makeshift shanties, the national project of restoring dignity to the mass of people stripped of it under apartheid has failed.[1]

It is not only poverty that denies them their dignity, but inequality. In a relatively prosperous country such as South Africa, the massive disparities in income and wellbeing amplify the failure to restore human dignity. South Africa has one of the highest Gini coefficients in the world.[2] While the poorest might not be aware that they only earn around 2% of the national income while the richest earn 70%, or that this figure has barely changed since 1995, they nevertheless witness the increasingly conspicuous consumption of not only historically privileged whites in enclave suburbs, but also a black political elite, largely those with direct party affiliations, enjoying the benefits of patronage and power (Bhorat, Van der Westhuizen, and Tsang 2013). Until recently these contradictions seemed contained. Though service delivery strikes in neglected townships have been frequent over the last decade, come election time the populace has returned the party of liberation to power with an overwhelming majority in four elections. Populists—some within the dissenting leadership of the African National Congress Youth League (ANCYL), despite conspicuously benefitting from existing systems of patronage—have been quick to exploit the failure of economic transformation to challenge the leadership of the party. With slogans such as "economic freedom in our lifetime," they call for the nationalization of mines and the restoration of the wealth of the land to the people. The political leadership sought to quell the emerging tears within the social fabric of the country resulting from national conditions of structural unemployment and weak growth in a global recession that was finally beginning to bite in South Africa, with the promise of the creation of five million

---

[1] South Africa has been wracked by service-delivery protests in marginalized areas of the country where municipalities have either failed to spend their budgets or lost the funds to corruption. Perhaps the most symbolic evidence of this failure is the public provision of toilets and sanitation without walls in provinces under the leadership of both the African National Congress (ANC) and the Democratic Alliance (DA), thus denying people the most fundamental privacy, which, in the literature, is one of the underlying principles of human dignity. National government however has also not provided the necessary oversight to provinces—with books not yet delivered to schools halfway through the school year in some provinces and with the national basic education department not acting on cases of corruption and negligence.

[2] According to the Income and Expenditure Survey, the Gini coefficient, which measures the gap between richest and poorest, increased marginally from about 0.66 to 0.70 between 1993 and 2008. During the same period in Brazil, the Gini coefficient decreased from 0.64 in 1993 to 0.52 in 2008 (Leibbrandt and Finn 2012). South Africa remains one of the world's most unequal societies (NPC 2011a).

jobs by 2020 in the New Growth Path (2011), the macro-economic plan of the current administration and a party manifesto for the next election referred to as the "second transition"—from political to economic freedom.

But the contradictions could no longer be contained. In the mining industry, the backbone of South Africa's extractive resource-based economy, conditions were ripe for unrest. Unlike its BRICS partners (Brazil, Russia, India, and China), South Africa missed the commodities boom. Instead, an uncertain investment climate, due not least of all to calls for nationalization, aging infrastructure and mines, and what are perceived by investors to be burdensome regulations, led to a contraction in the mining sector. While the world's top 20 mining countries achieved an average growth rate of 5% a year, South Africa's mining sector shrank by 1% a year, according to South Africa's Chamber of Mines (Spector 2013). Particularly hard hit was the platinum sector, where intractable wage disputes resulted in challenges to the hegemony of the major union federation in the country and one of the ANC's Tripartite Alliance partners, Congress of South African Trade Unions (COSATU), the other being the South African Communist Party. Through its political networks, COSATU had been able to hold together the fragile arrangements that have supported the pact between mining capital and the new power elite reached in the transition from apartheid to democratic rule.

On August 16, 2012, 34 mineworkers were shot dead by heavily armed police firing from the ground, armored cars, and even a helicopter. In total, more than 44 people were killed over the week, 78 others suffered bullet wounds, and 270 mineworkers were arrested and initially charged with murder. No police were injured during the main confrontation, but two policemen had been killed, and severely disfigured, the preceding weekend.[3] This happened near a small town called Marikana, on the grounds of the Lonmin platinum mine (listed in London) in northwest South Africa's "platinum belt," which, according to *Bullionstreet*,[4] is home to 80% of the world's supply of platinum with a current output capacity of 5.5 million ounces per annum.

---

[3] For a more detailed description, see Patrick Bond's "South African Political Economy after the Marikana Massacre": <http://globalfaultlines.org/2012/10/21/south-africas-political-economy-after-the-marikana-massacre-by-patrick-bond/re-emerged>.

[4] *Bullionstreet,* a New York electronic mining magazine, wrote on Thursday, July 5, 2012 that: "Projected strikes at the platinum belt in South Africa could reduce supply dramatically in world." <www.bullionstreet.com/news/projected-strikes-at-sa-platinum-belt-to-boost-prices/2239>.

After several weeks of prevarication, the President of South Africa, Jacob Zuma, appointed a senior retired judge to head a Commission of Enquiry into the events. While the country awaits the final report, the press and academic and social commentators attribute numerous explanations to what happened at Marikana: a leadership vacuum in the mining house, the union, and the police; violent rivalry between the official National Union of Mineworkers (NUM) and the opposing independent union, the Association of Mineworkers and Construction Union; poor police training; and various types of instigation by marginal socialist formations, even by "traditional leaders."

Yet, these appear only to be symptomatic of a far more fundamental fault line in the "bargain" struck between the ANC Tripartite Alliance and white business (mining capital) that underlies power relations in post-apartheid South Africa—as mining capital had done previously with the apartheid government (Wolpe 1972; Legassick 1974; Davies, Kaplan, Morris, and O'Meara 1976; Terreblanche 2012). This "elite compromise" underpins the system of political legitimization and economic accumulation on which the sustainability of South African capitalism, and particularly the mineral energy financial complex, depends. Critical to this arrangement is the balance between the interests of mining, the Party, and organized labor, specifically COSATU. These formerly competing interests are also no longer distinct, with former union bosses now bosses of the big mining houses through black economic empowerment deals, and party bosses within government.

To see these linkages is to understand that the "threat" posed by unorganized labor during the illegal strikes was not only to COSATU and indirectly to the ruling Alliance but also to the very stability of the country. The control of dissent under conditions of extreme poverty and inequality now hinges on the generation of super-profits, with targeted welfarist redistribution through the transfer of taxes from the wealthiest through the expanding social grants system. Marikana represents the willingness, indeed need, to resort to the most extreme form of state coercion, not used by the State since the end of apartheid, to safeguard this tenuous stability. There are deep fractures in the political economy of the country, which has been held together by this elite compromise and is under strain. The use of state violence has exposed not only the relationship itself, but the inherent contradictions within it.

Economic growth, inequality, and human development

Crises such as Marikana, which was arguably the greatest since the end of apartheid, will continue to dog any government, as long as economic inequality in South Africa remains among the highest in the world. Historic domestic inequality is compounded by growing global inequality. In contrast with high growth rates seen around the world over the previous three decades, the South African economy did not see growth rates comparable to many of the successful economies of the North and certainly not the double-digit growth rates of several emerging economies.

During the first decade of the post-apartheid era, gross domestic product (GDP) grew at a "modest rate," averaging 1%, though edging up more recently to 3%. This has, however, been the longest period of positive growth in South Africa's history (Bhorat and Van der Westhuizen 2010). How did this growth happen? The envisaged post-1994 economic policies for the development project stated that the economy would require steering onto a new development path, which, among other things, would reduce dependence on resource sectors through increased industrial growth and diversification.

However, in a thorough review of the South African economy in the post-apartheid era, Mohamed (2009, 2011) states that South Africa experienced the "wrong type" of economic growth from the end of apartheid and particularly during the five years prior to the 2008 financial crisis. Economic growth was associated with high unemployment and growing inequality, and because it required growing private-sector indebtedness and was accompanied by a decline in productive services and manufacturing, it was also unsustainable (Mohamed 2011).

According to Mohamed (2011: 36–37), "increased flows of hot money into and out of the economy favoured the growth of a services sector linked to increased debt-driven consumption and financial real estate speculation and a decline in manufacturing and productive services." The trends in the South African economy have been very different from those in the high-growth East Asian economies, and also the others in the BRICS group,[5] of which South Africa has only recently become a member. In fact South Africa, with a considerably smaller economy than any of the other BRICS countries, is better grouped with countries such as Portugal, Ireland, Greece, and Spain

---

[5] The BRICS group refers to an economic and political bloc of emerging economies—Brazil, Russia, India, China, and South Africa (which joined the bloc in 2011).

(the so-called PIGS), which, like the US economy, have large trade deficits that make them dependent on foreign borrowing and capital inflows (Mohamed 2011).

Another key factor in the South African economy, to which Bhorat and Jacobs (2010) have given considerable attention, is the change in the skills profile. The National Planning Commission (NPC) Diagnostic Report (NPC 2011a) shows that job growth between 1995 and 2009 saw a 50% increase in high-skilled jobs and a 20% decrease in low-skilled jobs. The implications of this in the dynamic high-tech ICT sector are discussed further below. Using data for the period 1970–2005, and updated to 2009, Bhorat and Jacobs (2010: 20) argued that:

> ...this growth path has been built on a rising demand for skilled labour with a steady erosion in the demand for unskilled or under-skilled workers. The modern era in the South African economy has thus been defined by a growth path with a constant increased demand for educated workers at the expense of those with lower level of human capital. In trying to link the nature of South Africa's growth path to the human capital endowments of households, we showed that households at the top end of income distribution benefited more from growth than those in the middle and bottom end of the distribution. In particular, better educated households gained more from this economic growth than households who are lesser educated so effectively defining a growth path in South Africa manifest in generating high returns to the educated, at the expense of the less educated.

The stated goal of post-apartheid economic policy was to reduce poverty, inequality, and unemployment. A 2% growth should lead to a 1–7% reduction in poverty, depending on the successful implementation of particular countries' redistributive policies (Bhorat and Van der Westhuizen 2010). In South Africa, poverty declined from 52% in 1995 to 49% in 2005 and, in the lower poverty group, there was a 7% decline (31% to 24%). In addition, there were definite gains in poverty reduction, particularly in African female-headed households (Bhorat and Van der Westhuizen 2010). All people, regardless of race, experienced increases in expenditure, which was seen as an indication that growth was "pro-poor."[6]

Despite the modest gains in poverty reduction, the inequality gap did not decrease; instead, it increased between all groups. Overall it increased from 0.64 in 1995 to 0.70 in 2008. This led Bhorat and Van der Westhuizen (2010)

---

[6] But an African female-headed household still yielded vastly higher headcount and poverty-gap ratio estimates in both 1995 and 2005.

to conclude that while South Africa in 1994 was one of the most unequal societies in the world, by 2008 it was probably the most unequal. So, although it increased for all groups, on skills and technology gaps in South Africa the affect on different groups was uneven. The latest World Bank report (2012a) shows that a white child will receive better access to electricity; primary, secondary, and higher education; and sanitation than an African child—which has drastic effects on their long-term development and chances of future growth. According to Bauer (2012), "South Africa's weak performance on providing employment opportunities is hampered not only by slow job creation but also by a highly unequal access to the limited number of opportunities. Global comparisons show South Africa to be an outlier in terms of both the level and inequality of employment opportunities."[7]

While spending on education and health remained fairly constant in real terms, social grants (excluding administration) now consume 3.2% of GDP, up from 1.9% in 2000. The total number of beneficiaries increased from 3 million in 1997 to 15 million in 2010 (Woolard and Leibbrandt 2011).[8] The share of households in the first income decile with access to grant income increased from 43% in 1995 to almost 65% in 2005, and even for households in the sixth decile, grant income increased from 19% in 1994 to 50% in 2005.

Using 2010 income data Bhorat, Van der Westhuizen, and Tsang (2013) confirm that there is no change in poverty levels but an increase in income inequality over the previous five years. However, they find that delivery of social grants to primarily African households assists in ameliorating poverty and inequality increases and that this is funded through taxing the rich who have gained from economic growth, as can be seen in Figure 6.1. The middle of the distribution curve has lost out from economic growth. From a race point of view, this now affects largely recession-hit Indian and white racial groups, who are predominantly in the middle-income range and largely not benefitting from social grants. Moeletsi Mbeki (2009: 87) argues that, ironically, despite claims by the ANC government that "social grants make people happy" by putting food on the table, in reality recipients become more insecure due to the possible withdrawal or reduction of their grants.

---

[7] See <http://mg.co.za/article/2012-07-24-entrenched-inequality-of-opportunity-threatens-sas-future>.

[8] More recent estimates suggest that 25% of the population are on social grants and that grants represent 40% of household income in the poorest quintile (Woolard and Leibbrandt 2011).

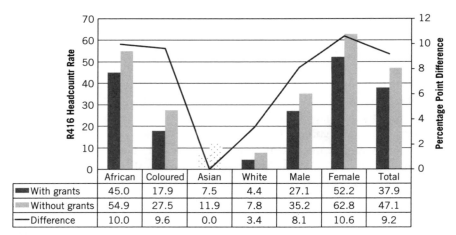

	African	Coloured	Asian	White	Male	Female	Total
■With grants	45.0	17.9	7.5	4.4	27.1	52.2	37.9
▨Without grants	54.9	27.5	11.9	7.8	35.2	62.8	47.1
—Difference	10.0	9.6	0.0	3.4	8.1	10.6	9.2

Figure 6.1 Income poverty with and without social assistance: head count rate at lower poverty line, 2010

Source: Bhorat, Van der Westhuizen, and Tsang. (2013). Development Policy Research Unit, University of Cape Town.

South Africa has followed a mixed growth path that has increased both income and inequality, and this is echoed in the area of human and informational development. Education and health are two key indicators for measuring human development. The NPC Diagnostic Report (2011a) states that: access to education is now nearly universal; there has been a steady increase in basic literacy; there is much better equity in school funding; 80% of learners aged five are in grade R; and most poor children receive school meals.[9] However, there are huge variations in education inputs—as the recent failure of state schools in some provinces to receive text books highlights—and school outcomes, with only 1% of African schools performing adequately on high-school-certificate (school-exit) levels. Of particular concern is mathematics, in which South Africa ranks 137th out 139 countries (WEF 2010), and is therefore outperformed by most other African nations. Although the public schooling system itself is extremely uneven, education excellence is concentrated in a small, but highly sophisticated private schooling system, the products of which are overrepresented in the

[9] However, these school meals were the first to be cut when provinces overran their budgets and had introduced emergency austerity measures. The strong unionization of teachers meant jobs could not be touched.

high entry level areas of the tertiary education system and, as a result, the top end of the economy.

Likewise, despite a world-class private health-care system in many respects, South Africa's performance has actually deteriorated on a number of health indicators. The HIV/AIDS rate is 10.5% (5.24 million in a total population of 50 million in 2010), which is among the highest in the world; infant mortality rates are high but have decreased slightly from 57 live births per 1,000 in 2001 to 47 per 1,000 in 2010 (Stats SA 2010).

Overall, South Africa is one of a few countries in the world where life expectancy declined between 2001 and 2005, though by 2012 it had improved from 54 to around 60 years of age. The Lancet attributes this turnaround to a combination of factors such as specific policy and program changes in four of the so-called colliding epidemics: HIV and tuberculosis; chronic illness and mental health; injury and violence; and maternal, neo-natal, and child health.[10]

The NPC Diagnostic Report (2011a: 20–1) concludes that South Africa "faces a large and growing burden of disease, a collapsing public health system, largely due to policy mistakes—and the biggest concern is the massive shortage of skilled staff."

One way of demonstrating that GDP growth does not directly translate into human development is to compare the ratings of different countries against GDP and United Nations Development Programme (UNDP) indicators. For two of the "African success stories," Botswana (−65) and South Africa (−51), the difference in ranking between GDP and human development is startlingly negative, while countries such as Costa Rica (+19) and Chile (+15) are doing much better. Table 1 shows that in poorer African countries there is less of a discrepancy, and it is interesting to note that there is a considerable difference between Finland (+11) and the US (−4).

In summary, the post-1994 South African democratic growth model operates through extensive social grants at the bottom end, with few benefits at the middle of the income distribution curve and the main growth at the de-racializing top end. Based on this growth path, Bhorat and Van der Westhuizen (unequal income distribution) and Mbeki (the disempowerment of welfarism) all express concern for the future of democracy. According to Mbeki (2009: 87), "the danger in this is that to sustain self respect, the unemployed and those on welfare may support demagogues who claim to

---

[10] See <www.timeslive.co.za/lifestyle/family/2012/11/30/life-expectancy-in-south-africa-rises-to-60-report>.

be marginalized and replace the ruling elite with nationalization and a 'people friendly government'." Bhorat and Van der Westhuizen (2010: 67) also ring a warning bell: "with declining tax revenues and rising fiscal deficits, it is unclear whether the current growth model is desirable or sustainable, and raises the alarm that these persistently high levels of inequality may give rise to social conflict and ongoing challenges around the nature and trajectory of the country's growth path."

The implications of these economic and social outcomes after two decades of freedom for the project of restoring dignity are profound. As Amartya Sen's now seminal work declares: "freedom" means "the removal of conditions of un-freedom; poverty, tyranny, poor economic opportunities as well as systematic social deprivation and neglect of public facilities" (1999: 3). Key to freedom for Sen is the notion of capabilities—the processes and opportunities that include aspects such as poverty and income inequality, but also capabilities in terms of education and health—core areas of poor performance for South Africa in global development indicators. This provides the economic and social backdrop for the investigation into South Africa's level of informational development that follows.

Informational development: ICT and higher education

A substantial body of academic and technical literature provides evidence of the relationship between informationalism, productivity, and competitiveness for countries, regions, and businesses. However, this relationship only operates under two conditions: "organisational change in the form of networking; and the enhancement of the quality of human labour, itself dependent on education and quality of life" (Castells and Cloete 2011: 3). To address this, we look at two sectors in South Africa: information and communication technology (ICT), which is key for networking; and education, particularly higher education, which is in the words of Castells, the "engine of the knowledge economy" (Castells 2001, in Muller et al.).

ICT

Recent studies demonstrate that a 10% increase in broadband penetration accelerates economic growth by 1% in developed economies and by 1.38%

in developing economies (Kim, Kelly, and Raja 2010). Koutroumpis (2009) demonstrates the existence of several levels of return from broadband infrastructure based on the level of penetration. He asserts that there is evidence of a critical-mass phenomenon in broadband infrastructure investments. The penetration level that he identifies is a critical mass of 20% of the population connected to the network, compared to the 40% for voice services identified by Röller and Waverman (2001). According to Koutroumpis, this percentage creates a vision for countries to capitalize on the beneficial effects that the network can provide, and it implies a 0.89% aggregate growth rate as a result of broadband externalities. Raul Katz (with Suter 2009 and Koutroumpis 2012) has demonstrated ICT's positive impact on job creation—initially as a demand for low-level skills required for the construction of networks, but subsequently for the higher-level skills associated with expanding communication services.

As alternative measures of progress to economic growth and GDP have become popularized, not least of all by Joseph Stiglitz[11] and Amartya Sen, nascent work applying notions of "happiness" to the ICT sector have emerged. Taken with the Gross National Happiness Index concept underpinning development strategies in Bhutan, studies have sought to identify and quantify the factors other than wealth that contribute to wellbeing or quality of life. Critical of GDP measures and seeking better links to individual welfare, Rohman and Bohlin (2011) found that while Internet access appears not to have a significant impact on quality of life, the experience of technology (exposure to mobile phone) did improve quality of life in Indonesia. The Chartered Institute for IT shows that access to information technology has a "statistically significant, positive impact on life satisfaction" and that women and those with low incomes and few educational qualifications benefit most from access to IT. On the basis of such empirical data (acknowledging the problems of reverse causality) and using the existing literature on happiness, Koo (2013) builds a theoretical case for the relationship between the Internet and happiness by demonstrating how sociability and empowerment, crucial determinants in measuring one's happiness, are enhanced by Internet use.

With these global demonstrations of the linkages of ICT to growth, individual welfare, and wellbeing, what are the outcomes of two decades of telecommunications reform and ICT sector development in South Africa?

---

[11] Joseph Stiglitz, "The Great GDP Swindle" <www.guardian.co.uk/commentisfree/2009/sep/13/economics-economic-growth-and-recession-global-economy>.

Nico Cloete and Alison Gillwald

Just as South Africa, with its abundance of natural resources, failed to capitalize on the global commodity boom of the last decade, so too it failed to capitalize on the global expansion of the information and knowledge economy—despite being ahead of the curve in this area 20 years ago. The early commitment to the development of an information society and knowledge economy by the African National Congress (ANC) in the first decade of democratic government appears to have evaporated. Information communication technologies appear to have slipped from the national agenda under the current administration: this, during a period which globally saw the ICT sector grow at double-digit rates, despite the declining growth rates that have accompanied the global recession in many of the advanced and middle-income economies.

The neglect of the ICT sector at a time in which several other countries made it a strategic priority has seen South Africa's steady descent down global indices, while other countries that have prioritized have leapfrogged past it. A comparable country in the early 1990s to current world broadband leader Korea in terms of GDP per capita and telecom penetration, by 2002 South Africa was down over 30 places and ranked 77 in the International Telecommunications Development Index (ITU 2004).[12]

By 2010 South Africa had slipped down to 91st position on the Index, while Korea was ranked at the top of the Index for broadband penetration (ITU 2002–12). Likewise, since 2004, South Africa has fallen from 34 of 138 countries measured in the World Economic Forum e-readiness Report (WEF 2012) to 72 in 2012 and was ranked at 94 in terms of the ICT usage component of the multidimensional study.

Once the African leader in telecommunications, South Africa is now ranked below several of the North African best performers in relation to various ICTs and some of the East African island states. In terms of broadband, countries such as Tunisia and Morocco and island states such Mauritius and the Seychelles now outstrip South Africa on broadband penetration. Also, several of the other major African markets—Ghana, Kenya, Nigeria—are demonstrating far greater dynamism as a result of more enabling policy and effective regulation.

---

[12] <www.itu.int/ITU-D/ict/doi/index.html>.

Access, use, and affordability indicators

Universal access and cost competitiveness are the primary, overarching objectives for telecommunications policy in South Africa. Cost-competitiveness refers to the provision of a variety of high-quality, low-cost services. Universal access comprises two aspects: physical proximity and affordability (Genesis Analytics 2009), both of which are also affected by cost-competitiveness. Globally, in the last five years, with the pervasiveness of broadband services, universal access and service policy challenges have shifted from being purely questions of access to those affecting the ability of citizens to benefit from these enhanced communications services optimally, not only as a result of cost, but also in relation to the necessary education and skill sets required.

Table 6.1 provides data from the 2012 Census ICT data together with the data from a survey by Research ICT Africa, which collects nationally representative individual as well as household data, which, with the rise of mobile phones and with Internet connectivity, provides a more accurate reflection of access and usage.

While these mobile indicators are high by any standard, aggregated they mask the unevenness of both access and usage patterns among different income groups, different sexes, and different localities (urban vs. rural). As South Africa is highly urbanized, the policy questions are not only about ensuring coverage in remote rural areas but also the unevenness of access

Table 6.1 ICT ownership in South Africa

Stats SA Census	2007	2011
Cell phone ownership	73.3%	88.9%
Households with fixed line	17.2%	14.5%
Households with computer	13.9%	21.4%
Households with radio	79.5%	67.5%
Households with television	66.5%	74.5%
Households with Internet	NA	35.2%
RIA Household Survey	2007	2011
Households with Internet	4.8%	19.7%
Individuals (15+) with Internet	15%	33.7%

Source: Compiled from SA Census 2011 and RIA 2011 ICT Access and Use Survey.

and usage among different income groups and social groups. While gender disaggregation of access and use shows more men owning mobile phones than women in South Africa, the figures are very similar, but as the complexity and/or the cost of technology becomes greater, such as with PC ownership and use, and Internet access and use, this shifts considerably so that men have considerably more access than women, spend more (even with mobile phones), and use the technology more optimally both in functionality and frequency and time. Although this is in line with (the limited) gender-disaggregated studies in other parts of the developing world, what modeling of this data reveals is that the determinant of this unevenness is not gender but the underlying unevenness in access to education and therefore the inequality of income. Being a woman does not significantly affect access and use of ICT—education and income does. Men and women with the same level of education and income utilize ICTs similarly, but the fact that women are concentrated among those nationally marginalized from education and income-generating activities is what explains the lower levels of adoption among women of ICTs, particularly as these become more sophisticated. This is particularly evident in the income disparity demonstrated in Figure 6.2, and the increasing inequality in education outcomes from primary through tertiary education (which in the African context is the threshold level for computer use [Schmidt and Stork 2008]).

The slow deployment of fixed broadband service (ADSL) and its high cost meant that wireless broadband services rapidly have become the primary form of broadband access over the past five years. Unlike in mature northern economies where wireless broadband was primarily a complementary nomadic/mobile offering to fixed broadband, which with ubiquitous copper networks or cable networks had been rapidly upgraded for high-speed Internet, wireless Internet access was often the only, and certainly the quickest way to be connected. While wireless broadband adoption in South Africa was initially constrained by the requirement of a computer into which wireless dongles are plugged, the entry of feature and smart phones into the market over the last few years means that South Africans are accessing the Internet for the first time in significant numbers from their mobile phones. This is so even when the national figure is disaggregated by locality, income, and gender. What is also clear from the data and focus groups is that social networking is driving the uptake of the Internet.

The resultant surge in data users and increased data traffic has placed the backhaul networks of mobile operators, historically dimensioned for voice, under extreme pressure. So while only a few years ago the greatest access

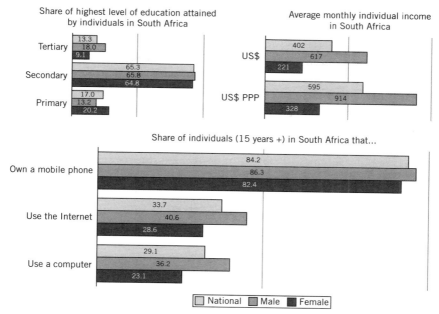

Figure 6.2 Gender disaggregated statistics on ICT access, education, and income

Source: Research ICT Africa 2011 ICT Household and Individual Access and Use Survey.

and expense as a result of the monopoly provisioning on the only SAT 3 cable was the high cost of international bandwidth, with multiple undersea cables now available the biggest challenges are cost and availability of national backbone and backhaul infrastructure, and of course the availability of high demand spectrum in the local loop. Immediate relief provided by wireless and mobile services to bandwidth-starved South Africans, however, has been stymied by the lack of access to next generation spectrum (LTE) as a result of the bungling of the migration of analogue terrestrial broadcasting to digital—a process that started over a year ago.

The longer-term policy ramifications are considerable. The lack of development of always-on, high speed, and quality bandwidth in the access networks (last mile) required by business, and particularly Business Processing Outsourcing and other job-creating, ICT-enabled service industries constrains informational development, and is a major determinant of global competitiveness.

Affordability

Affordable access to communication services has also remained elusive, with the cost of communication services—from fixed to mobile to leased lines and broadband—always above global averages.[13] This can largely be attributed to South Africa's lack of market reform during this period, despite the overwhelming evidence that effectively regulated competitive markets result in price decreases, improvements in service quality, faster rollout of infrastructure, the implementation of new technologies, and more choice for consumers. As a result, prices remain high despite the regulated reduction of termination rates (interconnection prices) over a three-year glide path by more than 60%. The reductions have been far too little, too late, and have resulted in prices a long way from those of an efficient operator. More effectively regulated termination rates in sometimes more competitive mobile phone markets elsewhere in Africa have lowered end-user prices to affordable levels. Competitive pricing has subsequently expanded markets, spurred innovation, and created the critical mass essential for affordable mobile money and banking services.

While this is the price that affects the majority of the population, high prices are not only evident in the mobile segment of the market. While the price of international bandwidth has dropped significantly with the landing of competing undersea cable operators in the country, broadband prices remain high by lower middle-income country standards, even on African pricing indices.

The negative policy outcome with regard to bridging the digital divide is especially evident when looking at broadband penetration. South Africa trails behind countries with similar GDP per capita rates such as Argentina, Poland, Mexico, Turkey, and Brazil; the lowest price of broadband in South Africa is higher than the highest price in most other lower middle-income countries (Figure 6.2). Even South Africa's pre-eminence on the continent in ADSL penetration has been lost to North African countries such as Tunisia and Egypt.

Arguments by South African operators, that they cannot be compared specifically to African operators because they are offering high-quality services demanded by consumers in South Africa, are also erroneous. According to the latest report of Ookla, an international broadband testing company, South Africans are on average only getting 74% of the speeds they sign up

---

[13] See Esselaar et al. (2010).

for, which is lower than the global average of 85%. Ookla's household promise index ranks South Africa number 55 out of 64 countries.[14] The Research ICT Africa *Broadband Quality of Service in South Africa Study* (2013) also demonstrates that not only are South Africans paying higher prices but they are seldom receiving the bandwidth advertised; that unusually, but in line with the dependence on wireless broadband, the throughput on GSM 3G and LTE networks is better than on ADSL, but overall there are problems with latency and jitter that make the optimal use of cloud services and certain time-specific applications and services impossible (Chetty, Calandro, and Feamster 2013).

Analysis of ICT policy outcomes

South Africa has not benefitted from the comprehensively or effectively implemented regulated market reform models that, in many emerging and developing economies, have driven uptake, driven down prices, and under-pinned economic growth, and continue to do so. Nor has South Africa benefitted from a strong and viable alternative vision that the establishment of a state-owned broadband company such as Broadband Infraco was meant to develop as an instrument of the "developmental state." It was simply presented by the Department of Public Enterprises in 2007 as a fait accompli—without any consultative policy process or reference to the regulated sector in which it was to operate. This, coupled with the attempt to salvage the defunct state signal distributor Sentech by setting it up as a privileged wireless broadband provider, left the sector stranded between two contradictory, or at the very least, uncoordinated strategies, without the potential benefits of either and none of which acknowledged the structural constraints, particularly aggregate demand for skilled labor.

This goes at least some way toward explaining the negative developmental outcomes in South Africa over the past few decades. From the Reconstruction and Development Programme (RDP) (1994)—in which ICT was at least featured in redress strategies—their presence has diminished in each successive macroeconomic plan, from the Growth Employment and Redistribution (GEAR) program (1996) to the Accelerated and Shared Growth (ASGISA)

---

[14] Ookla Netindex, <www.netindex.com/download/2,46/South-Africa/>.

policy (2008) and the New Growth Path (2010). This is indicative of these sectors' declining significance on the national agenda.

Barely a footnote in the president's 2012 State of the Nation address, ICT has been relegated to a bit part and is sometimes entirely absent on the national developmental stage.[15] This is despite the president referring at length in the State of the Nation address to the establishment of a Presidential Infrastructure Coordinating Commission (PICC), which has identified and developed infrastructure initiatives for state-owned enterprises as well as national provincial and local government departments that have been "clustered, sequenced, and prioritized into a pipeline of projects of strategic integrated projects" (Republic of South Africa, Parliament 2012). Although there was a one-line reference to associated projects focusing on health and basic education ICT infrastructure, as well as regional integration of information and communication technologies in the five major geographically focused programs, the infrastructure projects are in fact focused on ports, roads, and dams. This aligns with an economic strategy geared toward industrial growth and extractive mining, particularly ensuring that mined raw materials can reach ports for export. There is no longer any reference to the infrastructure required for the development of an information society or a knowledge economy.[16] Certainly the linkages between development, education, and ICTs in the informational era is not acknowledged.

---

[15] After more than a decade in the policy doldrums, the ANC's "Second Transition" document includes a component on communications, which speaks about it as strategic infrastructure for the developmental state. It acknowledges for the first time, however, perhaps on the back of the National Planning Commission's Diagnostic Report (2011a) and Development Plan (2011b), that South Africa now lags behind several other African countries and that if ICT is to fulfill its strategic imperative, broadband will need to be far more accessible and affordable—as available as water and electricity. How this is to be achieved, however, remains unclear. For example, having signalled to Korea Telecom a willingness to privatize 20% of Telkom (essentially a bailout for the ailing operator), in June 2012 a R3 billion Korean investment was rejected—despite its intended purpose to provide a much-needed cash injection as well as vital skills and technology.

[16] Despite telecommunications and broadcasting being a *national* jurisdiction, in the State of the Western Province Address, the only province not held by the ruling ANC, the Democratic Alliance (DA) has prioritized broadband extension throughout the province in order to create a "smart" province as a role model for the rest of the country. According to the DA, far more investment in fast and affordable broadband infrastructure is necessary if South Africa is to become an internationally competitive knowledge economy, improve productivity, and enjoy access to new markets. (Western Cape Broadband Initiative Prospectus 2012, unpublished.)

Education

Primary education is the first building block of capability and South Africa actually starts off quite well with a net enrollment ratio of 85%, which puts South Africa at 115 on the WEF (2012/13) ranking. Unfortunately, the quality is ranked at only 132 out of 144 countries. When it comes to mathematics, a key skill for further education and employment, South Africa ranks even worse, 137 out of 139 (WEF 2010), meaning South Africa is outperformed by almost all other African countries.

In a review for the National Planning Commission, Taylor (2011) states that the South African primary school system is significantly underperforming relative to its regional counterparts given its large relative advantage in material resources. South Africa is still a tale of two school sub-systems: one which is functional, wealthy, and able to educate students; the other being poor, dysfunctional, and unable to equip students with the necessary numeracy and literacy skills they should be acquiring in primary school. This inequality of school provision has consequences for the labor market, poverty, and hereditary poverty. This pattern has strong racial overtones: Residents of poor and predominantly black neighborhoods frequently attend schools with a lack of discipline, weak management, and few competent teachers.

Central to the highly productive, globally connected sector of the economy are high-level skills and extensive participation in higher education. The NPC's new National Development Plan is so enthusiastic about knowledge production that it declares that "knowledge production is the rationale of higher education" (NPC 2011b: 271), indeed a radical departure from the traditional "rationale" of higher education in Africa—that is, disseminating (teaching) knowledge from somewhere else—as well as a departure from the post-1994 focus in South Africa, where higher education was seen mainly as an equity instrument (mobility for the historically disadvantaged) (Cloete et al. 2011). Higher education influences a country's innovative capacity and many countries—including rapidly developing nations such as China and India—have been persuaded to put knowledge production, innovation policies, and higher education at the core of their development strategies (Pillay 2010).

From assessments of the South African system by the Harvard panel on ASGISA (Dube et al. 2007), a World Bank project (Fisher and Scott 2011), and the Centre for Higher Education Transformation's (CHET) recent work on differentiation (Badsha and Cloete 2011), the South African higher education system can be characterized as medium knowledge producing and differentiated; with low participation and high attrition rates; with insufficient capacity for adequate skills production; and with a small, chronically in-crisis sub-sector (mainly institutions from the "historically disadvantaged" universities). The two central issues requiring new approaches and new policies are knowledge production (mainly the production of doctoral graduates and publications accredited by the Institute for Scientific information [ISI]) and participation (the proportion of 18- to 24-year-olds who are in tertiary education).

Knowledge production

Globally, the South African higher education system was placed by the Shanghai JiaoTong ARWU 2008 country rankings in the 27–33 range, along with the Czech Republic, Hong Kong, New Zealand, and Ireland; the top university (Cape Town) was in the 200–300 range. In global terms, Africa's proportion of publication output is declining, although the top six African countries are retaining their proportion of around 1.7% (Web of Science 2010). South Africa is still the dominant producer (37%), followed by Egypt (27%) and Nigeria (12%). However, as is the case with ICT connectivity, South Africa's lead is being eroded, particularly by North Africa. In the World Economic Forum (WEF 2012) global competiveness rating, South Africa is ranked at 52, in the same league as Russia (67), Brazil (48), and India (59), but well behind China (29). In terms of efficiency enhancers, the education and training system is rated 140 out of 144 countries, but 51 in terms of the local availability of specialized research and training. The most problematic business deterrent is an inadequately educated workforce (WEF 2012/13).

On the subject of knowledge production and relevant skills, an as yet unpublished World Bank (2012a) assessment describes South African higher education as a "low participation–high attrition system" with the following problems.

Applying the knowledge economy paradigm to South Africa, its weak post-apartheid growth can be attributed to the deterioration of relative performance of two key indicators, namely innovation and education.

The shortage of high-level skills has been a huge hindrance for innovation and technology absorption.

One of the biggest contributors to the sub-optimal performance of the South African economy is a human-capital trap. Massive investments in the education system have not produced better outcomes in either academic performance or graduation rates.

South Africa has drastically scaled up investment in knowledge generation since the end of apartheid. This trend has not been matched by an equally rapid increase in research and development (R&D) personnel.

Participation in higher education

Table 6.2 illustrates the remarkable relationship between higher education participation and the stage of economic development and global competitiveness. South Africa's participation rate[17] of 15.4% is significantly lower than that for comparable middle-income countries, although much higher than the average of around 6% for sub-Saharan African countries.

Participation in the South African tertiary education system crept up from 12% in 1994 to around 19% in 2011, if new data on further education and training colleges are included (Sheppard 2011). During the same period, the Brazilian system "exploded" from 14% up to 25%—mainly through private provision stimulated with tax concessions. Three major causes for the lack of expansion in South Africa include: the absence of a post-school, pre-university college-type system that can absorb students who pass the formal "matric" school-leaving exam, but who do not qualify for entrance into university; the low throughput rate from the school system of students who are adequately prepared for university studies; and the almost insurmountable restrictions on private higher education provision. Crucially, with the absence of a post-secondary school college sector, South Africa is not producing the mid-level generic skills (what Castells [2001] calls self-programmable skills) that are crucial for the knowledge economy.

In Africa, higher education is key for growth (knowledge production and skills), redistribution (equity), and democratic participation. Kofi Annan, then secretary-general of the United Nations, recognized the key role for the university as a knowledge institution in Africa by stating that: "The university must become a primary tool for Africa's development in the new century" (quoted in Bloom et al. 2006: 2). This was endorsed when,

[17] UNESCO definition of enrollment in tertiary education as a proportion of the 18- to 24-year-old cohort.

Table 6.2 Stage of development, tertiary education participation rates, and competitiveness

Country	Stage of development (2012/13)	Gross tertiary education enrolment rate (2012/13), with ranking	Overall global competitiveness ranking (2012/13)
Ghana	Stage 1: Factor-driven	12 (103)	114
Kenya	driven	4.1 (130)	106
Mozambique		1.5 (139)	131
Tanzania		2.1 (137)	113
Uganda		4.2 (128)	118
Botswana	Transition from 1 to 2	20 (119)*	76
Mauritius	Stage 2:	25.9 (82)	55
South Africa	Efficiency-driven	15.4 (101)	54
Costa Rica		25.6 (81)	56
Chile	Transition from	59.2 (38)	30
China	2 to 3	26.0 (79)	27
Finland	Stage 3:	93.7 (3)	7
South Korea	Innovation-driven	103 (1)	22
United States		94.8 (2)	4

* According to Botswana Tertiary Council, participation rate is 20+

Note: Income thresholds (GDP per capita in USD) for establishing stages of development (WEF 2010: 10): Stage 1 Factor-driven: <2,000; Transition from Stage 1 to Stage 2: 2,000–3,000; Stage 2 Efficiency-driven: 3,000–9,000; Transition from Stage 2 to Stage 3: 9,000–17,000; Stage 3 Innovation-driven: >17,000. Key at Factor level is health and primary education, for Efficiency it is higher education and financial markets, and for Innovation, business sophistication and R&D.

Source: World Economic Forum (2012/13) for 144 countries

in advance of the UNESCO World Conference on Higher Education in 2009, a group of African education ministers called for improved financing of universities and a support fund to strengthen training and research in key areas (MacGregor 2009).

The maintenance of an elite higher education system, without a post-secondary college sector, suggests that higher education mirrors the narrow elite-formation model of black economic empowerment (BEE), which created a small, globally connected and very wealthy group (Bhorat and Van der Westhuizen 2010) and a large group of youth without skills to participate productively in the economy. This was rather dramatically illustrated by a 2009 CHET study showing that 2.8 million youths between the ages of 18 and 24 were "not in education, employment or training"—the so-called NEETs (Cloete 2009). A subsequent article in the South African *Mail & Guardian*, "Idle Minds, Social Time Bomb," drew attention to the potential of 2.8 million youths to cause serial social disruption (Gower 2009). The impact of this study was "enhanced" when the 2009 crime statistics showed that the average age of a house robber is between 19 and 25 years, and that of all arrested robbers 90% were NEETs (Cloete et al. 2011). The 2011 Arab Spring in North Africa further spotlighted this issue and added a political dimension of urgency.

The most recent major policy papers in South Africa, the Green Paper from the Department of Higher Education and Training (DHET 2012) and the National Development Plan (NPC 2011b), both responded by stating that increased participation (to at least 30%, up from the current 17%) is a minimum target and that the poorly functioning further education and training (FET) sector must be revamped and expanded—from 400,000 to four million by 2030. Both policy papers, for the first time in the post-apartheid era—albeit with some unresolved tensions between channeling funds to the poorly performing, historically disadvantaged institutions versus strengthening the high knowledge-producing institutions—agree that both knowledge production and participation must increase dramatically.

As will be discussed in the next section under "Politics and policy," the question remains whether this will be yet another virtuous, but unimplemented policy.

Politics and policy

What is the South African development model?

Responding to the above question at the Stellenbosch Institute for Advanced Studies (STIAS) seminar,[18] a senior member of the National Executive Committee (NEC) of the ruling ANC said: "We started this route (deliberately

[18] For a program and participants of the STIAS seminar, see the CHET website: Informational and Human Development, <www.chet.org.za/events>.

or otherwise) with a rather fuzzy sense of our destination, and hence a disconnect between means and ends and a dangerously short-termism in our strategies and programmes." A senior government official from the Treasury answered differently: "the development model is what we fund and in every one of the 'pillars' of the Reconstruction and Development Programme [RDP] (1994) budgets have doubled or tripled since 1995."

The notions of development spelled out in the RDP are: "The RDP would link growth, development, reconstruction, redistribution, and reconciliation into a 'unified programme,' held together by a broad infrastructure programme that would focus on creating and enhancing existing services in the electricity, water, telecommunications, transport, health, education, and training sectors." According to this view, problems arose due to a lack of capacity to spend the budgets—in other words, a lack of implementation capacity. One of the ANC executive members echoed this in a presentation at the seminar about a lack of leadership quality during the transition, but he did not provide reasons for this lack. The question is really whether the RDP can be traced as the development model underpinning the macroeconomic strategies that follow. There appears to be little to connect the RDP with consecutive growth models such as the Growth, Employment, and Redistribution (GEAR 1997),[19] the Accelerated and Shared Growth Initiative (ASGISA 2005),[20] or the New Growth Path (2011),[21] other than the very broadest concepts of reconstruction, growth, and redistribution.

Offering an entirely different explanation at the same seminar was Moeletsi Mbeki, who claimed that the real "bargain" or pact between the ANC and the Afrikaner nationalists and English capital was to maintain the development model of the previous regime, namely the minerals-energy complex (MEC). South Africa, which has one of the highest endowments of minerals in the world, developed an economy driven by the extraction of minerals (gold, diamonds, coal, platinum, steel), without any further beneficiation—through cheap electricity and chemicals. Most of the assets of the economy are derived from exporting these metals.[22]

---

[19] See GCIS <www.info.gov.za/view/DownloadFileAction?id=70507>.
[20] See GSIS <www.info.gov.za/asgisa/>.
[21] See <www.info.gov.za/view/DownloadFileAction?id=135748>.
[22] Previously most of these exports went to Europe, but that has changed dramatically. China is now South Africa's biggest trading partner and this is so important that, despite South Africa's constitution and pride in human rights, it refused the Dali Lama a visa, to the consternation and condemnation of commentators such as Archbishop Emeritus Desmond Tutu.

At the pre-democracy negotiations, it was agreed that the MEC would be preserved in exchange for a Black Economic Empowerment plan that would incorporate a minority of blacks into the business elite. This would maintain the availability of cheap labor—not through oppressive apartheid laws, but through a massive expansion of the welfare system and through globalization—and cheap imports of consumer goods (Mbeki 2009).

These metal exports were a huge blessing for South Africa in terms of capital accumulation through foreign investors and the construction of physical infrastructure.

The MEC is not a post-apartheid invention. A series of seminal class analyses as far back as the seventies revealed the alliance between the apartheid state and what was seen as historically white English, liberal capital and foreign capital in the mining sector which has underpinned the economy for over a century (see Wolpe 1972; Legassick 1974; Davies et al. 1976). Reviewing earlier work examining the state capital relations, Terreblanche (2012) describes the MEC as a course of capitalist development since the 1870 minerals revolution (the discovery of diamonds and gold) upon which extraction came to be based on the extreme exploitation of African migrant labor. The MEC was initiated and led by English and foreign capital and did not only concern itself with mining, but significantly affected both the economic and political models of development. Not only was it the basis of the Anglo-Boer War (1899–1902), but it led to the notorious 1913 Land Act which effectively removed individual property rights from Africans, and to the Rand Revolt of 1922 when General Smuts, the Boer prime minister, was prepared to use military aircraft to bomb white striking mineworkers in the hills around Johannesburg; state violence eerily reminiscent of the Marikana massacre.

What is evident is a continuous "development path" in which successive nationalist political leadership, whether white or black, has been under constant pressure from English-led global mining capital conglomerates. Terreblanche concludes that "although the contribution of the mining industry to the South African economy has been enormous, its destructive impact on African society, and its negative ecological externalities must not be underestimated" (Terreblanche 2012: 49). Mbeki concurs and adds that the greatest weakness is the much-described "Africa resource curse"—the dependence on cheap, low-skilled labor (Mbeki 2009: 76–7).

Nico Cloete and Alison Gillwald

Fragmented development

One of the effects of the South African "elite pact" is that development in information technology has been fragmented with informationalization of high-end economic and social activities only. The financial system, for example, is dynamic and informationalized. Society at large is not. Nor is the economy at large. For example, South Africa has a world-class, highly efficient tax system and a very well-run Treasury,[23] necessary for the current clientele channels required to enable the redistribution critical to maintaining social stability through cash grants and other welfarist mechanisms.[24]

Similarly to ICT, education and particularly higher education is partially informationalized, with five universities in the Shanghai Top 500, and South Africa, with Australia, will jointly host the world's largest radio telescope, the Square Kilometer Array (SKA)—which will be one of the world's biggest science experiments by 2016.[25] However, the tertiary participation rate is still around 20% and three million youths between 18 and 24 years of age are not in education, training, or employment.

The disconnect between this informationalized, financial, and resource extractive economic sector from human development is rather starkly illustrated by the 2012 World Economic Forum Global Competitiveness Index rankings. Overall, South Africa ranks 52 out of 144 countries. On one hand it ranks at 1 in auditing standards, securities exchange regulation, and legal rights, and at 2 in soundness of banks and financial services. On the other, it ranks at 133 for primary education and life expectancy, 134 for business costs of crime, 140 for education and training quality, and 143 for quality of mathematics and science education. And the WEF (2012/13) adds that the biggest deterrent to doing business in South Africa is the "inadequately trained workforce."

A model of development exists, but it is not the "fuzzy" empowerment model implicit in the Reconstruction and Development Plan of 1994. Currently there is a disjuncture between informational development and human

---

[23] "Many observers, both internal and external will say that we have a world-class tax system and that the tax rates in South Africa are competitive with the best in the world. In that sense we do not come second to anybody." *Financial Mail* interview (February 29, 2004) with Pravin Gordhan, South African Receiver of Revenue.

[24] The social grant and pension administrative system is informationalized with a state of the art biometric system that operates even in rural areas. SA Government News Agency (2013/04/02).

[25] <www.southafrica.info/about/science/skashared-250512.htm#ixzz2PJqKPL8z>.

development which will impede any national development plan in the context of building a modern economy—and the model of development has high human and environmental costs. Even in the mid-term, without more broad-based economic and education empowerment outcomes, the current path seems unattainable as a model for growth.

The developmental state?

In leading informational economies all over the world, the state has played a central role in developing a forceful supply-side policy through investment in education—critical to citizens' ability to adjust to the change brought about by technological innovation—and investment in the necessary infrastructure, such as telecommunications (Gillwald 2009). In the informational era, as information generation, processing, and transmission become the fundamental sources of productivity and power, so too does the development of communication networks and quality education to drive the development of the economy and society (Castells 2001).

Gumede (2010) argues that policy-formulation processes and institutional mechanisms that have evolved since 1994 indicate that South Africa is aiming to be a developmental state—the establishment of the National Planning Commission in 2009 is but the latest of such institutional mechanisms. Although the term "developmental state" was used rhetorically in ANC strategies as far back as the RDP, it was only around 2008 that it was proposed by President Thabo Mbeki in response to criticisms of the GEAR, as the form of state necessary to deal with the structural economic challenges facing the country, particularly poverty and unemployment (Gillwald 2009). It was only in the attempt to make a clean break from GEAR that it was formally adopted and became the pillar for the next two macroeconomic policies, ASGISA and the New Growth Path.

But is a state developmental simply by declaring itself so? Castells draws on the now classical concepts of the development state—legitimacy, delivery, authoritarianism, and a social (identity) project—to determine when a state is *developmental*. He says it is so when the state located in a specific historical context establishes as its principle of legitimacy its ability to promote and sustain development, understanding by development the combination of steady high rates of economic growth and structural change in the economic system, both domestically and in its relationship to the international economy (1996 vol. 1: 182).

It is clear from the evidence above that the South African state from this perspective is not developmental. The unrest and dissent that erupts through the patchwork of placatory social grants and international event windfalls, such as the 2010 World Cup, challenges the legitimacy of a state that has been unable to address the problems associated with structural unemployment, undersupply of skills, extractive industries and export dependence within the domestic economy, and as a result, its lack of global competitiveness as well.

The reasons for its inability to do so can be found not least in the dearth of bureaucratic capacity required by a developmental state. The National Planning Commission emphasizes the need for a capable state. It makes clear it will not deliver on its developmental objectives without it. In the Diagnostic Report (NPC 2011a), the NPC notes that in order to "bring about a capable developmental state that can give effect to the national plan, it is necessary to identify areas where government is failing to provide realistic strategies for overcoming limitations in state capacity." But can this be achieved with the highly politicized appointive bureaucracy that has emerged over the last two decades? The strategy of ANC cadre deployment to meet these political objectives of transformation, often without sufficient capacity and competency, has had a devastating effect on democratic institutional building, service delivery, policy formulation, and leadership.

In the successful developmental states of Northeast Asia, power is wielded unequivocally by an autonomous bureaucratic elite, drawn from the most talented at the best universities in the country, who "formulate broad industrial policy, identify the means for implementing it and ensure (highly regulated) competition in designated strategic sectors" (Schneider 1999). Explaining the failure of the developmental state in Latin America but apposite to the case of South Africa, Schneider points out that while appointive bureaucracies are major political players because of their discretionary power, they lack independent power bases and are not a coherent group with predictable interests: "Rather they are brokers, deal makers and idea peddlers..." (Schneider 1999: 14, quoted in Gillwald 2009).

Although the politicization of the bureaucracy has been justified on the grounds of redress and the need for a transformative political will within the public sector, the inability of the public service to deliver has been widely acknowledged within the South African Government, prompting various initiatives to build the human capital essential to the delivery of the national project by the developmental state (SAMDI 2006).

And what of the "national project" identified as the binding agent of the development state? Although the legitimacy of the state was crafted around the national project of redress, redistribution, and reconstruction—indeed, the restoration of dignity—in order to achieve these, the state had to structurally change the economy. Certainly from the 1990s, the national project for the liberation movement and subsequently for the country following its electoral victory was the building of a democratic, non-racial state through the transformation of the economy and society. This was built on a long history of nationalist and socialist resistance and was formalized in the African National Congress's manifesto for the 1994 elections, the Reconstruction and Development Programme (RDP). The RDP, geared primarily at alleviation of poverty through the redistribution of wealth, was the national transformation project, and in 1994, the South African state under the leadership of Nelson Mandela had the legitimacy to override other interests. However, it was precisely the absence of significant economic growth, and growing unemployment and a recurring currency crisis, that led the second democratic government under Thabo Mbeki to shift to a more pragmatic and orthodox macroeconomic framework, Growth Employment and Redistribution strategy (GEAR). Although this resulted in moderate growth in the economy, it failed to address the problem of structural unemployment and poverty, creating the crisis of legitimacy for the state. The party sought to address this from a policy perspective through the deployment of the concept of the developmental state, and subsequently, politically, through a change in leadership.

This however did not translate into an extension of the national project. The failures of transformation reflected in poor service delivery in a range of areas began to bite, and civil society tested the limits of state power on major social issues, such as HIV/AIDS "denialism" of which Mbeki was the main proponent, eroding the ability of the state to forge a national project. In fact, by the second democratic elections in 2004, there really was no longer a cohesive project of national transformation. While issues of redistribution and poverty alleviation continued to dominate the political agenda, the failure to address these on the ground manifested in increasing social unrest, which was contained through the development of an extensive welfare net by the state.

Nico Cloete and Alison Gillwald

What are the reasons for these negative developmental outcomes?

Many reasons for this have been advanced, but a prevailing view is that, starting with its Constitution, South Africa has world-class policies, but does not have the capacity to implement them. This assumption could be questioned on a number of grounds. First, as demonstrated in the preceding analysis, there is evidence that in many areas, from education to health to ICT, there has been a lot of "bad" policy—from policies that have weakened already weak sectors (curriculum reform and teacher retrenchments in education), to economic and ICT policies that are explicitly anti-redistributive, and redistributive policies that are disempowering.

Second, a study in eight African countries shows that with regard to higher education and development, there is, with the exception of Mauritius, no agreement on the development models of the other seven countries, or on the role of higher education in them. This study suggests that in a number of countries, South Africa included, implementation capacity may not be the central problem, but rather it is the lack of agreement on what needs to be done. In terms of implementation, the worst scenario is low capacity plus disagreement (Cloete et al. 2011).

Third, development plans for nearly a decade now have deployed the developmental state as the main driver. South Africa does not meet several of the criteria of successful developmental states that it seeks to emulate. Minimally, this includes having the institutional and bureaucratic capacity to develop appropriate policies and implement them; a collective project around which to forge a national identity; and a state with the legitimacy and autonomy to rise above sectional interests to drive development (Woo-Cumings 1999; Evans 1995). Instead, in South Africa apartheid legacies continue to compartmentalize identity along racial and ethnic lines, despite nation-building efforts reflected in references to "the rainbow nation" and other calls for a collective identity. This said, non-racialized class and interest groups have emerged post-1994. Reflecting the dualism in the economy and society, the beneficiaries of the uneven informational development within the country are connected to global cultural norms and focused on individualized personal development. This group is increasingly deracialized. The excluded group, however, is largely black and increasingly simply individualized consumers with a household debt-to-income ratio of 78%.[26]

---

[26] <http://blog.wilde-insights.co.za/?p=219>.

According to Castells (Chapter 1 in this volume), the more individual identity dominates and informationalism depends on entrepreneurs seeking personal development without concerns for human development of the territorial community, the more it leads to a deterioration of the living conditions of the community at large—in spite of the personal improvement of the innovators. The split between individual identity from collective identity results in the splitting of informationalism from human development.

In a provocative book on identity, Ivor Chipken (2007) asks, "Do South Africans Exist?," and after an extensive reflection on African nationalism, the national democratic revolution, cosmopolitan citizenship, racial democracy, nationhood, the people, and the impossibility of the national community, concludes that while there is a vibrant debate, that on occasion exceeds vibrancy, there is no clear sign of a "new South African" that can form the glue of a developmental state.

Fourth, a rather cynical counter-explanation is that, in line with the 1994 "bargain" between the ANC and big business, it is not possible to develop a connection between the logic of informationalism and the logic of welfarism (Mbeki 2009). In this case, many policy commission activities and processes are what Weiler (1984) calls "compensatory legitimation." For Weiler, commissions and subsequent polices are often an attempt to buy time and to create the impression of government action. You-tien Hsing (2010), drawing on her observations in China, talks about "policy as performance"—when the regime has no intention to enact change, but "performs" policy rituals in order to create the impression of an intention to change, or in South African parlance, to transform and empower.

The tension between practice and discourse is nowhere more clear than within the Presidency itself. As raised earlier in relation to ICT and higher education, in November 2011 the NPC, based in the Presidency, released the National Development Plan: Vision 2030, which asserts in its vision statement that South Africa must create a "virtuous cycle of growth and development that will aim at eliminating poverty and sharply reduce inequality by 2030" (NPC 2011b: 2). It further states that capabilities will be upgraded to enable sustainable and inclusive development, which will involve creating more jobs, expanding infrastructure, moving toward a low-carbon economy, improving education and training, and building a capable state (NPC 2011b: 5–6). This document contains, among others, proposals to improve knowledge production and participation in higher education and informationalism. Limited as this is, taken together, this could be seen as the first post-apartheid government policy statement that tries to strengthen the dynamic, knowledge-producing, technologically advanced ICT sector, and one that highlights the critical connection to human development, within a sustainable environment.

Concluding remarks

Can it simply be that the reason a broader, more inclusive informational development is not taking place in South Africa is because, at the level of decision-making, it is not considered important? The rejection of technology and innovation has a long history on the Left. In the 1980s, the Soviet Union failed to embrace the emerging information technology, which was one of the reasons for its collapse. Or is it simply an outcome of the "blanket" response to state–sector relations evident in the application of the "developmental state" without agreement or clarity on what it means? This fuzziness allows it to be all things to all people, and a successful rallying call after some of the perceived failures of GEAR, but that is not helpful in terms of implementing policy. This tendency toward empty rhetoric has failed to provide the nuanced and differentiated response required by modern states to deal with the increased complexity and dynamism of all sectors, but particularly ICT, resulting from changing production requirements and requiring differentiated modes of governance. Assessing the appropriate role for the state in different sectors is one of the primary policy challenges in South Africa (Gillwald 2009). To comply with international commitments and align itself with global trends, the government has made rhetorical commitments to both market reforms and the free flow of information that the new technologies have unleashed, yet remains fundamentally distrustful of them and of the specialist institutions to which, as a requirement of such reforms, they have delegated powers, such as sector regulators.

Informationalism cannot be achieved without a synergistic relationship between the dynamic, informational sector of development—which includes advanced services and knowledge-based economic activities—and the processes of human development—which include environmental sustainability and higher levels of participation in tertiary education. Essential to successful modern economies are the knowledge base, the quality of the workforce, social stability, and managerial efficiency. These are the sources of productivity and competitiveness—the key factors of wealth creation in a globally interdependent economy. If informationalism is limited to a small, globalized sector and if there is no "virtuous" feedback loop between informationalism and human development, South Africa will remain underdeveloped.

The extractive industries on which the fragile economic and political stability currently rest are unsustainable—socially, politically, and environmentally. Without a dynamic sector able to generate sufficient wealth to support public spending and thus improve social wellbeing, the state's fiscal problems will ultimately limit the process of redistribution of income and services, which is currently plastering over the structural problems in the economy, service delivery collapse in certain key areas, and the erosion of political transparency and public consultation.

The social grants that appear to flow from the human rights miracle of 1994, often seen as providing the safety net required by the spirit of the Constitution, affect the very dignity project itself: in the absence of conditions that enable human development, it robs people of their dignity and freedom, by denying them the capabilities to determine their own lives, as Sen (1999) has highlighted. This perpetuates the conditions for poverty and inequality associated with political dissent. While the legacies of apartheid will long linger in the economy and society and no doubt in the discourse of political mobilization, the sense of victimhood this gives rise to is paralyzing. The underlying principle of equality on which the dignity project rests and which has provided the rationale for the concepts of reconstruction, redress, and redistribution that have informed national planning for two decades is central to any plan moving forward.[27] But it will be impossible to move forward as long as a discourse of victimhood and entitlement supersedes performance. This was rather dramatically demonstrated during April 2013, when the senior minister responsible for national planning in the office of the President was publicly rebuked by the President after he made a case for "building government capabilities," but warned public servants not to blame apartheid for their lack of delivery and failure to meet citizens' expectations. The President responded the next day by saying: "To suggest we cannot blame apartheid for what is happening in our country now,

---

[27] This idea of the three Rs that underpin post-apartheid development planning being regressive rather than progressive came from a comment by You-tien Hsing, the author of the chapter on China in this book. Reflecting on the case of South Africa in contrast to China she asked why everything in South Africa was "re"—reconstruction, redress, redistribution—"why don't you just construct, produce, and distribute?"

I think is a mistake to say the least…it is impossible for change to be completed in just 20 years."[28]

The time has come for less backward-looking rationales to achieve equality and restore dignity. A social compact that seeks to ensure that citizens have the capabilities (substantive freedoms such as education, skills, and health) to exercise autonomy in the context of their hard-won liberties is more likely to result in a better distribution of opportunities within society than a system reliant on wealth redistribution, which is the economic basis for the current fraying social contract.

[28] "We Can Blame Apartheid, Says Zuma" (IOL News, April 11, 2013). <www.iol.co.za/news/politics/we-can-blame-apartheid-says-zuma-1.1498541>.

Chapter 7

Development, Democracy, and Social Change in Chile

Fernando Calderón and Manuel Castells

Introduction: new development in Latin America

Over the last two decades, Latin America has been fully integrated into the global economy, as the region has increased its competitiveness and stepped up its modernization.[1] After the lost decade of the 1980s, in which Latin America as a whole actually regressed in its share of the world economy, in the 1990s macroeconomic context, after the implementation of reforms aiming to control inflation, rationalize public spending, and strengthen the financial system, most economies stabilized and created the opportunity for sustained economic growth in spite of cyclical variations over the 1990–2012 period. Between 2003 and 2008, Latin America as a whole grew at an

---

[1] For a thorough analysis of the integration of Latin America into the global economy, see Ernesto Ottone's "The Non-Global Global Crisis: Latin America in the Globalization Process," in Castells et al. (eds) (2012). For a deep understanding of the sociopolitical conditions of development in Latin America, see Fernando Calderón's (coordinator) *Las huellas del futuro. Lideres y soberano* (2013) and *Los conflictos sociales en América Latina* (2011).

average annual rate of 4.5%. Furthermore, the 2008–9 financial crisis in advanced economies had a small impact in Latin America. There was indeed a decline of exports as a consequence of the recession in the United States and Europe, but it was only significant in 2009, and it was largely compensated by the growing importance of Asia for Latin American exports, so that in 2010–11, growth resumed at an average annual rate of 5% for the region as a whole. What is remarkable is that financial markets in Latin America were not overwhelmed by the turmoil and speculation that characterized the Western economies. The reforms undertaken in Brazil, Mexico, and Chile in the 1990s, and in Argentina and Peru in the 2000s, made financial institutions more robust. Government policies contributed to the avoidance of both stagnation and inflation for the first time in Latin American history, although this statement should be qualified by acknowledging the variations among countries.

However, the integration of Latin America in the global economy in the 1990s—while achieving macroeconomic stability and attracting foreign investment, ultimately stimulating growth—was obtained at a high social cost. In 2000, the percentage of population below the poverty level reached 44%, while income inequality increased substantially, and the informal economy was pervasive in most metropolitan areas. Structural reforms carried out throughout the region in the '90s produced negative outcomes in most countries: high inequality and poverty rates, a decrease in Latin America's share of global GDP, and weakened social cohesion. They also induced a political crisis that dented trust in political parties and severed democratic governance. Social protests against the neo-liberal model prompted the rise of neo-populist politics across the region, from Venezuela to Ecuador, Bolivia, Nicaragua, and Argentina.

Notwithstanding, some countries—particularly, Chile, Costa Rica, and Uruguay—that applied structural reforms in a heterodox fashion and whose institutions were stable performed significantly better during the first decade of the twenty-first century. From this variegated experience, four political trends have emerged:

1. *Conservative modernization*: renewal of the political party system, institutional reforms to reinvigorate respect for authorities, market-based economies, and close alliances with the US;
2. *Practical reformism*: renewal of the political party system, secular values, promotion of alliance building, state capacities focused on maximizing growth and social wellbeing, and strategic links with the US;

3. *Popular nationalism*: quest for political hegemony, dominant role of the state, massive popular rallies, charismatic leadership, and strong anti-imperialism sentiments, and;

4. *Neo-developmental indigenism*: bringing together the state's strategic role with communitarian peasant and urban popular organizations.

In economic terms, for the past ten years, the political classes of a few Latin American countries, such as Argentina, Bolivia, Brazil, Ecuador, and Venezuela, have promoted neo-developmental policies. These countries' states have been recovering their capacities as connectors between society and economy, while stimulating aggregate demand, controlling the operations of multinational firms, and strengthening regional integration.

Neo-developmental projects have found a fertile ground in the aforementioned countries and in various international arenas. At the national level, the project is based on an alliance between citizens, business, and the media, which has directed its efforts to consolidate regional integration, especially for the manufacturing industry and commodities markets. With the latter goals in mind, state enterprises have been nationalized or have entered joint ventures with multinational firms. Neo-developmental projects have also favored large-scale social programs focused on alleviating poverty—mainly through conditional cash transfers—and on small and medium-sized firms. Such a strategy has had positive outcomes in reducing the poverty level to 33% of the population, although inequality remains a daunting challenge for Latin America.

In the public sphere, emerging actors—associated, in many cases, with political parties or pro-government grassroots organizations—have replaced traditional bureaucracy and filled numerous high-profile positions. Neo-developmental projects have also given high visibility to multiculturalism, which, in turn, has promoted cultural traditions of native and African descendants, who were undermined and underappreciated not long ago.

The state has played a key role as facilitator of economic and sociopolitical processes pertaining to each country and its specific context. As a consequence, Latin American leaders have increased their autonomy from international government institutions. Of course, Brazil is a chief example and has become Latin America's leader and a relevant player in the global scene.[2]

---

[2] For further detail see Calderón 'La inflexion politica en el cambio sociocultural en America Latina' PAPEP PNUD Escenarios Politicos en Amarica Latina Siglo XXI (Buenos Aires, Argentina 2009).

However, between 1990 and 2010, two countries stood out as being able to engage in a dynamic model of economic growth while improving the conditions of human development: Chile and Costa Rica.

This chapter will focus on Chile because it has an added significance. Chile under Dictator Augusto Pinochet was presented as the archetypical example of the free-market development model that came to be known as neoliberalism. Here we can contrast two different models of development from two different periods within the same country: one that disregarded human development, and another that embedded human development within economic development. Furthermore, while economic growth continued in Chile after 2010, the rise of social inequality associated with both models of economic growth and the dysfunctional party system that excluded citizens from public debate led (in 2011–12) to the rise of powerful social movements in Chile that challenged the priority given to economic competitiveness over human development by the new, conservative government elected in 2010. Thus, by analyzing the Chilean experience between 1990 and 2012, we will be able to assess the interaction between human development and informational development, as well as the redefinition of both terms in the interplay between political democracy and new social movements.

After proceeding with this analysis of Chile, the text concludes by considering the relationship between human development, informational development, and political development in Latin America, as well as the lessons this analysis may provide for the international experience.

Neoliberal ideology and the reality of economic growth in Pinochet's Chile

In the term of Pinochet (1974–89),[3] Chile underwent a substantial transformation of its productive structure: it became largely integrated in the global economy, and, in spite of two major economic crises, it experienced relatively high economic growth at the cost of staggering human suffering and exploitation (1.7% annual GDP growth in 1974–83; 6.4% GDP growth in 1984–89; 23% inflation in 1989; 15% unemployment in 1989; 40% living

---

[3] For sources and analysis of Chilean development up to 2005, see Castells' *Globalizacion, desarrollo y democracia: Chile en el contexto mundial* (2005).

in poverty in 1989). This experience was hailed all around the world by neoliberal ideologues.

This model of economic growth can be characterized as an authoritarian, exclusionary, and liberal model of development. It was based on putting the resources and authority of the Chilean state at the service of private investors, selling public property, curtailing public spending, and opening the Chilean economy to the global economy with a significant increase of exports (an increase of 10% per year). It was based on the restriction of social and environmental legislation, the elimination of political freedom, and the reduction of wages and benefits to the minimum. In real terms, on a wage index of 100 in 1970, by the end of the regime in 1989, the level of wages had risen to 103. In short, it was economic growth with human underdevelopment. Informational development was never present as a policy or a business practice. Productivity growth was based on extracting more value from labor, not on technological or managerial innovation.

In fact, the achievements of this period of economic growth under Pinochet were outperformed in strict economic terms by the democratic model of development.

The Chilean democratic, inclusionary, liberal model of development

Democracy, albeit within certain limits, was restored in Chile in 1990. Between 1990 and 2010, the country was governed by a coalition of democratic parties (the Christian Democrats, Socialists, and Left Democrats, among others) organized in the Concertación Democrática. During this period, the economic performance of Chile in terms of economic growth, job creation, increase of exports, investment, and control of inflation improved considerably over the Pinochet period (GDP growth of 6% annually on average over 20 years; 10% annual growth of exports; unemployment dropped to under 9%; inflation went down to 2–3%). Financial stability was maintained, and public spending increased substantially. In addition, living conditions improved dramatically. Real wages—whose index (on a 1970=100 basis) was at 103 at the end of Pinochet's term—jumped to over 200 in 2009, the proportion of population below the poverty level went down to 15% (from 40%), and extreme poverty was almost eliminated (2%). Furthermore, a proto-welfare state was created, with substantial public investment in education, health, housing, urban services, and social welfare, while the privatized pension system was regulated and complemented by government policies. Education enrollment rates reached 100% in primary education and 90% in secondary education. The proportion of students enrolled in higher education doubled in the 1990s, and reached 24% for the cohort of 20–29-year-olds in the mid-2000s. However, this expansion of higher education was largely due to the creation of numerous private, for-profit universities, many of mediocre quality, with a high cost for low-income families, while middle-class students with better secondary education were admitted to better quality, less-expensive public universities. This unequal education led to the social crisis that we will analyze below. Health coverage improved substantially, although it remains uneven at the time of writing. Infant mortality decreased to 10 per thousand, and life expectancy rose to 80 years for women and 70 years for men. The pension system is still dominated by private insurance with profound inequalities, inducing an ongoing public debate in recent times.

While according to ECLAC (2012)[4] income inequality has remained among the highest in the region, after calculating indirect wages via redistribution in public and social services, economic inequality was reduced by approximately 30%.

At the same time, worker's rights were restored, a stable industrial relations system was established, institutional democracy was effective in ensuring clean elections, and an independent judiciary asserted the rule of law. The remnants of Pinochet's Constitution, which retained political privileges for him and for the armed forces, for the most part were phased out. By the time of the presidency of Ricardo Lagos (2000–6), democracy had been established, the armed forces had been institutionalized, the dictator had been brought under judicial prosecution (he avoided trial by claiming insanity), and most of the crimes of his dictatorship had been exposed and prosecuted.

Thus, it can be argued that Chile between 1990 and 2010 was a relatively successful democratic model of economic development combined with enhanced human development in a fully democratic state based on freedom and a system of industrial relations. Financial and fiscal stability were preserved. Environmental legislation was introduced. And yet, we can also characterize the model as liberal because it operated in a free-market

---

[4] ECLAC. (2012). *Social Panorama of Latin America 2011*. UN: Santiago de Chile.

environment, with an open economy that benefitted from accrued competitiveness in global markets. Furthermore, macroeconomic policies were characterized by liberal orthodoxy, and Chile signed free-trade agreements with the Americas, China, the European Union, and a variety of countries in Asia and Africa. Indeed, Chile became the most competitive and globalized economy in Latin America. Figure A in this chapter's Appendix displays the high rate of GDP growth between 1990 and 2011.[5]

Standards of living improved considerably in terms of income per capita during this period. Chile became the third-richest country in Latin America after Mexico and Argentina, and human development indicators improved substantially thanks to the expansion of education at all levels, and the increased coverage of health care.

At the source of the successful, stable model of economic growth in Democratic Chile, econometric and institutional studies have identified the following factors:

- Substantial increase of total factor productivity—way above the increase in productivity of labor and capital. This is typical of informational development, as economic growth under informationalism does not come from adding more capital or labor, but from adding more knowledge, technology, and effective management.
- Growth of productivity and competitiveness in the private business sector on the basis of the institutional and macroeconomic reforms undertaken in the 1990s.
- Social and political stability as a result of the political consensus to stabilize democracy, and the social pact between government, unions, and businesses. The basis of this agreement was a single major salary increase in 1990–2 followed by moderation in the wage demands of the unions.
- Continuation of a policy of open trade with the entire world economy, based on the competitiveness of Chilean companies.
- Anti-inflation policy with systematic budget surpluses and the creation of a stability fund from royalties obtained from copper exports to be used in

[5] Chile Human Development Reports, from 1996 to 2012, have analyzed the complexity of the tendencies and the relationships between the modernization of the economy and society. One of the main conclusions is the prevailing gap between human development and citizenship. For further detail, see Márquez, R. and Moreno, C. (2007), "Desarrollo sin ciudadanos: el modelo chileno de los últimos veinte años," in *Ciudadanía y Desarrollo Humano. Cuadernos de gobernabilidad democratic Vol. 1.* Siglo veintiuno editores: Ciudad de Buenos Aires.

case of emergency (e.g. earthquake) as well as in R&D (as a matter of fact, it was used more often for earthquake relief than for R&D).

- Increase in spending on programs that we could consider part of a welfare state, such as education, health, and housing, financed in a non-inflationary manner thanks to a substantial increase in taxes (an increase equivalent to 2% of GDP in the first period of democracy).
- Substantial increase of investment in the economy, which went from 19% of GDP under Pinochet to 27% in the democratic period.
- Control of financial flows imposing a tax on short-term investment by speculative capital.

This model of economic growth with human development continued under all the administrations of the Concertación, and at times under the Christian Democrats (1990–2000), the Left Independents (Lagos, 2000–6), and the Socialists (Michelle Bachelet, 2006–10).

In 2010, for the first time in Chilean democratic history, a conservative president was elected. Piñera, who had explicitly broken with Pinochet during his dictatorship, was supported by a coalition of the entire right, including ex-Pinochetistas. However, given the strong popular support for government social programs, Piñera kept by and large the social policies introduced by the Concertación alongside liberal economic policies. Indeed, his election was due more to his Christian Democratic opponent's lack of charisma and to the Concertación Coalition's political party crisis than to his own appeal to the population, in spite of his image as a self-made entrepreneur (he is the wealthiest man in Chile). It is widely expected that the 2014 presidential election will be won by ex-President Michelle Bachelet, who was unable to run for a consecutive term, but left office with an over-80% approval rate.

However, the 2014 election will take place in a very different social and political context because three major crises are looming on the horizon due to the Chilean model of development. First, informational development, a necessary condition for continuing down the path of competitiveness in the global economy, is at this point clearly insufficient to sustain high economic growth in the near future. Second, the lack of improvement of the educational system, both in terms of quality and cost, has become socially unacceptable for the students and their families. Third, the democratic political system has imploded, with a political class (of all ideological persuasions) unable to adapt to the participatory demands of a more educated and conscious Chilean society. As a result of these trends, a massive, active student movement entered the public debate in 2011 and continues to take its demands to the streets at the time of this writing, with overwhelming support among the population. Thus, a new model of development is being conceived in the minds of Chilean citizens—particularly among the young generation who grew up after the end of the dictatorship. This model we could label, in contrast to the two preceding models, as democratic, inclusionary, egalitarian, and participatory. The actual content of this prospective model will be clarified by the empirical analysis that follows.

The limits of informational development in Chile

Chile successfully withstood the 2008–9 crisis involving the Western economies. It kept growing at about 6% per year in spite of a devastating earthquake and tsunami in 2010—a disaster that showed the world the modernity of Chile, as fatalities were limited to about 600, rescue was swift, and the reconstruction process is now well underway and on schedule.

However, the ambitions of Chile to become the first fully developed country in Latin America can only be fulfilled if its informational capacity increases at the level required by its competitive challenges in the global market. In this sense, Chile is lagging behind in R&D investment and human resources development. A few export sectors, particularly in agro-business and minerals, are currently based on knowledge and savvy marketing (copper, salmon, seafood, wine, fruits and vegetables, and forestry products, among others). Manufacturing only accounts for 20% of Chilean exports and only 4% of these are in high-technology sectors—equivalent of half of the proportion in Argentina, one-third in Brazil, and one fifth in Mexico.

The huge quantitative expansion in education has not been followed by a similar improvement in quality, particularly in a higher education sector that is dominated by low-quality, costly, private universities. It is fair to speak of a deep crisis in the education system in Chile. The proportion of the population fully competent to manage information is about 2%, compared with 5% in Portugal and 25% in Finland. About 50% of the population does not understand what they read and cannot make inferences from their reading.

Public research is still largely bureaucratic and government institutions and their employment policies are dominated by patronage and clientelism. Only two universities, the Universidad de Chile and the Catholic University in Santiago, are among the top 500 universities in the world. Chile is far behind Mexico, Brazil, and Argentina in the proportion of graduates in science and technology. The innovation system is dominated by short-term strategies under control of private firms for their own immediate benefit. Thus, while there is in-house innovation for a number of Chilean companies led by an entrepreneurial mentality, business investment in research only represents 20% of R&D and accounts for less than 10% of researchers.

However, there have been significant efforts to engage in the path of informationalism:

- High level of imports in technology transfer, both in capital goods and in direct foreign investment. In this regard, Chile is ahead of all other Latin American countries.
- Investment in ICT represented 5.7% in the 2000s, at the level of Brazil or Finland, and way above the remaining Latin American countries.
- Telecommunication coverage, both for landlines and wireless, is the highest in Latin America.
- Diffusion of Internet connection from home and from schools is also the highest in Latin America. The government established some pioneering programs, such as Enlace, to support diffusion of the Internet in the school system, undertaken during the Lagos administration.

However, the neo-liberal mentality is still pervasive in the economic ministries and has been accentuated during the Piñera administration. The consequence is that technological modernization is left to market mechanisms and therefore is piecemealed, ineffective, and socially unequal.

The Limits of human development in Chile

If there is a critical feature of human development and its connection to informational development, it is education.[6] The Chilean democracy rightly identified this question as central and focused efforts and resources into a fast, massive expansion of the education system from the 1990s onward.

---

[6] For the social student movements, see Vera's "Epistemologías comunicacionales para comprender el movimiento estudiantil 2011 en Chile" (2012); Barahona et al. "Tracking the 2011 Student-Led Movement in Chile through Social Media Use" (2012); Somma's "The Chilean Student Movement of 2011–2012: Challenging the Marketization of Education" (2012); BBC Mundo Cono Sur "¿Por qué tiene tanta fuerza el movimiento estudiantil chileno?" (2012); and CERC "Barómetro de la política" (2011).

However, due to a lack of sufficient public resources and an unrestrained belief in the capacity of the market to handle education, much of the expansion, particularly in higher education, was left to for-profit, private universities; a new creation that delivered low-quality education at a high cost for the low-income families whose children did not enjoy a good secondary education and were therefore blocked from admission to public universities. As Table 1 in this chapter's Appendix shows, 76.58% of total expenditure in higher education in Chile is borne by privates, and 68.11% is shouldered by households. On average, private expenditure in tertiary education for OECD countries is 30.04%, which is 46 percentile points lower than in Chile. For instance, in Finland, only 4% of such expenditure falls on the private sector. Furthermore, annual tuition fees in Chile are comparable to those of Canada and New Zealand.

Thus, Chile became the epitome of a socially regressive trend that has been happening for years across the whole of Latin America: low-income groups subsidize public universities for the middle class while they have no option but to pay a substantial proportion of their meager budget to attend low-quality, private universities. Figure 7.1 displays the empirical evidence showing the increasingly problematic situation of higher education in Chile.

At the root of the problem is a high level of inequality in income distribution in Chile. In 2011, the autonomous income[7] of the highest decile was almost 36 times higher than the income of the lowest decile, and almost four times as big as the national average, as shown in Figure 7.2.

This high level of inequality is the result of the legacy of Pinochet's exclusionary model of growth, as well as of the level of inequality usually associated with fast economic growth in the early stages of development. However, education is precisely the factor that can correct inequality by leveling opportunities of social mobility via the incorporation of low-income groups into a skilled labor force. Yet in Chile, as in most of Latin America, the education system actually reproduces inequality. The low-income groups need to pay a higher proportion of their income to enroll in a university, and a significant segment of the population cannot access either private or public universities. Figure B in this chapter's Appendix displays the net coverage of

---

[7] **Autonomous income:** includes wages and salaries, earnings from autonomous labor, households' self-produced goods, bonuses, rents, interest earnings, retirement pensions, widows' pensions and transfers between private parties. For further detail see CASEN Households Survey definitions and methodology, <http://observatorio.mini steriodesarrollosocial.gob.cl/casen_def_ingresos.php>.

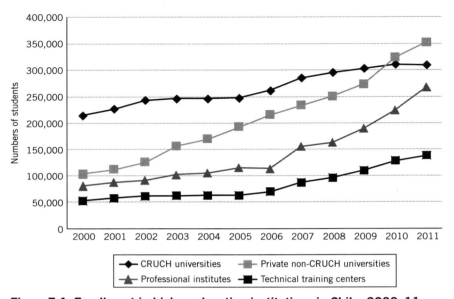

Figure 7.1 Enrollment in higher education institutions in Chile, 2000–11
Private universities' enrollment has grown faster than any other type of university
and accounts for the largest group of students.
Note: CRUCH Universities refers to the 25 public and traditional universities affiliated
with the Council of University Directors of Chile (CRUCH is its acronym in Spanish).
Source: Prepared by the authors, using data from Higher Education Information
Service, Ministry of Education.

Higher Education, i.e. the population of 18–24-year-olds attending higher
education in relation to the total age group, and the Autonomous Income
Distribution, both by quintiles. Even though the distribution of university
students by quintiles is somewhat less unequal than that of income, it shows
the significant difference in access. While 22.1% of those aged 18–24 in the
first quintile attended institutions of higher education, almost 60% of the
highest-income quintile was enrolled. In other words, the massive expansion
in higher education increases the educational level of the population, but
reproduces social inequality rather than correcting it. Criticism of this inequity
in the education system was the spark that triggered the massive student
protests in 2011.

In 2006, in order to subsidize loans for students in need, the government
established a system of loans with incentives for bank participation. An

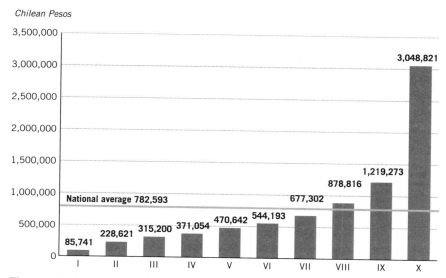

Figure 7.2 Autonomous income distribution by deciles of per capita autonomous income, 2011 (Chilean Pesos)

Source: Prepared by the authors, using data from the Economic Commission for Latin America and the Caribbean (ECLAC).

evaluation of this system by the World Bank in 2009 showed that it would have been cheaper for the government to provide full fellowships to students of the same amount as the loans. This is an illustration of how the ideology of market efficiency often increases cost and decreases quality. In a similar vein, studies have shown that the educational quality of private secondary schools is no higher than in public schools, with the exception of the elite schools. But even for these elite schools, their educational attainment in Chile is inferior to comparable institutions in other middle-income countries.

In sum: the democratic liberal policies of human development did not break completely with the authoritarian liberal policies. They borrowed the ideology of market efficiency while supporting the quantitative expansion of school enrollment. Therefore, the population of Chile became much more educated in terms of formal schooling in a short period of time, but their actual educational level, obtained at a high cost, did not meet basic standards of quality. On the positive side, the value of education became deeply internalized in the population, and this universal aspiration became the psychological incentive to fight for a better, more affordable education.

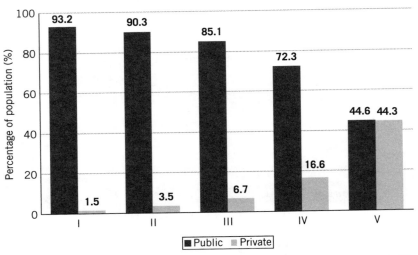

Figure 7.3 Health-care coverage by system and autonomous income quintiles, 2009
Source: Prepared by the authors, using data from the CASEN Households Survey 2009, MIDEPLAN.

Over time, other limitations of the liberal approach to human development emerged in public consciousness. In particular, high inequality also persists in terms of access to private insurance in the health-care system. Only 1.6% of those belonging to the lowest-income quintile are covered by the private system, as shown in Figure 7.3.

Moreover, marginal reductions in[8] income inequality at a time of high economic growth became insufficient for a population that had risen to assert their democratic rights. Figures 7.4 and 7.5 show the widespread perception of inequity in the distribution of the fruits of economic growth in Chile. Chileans show the lowest proportion in Latin America (6%) of those who think that the distribution of wealth is just or very just.

In other words, the skillful mix of government-led redistribution policies and market mechanisms practiced by the Concertación governments became out of control in 2010–11, making it clear that among the virtues of the market, there is one missing: a commitment to equalize opportunities and

---

[8] According to ECLAC data, between 2009 and 2011 Gini Coefficient went down from 0.524 to 0.516 (ECLAC-CEPALSTAT 2013).

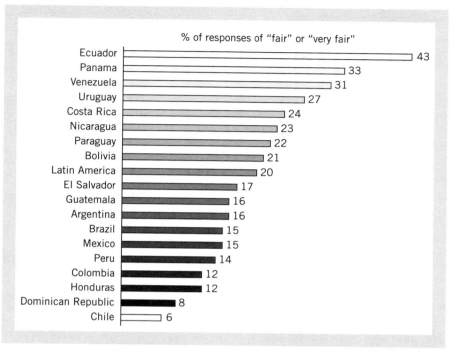

Figure 7.4 Percentage of the population considering the distribution of wealth as "fair" or "very fair" in these selected Latin American countries, 2010

Source: Latinobarómetro Survey, 1997–2011.

correct inequalities. Discontent with inequality and insufficient coverage of social needs was aggravated by the new Piñera administration's inefficient management of government policies. He appointed businessmen to key positions of government to run the administration as a corporation. The result was gross mismanagement of government programs, including the inability to execute in due time the budgets approved by parliament in 2010–11. The ideological attempt to align public management over the practice of business led to a chaotic disorganization of public services. A critical mistake in 2011 was the bureaucratic inability to pay for several months of fellowships due to over two million students, and the delay in covering the luncheon subsidies for hundreds of thousands of students. This was the spark that ignited the fire of popular indignation, inducing a massive student movement that became the standard-bearer of the frustrations and

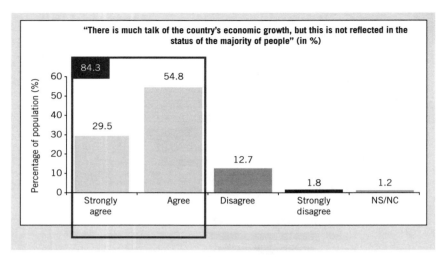

Figure 7.5 Percentage of the Chilean population that "agrees" or "strongly agrees" with the statement that the economic growth of the country does not reflect the real situation of the majority of the people

Source: Compiled from the metropolitan survey research from the Centro de Investigación en Estructura Social (CIES), University of Chile.

aspirations of Chilean citizens in a context of profound crisis of political legitimacy.

The rise of civic consciousness: new social movements in twenty-first-century Chile

The first period of Piñera's presidency was marked by a profound crisis of legitimacy in all Chilean institutions. Political democracy was now deeply entrenched and supported by most Chileans. But at the same time, a large majority of the population was critical of the way democracy was actually functioning. This is not necessarily Piñera's fault; rather, the incompetence of his administration triggered the rise of civic consciousness that brought together multiple grievances that had been boiling up for quite a long time during the Concertación governments. Figure 7.6 and those following tell the story.

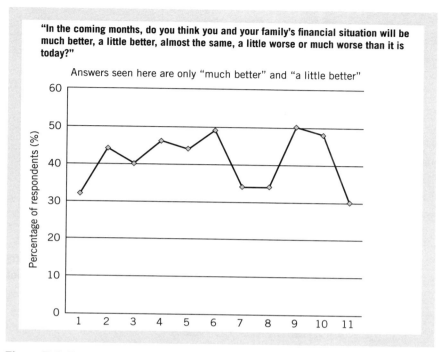

Figure 7.6 Proportion of Chileans who thought the economic situation of their family would be better in the coming months, 2011

Note: This indicator of economic optimism declined to its lowest level in ten years, despite continuing economic growth for the country as a whole.

Source: Latinobarómetro Survey, 2001–11.

In sum, there is lower satisfaction with life in general among the population in Chile than in most other Latin American countries, as shown in Figure 7.7.

The fundamental reason for dissatisfaction with the state of affairs in the country appears to be a crisis of trust in the government and in the institutions of society at large.

Thus, Figure 7.8 shows that there was a drop in the proportion of people who thought that the government was governing in the interests of the people, from 55% in 2010 to 29% in 2011—the largest drop in Latin America.

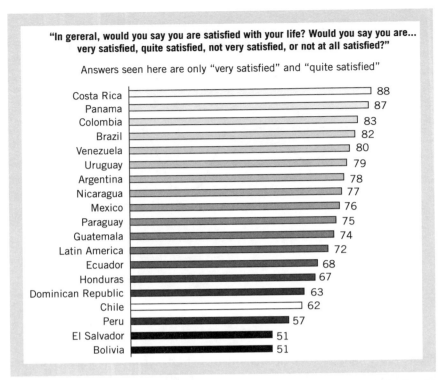

"In gereral, would you say you are satisfied with your life? Would you say you are... very satisfied, quite satisfied, not very satisfied, or not at all satisfied?"

Answers seen here are only "very satisfied" and "quite satisfied"

Costa Rica — 88
Panama — 87
Colombia — 83
Brazil — 82
Venezuela — 80
Uruguay — 79
Argentina — 78
Nicaragua — 77
Mexico — 76
Paraguay — 75
Guatemala — 74
Latin America — 72
Ecuador — 68
Honduras — 67
Dominican Republic — 63
Chile — 62
Peru — 57
El Salvador — 51
Bolivia — 51

Figure 7.7 Proportion of people who are "satisfied" or "very satisfied" with their lives
Source: Latinobarómetro Survey, 2011.

The crisis of legitimacy is not only political, it is institutional. Figure 7.9 shows the steep decline in trust between 2010 and 2012 in the police, the military, the justice system, parliament, government, political parties, and the church. The young generation felt alienated from the conservatism of institutions. Women (40% of whom are now employed) were particularly critical of the old order, including a church out of touch with the new Chile, as shown in Figure C in this chapter's Appendix. The armed forces, already tainted by their dictatorial past, were blamed for their boycott of president Bachelet during her efforts to manage the devastating earthquake of 2010.

Political parties were especially unpopular, and widely considered to look out for their own interests rather than the interests of the people. As for the Piñera administration, inefficient management of government policies

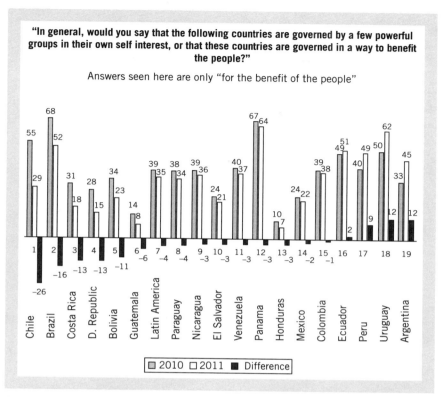

Figure 7.8 Proportion of people thinking the government governs in the interest of the people, 2010–11

Source: Latinobarómetro Survey, 2010–11.

quickly removed the meager capital of trust Piñera had at the time of the election. Chileans, in spite of sustained economic growth, came to be massively critical and skeptical of the state of the country, and also rejected the right and the center-left as their representatives (see Figure 7.10).

Consequently, only 12% of Chileans believe their democracy had improved in 2011 (see Figure D in this chapter's Appendix).

Furthermore, over 64% of Chilean people now question the model of economic growth that has prevailed in the country since 1990, as shown in Figure 7.11.

This rejection was particularly acute among the new generation, no longer living in fear under the shadow of the dictatorship. A new Chile had risen. It

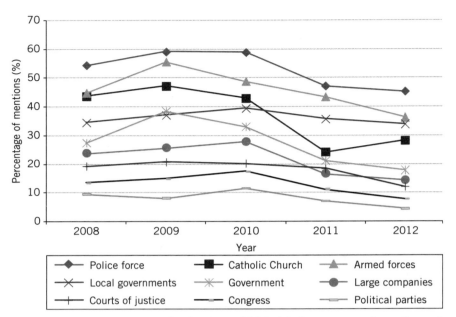

Figure 7.9 Trust in selected institutions, 2008–12. Percentage of mentions of "a lot" and "quite a bit."

Source: Public Opinion Survey, Institute of Social Sciences Investigation, Diego Portales University.

took the form of a student movement that occupied the streets of Santiago and the main cities of the country for over a year, with moments of high mobilization and others of pause and reflection.

Inspired by the student movement, multiple conflicts and social protests took place all over Chile: civil society occupied the public debate, displacing the discourse of economic growth as the only goal of development. The average number of social conflicts in Chile in the 2000s was 75 per year. In 2011 and 2012, the number and the intensity of the social conflicts increased several times. In 2010, Chile was the country with the lowest level of social conflict in the region, but with the highest level of repression (Calderon 2012).

The Chilean student movement started—as have most movements in the twenty-first century—within the social networks of the Internet, but soon expanded into public space and engaged in demands and negotiations with the government. The unified goal of the movement was to demand free, quality public education. In the short term, its participants requested the

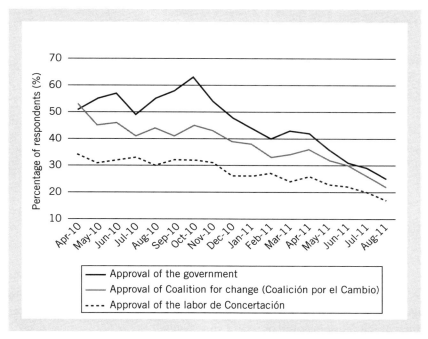

Figure 7.10 Approval of the government and political coalitions
Note: This graph shows a generalized crisis of institutional and political legitimacy: the decline of trust in the opposition is even more pronounced than that for the conservative government.
Source: Survey Adimark GfK—April to August, 2011.

immediate payment of larger and more numerous scholarships, in addition to the lowering of loan costs. They also fought for participation in the design and management of education policies and of the universities, as well as for government control of private universities. They extended their goals to the reform of public services at large, asking for better and cheaper health care, a public pension system, and subsidies for housing and public needs. In sum, they articulated a traditional social democratic program of government policies to cover the social needs of the population, financed by taxation of the rich, to lower social inequality. In fact, although the program of the movement was only precise in its educational demands, the tone of the public debate it inspired in society and the media envisioned a new model of development, moving away from the liberal approach to social policies and

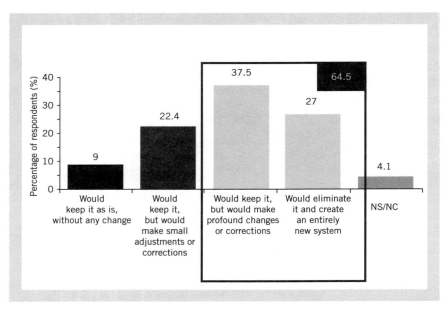

Figure 7.11 "If you could do something with the current economic system, which of the following options would you choose?"

broadening the avenues of citizen participation beyond the limits of a democracy controlled by the main political parties. This is why we suggest labeling their proposed model the **Chilean democratic, inclusionary, egalitarian, participatory model of development**. This model also included components of informational development, since they emphasized the role of research in universities and the need to improve the quality of education, the weak link of informationalism in Chile. Even if the charismatic leader of the movement, a young woman named Camila Vallejo, was a member of the Communist Party, the ideological composition of the movement was highly diverse and included anarchists, leftists, and students who were simply rejecting the university and society at large. There was a high level of tolerance within the movement, the debates were civil and public, and most decisions were made in assemblies. It was a self-reflective movement in that it proceeded to elaborate thorough analyses of Chilean society and extended its critique to institutional sexism and racism. It brought back to the forefront of public debate the rights of the Mapuche minority and due respect for indigenous, communal forms of self-government. What is meaningful is that this highly self-conscious movement received the support, over a long period of time, of over 85% of citizens, to the point that President Piñera himself praised the movement in his public address to the United Nations, in the hope that time and fatigue would lead to its demise. Although this is the case, the government resorted to harsh police repression on several occasions. Indeed, for the governing right, the hope was (and is) that the opposing parties are scoring at an even lower level among voters, and are equally criticized by the student movement.

There is a chance, however, of a future connection between the model of development put forward by the Chilean social movements, and the future development of Chile. Michelle Bachelet, returning from her high-level post heading women's rights programs for the United Nations, is expected to run for president in 2014 on a platform compatible with many of the demands of the movement. She is known for being critical of her own party's inability to regenerate itself. Therefore, there could possibly be a connection between an influential social movement, expressing the values of the new generation, and a charismatic candidate known for her independence, regardless of her Socialist affiliation. If this happens, Chile may again be a testing ground for an innovative model of development, bringing together economy, knowledge, social justice, and society under the impulse of a hopeful young generation.

Chilean development: past, present, and future

The Chilean experience displays, over a period of 35 years, two-and-a-half distinctive models of development, as well as a new vision of development.

The first model, under Pinochet, was entirely based on a strategy of market-led growth in a global economy, disregarding human development. It succeeded in stimulating economic growth and modernizing the economy, but at the price of two major recessions in a 15-year period and staggering social and environmental costs, thus destroying the democratic institutions and undermining future development by overlooking informational policies.

The second model kept much of the economic liberal orientation of the preceding model but obtained better results in terms of economic growth, inflation control, productivity growth, and employment. It added a second dimension by giving a major impulse to human development and political democratization. It can be shown that the improvements in human development were major factors in achieving high economic growth.

Therefore, the second model shows a virtuous circle between human development and economic growth.

However, in spite of some informational components in the democratic model of development, we cannot see that an informational development strategy has been truly present in Chile. And it revealed over time some fundamental flaws in human development as a result of excessive belief in the ability of the market to guide development for the welfare of the nation.

Thus, the future development of Chile depends on its institutional and entrepreneurial capacity to stimulate informational development and to connect this process to both human development and economic growth in the framework of a participatory democracy suited to the Internet age. It is not a dual model, but a triangular model (informationalism, human development, and institutional reform) that is required for Chile to be a truly developed country in spite of its history of isolation on the southernmost tip of the American continent. The rest of the world may learn from the lessons of its contradictory recent history.

Conclusion: implications for the relationship between development, informationalism, and democracy in Latin America

Within the last decade, Latin America has enjoyed a period of sustained economic growth, largely due to its integration into the global economy as an exporter of valuable commodities: minerals, energy, raw materials, and knowledge-intensive agricultural products, taking advantage of the fast growth in Asian economies that are dependent on food staples, raw materials, and energy to sustain their expansion. Brazil, Mexico, and Costa Rica also add a large share of manufactured goods to their export mix. It can be said that, overall, globalization has helped economic growth in Latin America. It is also true, however, that the one-sided character of this process of global integration led by market demands left behind a substantial proportion of the population. In spite of some improvement, in 2010, over one third of the Latin American population was still living below the poverty level.[9]

---

[9] On average, between 1990 and 2011 Latin America's poverty rate has been reduced almost 20 percentage points: from 48.4% to 29.5%. This said, extreme poverty has been more resilient. Over the same period it decreased a little more than 10 percentage points: from 22.6% to 11.5%. See <http://estadisticas.cepal.org/cepalstat/WEB_CEPALSTAT/Portada.asp> (ECLAC 2013).

The contrast between a small middle class reaching a high standard of living with the conditions of the large majority of the population (40% of urban employment is in the informal economy) has led to a dramatic increase in crime and violence as the criminal economy has taken root as an alternative way of life in most countries, with the significant exceptions of Chile, Costa Rica, and Uruguay. Cultural identity of marginalized communities has become a trench of resistance against unjust globalization. Social protests emerging from economic and cultural sources have converged to transform the political landscape of Latin America. In most countries, traditional political parties are in a shambles as their corruption and nepotism have been exposed. A wave of social progress and political changes is spreading over the continent, creating new trends and incertitude of both the future and the quality of integration into the global economy, and even challenging the stability of democratic institutions. In some countries, particularly Mexico, Colombia, and Guatemala, transnational organized crime has deeply penetrated the institutions of the state to the point of making it dysfunctional. However, Brazil, Uruguay, Argentina, and Costa Rica have, until now, managed popular demands by channeling them into the democratic political system. Chile was able for some time to tame social tensions while achieving a high rate of economic growth, until failures in human welfare, as a consequence of its excessively liberal orientation, induced a major social movement that is undermining the legitimacy of political institutions. Indeed, there are still immense social needs to be satisfied in Chile and in the region as a whole, and these needs require the capacity to bring together informational development, human development, and participatory democracy. For some time, Chile was successful in improving social conditions and inducing economic growth with limited investment in informational development. However, over time, the sustainability of global competitiveness requires much more decisive government guidance in research, innovation, technological modernization, and human capital formation. The quantitative expansion of higher education with little improvement in quality and research is creating a bottleneck that may jeopardize economic growth itself. Moreover, the limitations of a market-driven orientation in tackling major social issues such as education, health, and pensions, instilled widespread social dissatisfaction among a Chilean population that recovered its assertiveness and mobilized as an active civil society. The traditional political parties were not able to respond to the demands of this civil society, particularly to the projects and dreams of a new generation. Under the administrations of both President Ricardo Lagos and President Michelle Bachelet, the normalization of the Chilean democracy was achieved and the basis of a limited welfare state was laid out. However, the difficulties of the Piñera administration in fully understanding the transformation of the Chilean society, and the rejection of citizens vis-a-vis the political class at large, resulted in a major social movement that opposed the model of development and called for a deepening of democracy. What is significant is that this protest, supported by 85% of the population, took place alongside the continuation of economic growth. Thus, Chileans are projecting their future beyond the limits of growth for the sake of growth, and a democracy reduced to electoral procedures; beyond even the respect of civil rights. The thesis that economical increase can be traduced in political power becomes weak.

In comparison with the dictatorship of Pinochet, the achievements of democratic Chile were remarkable. But history never stops. As soon as Chileans felt secure in their democracy and assured of their chances of prosperity, they asserted their aspirations toward deeper human development and participatory forms of representation. Indeed, they engaged in a public debate about institutional change.

The importance of the lessons of the Chilean experience for Latin America as a whole cannot be overlooked. Economic development, informationalism, human development, and democracy must go hand in hand in a synergistic relationship for each dimension of this development model to succeed. Without informationalism that includes human development, economic growth cannot be sustained in the current global economy. Without economic growth, human development cannot be afforded. But without a redistribution policy that provides human development for the population at large, societies rebel against the one-sided logic of economic growth for the benefit of the upper-income groups. When economy and society diverge in their dynamics, the political institutions come under stress and democracy appears to many as an empty shell. Under such conditions, the democracy obtained over three decades of strenuous efforts could be eroded. But for democracy to respond to this challenge, it needs to reform itself in institutions, in policy, and in personnel, starting with the renovation of an obsolete and morally bankrupt party system.

Unless the four terms of the developmental process (economic growth, informationalism, human development, and participatory democracy) are connected in a sustainable form under the strategic guidance of a renewed political agency, Latin America could indeed regress to the stagnation and poverty of the 1980s: it could fall back into a cycle of corrupt democracies followed by authoritarian populism; it could sink into a crisis of institutions overtaken by criminal cartels; and it could degenerate into violence and ethnic hatred. Yet, building on the lessons of Chile (both positive and negative), adding the decisive component of informational development, and reinventing democracy in Latin America could also evolve toward a new model of economic growth with social redistribution and institutional reform. This study has tried to identify the components of this virtuous circle of development formed by knowledge-based economic growth, a *sui generis* welfare state, and informationalism. These are the constitutive elements of a new Latin America able to connect to a multilateral system of interactions in the global networks of wealth and power that could bring prosperity and sharing to humankind in the twenty-first century.

APPENDIX

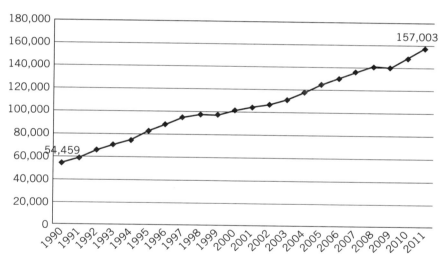

Figure A Real gross domestic product, 1990–2011 (millions of 2005 US dollars)

Source: Prepared by the authors, using data from the Economic Commission for Latin America and the Caribbean (ECLAC)

Table 1 Distribution of expenditure on higher education and annual tuition fees, selected countries, 2009 Percentages and US dollars converted using PPP

Country	Share of private expenditure	Share of households expenditure	Average annual tuition fees charged in public institutions
Chile	76,58	68,11	3,140[*]
Korea	73,91	49,15	5.193,44
United Kingdom	70,38	58,07	4.713,33
Japan	64,73	50,68	4.602,38
United States	61,93	45,30	6.311,85
Australia	54,58	39,13	4.222,32
Israel	41,83	27,27	m
Canada	37,12	20,22	3.773,52
Russian Federation	35,39	27,42	m
New Zealand	32,09	32,09	3.031,43
Italy	31.43	23,81	1.289,06
Mexico	31,31	30,95	No tuition fees
Poland	30,26	22,78	m
OECD average	30,04	0,00	m
Slovak Republic	29,96	11,66	Maximum 2.707
Portugal	29,06	22,29	1.258,73
Netherlands	28,04	14,93	1.860,64
Spain	20,91	16,78	1.052,05
Czech Republic	20,08	8,77	No tuition fees
Estonia	19,83	18,20	m
Argentina	19,36	12,87	m
France	16,95	9,70	190 to 1.309
Ireland	16,21	13,80	From 2.800 to 10.000
Germany	15,61	0,00	m

Slovenia	14,93	10,77	m
Austria	12,32	2,90	858,81
Belgium	10,26	5,48	608,38
Sweden	10,21	m	No tuition fees
Iceland	7,99	7,35	No tuition fees
Denmark	4,57	m	No tuition fees
Finland	4,23	m	No tuition fees
Norway	3,90	3,03	No tuition fees
Switzerland	m	m	888,75
Luxembourg	m	m	m

Notes: * academic year: 2005; m: missing
Source: prepared by the authors using data from OECD databases

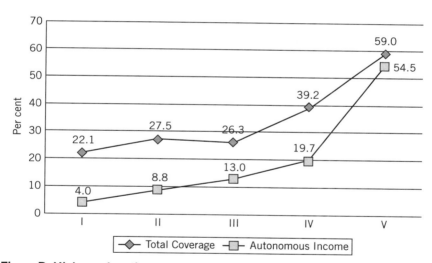

Figure B Higher education net coverage by autonomous income quintiles, 2011

Source: prepared by the authors, using data from the CASEN Households Survey 2011, Social Observatory, Ministry of Social Development

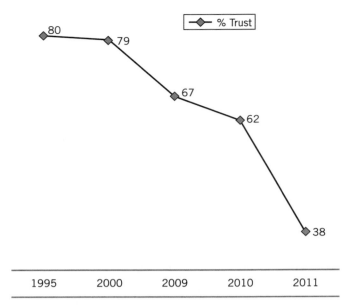

Figure C Trust in the Catholic Church
Source: Latinobarómetro Survey, 2011

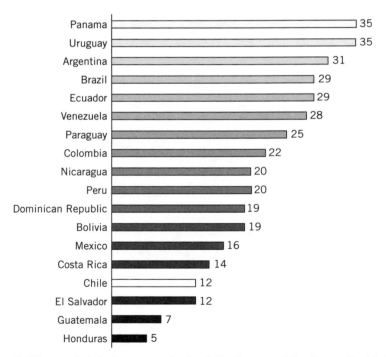

Figure D "Do you think democracy in the following countries has gotten better, stayed the same, or gotten worse?" (Answer shown here: "Gotten better")
Source: Latinobarómetro Survey, 2011

Pacifism, Human Development, and Informational Development: The Costa Rican Model

Isidora Chacón

Introduction

Costa Rica: A unique development experience

One of the most striking paradoxes of development refers to the dispropor-tionate use of scarce resources in military expenditures whose main purpose is, too often, to support domestic domination rather than national defense.

This has been the case for most of Latin America, and particularly for Central America. There is, however, one major exception, in fact a unique case in a global perspective: Costa Rica, one of the few countries in the world without armed forces. As it is known, Costa Rica abolished its armed forces in

1949, after the bloody civil war of 1948, and never again reinstated an army.[1] This is particularly striking when we consider that Central America has been, and continues to be, one of the most turbulent and violent regions in the world, in terms of civil wars, guerrilla warfare, wars between countries, and covert interventions by powers external to the region. Furthermore, not only has Costa Rica preserved its internal and external peace, it has contributed decisively to peacemaking in Central America.[2]

What has come to be known as the Costa Rican Pacifist Model (Sala 2008) helped to stabilize the country as a constitutional democracy, without any disruption since 1949. Costa Rica is also a unique case in Latin America in terms of having created a comprehensive welfare state, with universal, public health coverage, full scholarization in primary education, almost full scholarization in secondary education, and a wide network of public services in housing, poverty alleviation, and other areas of social need. There is in fact a direct connection between the abolition of the armed forces and the process of development of the welfare state, since the 1949 Constitution.

National security issues are addressed by a police force, relatively professional but grossly underequipped, that takes care of internal security matters but does not have the capability of engaging in any large-scale military operations, as became apparent in the brief occupation of a portion of Costa Rican territory by Nicaraguan troops in October 2010. The control of the activities of transnational drug cartels are handled with the support of United States agencies with the condition of not stationing armed units in Costa Rican territory. The security needs of the Costa Rican state have been met by an active diplomacy, based on multiple international agreements and the support of international organizations.[3]

---

[1] It is true that the abolition of the army in Costa Rica occurred in the context of other factors weakening the army itself, including the gradual loss of officer positions and senior privates and pay parity between soldiers and policemen, which developed primarily during the situation of 1948 and 1949 that culminated with the abolition. Further contributing factors were the inability of the Governing Board to reorganize the army according to their interests, the reaction of the lower classes of the opposite party, and foreign military pressure to act on the territory of Costa Rica.

[2] This role is exemplified by the mediation of President Arias in the negotiations that led to the Peace Plan of Esquipulas in 1987, a plan that set up the bases to the civil wars in El Salvador and Nicaragua, and established various mechanisms to keep peace in the region. President Oscar Arias received the Nobel Peace prize, and the Principe of Asturias prize for his role in peacemaking, and he continued, in his second tenure as president, to mediate in other conflicts, such as the internal strife in Honduras in 2010.

[3] For an explanation of the mechanisms through which Costa Rica deals with its security threats in the absence of armed forces, see Appendix 1.

The management of international cooperation by Costa Rican agencies has not been exempt from organizational problems and misled decisions. Yet, overall, they have succeeded in keeping the country's peace without armed forces for over six decades.

In the context of this paper I am not arguing that this could necessarily be a feasible strategy for other countries, because the consideration of such a possibility would require engagement in the analysis of the current conditions of war and peace at the international level, a topic that exceeds by far the purpose of the research undertaken here in the framework of the comparative study of the interaction between human development and informational development. Rather, what I am focusing on here are the implications of the pacifist model of the modern Costa Rican state for development at large and for human development in particular.

Implications of the pacifist model for public policies

The pacifist model of development adopted by Costa Rica is based on three major features that derive directly from the fundamental policy choice of dismantling the coercive capacity of the state.

The first and most obvious implication of the pacifist model for public policy **is a decisive shift in the use of public resources away from military spending to giving priority to social expenditures.** Indeed, this new approach is mandated, in the Costa Rican Constitution of 1949.[4]

The second major implication of the pacifist model is that political stability cannot be assured by the coercive capacity of the state, as was the case more often than not in earlier periods of Costa Rica's history (Amoretti 2007) and even more so in the neighboring countries (Fonseca 2001). Instead, stability had to be based on political legitimacy as well as on broad popular support of the institutions of the state, regardless of social and ideological differences and conflicts between social groups and political actors. And this support of the democratic institutions is largely a function of a higher level of human development, and of a moderate level of social inequality, as shown in Figures 8.1 and 8.2 on the basis of data from the Human Development Reports for Latin America as a whole.

---

[4] Still the supreme law of the country, which states that 4% of GDP must be invested in education (it was increased to 6% in 1973, and 8% in 1991). Furthermore, a minimun level of spending on health and social security was later set by decree.

Isidora Chacón

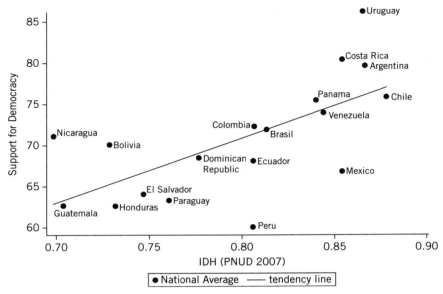

Figure 8.1 Effect of HDI on support of democracy

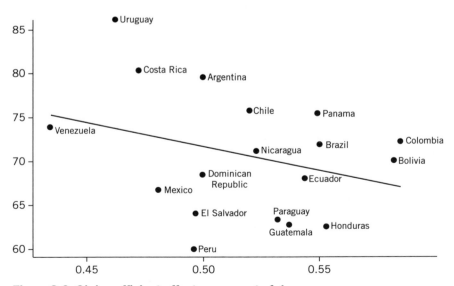

Figure 8.2 Gini coefficient effect on support of democracy

208

The third consequence of the choice of establishing the legitimacy of the state on human welfare and political democracy **was that the Costa Rican state needed to induce enough economic growth to finance the expansion of the welfare state on the basis of the country's resources**. Thus, **a key component of the Costa Rican model was the gradual formation of an active, interventionist state** that built a significant infra-structure in energy, telecommunications, transportation, agriculture, training, higher education, and research (Román 2009). Indeed, Costa Rica offers one of the highest indexes of "statism" in Latin America (see Figure 8.3). Statism is understood as the level of state intervention in the economy and in programs of human development.

It is interesting to observe that Chile, Costa Rica, and Uruguay, the three most developed welfare states in Latin America, are among the top four in the statist index. Moreover, Chile is the leading country in economic growth in

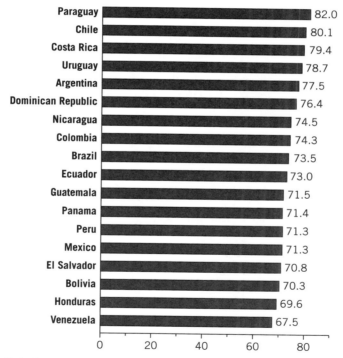

Figure 8.3 Index of statism, selected Latin American countries
Source: Americas Barometer by LAPOP
Note: 95% confidence interval (design-effects based)

the last 20 years, and Costa Rica ranks in the upper tier of rates of economic growth in the past 40 years. This implies that there is no contradiction between state intervention, economic growth, and the welfare state. Instead, it appears to be a positive feedback loop between the three processes.

Recent studies have shown the high correlation between active policies of economic growth, satisfaction with democracy, and support for the political institutions in Latin America as a whole (Calderón 2012). In this context, Costa Rica started to build early on a virtuous circle between economic development, human development, and political democracy. But the key component is not economic growth per se, but the economic capacity of the state to use the resources of economic growth to alleviate poverty in the country. Indeed, as shown in Figure 8.4 for the whole of Latin America, social cohesion and political legitimacy are strengthened by the perception that government policies are geared to fight poverty.

How much do you think the current government fights poverty?

Therefore over the last four decades Costa Rica has developed, to a large extent, a state that has led the modernization of the country, funded the welfare state, and was able to endure the shock of the country's competitive integration into the global economy.

In this chapter I will examine the three key components of this development model, laying down the conditions of its historical formation and

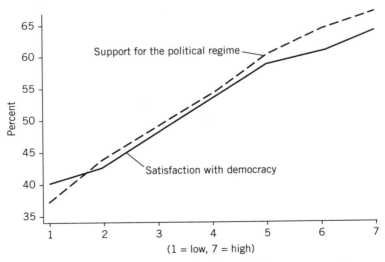

Figure 8.4 Relationship between satisfaction with democracy and support for the political regime, 2010

measuring its achievements, as well as showing the contradictions that emerged over time in each dimension of the model, and the policy debates aimed at overcoming these contradictions.

The rise of a tropical welfare state

Government policies in Costa Rica since 1950 have implemented in general terms the constitutional mandate of constructing a welfare state in the unlikely context of a poor country in the midst of Central America. This emphasis of public policies on improving human welfare is shown in the statistics of the proportion of public spending over GDP in health and education, the key components of human capital formation, particularly when compared with other countries in Central America and in Latin America. As a result of this relative coverage of human needs, there is greater social stability in Costa Rica than anywhere else in Latin America.

The result in the medium and long term was the increase of Costa Rica's ranking in the Human Development Index (HDI), which led the country to third place among the countries of Latin America in 1995 with a value of 0.794. In 1996, the country fell to fourth place on the scale, even though the value of the index improved to 0.830 (Table 8.1). In 2010, methodological changes in the construction of the HDI slightly lowered the relative ranking of the country to sixth place for the Latin American region, with a value of 0.725 in the index. This re-classification in the overall ranking results from the method used to calculate educational attainment for the school system. The combined gross enrollment in education was calculated on the basis of the years of education that a child can expect to receive given the level of current enrollment, corrected by the rate of high school dropout. Because the level of enrollment was already very high, and the dropout rate increased, the attainment index scored at a lower level even if the overall educational level in Costa Rica remained among the highest in the region (Table 8.2).

Nonetheless, while Costa Rica remained in the upper tier of the HDI scale in Latin America, it showed a certain stagnation in the improvement of the education system at the secondary level with a dropout rate of 10.2% (2010).

The foundations of any welfare state are public health, pension funds, social subsidies for citizens in distress, and public education.

A key component of the welfare state in Costa Rica is the **social security system,** which provides three sets of benefits.

Table 8.1 Costa Rica and Central American countries: HDI 2007, report 2009

	HDI	HDI position	LE*	LE* position	Adult literacy	Literacy position	Registration	Registration position	GDP per cap	PIBp position c
Argentina	0.866	2	75.2	6	97.6	2	88.6	2	13.238	3
Bolivia	0.729	16	65.4	17	90.7	11	86.0	5	4.206	16
Brazil	0.813	8	72.2	12	90.0	12	87.2	4	9.567	8
Chile	0.878	1	78.5	2	96.5	3	82.5	7	13.880	2
Colombia	0.807	9	72.7	10	92.7	9	79.0	10	8.587	9
Costa Rica	**0.854**	**4**	**78.7**	**1**	**95.9**	**4**	**73.0**	**15**	**10.842**	**7**
Ecuador	0.806	10	75.0	7	91.0	10	77.8	11	7.449	11
El Salvador	0.747	14	71.3	15	82.0	16	74.0	13	5.804	13
Guatemala	0.704	17	70.1	16	73.2	18	70.5	18	4.562	14
Honduras	0.732	15	72.0	13	83.6	15	74.8	12	3.796	17
Mexico	0.854	4	76.0	4	92.8	8	80.2	8	14.104	1
Nicaragua	0.699	18	72.7	10	78.0	17	72.1	17	2.570	18
Panama	0.840	7	75.5	5	93.4	7	79.7	9	11.391	5
Paraguay	0.761	13	71.7	14	94.6	6	72.1	16	4.433	15
Peru	0.806	10	73.0	9	89.6	13	88.1	3	7.836	10
Domin. Rep.	0.777	12	72.4	11	89.1	14	73.5	14	6.706	12
Uruguay	0.865	3	76.1	3	97.9	1	90.9	1	11.216	6
Venezuela	0.844	6	73.6	8	95.2	5	85.9	6	12.156	4

Note: *LE = life expectancy

Table 8.2 HDI 2010, report 2010, new methodology

	IDH	IDH position	LE*	LE* position	Years education	Years educ. position	Years educ. hoped for	Position educ. hoped for	Gross Nat. Income per cap	GNI p.c. position
Argentina	0.775	2	75.7	6	9,3	4	15.5	2	14.603	1
Bolivia	0.643	14	66.3	18	9,2	5	13.7	7	4.357	16
Brazil	0.699	8	72.9	12	7,2	13	13.8	6	10.607	8
Chile	0.783	1	78.8	2	9,7	1	14.5	3	13.561	4
Colombia	0.689	11	73.4	11	7,4	12	13.3	11	8.589	9
Costa Rica	**0.725**	**6**	**79.1**	**1**	**8,3**	**8**	**11.7**	**15**	**10.870**	**7**
Ecuador	0.695	10	75.4	7	7,6	11	13.3	10	7.931	12
El Salvador	0.659	13	72.0	16	7,7	10	12.1	12	6.498	13
Guatemala	0.560	18	70.8	17	4,1	18	10.6	18	4.694	14
Honduras	0.604	16	72.6	14	6,5	15	11.4	16	3.750	17
Mexico	0.750	5	76.7	4	8,7	6	13.4	9	13.971	2
Nicaragua	0.565	17	73.8	9	5,7	17	10.8	17	2.567	18
Panama	0.755	4	76,0	5	9,4	3	13,5	8	13.347	5
Paraguay	0,640	15	72,3	15	7,8	9	12,0	13	4.585	15

(continued)

Table 8.2 Continued

	IDH	IDH position	LE*	LE* position	Years education	Years educ. position	Years educ. hoped for	Position educ. hoped for	Gross Nat. Income per cap	GNI p.c. position
Peru	0,723	7	73,7	10	9,6	2	13,8	5	8.424	10
Domin. Rep.	0,663	12	72,8	13	6,9	14	11,9	14	8.273	11
Uruguay	0,765	3	76,7	3	8,4	7	15,7	1	13.808	3
Venezuela	0,696	9	74,2	8	6,2	16	14,2	4	11.846	6

Note: LE* = life expectancy

Methodological changes 2010 report concerning reports 1990–2009:

1) The average years of education substitute for adult literacy;

2) The combined gross enrollment was restated as the expected years of education, or years of education a child can expect to receive given the current enrollment;

3) Gross national income (GNI) per capita replaces the gross domestic product (GDP) per capita;

4) To add, the three components were changed to a geometric mean (which measures the typical value of a set of numbers). This poor performance in any of the components is now directly reflected in the value of the index and there is no perfect substitutability between them. Capture how balanced the performance of a country is in three areas.

First, **health benefits** are provided by the National Insurance Institute and the Social Security Fund. Together these constitute public health insurance with free, comprehensive universal coverage. The origin of the public health sector in Costa Rica was the creation of the Social Security Fund in 1943, which instituted a system to provide universal coverage. In 1983, the government issued an Executive Decree 14313-PLAN SPPS (called the Constitution of the Health Sector) with the aim of providing comprehensive care for the population, the social production of health care, and the rational use of resources, in order to preserve health and improve the quality of life of citizens. This comprehensive public health system can be credited with the substantial improvement of the health of Costa Ricans, as showed by an infant mortality rate of 8.84 per thousand and a life expectancy of 79.1 years in 2009.[5]

The second component of the social security system covers **economic benefits**: pensions and subsidies for special groups in distress.

Thirdly, **there are social benefits programs to help families facing critical economic situations**. To respond to these needs, the system provides contributions in cash, kind, and services.

Overall, the social security sector represents about 9.3% of GDP. Government spending as a percentage of GDP has been maintained at a high level over the last two decades. Health expenditures have increased from 4.9% of GDP in 1990/91 to 5.4% of GDP in 2007/8, in the context of high growth of GDP.

The education sector has been a fundamental backbone of the Costa Rican Republic since its inception. As stated above primary and secondary education in state schools has been universal and free since 1949. Scholarization levels reach 100% in primary education and 90% in secondary education. Higher education is based on four large public universities of good standing in the Latin American context, particularly the University of Costa Rica, ranked among the top twenty universities in Latin America. The cost of public college education for families, whose monthly income is located in the national average and who pay the full tuition at public universities, is 2.82% of their annual household income, compared with 22.7% in Chile. These Costa Rican universities offer fellowships to students in need. The system is completed by over 50 private universities of diverse quality.

Overall, in the area of education, Costa Rica has achieved results well within the standards set by the United Nations' Millenium Development Goals (Programa Estado de la Nación en Desarrollo Humano Sostenible 2009), as

---

[5] According to the Household Survey from the National Institute of Statistics and Census: 81.8 for women and 76.8 for men.

Table 8.3 Costa Rica: Second Monitoring Report to Achieving the Millennium Development Goals – some indicators, 2009

Year	target 2.1 2.2 Proportion of students entering first grade who reach last grade		target 2.2 2.3 Literacy rate of people aged 15 to 24 years		meta 2.3 (a) 2A.n4) Net enrollment rate in the transition cycle (at six years old) ta 2.3 (a)		meta 2.3 (b) 2A.n5) Net enrollment rate in the interactive cycle II (five years old)		goal 2.4 2A.n6) Gross enrollment rate in secondary education	
	obser-ved 1	expected progress	obser-ved 2	expected progress	obser-ved 3	expected progress	obser-ved 3	expected progress	observed 3/ 4/	expected progress
1990	76.7	76.7	n.d.		61.7		5.1		53.6	
1991	78.9	77.6	n.d.		64.0		4.8		55.2	
1992	80.0	78.6	n.d.		62.6		5.5		57.5	
1993	80.2	79.5	n.d.		65.6		5.4		57.4	
1994	81.4	80.4	n.d.		67.1		4.9		57.6	
1995	82.3	81.4	n.d.		68.8		4.8		58.2	
1996	83.1	82.3	n.d.		70.9		5.1		56.8	
1997	84.2	83.2	n.d.		75.7		5.4		58.4	
1998	85.1	84.2	n.d.		80.5		5.5		58.2	
1999	85.6	85.1	n.d.		83.6		5.8		58.1	
2000	86.0	86.0	97.6	97.6	82.1		6.7		60.8	
2001	85.9	87.0	n.d.	97.7	88.3		20.3		62.7	

Year										
2002	86.8	87.9	n.d.	97.8	89.4	92.8	26.8		65.8	
2003	86.9	88.8	n.d.	97.9	92.8	94.8	33.0	33.0	68.8	68.8
2004	88.6	89.7	n.d.	98.0	90.8	96.9	37.1	35.2	72.5	70.5
2005	88.0	90.7	n.d.	98.1	93.0	99.0	43.4	37.6	76.4	72.2
2006	89.1	91.6	n.d.	98.2	95.1	99.0	47.3	40.1	78.4	73.8
2007	90.7	92.5	n.d.	98.3	92.7	99.0	46.0	42.9	79.0	75.5
2008	92.2	93.5	n.d.	98.3	93.0	99.0	53.7	45.8	79.4	77.2
2009	n.d.	94.4	n.d.	98.4	92.8	99.0	55.4	48.8	82.7	78.9
2010		95.3		98.5		99.0		52.1		80.6
2011		96.3		98.6		99.0		55.7		82.3
2012		97.2		98.7		99.0		59.4		83.9
2013		98.1		98.8		99.0		63.4		85.6
2014		99.1		98.9		99.0		67.7		87.3
2015		100.0		99.0		99.0		72.3		89.0

Source: Costa Rica: II Informe de Seguimiento al logro de los Objetivos de Desarrollo del Milenio, 2009

Table 8.4 Costa Rica: Second Monitoring Report to Achieving the Millennium Development Goals – some indicators, 2009

year	2.1) Net enrollment rate in primary education 1/	2.3) Literacy rate of 15 to 24 years, women and men 2/		2A.n1) Average time that students graduate from primary 3	2A.n2) Dropout rate in primary intra-annual 4/	2A.n3) Percentage of repeat-ing in primary 4/	2A.n7) Percentage of students who start school and finish 3	2A.n8) Education spending as a percentage of GDP/
		men	women					
1990	98.5	n.d.	n.d.	7.8	4.7	11.3	39.9	3.8
1991	99.6	n.d.	n.d.	7.8	4.5	10.5	39.3	3.7
1992	100.0	n.d.	n.d.	7.9	4.6	9.6	40.5	3.9
1993	100.0	n.d.	n.d.	8.0	4.1	8.1	40.1	4.1
1994	99.6	n.d.	n.d.	7.9	4.2	8.7	37.8	4.3
1995	99.8	n.d.	n.d.	7.7	5.0	9.3	37.6	3.8
1996	100.0	n.d.	n.d.	7.6	4.5	11.4	39.9	4.4
1997	98.7	n.d.	n.d.	7.3	4.5	10.1	41.3	4.4
1998	98.5	n.d.	n.d.	7.2	4.9	10.0	43.8	4.5
1999	98.8	n.d.	n.d.	7.2	4.4	9.5	46.5	4.1
2000	99.3	97.2	98.0	7.2	4.1	8.2	43.8	4.7
2001	99.4	n.d.	n.d.	7.2	4.5	8.4	43.1	5.1
2002	99.8	n.d.	n.d.	7.1	4.0	7.6	44.2	5.5
2003	99.8	n.d.	n.d.	7.1	3.9	7.5	44.2	5.5
2004	99.7	n.d.	n.d.	7.0	3.3	7.4	43.6	5.4
2005	100.0	n.d.	n.d.	7.0	3.4	7.5	43.1	5.2
2006	100.0	n.d.	n.d.	6.9	3.8	7.6	43.5	5.0
2007	100.0	n.d.	n.d.	6.9	2.5	7.9	43.1	5.2
2008	100.0	n.d.	n.d.	n.d.	2.9	7.4	n.d.	5.7
2009	100.0	n.d.	n.d.	n.d.	3.0	6.3	n.d.	6.8

Source: Costa Rica: II Informe de Seguimiento al logro de los Objetivos de Desarrollo del Milenio, 2009

Table 8.5 Costa Rica: education coverage

	1950	1960*	1970*	1980*	1990	2000	2010*
Illiteracy rate (%)							
population 10 years +	21.2	14.3	10.2	6.9	n.d.	4.8	n.d.
population 15–24 years	17.4	11.0	4.9	2.9	n.d.	2.4	n.d.
Assistance to regular education (%)							
population 7–24 years	33.5		58.6	51.8	58.2	65.9	72.3
population 7–17 years			74.8	71.0	78.9	83.3	92.1
Average schooling (years)							
population 25–34 years			5.5	7.5	7.9	8.2	9.3

Note: 1960 Figures are of 1963, 1970 of 1973, 1980 of 1984 and 2010 of 2009.
Source: own Figures of the National Population Census 1950, 1963, 1973, 1984 and 2000 household surveys in 1990 and 2009 (National Institute of Statistics and Census, INEC-)

shown in Tables 8.3, 8.4, and 8.5. And we know that education is the foundation of both human development and informational development.

Costa Rica: a working democracy

The level of political legitimacy in Costa Rica is one of the highest in Latin America, as shown in the report of UNDP on democracy in Latin America (Programa de las Naciones Unidas para el Desarrollo 2004) on the basis of the Electoral Democracy Index (see Figure 8.5). This Index considers voting rights, free and clean elections, and election to key positions in public office. In all of these areas, Costa Rica shows one of the highest rankings in Latin America for the period studied (1990–2002). In fact, political legitimacy has been strong since 1949, the beginning of a sequence of sixteen democratically elected presidential terms.

The transparency of elections and the effective implementation of social policies generated a dynamic in which these elements provided a framework for developing a more equitable society. Democracy and the welfare state reinforced each other, inducing strong social cohesion and preventing any temptation to resort to the reinstatement of the army as a means of social

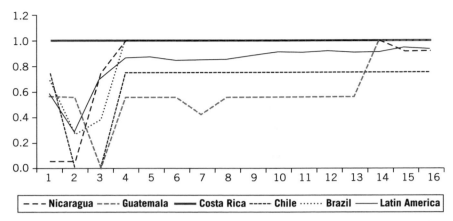

Figure 8.5 Electoral Democracy Index—five countries and Latin America average

Source: United Nations Program for Development (2010), Democracy in Latin America: Towards a Citizens' Democracy.

control. As shown in Figure 8.6, support for democracy in Costa Rica is the second highest in Latin America, after Uruguay.

This high level of political legitimacy has been achieved as a result of the following processes:

Free and clean elections

Costa Rica has been a fully democratic country since 1948, governed by the rule of law, with free elections whose outcome has been accepted by the candidates. There has been clear acknowledgment of its democratic practice by international organizations (Organization of American States 2010), and over two-thirds of citizens have consistently participated in the electoral process for the election of presidents, parlamentarians, and municipal councillors.

However, for the elections since 1998, the level of abstention has been relatively high (see Figure 8.7). This relative decline of electoral participation could be seen as a sign of political apathy, but it could also signal a certain level of satisfaction with the governance of the country. At any rate it should be considered an indication of disengagement of the citizenry vis-à-vis the conduct of public affairs. Yet, in spite of this democratic fatigue, Costa Rica continues to enjoy a level of institutional stability and political legitimacy unparalleled in the last half-century in Latin America.

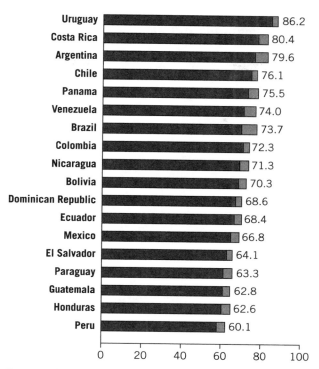

Figure 8.6 Support for democracy, selected Latin America countries

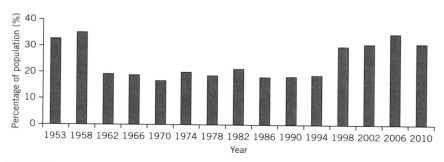

Figure 8.7 Costa Rica: abstention in presidential elections, 1953–2010
Source: Author elaboration with data from the Supreme Electoral Tribunal, Costa Rica

221

Isidora Chacón

Relatively clean public administration

According to Transparency International, Costa Rica scores high on the non-corruption scale in comparison with other countries of the region (Transparency International 2001 see Table 8.6). However, in the 1990s there were strong indications of corruption in favor of multinational corporations at the highest level of the state, and of transnational crime at the lower levels of the administration. When two ex-presidents appeared to have been tainted with corruption, they were prosecuted and convicted along with some of their collaborators. The judicial mechanisms of control functioned efficiently to contain the spread of corruption before it could make the whole state dysfunctional (Transparency International 2010; Inter-American Development Bank 2007; Programa Estado de la Nación 2009; Judge Teresita Rodríguez, personal communication, 2010).

The stabilizing influence of a full-fledged welfare state

Universal, free access to health and education, financed and managed by the state, as discussed in the preceding section, has been a key feature of the Costa Rican model, in sharp contrast with most countries in Latin America.

Table 8.6 Transparency International Corruption Perception Index 2010. Selected Latin American countries' world rankings

Country	Score	rank
Guatemala	3.2	91
El Salvador	3.6	73
Honduras	2.4	134
Nicaragua	2.5	127
Costa Rica	**5.3**	**41**
Panama	3.6	73
Mexico	3.1	98
Colombia	3.5	78
Chile	7.2	21
Uruguay	6.9	24

Source: Corruption Perceptions Index, 2010.

Together with a large network of government-funded programs, this redistributive policy has been essential for human development, and for the social and political stability that characterizes the country.

An effective political agency with a deliberate strategy implemented over a long period of time

The political actor that articulated the public policies and created a coherent development strategy was the social-democratic Partido de Liberacion Nacional. It was organized in the late 1940s by its charismatic leader, Don José Figueres, and became the dominant force of the country for three decades (Sala 2008), with the exception of a brief conservative interregnum. The PLN is still in government nowadays in spite of the growing strength of neoliberal candidates in recent elections.

The Costa Rican developmental state

The public funding of the human development strategy that made social stability and political democracy possible would not have been feasible without ensuring sustained economic growth to provide the necessary resources for a sizable level of government spending without triggering uncontrollable inflationary pressures. Indeed, the financing of widespread state intervention and of the growth of the welfare state was the most difficult issue to solve for the Costa Rican social democrats, given that Costa Rica was a poor country, with few natural resources, and largely dependent on traditional exports, mainly coffee and bananas (Quesada 1999). The PLN governments used essentially four mechanisms to generate the necessary resources:

1. **The development of a strong, solvent, and competitive national banking system, starting with the nationalization of all banks and the strict regulation of financial institutions** (Quesada 1999; Brenes 1990).
2. **The creation of an efficient tax collection system** (Contraloría General de la República 2002).
3. **The borrowing of capital from international markets and donors**, including funding from international aid (Quesada 1999).

4. **The construction of an infrastructure in water supply and sanitation, energy generation and distribution, and telecommunications.** In this regard a particularly important role was played by the Instituto Costarricense de Electricidad (ICE), a public corporation created in the 1950s to manage the generation and delivery of energy, mainly electricity from hydraulic power. ICE was also charged with the development of telecommunicatons in Costa Rica, including in the 1990s the diffusion of Internet access and mobile communication.

This active intervention of the state in the economy was particularly critical after the crisis suffered by the traditional model of economic growth in Costa Rica in the 1980s as a result of the shock suffered by Latin America as a consequence of the process of globalization, liberalization of trade, and financial volatility in the global capital markets. The model of economic growth largely based on the expansion of the domestic market and traditional exports came into question in the 1980s when the financial crisis that hit Latin America dried up the sources of international lending and brought many of the domestic banks to the edge of bankruptcy. Public debt became unbearable. The response of the Costa Rican state to the crisis of the growth model in the 1980s was to become developmental (Johnson 1995), engaging in a new strategy of building competitiveness in the global economy.

The main developmental strategy was diversification of the economy, as new sectors of activities (e.g. organic produce, fresh flowers for export, microelectronics, medical instruments, etc.) received support from the state, breaking the long hold that the "cafetaleros" had on government subsidies and favors. (Estado de la Nación 2009; INEC 2009). This diversification is indicated by the changing sectoral structure of the economy (Table 8.7) and the changing distribution of the labor force (Table 8.8). Particularly noticeable is the substantial increase in participation of women in the labor force, an indicator of the modernization of the country.

It is significant to observe the reduction of the contribution of the primary sector to the GDP (down to 7% in 2010 from 39% in 1950), and the rise of the secondary sector to 25% in contrast to 18% in 1950, with a relatively high level of productivity, as the level of employment in the secondary sector increased only from 16% in 1950 to 19% in 2010. The tertiary sector has substantially grown in both share of GDP and share of employment. However, as is well known in development studies, the internal composition of the tertiary sector includes vastly different economic activities, from social services to personal services, and from advanced business services to

Table 8.7 Costa Rica: GDP structure by sectors

	1950	1960	1970	1980	1990	2000	2010
GDP per capita (USD 2010)	1.684	2.219	2.865	3.811	4.532	6.011	7.842
GDP structure (%)	100	100	100	100	100	100	100
Primary sector[1]	39	26	23	18	13	9	7
Secondary sector[2]	18	20	24	27	30	31	25
Tertiary sector[3]	43	54	53	55	57	60	68

Notes:

[1] Crop and livestock production and fishing.

[2] Manufacturing, construction and electricity, gas and water. It also includes mining and quarrying, but it is a minor activity in the country.

[3] Services.

Source: own production Figures and exchange Central Bank of Costa Rica (BCCR) and INEC and CCP population (2008) National Institute of Statistics and Census and Central American Population Center (2008). Estimates and projections of population by sex and age (updated Figures)1950–2010. San Jose: National Institute of Statistics and Census (INEC) and Central American Population Center (CPC) at the University of Costa Rica (UCR).

Table 8.8 Costa Rica: employment structure by sectors

	1950	1960*	1970*	1980*	1990	2000	2010
Total employees (thousands)	272	395	565	794	1.017	1.456	1.902
Employment structure (%)	100	100	100	100	100	100	100
Primary sector[1]	55	49	38	31	26	17	15
Secondary sector[2]	16	19	20	20	26	22	19
Tertiary sector	29	32	42	49	48	61	66
Employees/total population (%)	34	30	30	33	36	38	42
Women/total employees(%)	15	16	20	22	28	33	37

Notes: 1960 figures are for 1963; 1970 figures for 1970 and 1973; and 1980 figures from 1980 to 1984.

[1] Crop and livestock production and fishing.

[2] Manufacturing, construction and electricity, gas and water. It also includes mining and quarrying, but it is a minor activity in the country.

Source: own Figures of the 1950 National Population Census, 1963, 1973 and 1984; household surveys 1990, 2000 and 2010 (National Institute of Statistics and Census, INEC).

informal activities. Tourism is a decisive component of the Costa Rican export economy (export of services), and within tourism coexist subsectors of low value added (domestic tourism, largely oriented toward beach tourism) with sectors of high value added (eco-tourism, particularly).

Therefore, to comprehend the deep transformation of the productive model of Costa Rica we need to refer to **the strategic initiatives of the state to create modern, export-oriented sectors, and to provide the human resource base for their competitiveness**. I outline below the most important of these initiatives.

First, the support of the state to a nascent informational economy that has gradually expanded, building on the Costa Rican strength in human capital. This human capital formation relies on a relatively good public education system, and some good quality universities and R&D institutions (such as the University of Costa Rica or the Instituto Tecnológico de Cartago). The result has been increased productivity in agriculture, manufacturing, and services, and the opening of new lines of high-value exports (Prosic 2011). This human resources basis has made the transformation of the model of economic growth possible by the following mechanisms:

a) **Attracting foreign capital in advanced manufacturing and services**. The success of this strategy is strikingly exemplified by the choice of Costa Rica by Intel in 1994 for the location of an advanced microelectronics facility, the most important high-technology plant in the region (PROSIC 2011; CONACOM 2007). Among the factors that accounted for Intel's locational choice, the company cited the political and social stability of the country, high quality of life, low levels of corruption, high levels of economic freedom, and relatively high levels of education (Intel 2006). Intel's installation in Costa Rica took place in the face of competition from countries like Indonesia, Thailand, Brazil, Argentina, Chile, and Mexico. To attract Intel to Costa Rica, the government partnered with the Harvard Bussines School, INCAE (the Costa Rican Business School) and CINDE (Costa Rican Coalition for Development). Additional factors in the locational choice of Intel were tax incentives from the government, the possibility of fast construction of cost-effective facilities, and access to a well-trained labor force. In 1994, Intel invested 300 million USD to build the microelectronics assembly and testing plant in Costa Rica. The plant became fully operational in 1997. Around the plant, located in Heredia (a locality in the San Jose metropolitan area), a technology cluster has developed, in collaboration with the main universities and technology institutes in the area. In 1998 Intel started with 500 employees. In 2011 it had generated almost 3000 direct jobs and 2000 indirect jobs in its network of suppliers and the firms in the cluster. In 1998 Intel's exports accounted for 67% of exports of Costa Rica's free zones. However, due to the expansion of the local companies in the cluster, Intel's share of exports was reduced to 40% in a context of rapid expansion of the microelectronics industry. There are 358 additional companies in the electrical and electronics sector in Costa Rica, such as Bticino, Trimport Electronic, Atlas, etc., and more than 775 electronics products are exported to over 90 different destinations. By 2007, 34% of Costa Rican exports were in electrical and electronic products. Although the volume of electronic exports continued to increase, the share of electronics fell to 25% by 2011, but other advanced technology manufacturing such as precision instruments and medical equipment increased to 11.9%, so that overall, manufacturing exports accounted for three-quarters of total exports in 2011, of which more than 50% were high-technology products. This is a textbook case of the significant multiplier effect that the location of a high-technology plant of a multinational corporation can have on local manufacturing industries, provided the right conditions are met. These right conditions include the existence of a network of qualified suppliers, and of a growing pool of highly skilled labor. In 2011, Intel developed new microlectronics products in its Costa Rica facility, including a new transistor with the 3-D technology Tri-Gate, and a new model of personal computer, the Ultrabook. As a result of this technological and economic dynamism, Intel came to account in 2010 for 6% of Costa Rica's GDP, and for 28% of the added value of the manufacturing sector. In 2011, Intel exported products to a value of 1.89 billion USD. Furthermore, with the expansion of the microelectronics cluster, microelectronics production as a whole reached in 2009 34% of Costa Rica's exports (see Table 8.9).

b) **Using an upgraded technological infrastructure to develop new activities in advanced services and non-traditional agriculture** (Sauma and Sánchez 2003). Thus, in 2011, 22% of exports were agricultural products, but about 17% were fresh produce, whose main component was organic produce. It has to be noted that organic agriculture for export is highly informational, not only because of the need for strict cultivation control, but because the certification and labeling of produce in the export markets, which involves information processing and legal expertise, represents a decisive input, and a major cost, in the production process.

c) Taking advantage of Costa Rica's endowment of unspoiled nature to create a large, export-oriented tourist industry, mainly based in high-value eco-tourism, supported by the government's conservationist environmental

Table 8.9 Costa Rica: structure of exports (% over total exports by sector) 2007–11

Sector	2007	2008	2009	2010	2011
Livestock and fisheries	2.0	2.1	2.0	2.5	2.5
Fish and fillets	0.9	1.0	1.1	1.0	1.0
Dairy	0.5	0.5	0.4	0.8	0.9
Meat	0.5	0.5	0.5	0.5	0.5
Others	0.1	0.1	0.1	0.1	0.1
Agricultural	20.0	21.9	21.0	22.8	22.8
Fresh	14.6	15.6	16.2	17.6	16.9
Coffee, tea, and spices	2.8	3.6	2.3	2.8	3.6
Plants, flowers, and foliage	2.1	2.1	1.9	1.8	1.6
Others	0.5	0.6	0.5	0.5	0.6
Industry	78.0	75.9	77.0	74.7	74.8
Electrical and electronics	34.0	29.7	29.5	26.1	25.3
Food	8.3	10.3	11.9	11.7	12.4
Medical and precision equipment	10.6	10.7	10.9	12.4	11.9
Chemistry	5.5	6.2	7.0	6.2	6.3
Metalworking	3.9	4.1	3.5	3.4	3.9
Plastics	5.4	3.8	3.0	2.5	3.0
Textiles, leather, and footwear	2.1	2.2	2.4	2.7	2.6
Rubber	2.0	2.2	2.4	2.3	2.4
Paper and cardboard	2.0	2.2	2.0	2.3	2.4
Non-metallic mineral products	1.0	1.1	1.0	1.0	1.0
Jewelry	0.7	1.0	1.0	0.7	0.9
Timber	0.4	0.5	0.7	0.9	0.7
Mineral products	0.7	0.5	0.7	0.9	0.7
Transport material	0.4	0.4	0.3	0.6	0.6
Others	0.9	0.9	0.9	1.4	0.7
Total	**100.0**	**100.0**	**100.0**	**100.0**	**100.0**

Source: Ministry of Economy and Trade, 2011

policy, in cooperation with international environmental networks and with the support of multilateral agreements. Regarding the protection of the environment in Costa Rica, the policy emphasized the creation of national parks and protected forests, as well as selective reforestation in some areas of the country.[6] Protected areas in 2011 accounted for 26% of the country's territory.

The government developed five lines of action aimed at promoting sustainable tourism: strengthening the protected areas (infrastructure, training, information); establishment of a Sustainable Tourism Certificate that carries with it the possibility of favorable lines of credit to hotels deemed to be sustainable; commissioning certification of Green Flags for beaches; approving packages of legislative and financial measures to encourage agro-ecotourism; and community tourism development programs (Programa Estado de la Nación 2007; MINAE 2002). The new tourism industry emerging from this strategy is what I label informational tourism. In 2010, tourism accounted for about 7% of GDP. Costa Rica has been a trendsetter in the tourist industry, as other Central American countries have started similar programs of eco-tourism. However, the shortcoming of this strategy is that it is extremely sensitive to contraction of demand resulting from the slowing of economic growth in the international economy.[7]

[6] With the Forest Act 4465, of 25 November 1969, benefits of forests and ecosystems were recognized through payment to those who provide environmental services to society by establishing and maintaining valuable ecosystems. In 1996, the Forestry Act 7575 came to mark a turning point recognizing the environmental services of forests. The PSA law describes a grant: "The payment is provided as compensation to land owners with forest or wishing to establish forest plantations. Environmental services they provide to the community:Mitigation of greenhouse gas emissions (reduction, absorption, carbon sequestration and storage); protection of water for urban, rural or hydroelectric; protect and conserve biodiversity for sustainable use; scientific and pharmaceutical research and breeding; genetic protection of ecosystems and life forms; natural scenic beauty for tourism and scientific purposes."

[7] According to the data of SICA, the first tourist destinations were Costa Rica (2 million), Panama (1.3 million), and Guatemala (1.2 million), while leading hiking countries were Honduras (1.1 million), Belize (764,600) and Guatemala (657,100). International visitors left 7.341 million dollars in the region, a 0.9% increase from the previous year accounting for about 5.9% of regional GDP. The increased revenues from tourism were for Panama ($2,552 million), Costa Rica ($1,961 million) and Guatemala ($1,378 million). 41.8% of the visitors came from other Central American countries, 37.1% from North America, 9.4% from Europe, 9% from South America, and the remaining 2.7% from other regions. It also increased the number of hotels and inns in the isthmus, from 7,187 to 7,298. The occupancy rate in 2010 was 56%, 6.9 points higher than in 2009.However, the average expenditure per tourist fell from $105 a day in 2009 to 84 in 2010, while the length of stay fell from 8.6 to 8.4 nights per person.By country, the average expenditure was $112 a day in Costa Rica, $48 in Nicaragua, $109 in Panama, $97 in Guatemala, $79 in El Salvador, and $60 in Honduras. The report did not provide figures for Belize, where in 2009 the average daily spending was $149.The SICA predicted that in 2011 tourism in Central American countries would record growth of between 4 and 10%. In 2010, Costa Rica received 2.1 million tourists who spent more than 2,000 million dollars in the country, representing about 7 % of GDP. (<http://www.imagazinetut.com>.)

d) The shift toward an informational model of development included the diffusion of mobile communication and Internet access in the population at large, a project undertaken by ICE, the public corporation in the telecommunications sector, although there has been in recent years a limited liberalization in the telecommunications market with the entry of a few private companies, particularly in mobile telephony. In 2010, about 53% of households had Internet connection at home, but cybercafes and Internet access from schools and work places raise considerably the proportion of Costa Ricans connected to the Internet. The rate of penetration of mobile telephony has reached over 75%. Figure 8.8 displays the steady progression of communication and information equipment in Costa Rican households.

Furthermore, another strategic initiative of the Costa Rican government to lead the transition toward an informational society has been the program in eGovernment, both in internal networking of the administration, and in networking with citizens in the information and delivery of government services (Prosic 2011).

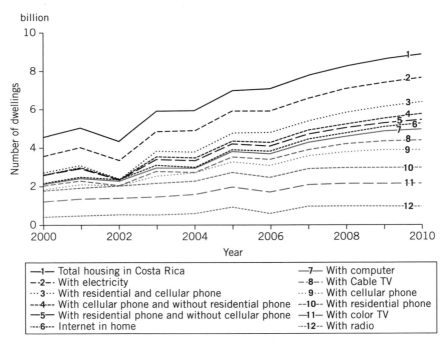

Figure 8.8 Evolution of equipment of households

Source: National Institute of Statistics and Census.

Thus, the informationalization of a few dynamic, export-oriented economic sectors is supported by the diffusion of information and communication technologies in the population at large, by the upgrading of the knowledge basis of the labor force, and by the digital upgrading of public administration. All together, these strategic initiatives set the stage for the transition to an informational mode of development.

The Costa Rican model of development

Over the last half-century, Costa Rica has been able to sustain a high rate of economic growth in spite of undergoing several crises as a consequence of downturns in the global economy. Between 1960 and 2008, Costa Rica achieved an average annual growth of 5.5%, overtaking Latin America as a whole and coming second only to the most dynamic economies of East Asia. Furthermore, while the economic crisis in the US induced negative growth (−1.3%) in 2009, the economy bounced back with growth rates of 4.2% in 2010 and 4.3% in 2011, led by growth of high-technology products and non-traditional agricultural exports. Consequently, per capita GDP in Costa Rica has increased steadily over time to reach in 2011 the level of 11,300 USD, up from 7,100 in 1999 (<http://www.indexmundi.com 2011>).

This long-term growth performance of Costa Rica can be largely attributed to the transformation of its export-oriented productive structure along the lines of what is labeled as informational development. In aggregate terms, the closest indicator of this transformation is the contribution of each factor to GDP growth: capital, labor, and total factor productivity (TFP). As it is known, TFP includes contribution of knowledge, management, technology, and the synergy resulting from specific forms of combination between capital and labor. Looking at Table 8.10, we can observe that over the whole period, TFP's contribution is higher than the contribution of labor. In the earlier stages of development, labor contribution was essential, as in all industrializing economies. Labor's contribution was gradually surpassed by contribution from capital and from TFP, with the latter becoming particularly important in the most recent period (2005–8 and—though not shown in the table—2010–11). The relevance of capital's contribution can be attributed to the role of public investment in the early stages of development, thus creating the foundations for the growth of productivity to lead economic growth in the future.

Table 8.10 Contribution of factors and productivity to GDP growth: Costa Rica, 1960–2008

Period	Growth	Capital	Work	TFP
1960–5	5.4	2.0	2.7	0.7
1975–80	6.2	3.1	2.0	1.0
1980–5	1.5	2.4	0.8	−1.8
1990–5	5.8	1.8	1.3	2.7
2000–5	4.1	2.3	1.5	0.3
2005–8	6.5	3.1	1.0	2.3
1960–2008	5.5	2.5	1.4	1.6

Source: Miguel Loría, Costa Rica Economy, 2011.

Thus, the model of development that has emerged in Costa Rica in the last two decades has relied on a synergistic relationship between human development and informational development that feed into each other: Human capital provides the knowledge and skills basis for informational development, and the new exports-oriented economy generates the wealth to finance human development under the conditions of proper taxation and adequate levels of social spending. The welfare state contributes to the maintenance of social stability that, in turn, strengthens political legitimacy. Figure 8.9 shows the set of relationships underlying the Costa Rican Model of Development.

However, the dynamism of the growth and redistribution model depends on the ability of the public sector to provide human resources in sufficient quantity and quality to generate a competitive knowledge economy, beyond the enclaves of high-technology firms and advanced tourist services. When some features of this model have come under question, the coherence of the model has been threatened and its synergy jeopardized.

Toward a crisis of the development model?

In recent years we have been witnessing a crisis of some of the features of the Costa Rican model of development.

- **The administration has become vulnerable to corruption**, including at the highest levels of government for a period of time (Ministerio Público

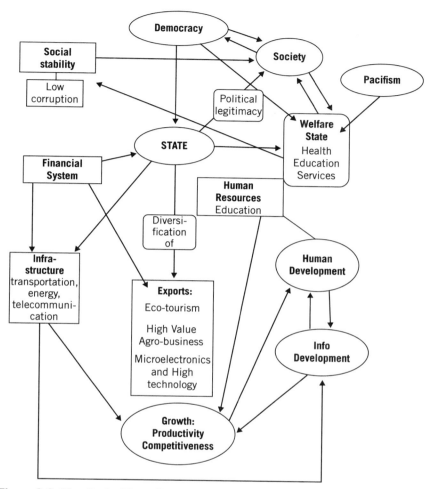

Figure 8.9 The Costa Rican Model of Development

2007). It is increasingly inefficient and bureaucratic and prone to clientelism on the basis of political networks of patronage. Furthermore, the municipal administration lacking resources and personnel is deeply clientelistic and often inefficient. The country faces a crisis of basic urban services: garbage collection, recycling, maintenance of public areas, etc. (El País 2011).

- **The welfare state may face financial shortages** if the new economic strategies competing in an open, globalized economy do not yield enough revenue, partly due to the fact that the informational sector is still very limited in capital and in job generation capacity.

- **The human resource base is lagging in relation to the needs of informational development**. A particularly worrisome problem is the low proportion of science and technology graduates in higher education institutions. Investment in research is clearly insufficient to sustain the path of informational development. In 2010 R&D investment represented a meager 0.53% of GDP. The University of Costa Rica, with its 42 research centers, is the institution that dominates research in the public sector, but only 7% of its activity is related to information and communication technology, engineering, and sustainable development. According to the National Indicators of Science, Technology, and Innovation, only 14% of the national research budget goes to engineering and technology projects (Financiero 873-MICIT). The enrollment rate in tertiary education is 25.3% and it is projected to grow in the coming years, but enrollment in technological and science areas is at a lower rate, and it does not meet the demand for technical and engineering skills (Programa Estado de la Nación en Desarrollo Humano Sostenible 2011). Graduates of basic sciences and engineering represent only 17.4% of graduates in public universities and 10.3% in private universities. According to the National Council for Science and Technological Research (CONICIT) and the Ministry of Science and Technology, the number of researchers is about 3,500 people in the public sector, with less than half (49%) actually doing research. Moreover, publications by Costa Rican researchers in Latin American scientific journals represent only 0.7% of total publications, although the figure should be evaluated in relation to the proportion of the Costa Rican population over the population of Latin America (0.8%) (Financiero 873-CONICIT).

Additional negative trends include increasing unemployment (standing at 10.4% in 2012); the rise of social inequality (Sauma 2010); the rise in crime, associated with the perception of greater insecurity (Poder Judicial 2010); and deterioration in the efficiency of the tax system that has diminished the capacity to generate revenue for the state. Thus, unless there is an overhaul of the tax administration, a fiscal crisis is looming on the horizon, undermining the continuity of the welfare state, the core of the current model of development.

In addition, Costa Rica faces new security challenges. In October 2010, Nicaragua invaded Costa Rican territory and cut a vast expanse of forest in

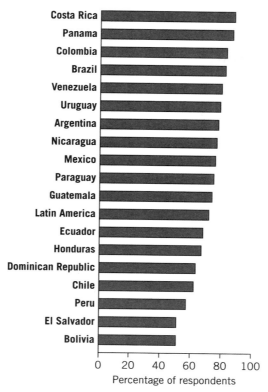

Figure 8.14 "In general terms: Would you say you are happy with your life? Would you say you are very satisfied, fairly satisfied, not very satisfied, not at all satisfied?" (Here only "very satisfied.")

to rekindle the intervention of the state in developmental policies. The social democrats, for the time being, have been able to steer a middle course, supporting the TLC, liberalizing some areas of the economy, and yet preserving the main elements of the welfare state legacy. They are trying to find new sources of productivity growth in informational industries and agricultural exports.

Costa Rica in 2012 is in fact at a crossroads and I cannot conclude at this point on the outcome of the ongoing debate.[9] However, we have enough

[9] On April 6th 2014, Luis Guillermo Solís, from Partido Acción Ciudadana, was elected President of Costa Rica with 78% of votes, thus ending the decade-long dominance of the social-democratic Partido Liberación Nacional. PAC was created on 2000.

data and experience on the model of development that has unfolded since the 1950s to draw a number of analytical lessons that could enrich the policy debate in the framework of the international experience.

Lessons from the Costa Rican model of development in a comparative approach

In order to place the analysis of the Costa Rican model in the broader framework of the relationship between informational and human development, I will consider the approach presented by Castells and Himanen in their analysis of Finland (Castells and Himanen 2002), and I will show the differences and similarities between the Finnish and Costa Rican cases.

I propose that what is specific is the singularity of the state, the key mediating institution in the process of development. The modern Costa Rican state was based on a pacifist strategy that makes it very different from other states in the world at large. Having said this, it was largely a state guided by a social-democratic ideology, not too different from the one prevailing in Finland, regardless of which party or coalition of parties are in government in Finland. This comparison has to be understood in the terms of a much lower level of economic and social development in the case of Costa Rica. Yet, in its particular social and geographic context, Costa Rica shows higher levels of human and informational development than most Latin American countries. It is my contention that the critical factor for this performance was the nature of the state, both a welfare state and a developmental state that succeeded in building political legitimacy and social stability on a foundation of human development. The special characteristic of the Costa Rican state comes from its ability to fund the expansion of its public sector in spite of the poverty of the country at the onset of the developmental process. I argue that the suppression of the armed forces enabled Costa Rica to free a sizable amount of resources that in other Latin American countries were destined to sustain an excessive warfare state largely used for domestic repression. While the original source of public investment in Finland was very different, what makes the two models similar is the priority given to social welfare (constitutionally mandated in the case of Costa Rica). In both cases, the welfare state

It is a progressive party whose success was predicated in the critique of the bureaucracy and corruption of the political class and was based on its proposal for a renewal of the state to make it more democratic, transparent, and efficient.

contributed to social stability and to political democracy. The difference is that democracy has been established in Finland since independence, while in Costa Rica there was systemic instability, as in other countries in its region, until pacifism and the welfare state created the conditions for the consolidation of democratic institutions.

Another basic similarity between the two countries is their strong national identity. Both being small countries (4.6 million in Costa Rica, 5.4 million in Finland) with a history of colonization and survival in a hostile environment, the nation-state is seen in both societies as the bulwark against all sorts of dangers, external and internal. Thus, the cultural basis for social cohesion, democracy, and state legitimacy provides a solid foundation for an interventionist state.

There are also striking similarities between the development models of the two countries in very different contexts and cultures. In both cases, a major economic crisis, derived from the changing conditions of globalization, threatened the economic basis of the welfare state. Finland had to survive the collapse of the Soviet Union (its main market) in 1991, and then create the conditions to join the European Union and compete in the global economy. Costa Rica had to overcome the shock of the financial crisis of the 1980s in Latin America, and then be able to integrate successfully in the process of globalization and liberalization of trade. In both cases, an interventionist state created the conditions for a shift to an informational mode of development. In the case of Finland, according to Castells and Himanen, to transform Finland into the number-one information society was a mobilizing project that actually succeeded in transforming the industrial basis of Finland, increasing productivity and competitiveness, and providing financial support for the expansion of the welfare state. In the case of Costa Rica, the project was less explicitly geared toward informationalism, but the government intervened decisively through public corporation programs in creating the productive infrastructure for technologically advanced economic growth, and ensuring the diffusion of new information and communication technologies among citizens and in the school system. Moreover, the strategic initiatives undertaken by the government focused on inducing a microelectronics cluster around Intel that became the main export engine of the country, very much like the formation in Finland of a telecommunications cluster around Nokia. In both cases the dynamism of the informationally transformed sectors (telecommunications and advanced services in Finland; microelectronics, medical instruments, eco-tourism, and organic agriculture in Costa Rica) have ensured high rates of growth in the last decade. Costa

Rica overcame the global recession of 2009 to grow again at over 4% per year in 2010 and 2011, while shielding its financial sector from the crisis of global finance. In both countries we can observe a positive feedback loop between human development and informational development: the welfare state provided the necessary human capital, and informational development made the welfare state financially sustainable, in spite of some shortcomings identified in this paper. There is however one major difference between the two countries: the much lower rate of R&D investment in Costa Rica, something that could jeopardize informational development once the benefits of technology transfer are exhausted. The Finnish state appears to have a more deliberate informational strategy and the institutional instruments to implement it (e.g. the Tekkes Foundation).

Meanwhile, the Costa Rican government seems to have lost the developmental drive of earlier periods in the construction of the country, and is lacking a determined policy in R&D and innovation. However, in both countries the modernized private sector is taking development into its own hands. Finnish companies are now investing globally, particularly in China, so that the crisis of Nokia is compensated by a new cohort of high-technology firms. Costa Rican companies have expanded beyond their role of suppliers to multinationals, and are making inroads in the export markets. Thus, the economic basis for the welfare state could be assured on the condition of a proper tax collection and efficient public management of the revenue collected. This key component of the virtuous circle of development seems to be in jeopardy in the case of Costa Rica, a major issue that could be an ominous trend for the sustainability of the dynamic model analyzed in this paper. Indeed, for Costa Rica to continue with its welfare state it needs to increase productivity and competitiveness in the economy by generating a full-fledged process of informational development, and it must modernize its public management to collect and use efficiently the revenue resulting from economic growth. Although there are some elements of this approach in the Costa Rican state, they are still limited, while the state is becoming increasingly corporatist, bureaucratic, and clientelistic. Thus, my analysis has shown both the sources of the relatively successful performance of the Costa Rican Model, and the sources of its potential decline.

Three major lessons for development policies seem to result from the analysis presented in this paper:

1. The virtuous circle between human development, informational development, productivity, and competitiveness seems to be verified in two very different cultural and institutional contexts.

2. The key for the implementation of this dynamic model is the existence of a democratic, active state that relies on the welfare state to ensure social stability and political legitimacy. Pacifism, be it extreme (e.g. the suppression of armed forces) in the case of Costa Rica, or practiced systematically as foreign policy in the case of Finland, is a major factor contributing to social stability, availability of resources, and political democracy.

3. The sustainability of the model depends on the ability of the state to renew itself, both in its internal functioning and in the strategic implementation of its policies. Relentless adaptation to the fast-changing conditions of globalization, technology, and culture, is a must for small countries, such as Costa Rica and Finland, to continue to show to the world that another way of development is possible.

PART THREE

Reconceptualizing Development

Chapter 9

Rethinking Human Development

Fernando Calderón

Background

The central idea of this chapter argues that the current goal of human development is both the autonomy and dignity of people.[1] From this starting point it is possible to analyze processes and developing policies. This goal would constitute the main demand of the people who seek new ways of life in the cultural, institutional, socio-economical, ecological, and political forms. Dignity would give a new meaning to development.

The text starts with conceptual arguments and empirical examples that aim to put dignity at the center of the debate. Afterward, the chapter re-analyzes the basic features of this pattern of development and proposes four strategic themes to strengthen the proposals of this approach: information-alism, environment, inclusion and social exclusion, and social conflict.

---

[1] The concept of "dignity as development" was originally proposed to our group by Professor Pekka Himanen.

Finally, it proposes the idea of a "human development agency." The chapter culminates with a corollary about the pedagogy of the proposal.

The argument is supported in the approach of the sociology of the actor and in the concepts and empirical findings of human development reports, particularly in the global reports and some regional and national reports promoted by the United Nations in which the author has participated. This chapter is also based on the discussions of the group that has worked on the project.

Why dignity?

In recent decades, human development has undergone significant developments worldwide. Particularly, statistical indicators of wellbeing in health, education, and income have improved. However, these advances usually have not been sufficient. Internationally, inequalities, both between countries and different social groups, have persisted and in some cases deepened, mainly because of the high levels of income concentration and social exclusion. Today, the situation of change and uncertainty associated with the global crisis tends to produce new inequalities even in developed countries. For example, in 2010 0.6% of the world's adult population that had a net worth of USD 1 million or more possessed 39.3% of the global wealth, whereas 69.3% of the world's adult population that had a net worth under USD 10,000 comprised only 3.3% of global wealth (Credit Suisse Research Institute 2012).[2]

This requires finding new perspectives and policies, combining national options with global politics that take into account the high levels of asymmetric interdependence that the phenomena of change and uncertainty have. The numerous demands of social protests around the world are highlighting development issues about dignity, human rights, and peace, as well as the search for prospects that go beyond instrumental, institutional, or economic answers to ongoing problems.

---

[2] Credit Suisse Research Institute. (2012). *Global Wealth Report 2012*, <https://www.credit-suisse.com/ch/en/news-and-expertise/news/economy/global-trends.article.html/article/pwp/news-and-expertise/2012/10/en/global-wealth-2012-the-year-in-review.html>.

The crisis in its many dimensions[3] is causing the emergence of new demands, criticisms, conflicts, and protests for dignity and human rights in numerous societies and cultures. It combines protests at local, national, regional, and global levels that, in addition to expressing discomfort, seek new ways of social life, and ultimately, cultural and political changes to the ongoing development options of the past 30 years.

According to Castells (2012:2–3),[4] the secular conflicts associated with current injustice are surfacing into a multifaceted rebellion, where there is humiliation provoked by the cynicism and arrogance of those in power, be it financial, political, or cultural, that brought together those who turned fear into outrage, and outrage into hope for a better humanity. A humanity that had to be reconstructed from scratch, escaping the multiple ideological and institutional traps that had led to dead ends again and again, forging a new path by treading it. It was the search for dignity amid the suffering of humiliation—recurrent themes in most of the movements.

Several studies and reports complement the above:

1. A study referring to India analyzes protests that demanded better health and education and sought to further development and address several issues related to human rights, focusing on gender relations (Patel 2010).
2. Levitt and Merry (2010)[5] examine how human rights were at the core of social movement mobilization in New York City, and in particular describe an effort to mobilize human rights to combat systemic race and gender discrimination. The authors argue that in certain contexts, human rights can provide relevant political resources to social movements in the United States. However, they do so in a diffuse way far from the formal system of human rights law. This case describes a new phenomenon in the United States: the mobilization of human rights campaigns by the social justice movements that have long relied on civil rights law.

---

[3] The financial crisis, the problems of democratic governance and national autonomy, the limits of multicultural coexistence options, the geopolitical changes in global power structures, the emergence of the state as an agent of global positioning of national economies, the distance between scientific and technological innovation and the institutional and educational systems, and the environmental crisis associated with an economic model based on consumption and environmental degradation.

[4] Castells, M. (2012). *Networks of Outrage and Hope: Social Movements in the Internet Age.* Polity Press: Cambridge.

[5] P. Levitt and S. Merry (2010). "Law from Below: Women's Human Rights and Social Movements in New York City," *Law and Society Review 44 (1)*:101–28.

3. Another investigation analyzed the conflicts and social protests in Latin America around social and cultural rights (Calderon 2012).[6] These conflicts share several features: platforms of exclusion and chronic inequalities, questioned by citizens; practical rationalities caused by social reproduction, coexisting with demands for greater effectiveness and efficiency, as well as systemic cultural conflicts; omnipresent states in all spheres of conflict, with limitations for prosecution, and societies with fragmented conflicts; new public spaces where tensions are represented in a contradictory manner, with conflicts that move to the information and communication networks with multiplying effects in the new scenarios of power. There is greater social complexity related to political systems and states with limited management capabilities.

4. The "Arab Spring" protests, in a different and intense way, embodied criticisms to the authoritarian forms of power, with demands for peace, dignity, and participation. The role of youth and activism in social networks was crucial. As the cyberactivist L.B. Mhenni (2011: 31) argued: "The Toila is a dream instrument for direct democracy, of citizenship. We want a world without bosses, where everyone can participate in decision-making, where everyone can produce changes in the reality."

5. The anti-nuclear peace movement in Japan, particularly after the Fukushima disaster, is another example. Recent studies show how the fears generated by the bombings of Nagasaki and Hiroshima influenced the experience of food contamination in 50 different types of protesters and social activists today, especially young people and women who are strengthening the pacifistic public opinion. The role of ICT has become crucial in these demonstrations (Hirabayashi 2012).

Thus, this renewed approach to human development that we are undertaking stems from the following ascertainment: public malaise, social demands, and massive protests throughout the world are highlighting the need to recuperate and reconstruct both dignity and individual and collective goals. Even though this path has been taken into account as an element of Human Development, it has become increasingly significant in the current context of global crisis.[7] It has also underlined the need of social actors' autonomy to attain their personal dignity goals.

---

[6] Calderón, F. (2012).
[7] For further detail see UNDP, (2000), *Human Development Report 2000. Human Rights and Human Development*. New York: Oxford University Press.

Another distinctive trait is the displacement of those demands into the information society, using the diverse social networks as means to express the claims and proposed solutions. It constitutes a very specific type of dignity fostered by global communications.[8]

In that regard, the human development approach, a holistic, interdisciplinary and normative framework,[9] should be redefined in terms of individual and collective actors' empowerment as the key to facing ongoing global changes. Furthermore, people's capacity to attain their autonomy and dignity goals must be strengthened in the short term.

This capability approach "sees human life as a set of doings and beings" (functionings) and it relates the evaluation of the quality of life to the assessments of the capability to function" (Sen 2003a: 4).[10] We consider these functionings as part and parcel of individuals' dignity.

In that respect, Sen's concept of real freedom refers to the development of people's capabilities to lead the kind of life they value, according to their aspirations.[11] Education and knowledge are fundamental, not only in terms of democratic socialization, or productivity, employment, and equality, but also in choosing the kind of life a person wants to live. Hence, education, the aforementioned choices, and development are closely related, especially in a context of rapid global changes and the increasing preponderance of the information society.[12]

Both the structural dynamics of globalization and its current crisis placed the question about human dignity and human rights, as the axes of a new social and political reform, at the center of the social demands and challenges of development, regardless of national and/or regional or cultural contexts or different levels of development. Dignity, understood as a person's sense of self-respect and esteem, is essential for individuals to form an integrated citizenship with others.[13]

---

[8] Such is the case of Chile's most recent student movements.

[9] As defined by M. Ul Haq in Fakuda et al. (2003).

[10] Sen, Amartya. (2003a). "Development as Capability Expansion," in S. Fakuda-Parr and A. K. Shiva Kumar (eds.), *Readings in Human Development*. Oxford: Oxford University Press.

[11] Sen, A. (1999). *Development as Freedom*. New York: Anchor Knopf, p.12.

[12] For further details see CEPAL, (1992), *Educación y conocimiento: eje de la transformación productiva con equidad. Libros de la CEPAL N° 33*. Santiago de Chile: CEPAL.

[13] On a more individual level than in the examples which follow, many human rights activists around the world work from this perspective of dignity and conflict (see <http://www.cdhrsupport.org/2012/02/20/how-the-humans-rights-movement-has-gone-global/, and http://monnews.org/?=3929>). Also, the reports of the Global Peace Index (2012) show advances and regressions in terms of peace and human rights globally. We can

Fernando Calderón

From a conceptual perspective, one of the main features of contemporary societies is a certain gap between instrumental and symbolic rationalities. This would be a sort of separation between culture on one hand, and economics on the other. In this separation, the relations of power are associated with economic restructuring and the "multi-global crisis" (Rojas 2011)[14] that is simultaneously becoming more dissociated and diffuse amid complexity, risk, and social vacuum (Castells 1997; Touraine 1997; Beck 2006; C. Rojas, 2011).

The point is to reintegrate substantive logic with the instrumental. I wonder about the possibilities of a fruitful articulation between the dynamics of change, associated with the technological information economy, and socio-cultural dynamics, linked to the new demands of quality of life emerging from the crisis and global change. The purpose is to explore the possibilities of a new historicity, understood as the capacity of a society to self-produce and to expand its mechanisms of action and participation. A renewed focus on human development, appropriate to the new circumstances, may constitute an important reference for policy proposals regarding the dignity of individuals and their societies. In this approach, actors, people, communities, and socio-cultural groups are both the subject and object of development.

This perspective assumes that the multi-global crisis does not eliminate the capacity of social action, but opens other possibilities. It also implies that socio-cultural actions can not only oppose the changing power relations, but can transform into options for participating in global change and giving a different meaning to development. Thus, quality of life and dignity of the people are in the very constitution of development goals; and not the markets or states. Quality of life expresses the need to be considered as a holder of a renewed human dignity, including collective and individual identities, social networks, and intercultural relations full of diverse

find significant regional, local, and urban experiences—as in Kerala, Barcelona, and Porto Alegre, for example—that work in the context of human development values. There are also important business experiences, especially in the small and medium scale, showing practices and advances that combine human development and informational elements. Furthermore, the valorization of dignity and human rights is also expressed at the institutional level through new laws, constitutions, and institutional arrangements, often associated with important NGO networks. UN-promoted Millennium Development Goals and various intergovernmental organizations have reached important agreements and policies, limited by the consequences of the crisis.

[14] It is called so due to the global diversities of ecological, financial, multicultural, and political crises.

aspirations and specific knowledge. Today, the active search for dignity gives a renewed meaning to the human development approach.

This approach is based on a constructivist theory that places at the center the subjectivities and capacities of societies and social actors, above the dynamics of markets and states. Furthermore, it is hoped that the markets and the state can work for the public and for the people and their societies. In this sense, the public space is valued as the place where people can make this kind of cooperative work. But it seems necessary to observe that the notion of the public is complex and constantly changing and being redefined in today's informational society, turning it more global.

In this regard, it is assumed that people are actors who constantly seek change and adapt to change, but not in a vacuum—rather, in specific institutional settings and with the burden of their respective subjectivities, which involve the recognition of the subjectivity of others who are different but equal. Only by enhancing the capacity for action and individual and collective reflection is it possible to advance the achievement of results in favor of democracy and development as a common understanding.

In the center of this social constructivist approach is located the actors' autonomy and personal freedom, which are values relating to politics and development. Subjectivity in particular is the one that refers to human dignity, and is not just an end in itself, but also an action. Better yet, it is an agency which optimizes particular interests that, together with expanding into the social compact, gain a collective character. But the collective commitments also allow for the achievement of individual goals and values. In this sense, the autonomy of the actor and the pursuit of liberty and its various options are not only efficient but fair, because they need and tend to involve the whole social compact. Dignity, as a value and practice, allows the evaluation of changes that occur, or have already occurred, but should also be understood as a value generator of changes.

Development as the empowerment of actors' capabilities

Development means creating the access necessary to empower actors' capabilities. In this regard, the goal of "possible" human development is to achieve an "acceptable society." In other words, a society where people can live a decent life and where actors are able to specify the manifest injustices (patent injustices) as a result of public deliberation, and as a method to define situations and options (Sen 1997 and 2000).

Fernando Calderón

The capacity of a person to be an actor is associated with the autonomy they have in choosing goals and achieving results in line with the process of searching for such results. This is the inseparable goal of achieving a "culture of solidarity procedural" (Pizzorno 1984). There lies the importance of the idea of citizen communication according with shared basic values such as human rights and dignity.

Himanen (2012b: 5) notes that:

Sen sets out from the concept of freedom, but he does not provide a reason for why people should be free. This notion, too, requires justification, which is the idea of dignity, that is, that all people are worthy of freedom. This is a reason to elevate dignity to be the most fundamental value—and, accordingly, to elevate the notion of a dignified life to be the most fundamental objective. Thus, all people have rights because they are 'worthy of rights' and 'valuable to have values'. A dignified life means a life with dignity.

The idea of "dignity" places in the center of development the subjectivities of people, and refers to the abilities of the people and their societies to decide on the orientations of their lives, according to their values and desires. In this sense, dignity is not univocal as it relates directly to the cultural possessions of people and their societies. Moreover, this development perspective also asserts that the formation of values and the evolution of social ethics based on solidarity strengthens development purposes and guides the relationship between the market and institutions.[15]

The recognition of cultural identity is a condition of human dignity and refers to multicultural pluralism of contemporary societies. It should be incorporated as a relevant capacity for development. From a cultural perspective on human development, dignity refers to the need to ensure and expand the possibilities of people in a constructive way in order for them to choose their preferred lifestyle, considering other ways of life. Moreover, it is impossible to think about an action or an agency in terms of a single actor, because action and agency are built with others. The importance of cultural identity is associated with the equity required for the realization of their dignity. The exercise of cultural identity by all people can lead to an extension of cultural diversity that allows them to have more options and a wider cultural spectrum (UNDP 2004b). From this approach, dignity means paying attention to the dignity of all, which necessarily involves considerations

---

[15] This idea is inspired by the concept of "real freedom" (Sen 1999). See also Rao and Walton (eds.) 2004.

of justice and equality. In this sense, the agency of dignity also refers to a reflexive identity that supposes the capacity to transform power relationships.

The human development approach seeks to focus both on the preservation of cultural heritage and the freedom for people to expand cultural spheres. However, it should be noted that cultural identity is not only one identity relevant to people; there are different identities related to religion, language, musical taste, eating habits, etc. Furthermore, depending on circumstances, identity is not just a discovery that sometimes involves a choice; it may result in restrictions (Sen 1999).

The exercise of cultural liberty is a right without limitations of recognition of a human specificity and is a condition of democratic sociability. It is essential to decide what is relevant in the cultural heritage and the different groups to which a person may belong. In this sense, it is crucial to resist the imposition of identity by others, but it is not feasible to assume an identity as one's own if it is not constructed in relation to others. We understand interculturalism as the fair coexistence between different people and as a shared value for each individual. It is a way of life.

Thus, cultural liberty refers to the cultural diversity inherent to all societies. It also underscores the relevance of expanding and guaranteeing people's options to choose the type of life they wish to live and to consider alternative lifestyles as well. "The importance of freedom links well with the need for equity in the pursuit of freedom," which necessarily includes the liberties of each person.[16]

To achieve a genuine cultural liberty people's cultural aspirations must be taken into account as well as recognized in a dignified and ethical manner. Social inclusion, collective aspirations, the right to privacy, the construction of identity, and recognition should also be included in a comprehensive notion of cultural liberty.[17]

At the same time, justice—supported by cultural diversity—should guarantee social actors individual aspirations and promote an environment in which citizen rights, equality, participation, political recognition, cultural liberty, and basic socioeconomic conditions thrive for all.

---

[16] UNDP (2004), *Human Development Report 2004: Cultural Liberty in Today's Diverse World*. New York: Oxford University Press.

[17] For a thorough analysis of culture and aspirations see Sen, A. in M. Walton and V. Rao (2004); for an examination of public deliberation's role in political culture see Calderón, F. in Walton and Rao (2004).

It is worth analyzing in detail this idea of dignity as a historical force of change, as a "place" of construction of meaning. According to Touraine,[18] the individual, to establish oneself as such, must struggle against forces that limit their subjectivity, such as the market, advertising, the fundamentalist logics, and the restrictions on the expression of diverse identities. By linking this perspective with Sen's approach, one might think that the agency would be built based on dignity.

The actor, meanwhile, is associated with a social position. The actor, whether collective or individual, can become the subject when they question an alienating logic that tends to reproduce their subordinate position in the social system. The actor is one person or one group that, based on its capabilities and its subjectivity, acts to achieve its goals while intervening to produce changes in its environment.

This development approach assumes the willingness of different actors to transform their society and, as such, would be associated with the idea of the capacity of society to transform itself. Here the development is largely the result of a conflict between forces contesting its orientation. Therefore, this proposal offers a vision of the conflict that is not clearly present in the traditional approach of human development, where conflict is treated in terms of opposition between development models, but not as opposition in

---

[18] Throughout his writings Alain Touraine has developed the notion of society's self reproduction as the core of the tension between reproduction and social changes. In "Producción de la societe (7:1973)," he states that "societies learn to sociologically acknowledge themselves when they self recognize as a product of their work and their social relations, when a group of social events are acknowledged as the result of social actions, decisions, transactions or a domination of conflicts." In *Le retour de l'acteur* (1984), Touraine analyzes the change of historicity provoked by the transition from an industrial society to a programmed society and the rising of new social conflicts, mostly of cultural and global nature. Actors oppose totalitarianism and torture as well as the political pseudo-rationalities of the powers that be, and in doing so they transition from revolutionaries to libertarians. In *Pourrons-nous vivre ensemble: Egaux et differents* (183: 1997), Touraine proposes his thesis of informational and knowledge societies' otherness. He also expands his theory of society's production in multicultural contexts and values positively UNDP's Human Development framework for introducing a new definition of modernity that emphasizes political liberty, creativity, and personal dignity. In "Apres la crisis," Touraine's fourth and most significant conclusion, the author asserts that in an increasingly global economy the only viable opposing forces "are universal rights, i.e. the right to exist, to freedom, and the recognition of those freedoms, whereas social and cultural identities are being threatened by the inhuman world of profit." In this regard, social life is threatened and weakened by financial capitalism, which is contrary to the interest of the population as a whole. Touraine, Alain. (1973). *Production de la société*. Paris: Seuil; Touraine, Alain. (1984). *Le retour de l'acteur*. Paris: Fayard; Touraine, Alain. (1988). *La parole et le sang*. Paris: Editions Odile Jacob; Touraine, Alain. (1997). *Pourrons nous vivre ensemble? Egaux et differents*. Paris: Fayard.

the power relationships, as a dispute between actors, and/or opposition between different political orientations.

The political recognition of equality between different cultures assumes a society of intercultural communication. The question is how to develop autonomous and responsible actors and how to know what the key institutions are.

The idea of dignity and autonomy of the actor is, therefore, essential to understanding the possibilities that the current crisis mutes into a development option that rests on the subjectivity of people. It is worth then specifying what dignity as a force of development is.

Himanen (2012b: 5) said that:

Another reason why dignity is here elevated as our central concept and value is because, in addition to freedom and justice, it is the fundamental basis of life values. In other words, it is the root of the following concepts: individual value (i.e. the freedom of the individual to be a subject), community value (i.e. the just opportunity for the subject to be part of a collective) and life values (i.e. the respect for life and human existence as a part of humanity). Here the concept goes much further than, say, the UN's Universal Declaration of Human Rights, which, though it is indeed divided into values relating to life, freedom and justice, views the notion of rights as the right of the living individual to life. In the present examination the notion of dignity additionally signifies the right of future generations to a similarly dignified life, which of necessity includes the notion of a sustainable environment. (Here it must be stressed that ecological sustainability is presented as our ethical responsibility towards the rights of future generations to the very possibility of a dignified life. On a conceptual level, this formulation does not pass comment on another important question, namely whether life other than human life has an intrinsic value of its own. The author certainly has his own stance on this matter, but with regard to the question of ecological sustainability the arguments offered above are more than sufficient.) Dignity is the fundamental concept, because it is the foundation of the values and rights outlined above, namely freedom, justice and life.

Dignity is associated with identities, aspirations, and discomforts; with questions, demands, desires, and anxieties of individuals and groups who seek to integrate their experiences to the public space and the public speech, and who seek their subjectivities and everyday experiences to be recognized as a fundamental part of social life by society as a whole.

As mentioned, subjectivity is particularly important as a counterpart to modernization and globalization. The multiple cultural and subjective manifestations are now a force that opposes and is in tension with the instrumental logic of globalization, the market, and techno-economics of information. Summarizing, subjectivity in many senses is opposed to the creation of a concentration of transnational power.

However, the absence of guarantees, the uncertainty prevailing in relations of power, and the fact that the agency of dignity is not granted must be stressed. A renewed human development approach, centered on people's dignity, should be understood in the context of a new "historicity field" where actors and interest groups debate and dispute the available development options. Those disputes have become particularly evident in the network society: local, national, and global actors are contesting society's course according to their preferences regarding the role of the state, free markets, and human hevelopment.

Having said this, globalization, particularly through changes in the industry and cultural markets and communication, has also had an impact on the expansion of subjectivities, establishing a new pluralism of societies and globalization. Subjectivity and demands for dignity, for their part, are the best guarantee for a renewal of politics, democracy, and citizenship.

Actors and new cultural movements are currently developing in relation to the expansion of their own subjectivities, which are set in relation to new domains of science, technology, knowledge, and network society. The demands of dignity are an intrinsic tension of the future of globalization itself. Precisely for this reason, dignity, the subject, and globalization are not separate phenomena. They are made in relation to a new historical tension in the context of which contemporary societies develop. In a world where democracy is a value unchallenged, the subject, person, or group does not build their subjectivity in a vacuum or in solitude; they do it in the middle of social relations and with other subjects who are different from them.

Collective action has become increasingly associated with individual demands or orientations. People seek to reconstitute themselves, assuming their own experience and building their specificity in opposition to new forms of power, and in this opposition give individual meaning to their collective existence. But individual actions are valued collectively as a common good.

Cultural freedom, understood as a common good, is also an undisputed principle of social equality. In this sense, men and societies seek to redefine their strengths against new forms of domination, and if they aspire to live in dignity, they know they cannot do so in an unjust society. Consequently, personal freedom and collective equality may constitute a common good. Each reinforces the other.

The idea of dignity is linked to the inter-subjective construction of the coexistence with equals. This statement is associated with the sociological thesis that different identities and orientations of actors are constructed in relationship to others. Thus, equality and difference are equivalent and both are associated with common good. In more current terms this would be associated with new experiences of local or municipal management, with the growing importance of horizontal communication technologies, and with the demands of new actors for dignity as the center of their concerns.

The idea of dignity is also closely related with the prevailing conflicts in the network society. Social networks have become spaces for communication and conflicts: discrimination and also the search for democratic recognition are present and dynamically interacting. Expressions of racism and cultural discrimination, but also demands for participation, emancipation, and dignity can easily be found on a social network. At the same time, people experience a constant tension when they participate in social networks. On one hand, there's a loss of intimacy and privacy; on the other, there are numerous opportunities for fructiferous interaction with peers and people with the most varied backgrounds. Even if private spaces are permeated by political, commercial, or institutional powers trying to impose their visions, social networks promote knowledge and free exchange of ideas and allow for the transformation of demands into real changes at the core of the same social networks.

From the point of view of democracy, the articulation of different subjectivities and cultures in a community of citizens is at the center stage. This is precisely why the expansion of citizenship is an important guarantee of equality. It is the subject of equality. Citizenship and equality are inseparable; they need to be renewed permanently, and are by definition incomplete.

The new cultural rights associated with the expansion of individual and collective subjectivities (of religion, ethnicity, gender, sexuality, migration, and ecology, among others), that redefine our societies as essentially multicultural, need to be integrated with social and political rights in order to become democratic. It is very difficult to expand subjectivities and cultural freedoms without the development of social citizenship—without the development of a dignity and a basic welfare of people. To enable people to develop their skills and subjectivity in order to choose as they please, the consolidation of basic conditions for a decent life is fundamental.

But it is also impossible to think about the expansion of social citizenship and recognition of the new cultural rights without a full recognition of the political status of each individual citizen. Precisely for this reason, building a community of citizens is the area of recognition of the expansion of new subjectivities. In a community of citizens, which is also increasingly global, the different specificities of each subjectivity are redefined in terms of the common conditions of citizenship. Inclusion policies in turn are legitimized by citizen participation in democratic life. The community of citizens is therefore an inclusive political unit, which is expressed in the construction of a public good that, on one hand, integrates the diversity and pluralism, but, on the other, gives to all these diversities one common status: citizenship, with rights and responsibilities. Thus, it is understood that all persons, regardless of their subjectivities, are considered citizens.

It seems essential to recognize that there are tensions and contradictions between the expansion of subjective particularities and the common universal element; the citizen. An international public sphere that guarantees unity by transcending the diverse subjectivities also influences the state. Hence, in democracy this integration between citizens and politics is linked to the political community of citizens. Political citizenship is the universal reference of the subjective pluralism of our societies. The same social and cultural movements seek recognition of their new rights of participation, distribution, and recognition, but their democratic realization is precisely associated with the political community of citizens. Today there is a curious social construction that links the national state and more open and internationalized public spaces with the demands and citizenship practices fully linking the local and the global.

Human dignity and human rights

As Habermas (2010) has insisted, human dignity is one and indivisible, as is every human being in particular. Only a policy that seeks substantive progress and cooperation at various levels of human rights and the various citizenships can aspire to respect equally the dignity of each person. This implies solidarity and cooperation between different individuals, and the assumption of common values.

In this sense, human rights lie at the core of a community of citizens so that it can demand respect for human dignity. However, this is insufficient if it is not associated with development, which involves actors and agencies of human development that promote a policy and economy based on people. This is why human development and human rights are complementary.

According to Sen, human development and human rights share a common motivation and can complement each other. "The first steps to appreciate that assessment of human development, if combined with human rights perspective, can indicate the duties of others in the society to enhance human development in one way or another. And with invoking of duties comes a host of related concerns such as accountability, culpability and responsibility" (Sen 2003a: 50 in Fakuda et al.).[19]

Here it is argued that human dignity is connected with rights and ethics and with the kind of economic development that makes these possible. And this is what is at stake in the global crisis. The current options seem insufficient and outdated.

The institutionalization of human rights and human development must be concurrent. The question is to know, in any particular case, what are the actors of the historicity and the emerging field of conflict.

The actor can be a provider of legal recognition (self-continent) that is self-determined: they live, feel, think, and act in relation to their own judgment (Habermas 2010: 12). In this sense the actor can transform their needs into actions operating in specific institutional fields. Dignity is a status of self-respect and respect for others and can be consolidated only with economic development that seeks social inclusion and participation. Only with better development patterns is it possible to achieve a sustainable and innovative human dignity.

Human rights are associated with a national community, and are connected with an increasingly global demand. The global overflows the national and hastens the universalization of human rights. This means the search for a new social global institutionalized order and a pattern of human development to support it. Nowadays social conflicts have pervaded as both national and global in scale, and in different levels and dimensions as social and economic violence and the lack of freedom and human capabilities.

---

[19] Sen, Amartya. (2003b). "Human Rights and Human Development," in S. Fakuda-Parr and A.K. Shiva Kumar (eds.), *Readings in Human Development*, Oxford: Oxford University Press. On a similar note, the 2000 Human Development Report argues in favor of a strong connection between human development and human rights. This report states that both approaches share a fundamental commitment to the promotion of liberty and dignity for all. At stake lies the redefinition of the latter notions in a context of crisis and changes provoked by the rising of the network society.

Fernando Calderón

The network as a public space

Currently, the movements that demand greater dignity and recognition of human rights are associated with the processes of transformation of new communication technologies and the network society. Today, the dynamics of the new conflicts and socio-cultural movements are expressed and developed in the information societies and seek to transform power relations both inside and outside the network. This is probably the most significant challenge of these new subjectivities, simply because the network is the new place to express and develop new forms of power. The network is thus, among other things, the sense of action of new 'alter-globalization' movements, leading to new forms of sociability and socialization, and as a result, to the reconstruction of the options of human development.

The patterns of socialization of new generations are different today than in the past. The relationship between education and employment is more complex and difficult. There have been mutations and ruptures of the monopoly of traditional schools, through homeschooling and new information and communication technologies, as well as new cultural subjectivities.

Conflicts are now increasingly related to the sociocultural uses of these new information and communication technologies. The new forms of sociability are paradoxical, because they are open to the world of the network but have the greatest impact among groups and restricted spaces—at least for now.

The new culture of technological sociability can change both subjectivity and the patterns of knowledge and everyday life of individuals and communities. However, this is not done in a void, but in the context of experiences of concrete historical social relations. This new subjectivity is now the new force of change.

In this sense, in a dignified society, to develop their skills and capabilities in the global world of techno-economics of information and social networks, human development policies need to reduce informational gaps and promote information capabilities and education that handles informational change codes and thus ensures a more equitable access to global networks of information and communication technology. This is a condition in which people, as autonomous actors, can reproduce their dignity and fight for it, or otherwise run the risk of being excluded and isolated.

These codes represent the management of skills and abilities to communicate on the network: adaptability, flexibility, horizontality, networking, innovation, articulation, multiplication, and exchanges—all of them requirements for proactive action in the information society as the main guarantee for building a dignified society.[20]

Our thesis argues that a new type of informational human development, meaning human development linked to the new technological intercommunication possibilities of handling personal and social relations and participation would be the best resource on which societies and individuals can count to deal with new forms of power and domination associated with changes in globalization and emerging maps of power.

A critical choice: dignity as real freedom

The main difference between schools of economic growth and human development is that the first is concerned about the expansion of income—measured by the Gross Domestic Product (GDP)—while human development focuses on the expansion of all the choices of individuals, whether economic, social, cultural, or political. While higher incomes can generate greater options, the relationship is not automatic. In particular, income may be unequally distributed in a society, so that low-income people will be severely restricted in their opportunities. But the fundamental reason why income growth may not translate into more options of human development is in the priorities identified by the society.

Hence, it is useful to compare the main emphasis of development perspectives as outlined in Table 9.1:

The human development perspective we are proposing analyzes the alleged automatic link between income growth and the over-sizing of the market. This link depends on the quality and distribution of economic growth and may be created through public policies such as social services expenditure and redistributive tax policy. But this also questions the over-valuation of the masses, the weakness of self-determination of people, and the overvaluation of the state, nation, or people, though not as an unknown historical force.

---

[20] According to CEPAL (1992), education and knowledge are of strategic relevance to achieve a productive transformation that also increases equity. Such a transformation requires a common platform as well as the extended use of "modernity codes," that is the management of basic abstractions, of the elemental arithmetic operations, and adequate reading comprehension.

Fernando Calderón

Table 9.1 Comparison between different emphases

	State	Market	Person
Main objective	Economic development	Maximization of revenue and profit	Expansion of capacities and opportunities for people to achieve total wellbeing
Primary concern	State	Markets	Human dignity
Principle that guides the actions	Participation of the masses	Efficiency	Autonomy, equity, freedom, and citizenship
Emphasis	Aims to achieve objectives	Means to achieve objectives	Purposes to achieve objectives
Cultural identity	National popular identity	Consumption culture	Interculturalism
Aims of education, health, and nutrition	Means to modernize the state and society	Input for growth: investment in human capital contributes to growth	They are ends in themselves; access to them is a human right
Features / objectives of the government	Strong leadership National integration	The state should only promote the role of markets Respect for human rights associated with the market, e.g. property rights Economic stability	Democracy The state is essential in order to promote human development Respect for human rights and dignity
Economic growth	Determinant way of internal growth	An end in itself The benefit of society is subordinated to the objective of growth	Essential, but only if it benefits individuals equally It is a means of human development

Policies' main guidelines	Modernization of society through education	Deregulation and privatization Efficiency improvements	Expansion of the capacity of the agency of actors and institutions
	National integration and industrialization through import substitution	Investment in human capital Macroeconomic stability	The dignity and citizenship as the axis of development Reducing inequalities
	Mass mobilization		Restructuring of national budgets, regional and local human development Promoting employment
Strategies to eradicate poverty	Universal social policies	Spillover effect of growth Investment in social sectors	Strengthening of the poor as social actors Equal participation in society
	Employment Welfare state	Social protection networks	Access to goods and services
	Distribution of wealth and income	Targeting and improving social indicators, especially education	Benefits of growth given to the poor
Leading indicators	Improvement of social indicators, mainly education	GDP GDP growth rate Development index relating to gender	Human Development Index
		Inflation rate Debt/GDP	Multidimensional poverty index

Source: prepared by the author

To accomplish this, in addition to carrying out important political and economic reforms, the focus of attention should first concentrate on personal dignity. Second, it should be noted that human development has two aspects: i) the formation of human capabilities (health, knowledge, and skills), and ii) the use that people give to their capacities (employment, productive activities, or leisure). Societies must build human capacities and ensure equitable access to livelihood options. Third, it should make a careful distinction between means and goals: people are the goal and GDP growth is the essential way to expand the options. But the nature and distribution of economic growth should be measured in terms of how to enrich the lives of individuals. Fourth, human development covers the entire society, not just the economy: political, social, ecological, and cultural aspects receive as much attention as the economic ones (ul Haq 1995).

Democracy is associated with the issue of dignity in several ways: i) political participation is an integral part of life in society—the role of a citizen of a country or of humanity is always present; ii) democracy is a good area to discuss claims and demands, in determining the relative importance of various skills (including cultural liberty)—the participatory discussion should play a central role, in the pursuit of achievements of development; and iii) even if democracy is seen as an essentially Western concept, the history of religions and cultures that are not directly Western is full of securities referring to human dignity, tolerance, and reciprocity, and is much older and extensive.

The world today is prosperous and miserable at the same time. The severity of the divisions and exclusions threatens the existence of a sense of human identity.

As mentioned before, the critique against exclusion related to globalization is reflected in the movements of the "indignant" in Spain, and in the fighters for human rights and peace everywhere; movements that challenge a globalization that only concentrates power, and seek an alter-globalization based on the most emancipatory goals (Wieviorka 2008). While these movements argue for new globalizations, both are global phenomena as to their concerns and their members. The activists are from all over the world and come together to oppose what they perceive as serious global injustices. Anti- and alter-globalization movements are probably the most globalized moral movements today. It is essential to analyze the center of their protests, which does not refer to globalization itself, but to human inequality.

Consequently, the crucial question is related to the distribution of the potential benefits of globalization between rich and poor countries and between different groups in society.[21] Under the assumption that there are gains from cooperation between countries, it is important to ask whether the distribution of benefits is fair, and not simply if there are gains. In this regard, the domestic economic policies of rich and poor countries should be performed and reformed, and guided toward a more equitable international division of the benefits of globalization. Again, "the real issue is the distribution of the benefits of globalization" (Sen and Klisberg 2007: 21).

One conclusion in different reports is that for culturally diverse societies, with structural heterogeneity, development, and democracy, to be sustainable there must be a commitment to conflict management in a deliberated way. So, conflict management is required to move forward in a culture of deliberation. Through these deliberative spaces, it is possible to create pragmatic arrangements that promote human development. Society, in order to develop itself, needs to combine a pragmatic, pluralistic, and participatory approach (UNDP 2002; UNDP-Bolivia 2002; UNDP-Chile 1998; UNDP-Bulgaria 1998; UNDP-Sao Tome and Príncipe 2004; UNDP-Egypt 2002).

Finally, all of these ideas refer to the potential of social actors with possibilities of self-determination, with representative capacity of interests and demands, and with development orientations; actors that have the capacity to mobilize cultural diversity, based on a common development that requires consensus and commitment. It is difficult to think about a change of management without a covenant. This is precisely why a process of political renewal is essential for democracy. It comes to generate the political conditions for a new pattern of development that rests on the capacity and potentialities for action of societies; a development model based on the constructive power of politics.

---

[21] An analysis of long-term trends in world income distribution between countries shows that the distance between the richest and poorest country was about 3 to 1 in 1820, 11 to 1 in 1913, 35 to 1 in 1950, 44 to 1 in 1973, and 72 to 1 in 1992. What is more amazing is that the British in 1820 had an income of about six times that of the Ethiopians in 1992. Japan, for example, had scarcely 20% of US income in 1950, but 90% in 1992. Southern Europe has seen a similar trend—with 26% of US income in 1950 and 53% in 1992. Some Arab states have also seen big increases in income. The assets of the three richest people are more than the combined GNP of all of the least-developed countries. The assets of the 200 richest people are more than the combined income of 47% of the world's people. A yearly contribution of 1% of the wealth of the 200 richest people could provide universal access to primary education for all ($7–8 billion) (UNDP 1999).

Fernando Calderón

Strategic topics

The necessary renewal of the human development perspective both reaffirms the fundamental features that organize its theory and its historical adaptation, and at the same time introduces in its analysis and proposals emerging issues and current events, especially those related to social and cultural demands. Among the strategic issues that we desire to highlight and explore in this chapter are those of informationalism, environment, the patterns of social inclusion and exclusion, and new patterns of social conflict.

Informationalism

Related to informationalism,[22] Castells (1997) analyzes how the international economy has been globalized through the transformation of production, organizational, cultural, and institutional systems, based on a technological revolution supported by the creation of new forms of information and communication. With this, the world has been articulated as a unit in real time and this has changed all areas of human activity. This new dynamic is developed from networks of exchange and communication flows that include everything that increases its value and excludes everything that ceases to have value, and so the markets and profitability are transformed into the criteria that determine those who are excluded from or included into the global networks.

The frequency of technology in households can be seen to be increasing (see Figure 9.1). In the context of this informational dynamic, multicultural identities are expanding in complex ways as core principles of social organization and political action. Also, new individual identities "self-constructed" around personal projects are developing.

Policies and reflections of human development are important but limited, facing significant changes at a global scale. For example, the Human Development Report (HDR) 2001 focuses on the impact that technological advances are going to have in underdeveloped and poor countries. The

---

[22] "Informationalism: productivity, competitiveness, efficiency, communication and power from the technological capacity to process information and generate knowledge" (Castells 1997:19).

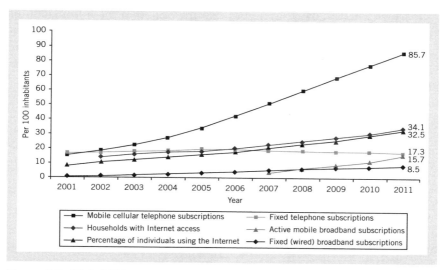

Figure 9.1 Global ICT development 2001–11

Source: ITU World Telecommunication/ICT Indicators database.

report argued that without appropriate public policies, such progress could be a source of social exclusion, rather than a tool for progress. In order for human development to have the support of new technologies, it is necessary to consider that: i) the technological divide should not follow the pattern of the division of income, since technology has been a fundamental tool in the progress of human development; ii) markets do not have enough power to create and diffuse the technology required to eradicate poverty; iii) developing countries face serious challenges in the management of the risks associated with new technologies; iv) the technological revolution and globalization are creating an age of networks, which is changing the way that technology is created and diffused; v) all countries, including the poorest, must implement policies that promote technological innovation; and vi) international initiatives and fairer global rules are required to create technological advances for the most urgent needs of the poor (UNDP 2001).

These ideas are important but insufficient. The challenges of global change require an intellectual renewal able to associate human development with informational innovation and multicultural democratic politics, and also with the needs of the network society theory.

In sum, Castells (2012: 22) argues that the notion of the information or knowledge society is simply a technological extrapolation of the industrial society, usually assimilated to the Western culture of modernization. The concept of the network society shifts the emphasis to organizational transformation, and to the emergence of a globally interdependent social structure, with its processes of domination and counter-domination. It also helps to define the terms of the fundamental dilemma of our world: the dominance of the programs of a global network of power without social control or, instead, the emergence of a network of interacting cultures, unified by the common belief in the use value of sharing.

Furthermore, human development and informational development can complement each other. Since informational development fosters competitiveness and knowledge, it has a positive effect on human development. At the same time, the promotion of competitiveness demands high levels of human development, particularly in terms of education. Both informational development and competitiveness rely on individuals' and society's capabilities. In the human development approach we are proposing, competitiveness and equity are mutually enhancing. The approach also entails societies and actors actively furthering interactions between competitiveness and human development. In fact, for political strategies to be sustainable in the long term they will have to simultaneously tackle human development and informational development.

A renewed perspective of human development needs to understand the new maps and concepts that account for the connections between the processes of change in the network society, and multiculturalism and the state.

The environment

Human development is linked to environmental degradation and to the emergence of climate change. Those themes present a particular and universal challenge at the same time, due to the need for renewal of the human development approach. The HDR 2011 emphasizes a sort of paradox between progress in human development, particularly in countries with higher rates of such development, and its enormous impact on environmental degradation. It's simple: with variations, more development means more

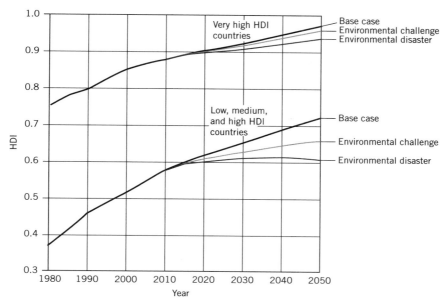

Figure 9.2 Environment and inequality threats to human development
Source: HDR 2011.

pollution; thus revealing the unsustainability of current patterns of economic growth in the medium and long term.[23] The unsustainability is obvious to everyone in the long term, but the most shocking results would be among the countries with the lowest levels of human development (UNDP 2011; UNDP 2007/8).

The HDR 2007/8 estimated that if all the inhabitants of the earth generated the same amount of greenhouse gases as some developed countries, nine planets would be needed (UNDP 2007/8: 3). According to UNDP (2011), there is a positive correlation between equity and sustainable development; thus, the greater the global equity, the greater the environmental sustainability. And equity is associated not only with welfare improvements, but

---

[23] The average inhabitant of a country with the highest human development index emits four times more carbon dioxide and twice as much methane and nitrous oxide than the people who live in countries with low, medium, and high indexes, and about 30 times the emissions of a person from a country with a low human development index (UNDP 2011: 3).

with the empowerment of development actors and the pursuit of personal dignity. The political question that should be posed is what is possible in today's circumstances. We present some reflections on such a topic:

1. The need to diversify the patterns of development according to goals and inter-cultural values related to democratic communities of citizens, stressing personal and collective dignity as a central value. That implies changing lifestyles and consumption patterns, and establishing a way of life re-integrated with nature.
2. A global public debate as a key resource for the achievement of such goals. Deliberation and dialogue per se are valuable not only in solving problems and developing goals, but also in evaluating results and participating in the construction process of results.
3. The management of this complex ecological policy must be flexible, but with clear goals, combining sustainability, equity, and productivity (Hirschman 1996).
4. The role of education and cultural knowledge is strategic in the proposal of an ecologic framework linked with a renewed focus on development. Such a framework is present in the intellectual field and in the new movements for dignity, especially among young people (UNDP 2009; Patel 2010).

All of the above criteria might be associated with the strengthening of the agency capacities of ecological movements, and with an increased legitimacy of international public opinion favorable to an ecologically sustainable development.

Social exclusion and inclusion

Social exclusion is understood as the lack of basic rights and the consequent deterioration of human dignity. The full enjoyment of those rights is a prerequisite for a society to be considered worthy. This perspective includes four issues: i) participatory limitations and societal disrespect indicate the absence of basic rights; ii) there is no emphasis on the results of the exercise of basic rights, but on equality in terms of freedoms in order to enjoy these rights; iii) a recognition that people have various capacities to exploit the opportunities available; and iv) the emphasis is placed on the goals, not on the means (so, for example, revenues are seen as one of the many ways that can contribute to social inclusion) (Klasen 1999).

In the approach we propose here, besides being a basic right, work gives social recognition; it is the core around the social dignity associated with an inclusive value system: those who are employed are members of a social and cultural community and are recognized as full citizens. Thus, as Sen (2000) argues, the adverse effects of the loss of employment are not just a lack of income but a consequence in terms of the loss of skills, the breakdown of social bonds, and the decreasing of individual freedoms. Work generates identity, reinforces dignity, and elevates agencies' capabilities for social action.

In Latin America, for example, inequality and social exclusion are the most important negative effects of structural reforms associated with heterogeneous experiences of globalization (UNDP 2004a; Calderón 2007b). As a general trend, the economic dynamics of recent decades were exclusive: many of the young people have been excluded or included unfavorably (Kostzer 2008). While in recent years the situation has improved, especially because of the reduction of poverty, Latin America remains the most unequal region in the world (ECLAC 2010). The great majority of people in different countries are located between exclusion and unfavorable inclusion.

To face the challenges that involve this complex reality of the dynamics between exclusion and inclusion, we need a change of perspective. The HDR 1993 (UNDP 1993) showed that the dynamics of exclusion from the labor market were directly related to the dynamics of economic competitiveness and these were some of the main limits to development.

The human development approach emphasizes the need for a concerted effort between the state and the market, and suggests some parameters that should govern the relationship between the state, the public, and the market. This requires a reflection regarding the role of the state and the markets in terms of people's development. Markets are essential for the exchange of goods and services. However, are they completely free and capable of promoting social inclusion for everyone? What kind of influence do they have on development and income distribution? As shown in the HDR 1993, markets do have barriers and they are neither automatically nor inevitably favorable for the people.[24] Thus, even if they are operating efficiently,

---

[24] UNDP. (1993). *Human Development 1993, People's Participation*. New York: Oxford University Press.

markets can provoke an increase of poverty, inequality, and unemployment. They can also neglect environmental sustainability and intergenerational concerns. The human development approach not only needs efficient markets, but also markets that take into account equity and sustainability. In that regard, we argue that ethics and politics via social actors—individually and collectively—seek to influence markets in order for them to incorporate the human development paradigm.[25]

Meanwhile, the state—and especially the welfare state—has been a significant participant in many historical processes, promoting social integration and providing institutional guarantees for public life. However, its actions are frequently hindered by inefficient bureaucracies and dominant economic interests. Only a complex, critical, and autonomous citizenship can impose limits on the state's tendency to concentrate power or reorient markets toward a more inclusive framework. In this regard, development models focused solely on the state or markets are insufficient in terms of human development.

If human development is not associated with innovation and the creation of a state of the public in terms of the welfare of society, the limitations are obvious.

For Sen, exclusion must be understood within the broader context of social relations and poverty, understood in terms of deprivation of capabilities. Similarly, poverty cannot be considered only as a lack of income but as "impoverished life;" that is from a relational perspective that takes into account the multiple dimensions of poverty and exclusion. Under this approach, people not only appreciate and need income, but also aspire to not be excluded from social relations. Hence, in this approach, social exclusion integrates the poverty of capabilities (Sen 2000). If exclusion is part of poverty then it becomes central to participation in social life and interaction with others. The impossibility of participation constitutes a privation itself. The exclusion also can be seen from a cultural and political perspective as the impossibility of or the limits to choosing a way of life (UNDP 2004b).

At the same time, being excluded from social relations can lead to other economic privations, further limiting opportunities for people. For example,

---

[25] The HDR 1993 argues that markets should be favorable to the public. Thus, three market failures should be regulated: i) market failures provoked by monopolies, pricing controls, and inefficient state intervention; ii) disparities among people participating in the markets, due to racial exclusion or insufficient capacities; and iii) externalities such as pollution or communicable diseases prevention (UNDP).

unemployment may generate impoverishment in economic terms, which in turn can generate deprivation—for example, by restricting access to knowledge, thus establishing a sort of vicious circle in which one type of exclusion leads to another. In sum, the various types of exclusion (economic, social, educational, cultural, labor, etc.) feed back frequently and lead to the exclusion of the possibility of living a life of dignity and full citizenship.

It is necessary to consider the dynamism that the exclusion acquires in a rapidly changing world. The processes of globalization, informationalism, and network communication permanently incorporate new groups to economic interaction, in a social and cultural setting, aside others. In this sense, globalization presents both risks and opportunities, though the opportunities can only be accessed by those who are not excluded (Sen 2000). The processes of globalization should be thought of in terms of human development.

In this context, crisis, uncertainty, and risk are data from the new conditions of development in globalization. Nobody is totally free from exclusion. Even those who participate in the formal economy and politics maintain dependent relationships and uncertainty given the fluctuations of the economy. This situation strongly affects agency capabilities of individuals and social actors. Today there is no guarantee of equity or social mobility, because the world is experiencing a greater risk due to the global scope of the economic crisis. Thus, the dynamics between inclusion and exclusion are embedded in a context of constant change, risk, and uncertainty; problems that a development approach has to face.

Added to this is the "unfavorable inclusion" in developed economies, because of the high risk of leading to exclusion. For example, demands for better or fairer conditions of employment or a more egalitarian social participation are linked to an unfavorable situation of inclusion, not of exclusion. However, it should be clear that unfavorable inclusion and exclusion are not the same problem; for example, a person who is included unfavorably by unfair labor conditions under which work may be excluded in other aspects of social life.[26]

We argue that both the benefits and costs of globalization and global crisis are currently at stake. In this regard, not only the allocation of costs and resources, but also the political orientation of development policies and crisis

---

[26] For further reference see the Statistical Annex: a Multidimensional Poverty Index, which shows the importance of social exclusion in global development, and Sen, A. "Temas Claves Del Siglo XXI," pp. 28–30.

impact on the balance of power.[27] The notion of unfavorable inclusion reflects the ambivalence of the most relevant social outcomes of the global crisis. On one hand, austerity plans implemented in the European Union, and to a lesser extent in the United States, have inflicted significant costs on their citizens. On the other hand, expansive policies carried out in emerging economies, such as Latin America, and especially Brazil, have helped to lift more than 60 million people out of poverty. In both situations the evolution toward active inclusion requires consensual policies that promote development and equity, with emphasis on excluded or semi-excluded portions of the population. Additionally, policies should combine—as alter-globalization movements have long demanded—global and local issues. The Tobin tax, in this regard, constitutes a promising example of renewed and more ambitious Millennium Development Goals.[28] In sum, even with different "historical floors," developed economies should implement policies oriented toward reversing the negative trends in terms of social degradation, while emerging economies should focus on sustaining and expanding their recent accomplishments. This context is contributing to the redefinition of countries' relations and interdependence.

It is important to analyze the relationship between socio-economic exclusion and political-cultural exclusion. The progress made by economies of Southeast Asia, whose success is often presented as an example to emulate in Latin America, is related to the ability of their governments to avoid exclusion in the field of education and basic social opportunities, although in the political field the inclusion has been limited, which is the most serious problem of human development in these countries.

Social conflicts

Current social conflicts are in the center of the strategic topics and are being fully redefined by the impacts of globalization. Even more, they are mainly the results of a distributive conflict associated with the impacts of globalization. Social conflict is redefined by the current global crisis in its various dimensions, and especially by the social consequences of certain economic policies that help global or regional financial capital. Today we are

[27] For further details see Beck's (2013) analysis of the Euro crisis and the German model.
[28] See 2003 Human Development Report.

experiencing a change in the global political system of decision-making and this affects the various matrices of emerging social order. We live in a multi-polar world, with emerging economies like China, Russia, South Africa, India, and Brazil. The multi-cultural crisis and the limitations of an inter-cultural coexistence acquire many forms in Europe and the US, especially between the West and the Arab-Muslim world. Ultimately, it redefines the ecological crisis and the serious difficulties on the part of central economies to achieve political agreements on climate change impacts.

All of these crises, changes, and conflicts tend to have systemic and global effects. In Latin America, for example, a recent study concluded that there not only exists the maintenance of extensive and intense conflicts over social reproduction and inclusion, institutional legitimacy, and multicultural order, but also conflicts combining a national logic against states and international powers with another based on the global as a function of an anti- or alter-globalization. Also, most of the power agendas, policy options, and conflict narratives are built into a new increasingly interactive and technological public space of communication networks (C. Rojas 2011).

Several studies have shown that the different demands and social conflicts in this time of crisis tend to multiply and become fragmented. They are the result of changes in the process of globalization, and politics and classical development options have not been able to process and manage demands quickly in the people's everyday lives.

Overall, the changes appear to be related to the limits of a cultural pattern of consumption associated with a reification of the market as the core of social life: a structural limit of the reproduction of environment to an accelerated social differentiation with high levels of concentration of income, resources, and economic power; and ultimately to a social polycentrism that has an enormous capacity to be governed by the current political options.

Today the logic of conflict and social action is expressed in a plurality of actors, many of them circumstantial, that tend to move toward information and communication networks. Thus the social networks are becoming places where people can express and develop relations of conflict and power and not only of the information and knowledge societies but also of industrial and pre-capitalist societies and economies.

In one study of recent conflicts and movements in the network centered on the demands of dignity and change, Castells has characterized the move-ments as being connected and decentralized in networks in numerous and flexible ways; as building autonomous spaces that link the network with public space; as being local and global at the same time; as combining the search for new ways of life with the use of a "timeless time;" as being intercommunicative between different parts of the global network; as articulating the role of political deliberation between indignation and the demand for a new type of society and politics; as the search for unity and solidarity; as indicative of human beings' self-reflective nature and their search for societal values that indeed can have an effect on public opinion with consequences for the regimen and the political system. Ultimately what would be at stake is the possibility of autonomy from the subject and a new development pattern (Castells 2012). In general, reports and human development theory have given little room to the strategic role of conflicts in development. Rather, it is at the sub-regional or national level where the issue of conflict has emerged as one of the main factors of development. The social agency theory only implicitly assumes the tremendous power that conflicts have in the viability of development and change strategies.

The definition of human development in accordance with a new era is still a pending task. In the center of such changes are located the problems of exclusion and options for a renewed agency of development.

Toward a human development actors agency

From an agency perspective of human development actors, the central issue is the possibility that the excluded can transform their needs into demands and actions, and interact with society and in institutional spheres.[29] In this respect, the improvement of living conditions and the political integration of the excluded are democratic issues in relation to the state and all aspects and strategic issues listed.

For this reason, it is of great importance to promote inclusion and justice agency. The human development perspective raises the need to link exclusion and inclusion through the notions of dignity and equal rights. These notions can be linked directly to the exercise of active citizenship (Calderón 2007a).

Exclusion of political participation can be regarded as a privation and denial of political freedoms and civil rights. As a counterpart, political inclusion creates opportunities for the remaining areas to advance. However, citizenship has acquired a different dynamic from what it has been in classic and dependent societies. Citizenship has to face the transitions and conflicts

---

[29] For more explanation see UNDP (2009), Chapter 1.

in increasingly polycentric and changing societies (C. Rojas 2011). This produces an explosion of new needs and rights, related to a wider field than the classics of political or social citizenship: the right to education needs to link up with the right to work and redefine social citizenship as well. Gender rights, sexual minorities, cultural identity, environmental issues, and access to the information society, among others, are able to redefine the action in new areas.

The concept of citizenship agency can be an interesting resource to address these issues. This agency has the power to mobilize citizen capacities, in order to modify a particular context to promote more equal situations in the access to property and services and freedom of choice that will result in greater social inclusion.

A citizenship agency could generate, through structural conditions and specific policies, greater inclusion and social equality. Moreover, this type of agency could promote the renewal and sustainability of human development.

From this perspective, we are talking about a development in which the notion of the human being as an actor prevails; a force open to creative action, possessed of a will and capacity to transform the development in terms of their relationship with others, themselves, and their environment. It is a new type of coexistence: being part of—ultimately—a community of citizens.[30]

In other words, by increasing the degree of cultural inclusion, there are conditions for greater agency. If it decreases, the agency will be harder to apply. The decreased or unfavorable inclusion would produce a limited capacity of action or agency. In sum, agency and inclusion can shape the virtuous circle of development. This implies the presence of political mediation, since only politics can enhance a fruitful interaction between social inclusion and citizenship agency. The agency also assumes the presence of certain basic economic conditions. It is also possible that citizens are looking to articulate the recognition of identities and political, economic, and social rights of participation in the decision-making process. The more equalized and synergistic the balance between recognition, distribution, and participation, the greater the capacity for agency and human dignity. By contrast, the lower the level of balance and synergy, the lower the capacity of agency and the higher the exclusion.

---

[30] For a comparative and theoretical perspective on human development, see UNDP (2008), *Ciudadanía y desarrollo humano. Cuaderno I de gobernabilidad democrática*. Buenos Aires, Siglo XXI, and UNDP (2004b).

Then, each social context will show different situations and relationships that will result in different balances, even within the same community or social conglomerate. The determination of what is important in a citizenship agency is necessary to identify the desired level of articulation between recognition, distribution, and participation.

It is worth noting that there isn't a preordained hierarchy for the articulation between recognition, distribution, and participation. In fact, such articulation varies according to specific historical processes.[31] An agency index calculated for four cities of MERCOSUR—Asunción, Buenos Aires, Montevideo, and Rio de Janeiro—identified not only the strength of citizenship agency and the significant role of women, but also differences among the younger generations in terms of the relevance attributed to distribution and participation.[32]

If exclusion and quality of everyday life constitute the main challenges for human development, the articulation and translation of a rights recognition agency, and the distribution and participation necessary to confront these challenges mean that actors can transform their needs into demands and into actions that modify their reality. That is, they become actors in their own emancipation. But it also involves some subjective disposition toward an emancipatory development that allows articulate tradition with innovation and individualization with collective development. In this area, a renewed role of public space as a meeting place and cultural exchange is vital for the development of acceptable societies.

The construction of such agency capacity is directly related to the ability of an actor to combine their goals (guided by values) with their identities and problems or conflicts involved in achieving those goals. In particular, the study of the actor determines at least four areas of development:

- First, every actor seeks certain types of orientation, and from some of these orientations lives a participatory experience. The levels and forms of an actor's participation determine the strength of their goals.
- Second, every actor has their own temporal horizon, defined mostly by their actions, from the system of exclusion-inclusion relations. Thus, even when the actors have their own historical continuity and their own

---

[31] For a discussion on culture, public action, and deliberation see Sen, A. "How Does Culture Matter?" and Calderón, F. and Szmukler, A. "Political Culture and Development" in Walton, M. and Rao, V. (2004).

[32] MERCOSUR Human Development Report 2008/2009 (UNDP).

experiences, turning points, crises, and conflicts define their orientation or main motive.

- Third, the actors show a heterogeneous evolution, based on their distinct identities, unequal levels of development in terms of information, conscience, organization, and personal finances, from their town or community.
- Fourth, it is important to consider the impact of actors on social relationships and society, not only because of isolated actions, but also because of an area of conflict in which the actors involved modify themselves in order to achieve a goal (Touraine 1984 and 2005).

The actor is primarily a citizen. Their development as a person is inseparable from human development. The construction of their real freedom and dignity is inseparable from the collective life of their society. Sen (1998) identifies the conditions required to be an agent and the relationship between agency, personal freedom, and collective commitments. Wellness freedom is a particular type of freedom and therefore is defined as a person's ability to achieve many things and enjoy the welfare.

This concept should be differentiated from the freedom of being an agent who alludes to what the person is free to do and pursues the goals or values they consider relevant. The actor facet of an individual cannot be understood without considering their objectives, purposes, and obligations, and their conception of the good. While the freedom of welfare is one that can achieve anything in particular, freedom of agency is more general: it is the freedom to get whatever the person, as a responsible actor, decides to get.

Freedom involves the recognition of constitutive plurality of modern societies. This idea of freedom comprises two distinct aspects: power and control. In the first aspect, the liberty of a person can be valued on the basis of their power to achieve selected results, without reference to mechanisms or control procedures. Power does not care how elections take place as long as it can get the desired results. The effective power allows the counterfactual election: things could be done according to the knowledge that one has about what the individual would choose if they truly had control over the outcome. Control, however, refers to the ability to monitor the processes and mechanisms used. In a democracy, it is the exercise of the rights and obligations of citizens. It involves, in addition, a culture of solidarity in the proceedings.

These ideas help one to understand how to build a collective option, respecting and conjugating with the self-determination of people. The capacity building of a citizenship agency requires a deliberative process, since the agency must be built in relation to others. It is impossible, even in the most absurd scenario of solitude, to think about an isolated action. Any individual or collective action either at the real or imaginary level involves the presence of others.

In this context, actor and agency constitute a sort of dialectic of human development. As an actor's agency increases, they can deploy more capabilities of self-determination and generation of life choices, according to their values and aspirations. But they can also, on a subjective level, develop a critical and reflective sense of their own action, thinking of themselves as an articulation between innovation and tradition on one hand, and between individuality and collectivity on the other.

The world is experiencing the process raised by the crisis of globalization. The critical issues that affect the daily lives of people and governments are generated in part by global processes that transcend national sovereignty (Beck 2006). Not everybody or everything is globalized, but global networks affect everyone and everything. The growing gap between the space of energy and exclusion that is generated by the financial issues (global) and the space in which these issues are handled (the nation-state) is a source of the current development crisis. The deficits of efficiency, legitimacy, identity, and equity, which affect the institutions of governability, now are reinforcing the need to build multilateral and global governance areas. The global crisis has some characteristics that on one hand affect current political and economic schemes but, on the other, create new possibilities for discussing development issues at a national and global level.

Those challenges have been frequently posed by social protestors, but also through the limitations faced by international cooperation and lending agencies like the World Bank, the International Monetary Fund, and the United Nations, as well as the United Nations Development Programme.

As a result of this crisis, civil society and non-governmental actors develop mechanisms that defend the interests, needs, and values of citizens, and affect the response of governments. Today there is a public sphere that operates in an international political arena which is not subject to any sovereign power, and is configured by the variable geometry of relationships between states and global actors (multinational corporations, religions, cultural creators, and intellectual and global cosmopolitans). Thus it forms a "global civil society." And precisely therein one can make sense of the collective experiences of international social deliberation.

One of the problems generated by globalization and political change is the complexity and transformation of economies and societies versus the limits of politics and national state institutions to process the changes. Societies are increasingly polycentric, and politicians find important difficulties in deciphering and governing them. There are new political scenarios, but not as yet the appropriate maps to navigate them.[33]

The changes occurring in the dimensions of the agency and its relationships—capacities achievements, orientations, development guidelines, and development fields—are oriented toward individualization without ignoring new collective demands and recognition of others who come, increasingly, from other cultures. Multiculturalism and individualization, along with the redefinition of collective goals that nowadays are more sociocultural and practical and not strictly political, are already part of the stock of the new agency that is observed everywhere. These changes in the agency, in the context of the culture of techno-sociability, are redefining solidarity and collective goals, but are also causing tensions between public and private, between individual and collective, between tradition and innovation. Moreover, discrepancies are noted between the personal construction of individualization and the construction of autonomous individuals on the part of society. The social itself is being redefined.

In public space, the possibilities of building a development agency would be related to the renewal of policy, the recognition of structural conditions, and the subjectivity and culture that come with these processes. It therefore requires a political agenda to strengthen capacities, especially for young people to understand and act on their own processes of change and, therefore, on their societies. The right to political action, understood as a collective good, is both a social and a common good. As stated by Rawls (1971), a social arrangement is only fair when, in comparison with other social arrangements, people who are in the most disadvantaged position in society get a better position. Here, the integrating capacity of politics refers to politics as a democratic power generator, in which the different agents, or actors, exchange arguments and proposals to build options. Thus, a policy of and for the actors should be responsible for the diversity of subjectivities and structural conditions. This requires one to account for the new "politicity:" more local and focused on everyday life, concerned about environmental and cultural issues, and tending toward social inclusion that integrates education and employment, and the individual with the collective.

Development of the capacity of agency would only be possible in the public sphere, understood as the meeting place between society and state,

---

[33] For more information see Calderón and Lechner (1998) and Lechner (2002).

where political ties are developed through public participation, and where the communication between different points of view affects the evolution of political institutions. Public space is not only an instrumental space of encounters, but also the cultural heritage of ideas and projects of a society that is constantly feeding public debate. The development of a democratic political culture is crucial as it allows accumulating experience and innovation in democratic development. In this sense, the virtues and republican values that connect the public sense with the common good constitute a guarantee of sustainability of democracy and human development.

Corollary: toward a pedagogy in order to renew the perspective

Renewing the perspective presupposes, above all, the maintenance and adaptation of the grounds for the changes and challenges of a multi-global crisis. This rest in promoting a sort of culture of human development pedagogy focuses on the renewal of the agency capacities of individual and collective actors to combine both local with global spaces, and historical areas with cultural and technological innovation, in a logic of results centered on values of dignity, and in subjective open horizons. This implies somehow maintaining and strengthening, on one hand, a reflection guided by practical values of results, if you will, and on the other, a theoretical reflection based on open norms of human development aimed at achieving dignity as a condition of human freedom.

Dignity and freedom are both substantive and procedural. Substantive, because they are open to various options regarding human actors, their abilities to handle codes and skills in societies of risk in constant change governed by informationalism and globalization and its capacities of action and reflection in conflictive relationships in a democratic order. Procedural, because they involve deliberative experiences to choose options and goals in terms of results and because they allow the optimization of particular interests associated with a public world. Deliberation between differences is the way of substantive creation of human development. The agreements that may emerge from it will be more successful because of the higher contributions of multiple actors. Deliberation is an optimal procedure for human development because it is legitimate and effective for combining personal and collective choices.

The pedagogy of human development is a new way of thinking about the environment. It is an "ecologized" way of thinking, where the actor is part of nature and its changes are not opposed to it. The actor neither dominates nature nor destroys it. Nature is an intrinsic part of a renewed human development. It is necessary to change the way of thinking on the relationship between man and nature, among other things. The goals of freedom and dignity cannot exclude the preservation of ecological balance. Recovering philosophical ideas about nature like the Andean's, that seek a fruitful harmony between nature and human beings, is also a pending intellectual task.

This new pedagogy implies a policy that seeks to confront subjectivities and cultures, the complexities of contemporary reality, and, from there, to redefine the goals of human development in a spirit of austerity and peace.

In conclusion, from the perspective of a renewed human development, the global crisis, beyond its various components and dimensions, evidences that the current economic and financial development options based on cultural patterns of consumption, extraordinary levels of concentrated wealth, cultural and social exclusion, poverty, environmental degradation, and weakened political and democratic institutions, at both national and global levels, are not sustainable in the long term nor a practical response to the crisis. The emergence of new conflicts and demands centered on subjectivities and dignity of individuals and communities, as new conditions and dynamics of the network society and the economics of information and communication technology, seem to evidence the need to renew a pattern of sustainable human development based on the quality of life for people, peace, cultural pluralism, and common good. This would be a new type of welfare society based on human dignity, where the subjects of development are people, and their communities expand and renew their capabilities of agency, creatively linking human development with informational development and multiculturalism.

Concluding remarks

We have argued that current demands and sociocultural protests provoked by the global crisis are deeply rooted in a revaluation of people's dignity and various multicultural groups. These demands for dignity and the uncertainty and negative impact of the global crisis require the reengineering of the human development approach, endowing it with the possibilities that informational development creates.

In this regard, our most relevant concluding remarks are:

First, the link between capabilities and freedoms should be redefined according to people's subjectivity and dignity. Human dignity overall has become an essential value, not only at the local or national levels, but as a desirable universal asset. People are the fundamental actors for this development approach.

Second, goals of the aforementioned approach are feasible, but not a given, due to the inherent risks and uncertainties of our current societies. In particular, key goals are the following: i) increasing the political agency of development actors; ii) strengthening informational capabilities to interact proficiently in social networks; and iii) embedding dignity and human rights demands with an inclusive and intercultural informational development. In our approach, dignity is both universal and indivisible.

Third, our approach, based on the recognition of people's agency, takes into account the role played by the numerous sociocultural conflicts, regardless of their origin—local, national, global, economic, or environmental. The consequential conflict and uncertainty constitute the main space where the likelihood of this human development approach to become part of a new "historicity field" is defined. In the latter field, the orientations of the network society as well as of the techno-economy are being disputed by three main options: state-centered, market-centered, and people-centered.

Fourth, our approach proposes a renewed association between markets, states, and societies, where common welfare is prized as a public good and as a guideline for both markets and states.

Finally, this renewed human development approach contends that the main obstacles for human development advancing people's dignity are the absence or shortcomings of real and cultural freedoms and the prevailing, if not growing, inequalities. In particular, there is a significant increase of unfavorable inclusion; poor people from emerging economies and also from some developing economies have become semi-included. Thus, it is vital to achieve a genuine association between innovation, sociocultural inclusion, and environmental sustainability.

In summary, we argue in favor of a renewed human development centered on sociocultural actors' agency, seeking to play a significant part in the information society, through the articulation of innovation, equity, real freedom, and environmental sustainability. We are not on a quest for an idyllic world; we are just acknowledging that a better society is indeed possible.

Chapter 10

Dignity as Development

Pekka Himanen

What is the goal of development?

In this final chapter, we must come back to the question that was raised at the very beginning of this book, and which has been present throughout: what is development in the Global Information Age?

Ultimately, one is forced to ask the following fundamental philosophical question: What is the ultimate goal of a sustainable development model? Or, to put it another way: What is the values frame of such development? Ultimately, this is the answer to the question: what really is "development"? So this last chapter looks at the key issue of this book finally from an ethical viewpoint and will complete it by making the philosophical argument for "dignity as development."

Second, as we have argued in this book, in our new Global Information Age the question about development has to be raised in relation to the new theoretical framework that best describes the conditions of development in this age. As always, everything here will be tightly tied with the social scientific analysis on development that we have made throughout this book. So, viewed from this perspective, this chapter completes the social scientific framework we presented, starting in Chapter 1, especially from the viewpoint of the cultural link in development.

Third, the question also has very significant practical importance. The question of the new goals of development is currently being debated extensively among both researchers and policymakers from the UN to individual countries and organizations such as the World Economic Forum. In June 2012, in the UN's Rio+20 meeting (United Nations Conference on Sustainable Development), the decision was reached to formulate new goals for sustainable development. Consequently, the UN has been working to define these new goals in a way that would go beyond the industrial era's GDP and HDI. These processes have indicated their openness to additional contributions that would go beyond their already very valuable status.

In fact, the greatest problem in this otherwise extremely valuable research and policymaking discussion is that often it ends by presenting an ad hoc type collection of aims and indicators, which lacks a systematic philosophical argument on the goal of development as well as a well-grounded social scientific framework on what the requirements of development are in the Global Information Age.

To underline the connections, the chapter proceeds in three parts: (1) It makes a philosophical argument on the ultimate goal of development, for "dignity as development," using the elements of the development theories of John Rawls, Amartya Sen, and Joseph Stiglitz, and taking a step forward from there. (2) Throughout this book, we have sought to root all theory directly in the best empirical data. So, therefore, in order to operationalize the concept of "dignity as development," its links to the main elements of the social scientific theoretical framework for the Global Information Age used in this book are explicated, emphasizing now the cultural link. (3) Finally, based directly on the grounds of these two first parts of the chapter, the concept of "dignity as development" is operationalized in a preliminary way that also gives it policy connectivity.

The philosophical argument: dignity as development

Industrial society was long dominated by economic growth as the goal of development. However, undefined economic growth alone is no longer a sufficient aim, for the simple reason that such a thing has become ecologically impossible and aside from the fact that its relation to the sustained increase in wellbeing is unclear (the same applies to GDP as an indicator of development, as activity that diminishes wellbeing and is ecologically destructive also counts as growth in GDP).

At the outset of this examination is the contention that the fundamental aim of sustainable development is the furthering of the requirements of a dignified life. Now it is appropriate to define exactly what that entails.

This examination has used especially the three most significant recent theories of the wider aims of development: the two most influential theories from the late twentieth century are Amartya Sen's *Development as Freedom* (1999) and John Rawls' *A Theory of Justice* (1971). At the beginning of the twenty-first century, a third significant approach has developed: wellbeing economics and psychology, whose principal exponents include Nobel Prize laureates Joseph Stiglitz and Daniel Kahneman.

Rawls: Justice as Fairness

Rawls' *A Theory of Justice* (1971) is perhaps the single most influential opus of political philosophy in the twentieth century, a work in which he presents his theory of "justice as fairness." In later works Rawls was to define certain aspects of the theory further (e.g. Rawls 2001; for the development of Rawls' thinking, cf. Freeman 2007 and Weithman 2011, and for interpretations on his theory, see the article collections by Daniels 1975, Kukathas 2003, and Richardson and Weithman 1999).

In this book, this theory has been used as an ethical argument for a renewed wellbeing society as a basis for sustainable wellbeing, by linking it to the concept of *justice*.

Rawls begins his presentation by asking the reader to imagine humans in the "original position," asking from behind the "veil of ignorance:" what is a just society like? The starting point here is that, in this original state, humans do not know which position in society they will come to inhabit. Based on this, they first reach a consensus that a just society is driven by a set of principles that everyone can feel are just, regardless of which societal position they themselves inhabit. From this initial consensus, Rawls extrapolates the two famous defining principles that drive a just society. The first of these is the Liberty Principle and the second is the Equality Principle.

According to the Liberty Principle, every person has an equal right to basic freedoms in a manner that is compatible with the same rights of other people. These freedoms include the freedom of religion, opinion, self-expression, and self-realization, and, for instance, the freedom to own private property.

The Equality Principle is concerned with the principle of fair equality of opportunity. In this context, fairness means that what is at stake is not only a formal principle of equal opportunity; rather, crucially, all people should in practice have fair equal opportunities to access things such as education, whereby they may more completely realize their full potential. From the Equality Principle it follows that everyone should in practice have fair and equal opportunities for wellbeing.

Based on these principles, people enter into a "social contract" regarding the establishment of a just society. In this light, Rawls' thought marks a continuation of the philosophical "social contract" tradition of Thomas Hobbes, John Locke, Jean-Jacques Rousseau, and Immanuel Kant, in which the contract was established in order to replace the survival struggle of a "natural state" (see Hobbes *Leviathan* [1651]; Locke *Second Treatise of Government* [1689]; Rousseau *Du contrat social* [1762]; Kant *Die Metaphysik der Sitten* [1797]).

Sen: Development as Freedom

Similarly, in the field of development philosophy the most influential analysis of the twentieth century is Amartya Sen's theory of "development as freedom" (e.g. Sen 1980, 1999; for later developments, see Sen 2009; for the continuation of Sen's line of thinking cf. e.g. Ul Haq 1999; Nussbaum 2000, 2006, and 2011; Alkire 2002).

According to Sen's famous "development as freedom" thesis, development means increasing freedom. In other words, development entails, for example, ever-greater levels of freedom from hunger, disease, lack of knowledge, and poverty as well as increased freedom for self-expression and self-realization.

In this book, Sen's theory has been applied to the goal of economic development: the ethical ground for economic development is increasing such *freedoms* of wellbeing.

In a philosophical sense, Sen marks the continuation of a liberalist tradition of Adam Smith and John Stuart Mill. From the perspective of the present examination, it is important to note that for Adam Smith, often referred to as the "father of capitalism," economy existed to serve primarily ethical objectives. The famous contention at the heart of Smith's *An Inquiry into the Nature and Causes of the Wealth of Nations* (1776)— namely that, in economy, focusing on the fostering of self-interest will also produce the best results with regard to overall interests, when such self-interest is conducted in competition within the free market—argues the ethical case for self-interest by linking it to the fostering of collective interest in the best possible way. This is the ethical argument for capitalism. Indeed, Smith was at least as much a moral philosopher as he was an economic theorist, and he considered *The Theory of Moral Sentiments* (1759) as his most significant work. The moral theory he expounds in this work contends that, when it is correctly understood, self-interest takes other people into account, because humans are creatures who experience joy at other people's joy and sorrow at other people's sorrow. As a pair of works, *The Wealth of Nations* and *The Theory of Moral Sentiments* reveal a broader vision in which the function of economy is to serve essentially ethical objectives.

Sen's most significant contribution is in linking the notion of freedom to the concept of capability, i.e. to the notion of "freedom as capability." Freedom is *capability*. Capabilities are freedoms in the sense of real opportunities. Here, capability encompasses both the levels of the external real opportunity and the inner capacity.

Sen stresses that freedom is a rather empty notion unless it is linked to real economic, social, and cultural capabilities. For instance, the freedom of self-realization is meaningless if such a freedom does not include a real opportunity of gaining access to education in order to more fully develop oneself. The most famous example of Sen relates to famines. In practice, most famines are not the result of a lack of food; rather, they arise because people lack genuine capability, i.e. they cannot in practice afford to buy food that nonetheless exists. As an example, Sen refers to the 1943 Bengal famine, a crisis of which he had personal experience, in which three million people died of starvation. No one's negative freedom was infringed (i.e. nobody was prevented from buying food), but people nonetheless died of hunger and malnutrition because they had no positive freedom or real opportunity to afford to buy food (Sen 1981).

Sen's approach gives further practical tools for moral choices. Instead of Rawls' theoretical veil of ignorance surrounding individuals' original position, as a vehicle for moral choices Sen employs Smith's notion of the "impartial spectator," who assesses the action of the self by setting himself apart from it and observing it from the outside. The moral choice is therefore what the impartial spectator would do. Sen seeks to bring morality even further into the realm of practice, and it is to this end that he has recently updated his approach (Sen 2009). He continues to encourage the assessment of situations from the perspective of the impartial spectator, i.e. imagining what a situation would look like in the eyes of an outside observer. Notions of capability become the object of particular moral scrutiny. Most notably, Sen's impartial spectator is characterized by the fact that he compares different possible options: he asks which option is better (or worse). In this way he can choose, in practical situations, the option that is morally better (or less bad), regardless of what a "perfect" society may entail.

A dignified life as the goal: Dignity as Development

Both Rawls and Sen depict their chosen subject in a most valuable way. Rawls outlines the philosophical consequences of the concept of justice. Sen, meanwhile, does the same for the concept of freedom. On a practical level, they both provide strong philosophical arguments for largely the same rights as those listed in the UN's Universal Declaration of Human Rights (UN 1948).

The constraints of their arguments, however, arise from where each of them chooses to begin.

Rawls invites us to imagine ourselves in the original position and to ask from behind the veil of ignorance: what is a just society like? However, this in itself cannot be considered the "original position." Rawls jumps directly to the question "What is a just society like?" as if this were self-evidently something that all people necessarily ask. But where does the notion come from that society should be just in the first place? This requires a foundation. This foundation is the notion that all people have the same *dignity*. It is because of the fact that all people have the same value that they are all worthy of the same justice.

In the same way, Sen sets out from the concept of freedom, but he does not provide a reason for why people should be free. This notion, too, requires a foundation, which is the idea of *dignity*; that is, that all people are worthy of freedom.

This is the first reason why *dignity* has to be elevated to be the most fundamental value—and, accordingly, to elevate the notion of a dignified life that fulfills this dignity to be the most fundamental goal of development. Dignity means the *worthiness* of every human being. Therefore, *all people have rights because they are worthy of rights* (such as freedom and justice). A dignified life means a life with such dignity. (Etymologically, the word "dignity" derives from the Latin *dignitas*, "worthiness," whose root is the word *dignus*, "worth." For the history of the concept, see e.g. Rosen 2012.)

There are, however, several other important philosophical reasons for this. Both Rawls and Sen presented their theories of justice and development without taking into account the environment. This can be seen in the UN Human Development Index—extrapolated from Sen's theories—which, on a practical level, features no ecological values (cf. UNDP 1990). In practice, the Human Development Indicator is an aggregate of life expectancy, schooling, and income.

One of the key expressed assumptions in Rawls' theory on the other hand is that, with regard to the satisfaction of people's material needs, there is no significant material scarcity. Given the challenges of ecological sustainability, neither of these approaches is valid any longer.

Therefore, another key reason why dignity is here elevated to our central concept and value is because, in addition to freedom and justice, it is also the fundamental basis of life values.

Here the concept also goes much further than, say, the UN's Universal Declaration of Human Rights, which, though it is indeed divided into values relating to life, freedom, and justice, views the notion of rights as the rights of the living individual to life. In the present examination, the notion of dignity additionally signifies the right of future generations to a similarly dignified life, which of necessity includes the notion of ecologically sustainable values.

Therefore, philosophically, *dignity* is the fundamental concept, because it is the foundation of the values and rights outlined above, namely freedom, justice, and life:

	→	freedom
dignity	→	justice
	→	life

The above now makes it also possible to link the key concepts of a sustainable development model—sustainable wellbeing, sustainable economy, and sustainable environment—to their ethical foundation. The notion of justice was used as an ethical foundation for sustainable wellbeing that is based on a wellbeing society. Now the entire foundation of this value goal can be expressed, taking the concept of dignity as its ultimate basis:

dignity ➜ justice ➜ equality   ➜ sustainable wellbeing
                                                (wellbeing society)

In a similar manner, a sustainable economy, whose ethical imperative is the fostering of capabilities (in the sense of freedoms from hunger, disease, and poverty, and the freedom for self-realization, etc.), can be positioned thus within the framework of the notion of dignity:

dignity ➜ freedom ➜ capability   ➜ sustainable economy

Finally, the ethical foundation of ecological sustainability can be expressed in the following way, linked to the life values based on the concept of dignity:

dignity ➜ life   ➜ sustainability ➜ sustainable environment

There are, however, still other philosophical reasons for the concept of dignity.

Dignity is the heart of ethics: Caring and Reciprocity

Ultimately, one further important difference is that the concept of dignity is here seen not merely as the "heart of human rights" but also as the "heart of ethics." What is meant by this is that dignity should not be understood only as the intellectual basis of the other fundamental values but also as the emotional heart that brings ethics to life. The concept brings with it the dimension of *caring*: empathy. Without that emotional heart, ethics remains merely a set of abstract principles that are not lived truly in practice. Dignity is the sense of worth of oneself and the other. From the ethical viewpoint, caring is dignity operationalized.

This is another important difference to the approach of Rawls. Rawls may be correct in his thought experiment that if people were put in the original position and behind the veil of ignorance to debate the nature of a just society, they could achieve a consensus regarding the fundamental *principles* of justice. However, mere structural principles are insufficient with regard to practically lived ethics. Practical ethics is not merely about abstract thoughts or structural principles. It requires a heart: it requires the ability to *care*, the ability to empathetically place oneself in another's position. It is actually only through this ability to empathize with the possibility that we could have been born into the societal position of any other person, and that suffering that afflicts another person could equally afflict us ourselves, that the Rawlsian thought experiment comes to life. In other words, it is an ability to empathize with another person to such an extent that we could imagine that, "We would be 'we' the way we are now, but the other way around, so that you would be 'me' and I would be 'you'." The ability to empathize in this way already makes people start acting better. Ethics is not about mere words. Ethics is about acts. Ethics is the heart that makes us live our values truly. Without emotion, there is no motion. Without being moved, there is no movement.

In fact, the very idea of justice remains ultimately pretty empty unless humans are beings who can empathize with others. Why would a person otherwise concern themselves with the question of "justice" after the "original position?" For example, upon finally perceiving their good, real position in society, they might well reject the whole notion of justice: Why would they continue to concern themselves with whether something is "just" in regard to someone else? Maintaining justice in society requires that we have the ability to caringly empathize with others as similarly valuable persons like ourselves: as the same kind of human beings who share the same longing for a dignified life.

A similar need for further elaboration goes for Sen's concept of "freedom as capability." This notion encompasses an important level that is not made explicit. Namely, that the concept of "freedom as capability" requires as a complement the concept of *responsibility*: freedom is a right. Ultimately, this right is left empty if it is not linked to the other half of the coin: the notion of responsibility. For instance, the right to the freedom to make one's own choices is in fact also the duty of others not to restrict such choices. Similarly, the right to privacy implicitly signifies the duty of others not to impinge on those aspects of a person's privacy that they have not themselves made public. Otherwise these freedoms, also in the sense of "capabilities," are empty. This could well be argued to have already happened to both of the cited freedom rights through the current media: there is no longer privacy as a right because the mass and social media do not implement their corresponding duty to respect privacy, for example, related to personal life.

From the perspective of practical ethics, this is of crucial importance. Sen's notion of capability accounts for only one half of the matter. Rights must always also mean duties. We might call this the need for the operationalization of rights—similar to the above operationalization of ethical principles. The problem is illustrated by the example of the Universal Declaration of Human Rights: in addition to a declaration of human rights, we would actually also need a declaration of human duties. In other words: "you have the following right, and that implies the following duties..." For example, the fact that you have the right to practice your religion means that you have the duty to let others also practice their religion. From the perspective of the notion of dignity, this has to be our starting point: you have the right to a dignified life, and this, in turn, implies that you have a duty to give the same right to a dignified life to everyone else.

In order for ethics to work in practice, the notion of capability must thus be complemented with the notion of *duty*—in addition to *freedom* there must also be *responsibility*. The notion of dignity expresses this reciprocity: It is about both receiving the respect of dignity from others and giving the same respect of dignity to others. You may not take away from others what you want for yourself. The right to our own dignity is simultaneously also our duty to respect other people's right to their own dignity. Dignity is reciprocal.

Dignity is a globally uniting value in a multicultural world

Finally, there is yet another and very important reason for adopting dignity as the founding concept. From the perspective of the universality of ethics in our definitively newly global times, the additional strength of the notion of dignity lies in the fact that it is a notion shared by all cultures, faiths, and secular traditions (cf. Kühn 1993).

Here's how this heart of ethics is found in all the great systems of ethics:

- Judaism: "What is hateful to you, do not do to your neighbor: that is the whole *Torah*; all the rest of it is commentary" (Talmud, Shabbat 31a).
- Christianity: "Do to others what you would have them do to you, for this sums up the *Law and the Prophets*" (Matthew 7.12).
- Islam: "Not one of you is a *believer* until he desires for his brother what he desires for himself" (40 Hadith of an-Nawawi 13).

- Hinduism: "Do naught to others which, if done to thee, would cause thee pain: this is the *sum of duty*" (Mahabharata 5.1517).
- Buddhism: "Hurt not others in ways that you would find hurtful" (Tripitaka Udana-varga 5.18).
- Confucianism: "Tse-kung asked, 'Is there one word that can serve as a principle of conduct for life?' Confucius replied, 'It is the word *"shu"* – reciprocity. Do not impose on others what you yourself do not desire'" (Analects 15.23).
- Secular philosophy: "Act as if the maxim of thy action were to become by thy will a *universal law* of nature" (Immanuel Kant, Grundlegung zur Metaphysik der Sitten 2.3).

Notice especially that this same core of ethics is not just found in all great religions and secular systems of ethics, but it is actually hailed as their greatest principle. In Judaism, this principle is said to be "the whole Torah (teaching);" in Christianity, "the Law and the Prophets;" in Islam, a condition for calling yourself a believer. In Hinduism, it is "the sum of dharma (religious duty);" in Confucianism, "shu, the principle of conduct for life;" and in the philosophy of Immanuel Kant, "the categoric imperative."

Therefore, the concept of dignity offers a radically globally uniting goal: a global basis for a "dignity revolution of values," after the Western Enlightenment revolution of values—if one wishes to put this in a very big historical context (although all human rights also follow from this universal conceptual basis). Whereas the slogan of the Western Enlightenment was "liberty, equality, fraternity," now in the global values revolution it can be summed up with the word—"dignity."

The culture of dignity as a culture of freedom, justice, and life

Finally, the concept of dignity has been chosen as a unifying concept also because it can serve in the above way as the culture of a sustainable development model that our world now greatly needs: from sustainable environment to sustainable wellbeing to sustainable economy. Using the above concepts, the culture of dignity is a culture of freedom, justice, and life— the foundations of sustainable economy, wellbeing, and environment. Or, to use the alternative expressions from above, it is a culture of creativity, caring, and life.

This is a very important formulation. Because of the numerous connotations of the word "dignity," it is essential to underline that it is a *moral*, not a *moralistic*, concept.

Dignity means the worthiness of every human being as a *subject*. For example, freedom then means the *subject*'s right to freedom: *to make free choices about one's life that are consensual with the free choices of the other subjects.* In research literature, expressions such as autonomy, agency, etc. are also used for the same basic idea. What is talked about here is the subject's right to define their subjectivity.

Likewise, caring means the ability to see the world genuinely from the viewpoint of the *other subject*—whose wishes may be different from one's own. So it is to *do to the other subject as you would wish done to you as another subject.* In literature, expressions such as otherness also capture this notion. What is being discussed here is the subject's duty to see the other subject genuinely as another subject.

The reason why this clarification is so important is that, in fact, otherwise the moralistic concept of a "dignified life" could easily be used *against* the moral concept of dignity: for example, such as in expressions like "carrying yourself with dignity" (as in the medieval idea of emulating the external behavior of royal dignitaries) that could easily become simply a way for societal use of power to push its moralistically restricting mannerisms on the subject. A "dignified life" does not refer to external appearances. Dignity does not mean moralism, which is in fact a culture of shame, guilt, and envy, and therefore the complete opposite of dignity. Dignity means that you are worthy of freedom, justice, and life as a *subject*.

With the above important clarification made, we can then proceed to describe the key elements of such a culture of freedom, justice, and life—as a basis of a sustainable development model. Ultimately, a dignified life in the above moral (not moralistic) sense is a notion that both forms the cultural foundation of sustainable wellbeing, economy, and environment, while at the same time providing the "missing link" between them. This symbiosis can be best depicted by the following diagrammatic model of sustainable development (see Figure 10.1 below).

Culture of freedom = culture of creativity

On a cultural level, the notion of a dignified life represents a culture of *freedom*, i.e. a culture in which people can realize themselves and which might therefore also be called a *culture of creativity*. On a very practical level,

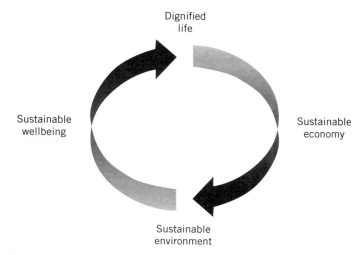

Dignified
life

Sustainable
economy

Sustainable
environment

Sustainable
wellbeing

Figure 10.1 Dignified life as the goal of the sustainable development model

this is also the cultural foundation of a sustainable economy. The culture of creativity is characterized by the idea that all people should have the opportunity to realize their individual potential to the fullest extent.

In practice, this implies the existence of education, research, and development systems that create the real freedom, i.e. the capability with which individuals can achieve their full potential. Thus self-realization can (in the case of economy) manifest itself through, for instance, innovation and entrepreneurship, as people put ideas into practice, and through a work and leadership culture, which encourages people to use the full gamut of their abilities. (Thus the cultural ethos of our information age differs radically from what Max Weber described as the "Protestant ethic" of the industrial age; cf. Himanen's 2001 analysis of "the hacker ethic" as the spirit of the information age for a more full description.)

Culture of justice = culture of caring

In a similar way, on the cultural level, a dignified life means a *culture of caring*, in which people empathize with others to such a degree that they can identify with the others' positions. This is the basis for the equality of opportunity, protection, and inclusion in wellbeing that follows from the notion of *justice*. Ultimately such a culture requires the ethical heart or operationalized dignity outlined above. In their essence, these are especially values related to a subject's life as part of a community. (See also Himanen 2005, 2007.)

Culture of life

At the foundation of ecological sustainability is a *culture of life*, a culture in which, in addition to respecting the lives of those living now, we also respect the lives of future generations. In other words, this is a culture of inviolability with regard not only to humans' physical inviolability (physical security, peace, etc.), but also to the inviolability of the environment, such that future generations will have the opportunity to live a dignified life. Thus, in their essence, these are especially values relating to the sustainability of all humankind. (See Himanen 2010.)

In the above way, in a culture of creativity, a person realizes the valuable within himself to the greatest possible extent in a way that, through a culture of empathy, connects to the recognition of the same value in all other people—and, then, through a culture of life, to a respect for the right to the same for the future generations.

On a cultural level, the functioning of a culture of dignity as a basis for a sustainable development model—that is, sustainable economy, sustainable wellbeing, and sustainable environment—can be summarized thus:

dignity → freedom (individual)	→ culture of creativity	→ sustainable economy
dignity → justice (community)	→ culture of caring	→ sustainable wellbeing
dignity → life (humanity)	→ culture of life	→ sustainable environment

Ultimately, such sustainable growth will serve the continued improvement of the requirements for a dignified life, and thus, on a conceptual level, a dignified life is both the foundation of the factors affecting sustainable development and the goal that links them together.

Wellbeing economics and psychology: Wellbeing as the Goal?

Finally, it is important to position the notion of dignified life in relation to the new framework of wellbeing economics and psychology that has lauded wellbeing (or "happiness" as a name of its highest degree) as the highest goal of development. Perhaps the most important work in this field has been the *Report of the Commission on the Measurement of Economic Performance and Social Progress* (Stiglitz et al. 2009), an analysis by a team of top economists guided by Joseph Stiglitz. The Stiglitz commission argued that the objective should be "to shift emphasis from measuring economic production to measuring people's wellbeing."

Research into the economics and psychology of wellbeing has resulted in significant scientific work questioning industrial society's notion of economic growth as the ultimate goal (for this extensive new literature, on the relationship between economic growth and wellbeing, cf. especially Easterlin 1974, 2004, and 2010; Stevenson and Wolfers 2008; Veenhoven and Hagerty 2006; Kahneman et al. 2006 and 2011; and on the empirical sources of wellbeing: Seligman 2002 and 2011; Csikszentmihalyi 1990 and 1996; Kahneman et al. 1999 and 2011). Development has to advance wellbeing.

Wellbeing is also viewed as an objective within the frame of a dignified life. This important body of literature has been applied in this book to the deepening of the content of the concept of wellbeing. The following three classic factors affecting the experience of wellbeing (and happiness) are especially important:

- autonomy: freedom, agency, empowerment
- sociability: social relationships and belonging to a community
- meaningful activity: work, free time, play

In fact, in this work, these have been added as important qualitative dimensions of the new wellbeing society, in addition to the more traditional quantitative ones of the industrial age:

$$\text{wellbeing} \quad \begin{array}{l} \rightarrow \text{autonomy} \\ \rightarrow \text{sociability} \\ \rightarrow \text{meaningful activity} \end{array}$$

There is something immediately alluring about the notion that "wellbeing should be the goal of development." Surely, the objective of development should precisely be wellbeing—or "happiness," as the name of its highest degree? What else could it be?

In the present examination, however, instead of wellbeing, dignified life has been chosen as the most fundamental notion. As already mentioned, it does include the concept of wellbeing; but wellbeing alone is not sufficient as a complete goal for development. The biggest problem of the concept of wellbeing is that it does not include all the dimensions that must definitely be seen as part of the ultimate goal of development, such as the concepts of justice and freedom argued for by Rawls and Sen. In the end, this problem is due to the philosophical fact that wellbeing is not an ethical concept. And because it is not an ethical value, it cannot serve as a foundation for the ethical categories of justice and freedom.

Even the empirical facts speak against this: for instance, in an authoritarian society people may experience both material and psychological wellbeing, even if they lack freedom and justice. If we posit that the definition of the notion of *wellbeing* also contains aspects such as political freedom—and go on to say that a person who claims to be well off cannot be really well off, if he is not free—then we would be guilty of stretching the notion so far that both conceptually and with regard to the empirical facts it would be rendered entirely meaningless.

In addition, the concept has another significant limitation. In fact, wellbeing is by its very nature a markedly hedonistic and utilitarian concept; something that is reflected in the decision of Nobel Prize laureate Daniel Kahneman to call his research "hedonic psychology." Accordingly, Kahneman's book, written in collaboration with two other leading wellbeing researchers (Ed Diener and Norbert Schwarz), is entitled *Well-Being: The Foundations of Hedonic Psychology* (1999). This brings us back to Jeremy Bentham, the father of utilitarianism, and his idea of a "hedonic calculus" as a principle guiding choices (*An Introduction to the Principles of Morals and Legislation* 1789). However, it is easy to imagine examples of persons who are not happy but still lead good and meaningful lives. The classic conundrum here was originally posed by John Stuart Mill: is it better to be a satisfied pig than an unhappy Socrates (Mill 1863)?

In addition, one can ask: Whose wellbeing (or happiness) are we talking about—that is, whose wellbeing (or happiness) matters? In fact, the concept of wellbeing requires the concept of dignity as its foundation: wellbeing is advanced for those who are seen as worthy of wellbeing. The goal of all people's wellbeing requires all people's dignity. In fact, the pioneer of utilitarianism, Francis Hutcheson, already made this connection when he stated that the principle of greatest happiness is linked to the concept of dignity: "the virtue of [action] is in proportion to the number of persons to whom the happiness shall extend (and here the dignity, or moral importance of persons, may compensate numbers)" (*An Inquiry into the Original of Our Ideas of*

Beauty and Virtue 1725). If all people don't have the same dignity, then their wellbeing or happiness does not have the same relevance either.

The most important observation from all of the above is that, in actual fact, wellbeing as an objective of development is a notion of a different dimension from that of justice and freedom. This crucial difference can be characterized in this way: freedom and justice are *ethical values*, whereas wellbeing is a *philosophy of life* objective. The most significant reason for the choice of dignified life as the most fundamental concept is that, philosophically speaking, it can be used as a foundation for both of these levels.

As outlined above, on the ethical level, the values of freedom, justice, and life are founded on the concept of dignity. On a philosophy of life level, wellbeing (or happiness) is one of the contents of a dignified life, that is, a worthy life. However, just as the concept of wellbeing is insufficient on the level of ethics, it is also insufficient alone as a philosophy of life objective. Wellbeing is not the only source of the experience of a worthy life.

It must also be complemented by other sources of a worthy life. The three key elements could be summed up in this way:

	→ wellbeing
dignity	→ flourishing
worthiness	
	→ meaningfulness

Wellbeing (and happiness as the name of its highest level) does give rise to the experience of a dignified, worthy life. However, it is also important to note that self-realization is an independent source of the experience of a worthy life. Flourishing and happiness are often linked together, but this is by no means always the case: let us take by way of an example the numerous artists and researchers throughout history who would not think of abandoning their creative work for anything despite the personal malaise that it may bring them. On the contrary, many of them would always choose their creative work, even in the certain knowledge that it means an unhappy life. Another indication of the distinctiveness of self-realization with regard to wellbeing can be seen in the fact that, according to the wellbeing literature itself, in the state of "flow" one does not actually experience any emotions, even happiness (Csikszentmihalyi 1990 and 1996; Seligman 2002 and 2011).

Pekka Himanen

Ultimately, the experience of dignity includes a level of meaningfulness beyond activity: life can be meaningful even if it is characterized neither by happiness nor flourishing. Indeed, happiness and flourishing are not wholly under our control. This we may call the fragility of life. Here is demonstrated a mystery of life: we may experience life as meaningful even if we are neither happy nor successful. In this sense, the deepest philosophy of life goal is not wellbeing but meaningfulness (i.e. a life that has a purpose, a "worthy life").

To summarize, the concept of dignified life serves as the ultimate basis for other goals of development in all three of the dimensions discussed (Figure 10.2):

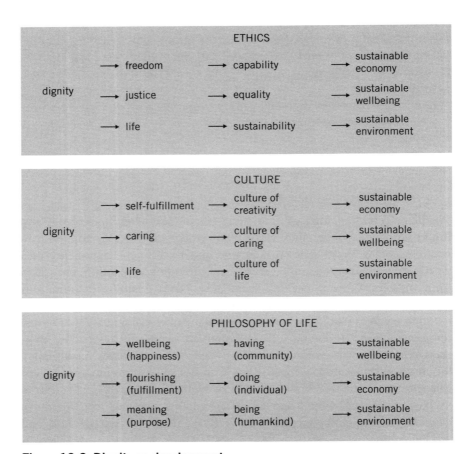

Figure 10.2 Dignity as development

Bridging dignity to the social scientific theoretical framework

The philosophical argument for why dignity should be seen as the ultimate goal of development (instead of its presently used alternatives that have been analyzed) has now been made. However, in this book, we also want to ground everything in the best theoretical knowledge that we have on the conditions of development in the Global Information Age. Therefore, it is still important to bridge the concept of dignity explicitly to the social scientific theoretical framework presented in Chapter 1 and supported empirically by the case studies.

In the context of the social scientific theoretical framework that has been guiding this book (starting from Chapter 1 by Castells & Himanen and including Chapter 9 by Calderon)—which has been built on the key concepts of informational development and human development and their cultural link—*dignity as development can be seen as a fulfillment of human worth*. Or to put it in more practical terms, *dignity as development can be seen as a fulfillment of our human potential in these areas of informational development, human development, and cultural development.*

Or, to employ the other terms that we have also been using, dignity as development can be seen as a fulfillment of human potential through sustainable economy, sustainable wellbeing, and sustainable culture—all of this of course having to take place in an ecologically sustainable way to make it a genuinely sustainable development model.

So, in practical terms, dignity as development can be interpreted as *sustainable fulfillment of human potential,* whether it is in the area of economic innovation and productivity growth toward a higher quality of life, or in the area of human development toward higher wellbeing in health, education, and social inclusion, and, of course, including the fulfillment of human potential in its cultural development, which ultimately links or delinks informational development and human development.

So, therefore, dignity as a concept is directly connected to the other key concepts of our theoretical framework on development. The following diagrams illustrate this connection. First, the relationship with our primary analytical terms—and, second, with their more practical translations (see Figures 10.3 and 10.4).

For the sake of operationalizing the concept of dignity, the following key features of our guiding theoretical framework should now be recalled—and complemented slightly further, with the view of being able to ultimately

Pekka Himanen

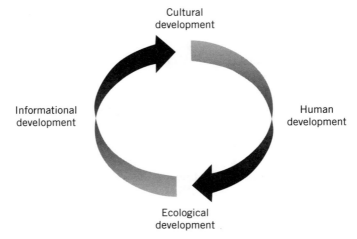

Figure 10.3 **The model of development in the Information Age**

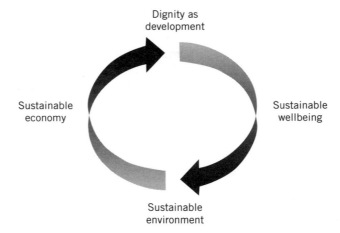

Figure 10.4 **Dignity as development**

choose the most relevant features of measurement for the Dignity Index grounded on this theory.

The concept of *informational development* is already explained in Chapter 1. It is a synonym for the concept of informationalism, as originally presented in Manuel Castells' theory of the network society (the trilogy *The Information Age*, 1st ed. 1996–8, 2nd ed. 2000–4, and updated in other publications after that). Informationalism is meant as a parallel to the concept of industrialism. They both refer to *the mode of development*. In the industrial society, development is based on the industrial mode of development. Likewise, in the informational society (which can also be referred to as "the Information Age" for the sake of convenience and to match the expression "the Industrial Age"), development is based on the informational mode of development.

From the viewpoint of economy, there are three critical factors of informational development that are increasingly important for economic development: that it is founded on (1) innovation-based (2) productivity growth driving economic growth using (3) the new forms of organizing knowledge made possible by information technologies. This theory of informationalism has been strongly supported by empirical research. Also in this book, Chapter 2 shows that the exceptionally strong informational development in Silicon Valley is based on the ability to strongly combine the three factors; the same is supported by the observations in Chapters 3 and 4 on the informational development in the Finnish model and in Europe.

For a long time, there already existed the assumption by Nobel economics laureate Richard Solow on the relationship of informational development and productivity. In his theory on growth, Solow suggested that in addition to labor and capital, technological advancement also plays a significant part in productivity growth (Solow 1956). Although the so-called "Solow residual"—a factor seen in the statistics as an additional explanation of productivity growth to labor and capital—supported this at a theoretical level, in respect to information and communication technology we long lacked a more specific demonstration of the relationship between informational development and productivity growth. This came to be called the "Solow paradox," which he personally summed up in the statement, "You can see the computer age everywhere but in the productivity statistics."

However, in the late 1990s, the situation changed. A particularly important analysis of the growth in informational productivity was made by MIT professor Erik Brynjolfsson, along with his colleagues. Brynjolfsson was finally able to demonstrate the strong correlation between informational development and productivity growth (Brynjolfsson & Hitt 1998 and 2003; Brynjolfsson & Yang 1999; Brynjolfsson & Saunders 2010; Jorgenson & Stiroh 2000 and 2002). Informational development shows up in productivity statistics in two ways: first, as the effect of ICT investments; and, second, less directly as part of the "Solow residual," which includes all use of technology in the broadest sense of the word (total factor productivity).

Pekka Himanen

Productivity growth is increasingly based on informational development, using innovatively the combination of information technology and the new forms of organization it enables. For example, while productivity growth in the United States for the two decades preceding the mid-1990s, 1975–85 and 1985–95, was about 1.5%, following the breakthrough of the Internet, during the subsequent decade it rose to 3% and has been on average 2.5% since 1995 (US Department of Labor STAN 2013).

Informational development as the mode of development means that the combination of the above three dimensions is increasingly the source of economic growth: therefore, indicators for these three dimensions of economy, innovation, and technology must be chosen to root the measurement of informational development in the Dignity Index to the best available empirical and theoretical knowledge.

As for human development as part of our social scientific theory, a framework has already been provided in Chapter 9 by Calderon. Our case studies supported empirically the conclusion that if society's investment in human development is very low, this also undermines broader informational development: the result is a divided society where only a very small segment is connected to the Global Information Age and the gap between this power elite and the rest of the population generates social tensions, as Hsing showed in Chapter 5 for the case of China, and Cloete & Gillwald showed in Chapter 6 for South Africa. A reason for this is that in this situation social inequity combines with a low general educational base, reducing the capacity for informational development. On the other hand, Chapters 7 and 8 on Chile and Costa Rica give hope that even an economically less-developed country can, through systematic policy-making, form some positive circle between informational and human development, even if the results are so far partial.

The most important notion here, looking at human development from a broader viewpoint of "dignity as development," is that even if the United Nations Development Program's Human Development Index (HDI) is a hugely valuable addition to the old GDP measure, for the reasons Calderon presents the whole concept of human development cannot really be reduced to a combination of only three basic indicators: life expectancy, basic amount of schooling, and income level (as is done in the HDI).

In the HDI, human development is calculated simply in the following way:

$$HDI = \sqrt[3]{LEI \cdot EI \cdot II}$$

in which:

$$LEI \text{ (Life Expectancy Index)} = \frac{LE - 20}{82.3 - 20}$$

$$EI \text{ (Education Index)} = \frac{\sqrt{MYSI \cdot EYSI}}{0.951}$$

$$MYSI \text{ (Mean Years of Schooling Index)} = \frac{MYS}{13.2}$$

$$EYSI \text{ (Expected Years of Schooling Index)} = \frac{EYS}{20.6}$$

$$II \text{ (Income Index)} = \frac{\ln(GNI_{pc}) - \ln(100)}{\ln(107,721) - \ln(100)}$$

Calderon makes a strong argument as to why this is not enough for the concept of human development. One must consider broader indicators of health, education, and the social dimension. Here, the notion of a more fully interpreted human development is elaborated further in order to be able to operationalize its measurement—in a way that reflects not only the traditional industrial welfare state's measures of deprivation elimination but also the informational wellbeing society's measures of the actual quality and experience of wellbeing (cf. especially Chapter 3 and the idea of human development agency in Chapter 9).

One analytical point has to be emphasized separately. As an Industrial Age measure of development, despite being much broader than the GDP, the HDI also has severe limitations because it does not take the ecological sustainability of development into account. Therefore, using the HDI one may have to give the name "human development" to a development that destroys our environment and thus our own wellbeing. This is clearly untenable in the context of the ecological crisis of the old development model. In the Dignity Index, no country can achieve a rating of the highest level of sustainable development if it performs very badly in ecological sustainability.

In the end, sustainable development requires a cultural link that combines informational and human development in a positive cycle. Again, these measures for cultural development must be built directly on a theoretical framework that is most tenable. Therefore, they must be built directly on the cultural framework presented at the beginning of this chapter: they include the culture of life, the culture of creative freedom, and the culture of justice.

With these additional remarks related to the social scientific theoretical framework and the concept of dignity, we are now ready to proceed toward the actual building of the new Dignity Index.

The Dignity Index: preliminary operationalization

The third and final part of this chapter's analysis will now operationalize the concept of "dignity as development" that has been presented above and grounded on both a philosophical and social scientific foundation.

While doing so, it is fully acknowledged that we already have a number of alternatives for the "old" GDP growth as a measure of development. In addition to the UN Human Development Index (UNDP 1990; Ul Haq 1999), these include among others:

- Genuine Progress Indicator (in which in principle the social and ecological cost of development is subtracted from the GDP, but the indicator is not systematically defined and in use);
- Gross National Happiness (the measure suggested by the King of Bhutan in 1972; it was first operationalized by Karma Ura and then universalized by the Canadian researchers Michael and Martha Pennock; still, it lacks a generally accepted definition);
- Happy Planet Index (New Economic Foundation: an aggregate of experienced wellbeing, life expectancy, and ecological footprint);
- Happiness Index (Gallup World Poll: subjective wellbeing);
- World Happiness Report Happiness Ranking (UNSDSN 2013, based on the Gallup World Poll Happiness Index, but analyzing the factors influencing it, edited by Helliwell, Layard, and Sachs);
- Your Better Life Index (OECD 2013b: an aggregate based on 11 themes; no uniform definition and calculated only for the OECD countries).

Related to these suggested alternatives to GDP, it is also important to keep in mind that GDP itself is also in fact a relatively new suggestion as a development measure that has in a short time been adopted as a surprisingly "self-evident" measure. However, it was formulated by Simon Kuznets only in 1934 for the US Congress in the context of helping the country to move economically forward from the Great Depression (see Kuznets 1934). Its international use started after the Bretton Woods conference in 1944, which established the current global financial institutions of the International Monetary Fund, World Bank, and the World Trade Organization, in the context of the post-World War II goal of reconstructing devastated economies.

In the current context of the Great Recession—which combines with three even deeper structural challenges of sustainable development: sustainable environment, sustainable wellbeing, and sustainable economy in the long run—there is an increased need for a new, more holistic measure to guide sustainable development (for the Great Recession see Himanen 2012 in Castells et al. (eds) 2012).

What differentiates the Dignity Index from all of the currently existing alternative indices that are all also very valuable (such as, e.g., the Human Development Index) are the following three criteria that have been used for its construction:

- The Index has to be directly built on a solid and systematic philosophical/ ethical argument on what development is.
- The Index has to be directly grounded on the most recent knowledge in social scientific theory, based on empirical data, that we know about development in the global information age.
- The Index has to be in practice useful in guiding actual policy-making in order to see each country's weaknesses and strengths so that better policy can be made to advance development.

This is how the Dignity Index has been built based on the philosophical and social scientific theories presented in this chapter and the book. What the Dignity Index then measures is development in the following three dimensions:

- Informational development
- Human development
- Cultural development

These components of the Dignity Index are important measures by themselves—as well as in terms of their subcomponents (therefore, the Dignity Index is not only an aggregate measure but also emphasizes that it is as important to focus on all of its sub-components separately). Finally, based on the combination of these three main dimensions, an overall Dignity Index can be calculated as a measure for any country's sustainable development—or "dignity as development."

At the same time, it is important to underline that in the context of this chapter this formulation of the Dignity Index is meant only as preliminary and is intended to illustrate what kind of categories should be included in an index based on this book's systematic philosophical and social scientific theory. (For further materials, a separate web page, www.dignityasdevelopment.org, is being established.)

The components of the Dignity Index

1. Informational Development

Based on the philosophical and social scientific theory presented above, the following key sub-components have been selected to indicate a country's level of informational development, as important determinants of the longer term sustainability of its economy in the global network society.

The first sub-component describes basic economic development, at the level of "hard" economic measures. The second sub-component describes innovation capacity for further economic development under the conditions of the global informational economy. And the third sub-component describes the development level of the technological infrastructure (ICT and knowledge) underlying that.

a) *Economy (Economic Development)*
  - GDP per capita (purchasing power parity)
  - GDP growth (annual real growth average)
  - Productivity (output per input working hour)

b) *Innovation (Innovation Development)*
  - Competitiveness index (the World Economic Forum measure)
  - Productivity growth (percentage)
  - Receipts of royalties and license fees (per capita in USD)

c) *Technology (Technological Development)*
  - Internet users (percentage of population)
  - Research and development investment (percentage of GDP)
  - Patents per capita (per million)

2. Human Development

Likewise, based on criteria outlined in this chapter and the book, the following key sub-components have been chosen as indicators of a country's level of a more fully understood human development.

Each of the sub-components describes the level of development on one of the three key components of human development: health, education, and social. Like in the choice of the indicators of the sub-components in general, the first indicator describes a very basic dimension of the sub-component—and is also very traditionally and generally established as such. The second and third indicators add deeper and more modern or fresh measures based on the philosophical and social scientific theory presented in this chapter and book.

a) *Health (Health Development)*
- Physical health: life expectancy (at birth in years)
- Health gender equality: maternal mortality rate (per 100,000)
- Psychological health: happiness (life satisfaction)

b) *Education (Educational Development)*
- Quantity of education: expected years of education (years of schooling)
- Quality of education: student performance (OECD PISA score for secondary level students)
- University level: scientific publications (citations Hirsch index)

c) *Social (Social Development)*
- Income inclusion: income inequality (Atkinson index)
- Health inclusion: social health differences (life expectancy inequality)
- Social belonging (youth unemployment)

3. Cultural Development

In accordance with the theory presented, for the cultural level the sub-components are the following three values following from the concept of dignity:

a) *Life (Culture of Life)*
- Natural life: sustainability by ecological footprint (CO_2 emissions)
- Physical life: peace (Global Peace Index)
- Social life: trust (trust of other people in society)

b) *Freedom (Culture of Creativity)*
- Autonomy: basic freedom of expression (Freedom House)
- Creativity: entrepreneurialism (GEM start-up entrepreneurship percentage)
- Openness: to others (percentage of foreign-born population)

c) *Justice (Culture of Caring)*
- Basic justice: rule of law (Freedom House)
- Gender justice: equality (representation of women in parliament)
- Global justice: foreign aid (percentage of GDP)

Statistical note

There have been three additional important statistical criteria for the selection of the above indicators:

- The indicators must represent the most modern research in their areas, from the most trusted international research institutions.
- The indicators must be as universally available and comparable as possible.
- The indicators must be kept up to date and as real-time as possible and must continue to be systematically updated annually or on another regular basis.

The purpose of the Dignity Index is to express the overall level of each country's development. The purpose of each of its three main components is to show how the country is doing in terms of informational, human, and cultural development individually. The purpose of the sub-components of these is to indicate how the country is performing in each more specific key area of that development.

In order to not get lost in statistics as an end in itself, in conclusion, the level of development of each indicator is translated from its mathematical figure to one of the following five levels:

- very high
- high
- medium
- low
- very low

The mathematical formulas used for calculating each indicator and translating them into the levels from very low to very high are included in the statistical Appendix to this chapter.

Dignity operationalized: Dignity Index for a selection of countries

As a conclusion to this chapter's operationalization of dignity, the following tables give a sample of how the countries included in this book's case studies are performing on the Dignity Index—both on an overall level and on each component separately.[1]

Tables 10.1, 10.2, and 10.3 show the Dignity Index divided into the three components of the countries' informational, human, and cultural development, before giving the overall "dignity as development" score (Table 10.4). The full source information for each indicator is listed in the Appendix.

And, finally, as a combination of all three components, the overall Dignity Index is calculated in Table 10.4.

Policymaking conclusions

For visualization purposes, the levels of development in each component and overall could also be expressed with the colors of red, yellow, and green (as in traffic lights), to give a quick indication of the situation.

The mere aggregate-level ranking in the Dignity Index is not alone the most interesting piece of information. In that regard, in fact, the most important observation is that *no country achieves in the Index its highest, that is "very high," level, which is the one that can be truly called fully sustainable. For this reason, it could be best said that the biggest political message is that the real number-*

---

[1] For the actual statistical data collection work for this chart, I must express my gratitude for the help of Dr. Isidora Chacon, with whom I've completed the hard work of compiling all of this data from its numerous sources. Any possible errors in data as well as the indicator selections, formulas, and calculations of the scores remain wholly my responsibility. Unfortunately, global statistics have the limitation that they are still mostly collected systematically based on the categories of the Industrial Age, so the construction of a Dignity Index fully in line with the new theory would require updating the indicators that are collected in the Global Information Age.

Table 10.1 Dignity Index—informational development

	INFORMATIONAL DEVELOPMENT OVERALL SCORE	1. ECONOMY overall score	GNI per cap. (PPP USD)	GDP Growth % (real annual)	Productivity (output per hour, US = 100)	2. INNOVATION overall score	Competitiveness Index (WEF index)	Productivity growth (index, 2005=100)	Receipt of royalties and license fees (USD per capita)	3. TECHNOLOGY overall score	Internet users (% of pop.)	R&D investment (% of GDP)	Patents per capita (per million)
			2012	2011	2012		2012	2005–11	2005–11		2012	2005–10	2005–10
NORTH AMERICA													
United States	VERY HIGH	High	43,480	1.8	100	Very high	5.47	108.2	387.1	Very high	81.0	2.8	707.6
EUROPE													
Finland	VERY HIGH	High	32,510	2.7	77	Very high	5.55	104.1	556.5	Very high	91.0	3.8	172.1
Sweden			36,143	4.0	86		5.53	103.4	619.4		94.0	3.6	147.1
Denmark			33,518	0.8	81		5.29	101.5	N.A.		93.0	1.8	27.9
United Kingdom			32,538	0.8	90		5.45	105.4	226.3		87.0	1.8	90.2
Germany			35,431	3.1	90		5.48	106.2	174.9		84.0	2.8	166.2
France			30,277	1.7	93		5.11	104.1	240.0		83.0	2.2	157.7
Italy			26,158	0.4	72		4.46	100.4	59.8		58.0	1.3	303.4
Spain			25,947	0.4	76		4.60	109.1	23.0		72.0	1.4	60.2
Portugal			19,907	-1.7	42		4.40	109.6	5.7		64.0	1.7	13.1
Greece			20,511	-6.9	50		3.86	100.2	6.1		56.0	0.6	42.2
Austria			36,438	2.7	86		5.22	108.7	92.6		81.0	2.7	134.6
Netherlands			37,282	1.1	96		5.50	104.0	320.8		93.0	1.8	117.6
Belgium			33,429	1.8	98		5.21	100.7	232.1		82.0	2.0	49.7
Ireland			28,671	1.4	90		4.91	120.3	574.2		79.0	1.8	54.4
EU-15 avg.	HIGH	High	30,626	0.9	80	High	5.04	105.6	240.9	High	79.8	2.2	109.7
ASIA													
China	MEDIUM	Medium	7,945	9.2	N.A.	Medium	4.83	N.A.	0.6	Medium	42.3	1.5	100.7
LATIN AMERICA													
Chile	MEDIUM	Medium	14,987	5.9	27	Medium	4.65	116.9	3.7	Low	61.4	0.4	59.6
Costa Rica	MEDIUM	Medium	10,863	4.2	N.A.	Low	4.34	N.A.	0.9	Medium	47.5	0.4	9.7
AFRICA													
South Africa	LOW	Low	9594	3.1	N.A.	Low	4.37	N.A.	1.3	Low	41.0	0.9	106.3

Table 10.2 Dignity Index—human development

	HUMAN DEVELOPMENT OVERALL SCORE	1. HEALTH overall score	Life expectancy (years at birth) 2012	Maternal mortality (per 100 000) 2010	Happiness (life satisfaction) 2012	2. EDUCATION overall score	Expected years of education 2010-11	Student performance (OECD PISA avg.) 2009	Scientific publications. (citations H-index) 2011	3. SOCIAL overall score	Income inequality (Atkinson Index) 2012	Inequality of life expectancy (% lost) 2012	Youth unemployment (% of 15–24 yrs) 2011
NORTH AMERICA													
United States	HIGH	High	78.7	21	7.2	Very high	16.8	496	1305	Medium	24.1	6.6	11.9
EUROPE	VERY HIGH	Very high				Very high				Very high			
Finland			80.1	5	7.4		16.9	544	352		11.3	3.9	19.3
Sweden			81.6	4	7.5		16.0	495	484		11.2	3.3	23.8
Denmark			79.0	12	7.8		16.8	499	399		11.0	4.4	15.7
United Kingdom			80.3	12	7.0		15.3	500	802		16.9	4.8	22.0
Germany			80.6	7	6.7		19.7	524	704		14.5	4.0	9.1
France			81.7	8	6.8		16.1	497	646		13.3	4.2	23.2
Italy			82.0	4	6.4		16.2	486	550		18.1	3.9	32.0
Spain			81.6	6	6.2		16.4	484	448		19.7	4.1	48.2
Portugal			79.7	8	4.9		16.0	490	218		20.8	4.9	31.7
Greece			80.0	3	5.8		16.3	473	247		18.1	4.8	51.5
Austria			81.0	4	7.3		15.3	487	355		12.7	4.2	8.8
Netherlands			80.8	6	7.5		16.9	519	545		12.3	4.3	7.8
Belgium			80.0	8	6.9		16.4	509	428		11.9	4.4	18.7
Ireland			80.7	6	7.3		18.3	497	254		13.8	4.3	35.3
EU-15 avg.	HIGH	High	80.7	6.8	6.8	High	16.6	500	459	High	14.7	4.3	24.8
ASIA													
China	MEDIUM	Medium	73.7	37	4.7	High	11.7	577	353	Medium	29.5	13.5	N.A.
LATIN AMERICA													
Chile	MEDIUM	Medium	79.3	25	6.6	Medium	14.7	439	181	Low	34.1	6.6	21.1
Costa Rica	MEDIUM	Medium	79.4	40	7.3	Medium	13.7	N.A.	97	Very low	37.9	7.8	21.6
AFRICA													
South Africa	LOW	Low	53.4	300	4.7	Medium	13.1	N.A.	216	Very low	63.1	28.4	55.0

Table 10.3 Dignity Index—cultural development

	CULTURAL DEVELOPMENT OVERALL SCORE	1. LIFE overall score	Ecological footprint (CO_2 emissions)	Global Peace Index (GPI)	Trust of others in society (%)	2. FREEDOM overall score	Freedom of press (Freedom House)	Creativity (GEM entrepreneur index)	Openness to others (% of foreign-born pop.)	3. JUSTICE overall score	Rule of law (Freedom House)	Gender equality (% of women in parliament)	Foreign aid (% of GDP)
NORTH AMERICA													
United States	MEDIUM	Low	7.2	2.06	37.0	Very high	18	0.717	13.5	Medium	1	17.0	0.2
EUROPE	MEDIUM	Medium				Medium				High			
Finland			6.2	1.35	58.0		10	0.564	4.2		1	42.5	0.6
Sweden			5.7	1.42	55.0		12	0.685	14.1		1	44.7	1.0
Denmark			8.3	1.24	60.0		21	0.763	8.8		1	39.1	0.9
United Kingdom			4.7	1.61	35.0			0.561	11.2		1	22.1	0.6
Germany			4.6	1.42	31.0		17	0.544	13.1		1	32.4	0.4
France			4.9	1.71	20.0		24	0.498	10.7		1	25.1	0.5
Italy			4.5	1.69	20.0		33	0.407	7.4		1.5	20.7	0.2
Spain			4.7	1.55	22.0		24	0.401	15.2		1	34.9	N.A.
Portugal			4.1	1.47	27.0		17	0.350	8.6		1	28.7	0.3
Greece			4.9	1.98	16.0		30	0.318	10.1		2	21.0	N.A.
Austria			5.3	1.33	29.0		21	0.454	15.6		1	28.7	0.3
Netherlands			6.3	1.61	46.0		12	0.616	10.5		1	37.8	0.8
Belgium			7.1	1.38	30.0		11	0.576	13.7		1	38.9	0.6
Ireland			6.2	1.33	30.0		16	0.631	19.6		1	19.0	0.5
EU-15 avg.	MEDIUM	Medium	5.5	1.51	34.2	High	18.4	0.526	11.6	High	1.1	31.1	0.6
ASIA													
China	LOW	Medium	2.1	2.06	57.0	Very low	85	0.281	0.1	Low	8.5	21.3	0.0
LATIN AMERICA													
Chile	MEDIUM	Medium	3.2	1.62	15.0	Low	31	0.414	1.9	Medium	1	13.9	−0.1
Costa Rica	HIGH	Medium	2.5	1.66	14.0	High	19	N.A.	10.5	Very high	1	38.6	−0.3
AFRICA													
South Africa	MEDIUM	LOW	2.6	2.32	17.0	Low	34	0.277	3.7	High	2	41.1	−0.3

Table 10.4 Dignity Index for selected countries, with rankings

	DIGNITY INDEX OVERALL SCORE	RANK
NORTH AMERICA		
United States	HIGH	3
EUROPE		
Finland	HIGH	2*
Sweden		
Denmark		
United Kingdom		
Germany		
France		
Italy		
Spain		
Portugal		
Greece		
Austria		
Netherlands		
Belgium		
Ireland		
EU-15 average	HIGH	4
ASIA		
China	MEDIUM	7
LATIN AMERICA		
Chile	MEDIUM	5
Costa Rica	MEDIUM	6
AFRICA		
South Africa	LOW	8

one ranking is left empty, as no country is yet sufficiently grounded on a sustainable development model in the Global Information Age. (* above indicates this)

Another important aggregate observation related to the Dignity Index is that, unlike, for example, in the UN's Human Development Index, the European Union is left behind by the United States (except Finland, for the moment). This is because in the Global Information Age a sustainable development model requires sufficiently strong informational development that is ultimately also a prerequisite for financing a high level of human development. Europe is here less renewed for the Information Age. For the reasons mentioned in the chapter on the Finnish model, its situation may also change, if it does not soon accomplish the listed renewals of its economy and wellbeing society.

As one more global observation one can note that, despite the strong economic growth of the Asian countries (such as China, which was analyzed as a case study), Latin America (for example in our case studies of Chile and Costa Rica) reaches higher levels of "dignity as development."

As we emphasized in Chapter 1, instead of there being one universal political answer that suits all countries, each country will have to make its policy specifically in its own context. On the most practical level, the sort of questions a policymaker should ask based on the Dignity Index include the following: Where are my country's weak points? What is the reason for low performance in these specific areas?

And then, going deeper to look at the country's situation in each of the individual components separately: informational development, human development, and cultural development. And from there, going to an even deeper level of the sub-components, such as innovation or education or the cultural sub-components.

And then, finally coming back to the big-picture level, one can ask: How is this all forming a virtuous or a vicious circle between informational and human development, mediated by cultural development? And ultimately: What should be done in practice to improve this, in order to achieve a sustainable development model—or "dignity as development?" These questions are part of what constitutes dignity-based leadership in the Global Information Age.

APPENDIX: CALCULATING THE DIGNITY INDEX

The following tables list the sources as well as the threshold values for each Dignity Index indicator and their levels: very high—high—medium—low—very low. Because in this Index we have wanted to emphasize the overall levels of development instead of marginal numerical differences, each indicator is normalized by assigning these levels the values of 3—2.5—2—1.5—1. In this way, we have intentionally sought to avoid the problem that comes in many forms of operationalizing indicators, namely that countries that are practically on the same level can get very different results in terms of their "ranking number." Naturally, it is also easy to think of using statistically more complex methods in the future development of the index, especially when new global statistical data reflecting the Information Age becomes available. This preliminary index is in fact also meant as an invitation for collective further development (to contact for that, see www.dignityasdevelopment.org).

The overall levels for each component, sub-component, and the aggregate Dignity Index are derived by adding these values and dividing by the total number of indicators. Based on this, the results are then again translated into the scale of very high—high—medium—low—very low, rounding the figure to its nearest equivalent (that is, 2.75 is the threshold for "very high," 2.25 is the threshold for "high," 1.75 is the threshold for "medium," 1.25 is the threshold for "low," and below that is ranked "very low").

The intent of this procedure is to grasp the overall level of development, instead of focusing on marginal decimal differences. In addition to the overall Dignity Index, the levels of its components and their sub-components are all presented separately, from informational to human to cultural development; this makes it possible to focus not only on the aggregate level but also on the specific sub-dimensions of development.

Appendix: Calculating the Dignity Index

	INFORMATIONAL DEVELOPMENT OVERALL SCORE	1. ECONOMY overall score	GNI per cap. (PPP USD)	GDP growth % (real annual)	Productivity (output per hour) US = 100	2. INNOVATION overall score	Competitiveness Index (WEF index) 2012	Productivity growth	Receipt of royalties and license fees (USD per capita)	3. TECHNOLOGY overall score	Internet users (% of pop.)	R&D Investment (% of GDP)	Patents per capita (per million)
			2012	2011	2012		2012	2005–11	2005–11		2012	2005–10	2005–10
NORTH AMERICA													
United States	VERY HIGH	High	43,480	1.8	100	Very high	5.47	108.2	387.1	Very high	81.0	2.8	707.6
EUROPE													
Finland	VERY HIGH	High	32,510	2.7	77	Very high	5.55	104.1	556.5	Very high	91.0	3.8	172.1
Sweden			36,143	4.0	86		5.53	103.8	619.4		94.0	3.6	147.1
Denmark			33,518	0.8	81		5.29	101.5	N.A.		93.0	3.0	27.9
United Kingdom			32,538	0.8	80		5.45	105.4	226.3		87.0	1.8	90.2
Germany			35,431	3.1	90		5.48	106.2	174.9		84.0	2.8	166.2
France			30,277	1.7	93		5.11	104.1	240.0		83.0	2.2	157.7
Italy			26,158	0.4	72		4.46	100.4	59.8		58.0	1.3	303.4
Spain			25,947	0.4	76		4.60	109.1	23.0		72.0	1.4	60.2
Portugal			19,907	−1.7	42		4.40	109.6	5.7		64.0	1.7	13.1
Greece			20,511	−6.9	50		3.86	100.2	6.1		56.0	0.6	422
Austria			36,438	2.7	86		5.22	108.7	92.6		81.0	2.7	134.6
Netherlands			37,282	1.1	96		5.50	104.0	320.8		93.0	1.6	117.6
Belgium			33,429	1.8	98		5.21	100.7	232.1		82.0	2.0	49.7
Ireland			28,671	1.4	90		4.91	120.3	574.2		79.0	1.8	54.4
EU-15 avg.	HIGH	High	30,626	0.9	80	High	5.04	105.6	240.9	High	79.8	2.2	109.7
ASIA													
China	MEDIUM	Medium	7945	9.2	N.A.	Medium	4.83	N.A.	0.6	Medium	42.3	1.5	100.7
LATIN AMERICA													
Chile	MEDIUM	Medium	14,987	5.9	27	Medium	4.65	116.9	3.7	Low	61.4	0.4	59.6
Costa Rica	MEDIUM	Medium	10,863	4.2	N.A.	Low	4.34	N.A.	0.9	Medium	47.5	0.4	9.7
AFRICA													
South Africa	LOW	Low	9594	3.1	N.A.	Low	4.37	N.A.	1.3	Low	41.0	0.9	105.3
Very high			40,000	3.5	90		5.25	106.0	400.0		80.0	2.5	200.0
High			30,000	2.5	70		4.75	104.0	275.0		65.0	2.0	150.0
Medium			20,000	1.5	50		4.25	102.0	150.0		50.0	1.5	100.0
Low			10,000	0.5	30		3.75	100.0	25.0		35.0	1.0	50.0
Very low													
Source:	UNDP (2013)		WB (2012)	WB (2012)	OECD (2013)		WEF (2013)	OECD (2013)	WB (2012)		ITU (2013)	WB (2012)	WIPO (2012)

	HUMAN DEVELOPMENT OVERALL SCORE	1. HEALTH overall score	Life expectancy (years at birth)	Maternal mortality per 100 000	Happiness (life satisfaction)	2. EDUCATION overall score	Expected years of education	Student performance (OECD PISA avg.)	Scientific publications (citations H-index)	3. SOCIAL overall score	Income inequality (Atkinson Index)	Inequality of life expectancy (% lost)	Youth unemployment (% of 15–24yrs)
			2012	2010	2012		2010–11	2000	2011		2012	2012	2011
NORTH AMERICA													
United States	HIGH	High	78.7	21	7.2	Very high	16.8	496	1305	Medium	24.1	6.6	11.9
EUROPE	VERY HIGH	Very high				Very high				Very high			
Finland			80.1	5	7.4		16.9	544	352		11.3	3.9	19.3
Sweden			81.6	4	7.5		16.0	495	484		11.2	3.3	23.8
Denmark			79.0	12	7.8		16.8	499	399		11.0	4.4	15.7
United Kingdom			80.3	12	7.0		15.3	500	802		16.9	4.8	22.0
Germany			80.6	7	6.7		19.7	524	704		14.5	4.0	9.1
France			81.7	8	6.8		16.1	497	646		13.3	4.2	23.2
Italy			82.0	4	6.4		16.2	486	550		18.1	3.9	32.0
Spain			81.6	6	6.2		16.4	434	448		19.7	4.1	48.2
Portugal			79.7	8	4.9		16.0	490	218		20.8	4.9	31.7
Greece			80.0	3	5.8		16.3	473	247		18.1	4.a	51.5
Austria			81.0	4	7.3		15.3	487	355		12.7	4.2	6.8
Netherlands			80.8	6	7.5		16.9	519	545		12.3	4.3	7.8
Belgium			80.0	8	6.9		16.4	509	42a		11.9	4.4	13.7
Ireland			80.7	6	7.3		18.3	457	254		13.8	4.3	35.3
EU-15 avg.	HIGH	High	80.7	6.8	6.8	High	16.6	500	459	High	14.7	4.3	24.8
ASIA													
China	MEDIUM	Medium	73.7	37	4.7	High	11.7	577	353	Medium	29.5	13.5	N.A.
LATIN AMERICA													
Chile	MEDIUM	Medium	79.3	25	6.6	Medium	14.7	439	181	Low	34.1	6.6	21.1
Costa Rica	MEDIUM	Medium	79.4	40	7.3	Medium	13.7	N.A.	97	Very low	37.9	7.8	21.6
AFRICA													
South Africa	LOW	Low	53.4	300	4.7	Medium	13.1	N.A.	216	Very low	63.1	28.4	55.0
Very high			80.0	5	8.0		16.0	525	500		12.5	5.0	10.0
High			70.0	15	7.0		14.5	475	350		15.0	10.0	20.0
Medium			60.0	25	6.0		13.0	425	200		17.5	15.0	30.0
Low			50.0	35	5.0		11.5	375	50		20.0	20.0	40.0
Very low													
Source:			UNDESA (2011)	UNDP (2013)	Gallup (2012)		UNESCO (2012)	OECD PISA (2009)	Scopus (2013)		UNDP (2013)	UNDP (2013)	WB (2012)

	CULTURAL DEVELOPMENT OVERALL SCORE	1. LIFE overall score	Ecological footprint (CO_2 emissions)	Global Peace Index (GPI)	Trust of others in society (%)	2. FREEDOM overall score	Freedom of press (Freedom House)	Creativity (GEM entrepreneur index)	Openness to others (% of foreign-born pop.)	3. JUSTICE overall score	Rule of law (Freedom House)	Gender equality (% of women in parliament)	Foreign aid (% of GDP)
NORTH AMERICA													
United States	MEDIUM	Low	7.2	2.05	37.0	Very high	18	0.717	13.5	Medium	1	17.0	0.2
EUROPE													
Finland	MEDIUM	Medium	6.2	1.35	58.0	Medium	10	0.564	4.2	High	1	42.5	0.6
Sweden			5.7	1.42	55.0		10	0.685	14.1		1	44.7	1.0
Denmark			8.3	1.24	60.0		12	0.763	8.8		1	39.1	0.9
United Kingdom			4.7	1.61	35.0		21	0.561	11.2		1	22.1	0.6
Germany			4.6	1.42	31.0		17	0.544	13.1		1	32.4	0.4
France			4.9	1.71	20.0		24	0.498	10.7		1	25.1	0.5
Italy			4.5	1.69	20.0		33	0.407	7.4		1.5	20.7	0.2
Spain			4.7	1.55	22.0		24	0.401	15.2		1	34.9	N.A.
Portugal			4.1	1.47	27.0		17	0.350	8.6		1	28.7	0.3
Greece			4.9	1.98	16.0		30	0.318	10.1		2	21.0	N.A.
Austria			5.3	1.33	29.0		21	0.454	15.6		1	28.7	0.3
Netherlands			6.3	1.61	46.0		12	0.615	10.5		1	37.8	0.8
Belgium			7.1	1.38	30.0		11	0.576	13.7		1	38.9	0.6
Ireland			6.2	1.33	30.0		16	0.631	19.6		1	19.0	0.5
EU-15 avg.	MEDIUM		5.5	1.51	34.2	High	18.4	0.526	11.6	High	1.1	31.1	0.6
ASIA													
China	LOW	Medium	2.1	2.06	57.0	Very low	85	0.281	0.1	Low	B.5	21.3	0.0
LATIN AMERICA													
Chile	MEDIUM	Medium	3.2	1.62	15.0	Low	31	0.414	1.9	Medium	1	13.9	−0.1
Costa Rica	HIGH	Medium	2.5	1.66	14.0	High	19	N.A.	10.5	Very high	1	38.6	−0.3
AFRICA													
South Africa	MEDIUM		2.6	2.32	17.0	Low	34	0.277	3.7	High	2	41.1	−0.3
Very high			1.0	1.50	60.0		20	0.650	15.0		1.5	45.0	0.9
High			2.0	2.00	45.0		30	0.600	11.0		2.5	35.0	0.7
Medium			3.0	2.50	30.0		40	0.550	7.0		3.5	25.0	0.5
Low			4.0	3.00	15.0		50	0.500	3.0		4.5	15.0	0.3
Very low													
Source:		GFN (2008)	GPI (2013)	Gallup (2012)		FH (2013a)	GEM (2012)	UNDP (2013)		FH (2013b)	IPU (2012)	UNDP (2013)	

	DIGNITY INDEX OVERALL SCORE	RANK
NORTH AMERICA		
United States	HIGH	3
EUROPE		
Finland	HIGH	2*
Sweden		
Denmark		
United Kingdom		
Germany		
France		
Italy		
Spain		
Portugal		
Greece		
Austria		
Netherlands		
Belgium		
Ireland		
EU-15 average	HIGH	4
ASIA		
China	MEDIUM	7
LATIN AMERICA		
Chile	MEDIUM	5
Costa Rica	MEDIUM	6
AFRICA		
South Africa	LOW	8
Very high	2.75	
High	2.25	
Medium	1.75	
Low	1.25	
Very low		

References

Adler Braun, Alejandro. (2009). *Gross National Happiness in Bhutan: A Living Example of an Alternative Approach to Progress.* <http://www.grossnationalhappiness.com>

Aghion, Philippe and Howitt, Peter. (2009). *The Economics of Growth.* Cambridge: MIT Press.

Ahonen, Guy, Hussi, Tomi, and Pirinen, Helka. (2010). Y-sukupolvi haastaa johtamisen Suomen työelämässä—syrjäytymisen kustannukset ja tulevaisuuden työelämään liittyvät mahdollisuudet, Työpoliittinen aikakauskirja, 4/2010.

Ahonen, Tomi. (2011). "Coining Term: 'Elop Effect' when you combine Osborne Effect and Ratner Effect," August 2011 <http://communities-dominate.blogs.com/brands/2011/08/coining-term-elop-effect-when-you-combine-osborne-effect-and-ratner-effect.html>

Alkire, S. (2002). *Valuing Freedoms: Sen's Capability Approach and Poverty Reduction.* New York: Oxford University Press.

Allen, Tim and Thomas, Allan (eds). (2000). *Poverty and Development into the 21st Century.* Oxford: Oxford University Press.

Amoretti, Luis Héctor. (2007). Los conflictos colectivos de carácter económico y social y sus medios de solución en el derecho costarricense. San José, Costa Rica: Litografía e imprenta LIL, S.A.

Arthur, Brian. (1994). *Increasing Returns and Path Dependence in the Economy.* Ann Arbor: University of Michigan Press.

Asmes, Barry and Gruden, Wayne. (2013). *The Poverty of Nations.* Wheaton: Crossway.

Avgerou, Chrisanthi. (2010). "Discourses on ICT and Development," *Information Technologies and International Development* 6(3): 1–18.

Badsha, N. and Cloete, N. (2011). *Higher Education: Contribution for the National Planning Commission's National Development Plan.*

Banya Honghsa, N. (2012). "The Peace and Civil Rights Movement in Burma." Available online: <http://monnews.org/?p=3929>

Barahona, M., García, C., Gloor, P., and Parraguez, P. (2012). "Tracking the 2011 Student-Led Movement in Chile through Social Media Use." Presented at Collective Intelligence conference, 2012 <http://arxiv.org/ftp/arxiv/papers/1204/1204.3939.pdf>.

References

Bauer, N. (2012). "Entrenched Inequality Threatens SA's Future." *Mail & Guardian*, 24 July 2012. http://mg.co.za/article/2012-07-24-entrenched-inequality-of-opportunity-threatens-sas-future.

Bay Area Council Economic Institute. (2012a). "Innovation and Investment: Building Tomorrow's Economy in the Bay Area," March 2012 <http://www.bayareaeconomy.org>

Bay Area Council Economic Institute. (2012b). "The Bay Area: A Regional Economic Assessment," October 2012 <http://www.bayareaeconomy.org>

Bay Area Council Economic Institute. (2012c). "Appendices to The Bay Area: A Regional Economic Assessment," December 2012 <http://www.bayareaeconomy.org>

BBC Mundo Cono Sur. (2012). "Por qué tiene tanta fuerza el movimiento estudiantil chileno?" Martes, 28 de agosto de 2012 <http://www.bbc.co.uk/mundo/noticias/2012/08/120827_chile_estudiantes_poder_vs.shtml>

BCS (British Computer Society). (2010). *The Information Dividend: International Information Well-being Index*. London: BCS Chartered Institute for IT.

Beck, U. (2002). *La sociedad del riesgo global*. Madrid: Siglo XXI.

Beck, U. (2006). *Power in the Global Age*. Cambridge: Polity.

Berek, Gunseli et al. (2011). *Inequalities, Development and Growth*. London: Routledge.

Beveridge, William. (1942). *Social Insurance and Allied Services*. London: His Majesty's Stationery Office.

Bhorat, H. and Jacobs, E. (2010). *An Overview of the Demand for Skills for an Inclusive Growth Path*. Midrand: Development Bank of South Africa (DBSA).

Bhorat, H. and Van der Westhuizen, C. (2010). *Economic Growth, Poverty and Inequality in South Africa: The First Decade of Democracy*. Cape Town: Institute for Democracy in Africa (IDASA).

Bhorat, H., Van der Westhuizen, C. and Tsang, D. (2013). *Poverty and Inequality Shifts in South Africa: A 15-year Review*. Cape Town: Development Policy Research Unit, University of Cape Town.

Bloom, D., Canning, D. and Chan, K. (2006). *Higher Education and Economic Development in Africa*. Washington, DC: World Bank, Human Development Sector, Africa Region.

Bobbio, N. and Viroli, M. (2002). *Diálogo en torno a la República*. Barcelona: Tusquets.

Bonoli, Giuliano and Natali, David. (2012). *The Politics of the New Welfare State*. Oxford: Oxford University Press.

Brenes, Lidiette. (1990). *La nacionalización bancaria en Costa Rica*. San José, Costa Rica: FLACSO.

Bresnahan, Timothy, Alfonso Gambardella, and AnnaLee Saxenian. (2001). " 'Old Economy' Inputs for 'New Economy' Outcomes: Cluster Formation in the New Silicon Valleys" *Industrial Corporate Change* V. 10, n. 4: 836–60.

Brett, E.A. (2009). *Reconstructing Development Theory: International Inequality, Institutional Reform and Social Emancipation*. New York: Palgrave/MacMillan.

Brickman and Campbell. (1971). "Hedonic Relativism and Planning the Good Society," in M.H. Apley (ed.), *Adaptation Level Theory: A Symposium*. New York: Academic Press.

Brynjolfsson, Erik and Hitt, Lorin. (1998). "Beyond the Productivity Paradox: Computers are the Catalyst for Bigger Changes," *Communications of the ACM*, August.

Brynjolfsson, Erik and Hitt, Lorin. (2003). "Computing Productivity: Firm-level Evidence," *Review of Economics & Statistics*, 85 (4).

Brynjolfsson, Erik and Saunders, Adam. (2010). *Wired for Innovation: How Information Technology Is Reshaping the Economy*. Cambridge, MA: MIT Press.

Brynjolfsson, Erik and Yang, Shinkyu. (1999). "The Intangible Costs and Benefits of Computer Investments: Evidence from the Financial Markets," MIT Sloan School of Management, December.

Bullionstreet. (2012). "Projected Strikes at SA Platinum Belt to Boost prices." <http://www.bullionstreet.com/news/projected-strikes-at-sa-platinum-belt-to-boost-prices/2239>

Calderón, F. (2007a). "Ciudadanía y desarrollo humano," in PNUD-PAPEP 2008, *Ciudadanía y desarrollo humano*. Buenos Aires: Siglo XXI.

Calderón, F. (2007b). "La inflexión política en el cambio sociocultural de América Latina," in PNUD-PAPEP 2008, *Escenarios políticos en América Latina. Cuadernos de gobernabilidad democrática Vol. 2*. Buenos Aires: Siglo XXI.

Calderón, F. (2011). *Los conflictos sociales en América Latina*. La Paz: Programa de Naciones Unidas para el Desarrollo/UNIR Foundation.

Calderón, F. (2012). *Tiempos de cambio. Consideraciones sociológicas sobre la democracia y el desarrollo humano*. Buenos Aires: TESEO—FLACSO.

Calderón, F. and Lechner, N. (1998). *Más allá del Estado, más allá del mercado: la democracia*. La Paz: Plural.

Calderón, F. and Szmukler, A. (2004). "Political Culture and Development" in Walton, M. and Rao, V. (eds), *Culture and Public Action*. Stanford: Stanford University Press.

Calderón, Fernando. (ed.) (2013). *Las huellas del futuro. Lideres y soberano*. Buenos Aires: Programa de Naciones Unidas para el Desarrollo, Siglo XXI.

Cardoso, Gustavo, Cheong, Angus, and Cole, Jeffrey (eds) (2009). *World Wide Internet: Changing Societies, Economies and Cultures*. University of Macau Press: 2009.

Cardoso, Gustavo. (Forthcoming). "Global Social Networks Research," Research Report, Lisbon: ISCTE-IUL/FCG.

Carnoy, Martin et al. (2013). *University Expansion in a Changing Global Economy: Triumph of the BRICS?* Stanford: Stanford University Press.

Castells, M. (1994). "European Cities, the Informational Society, and the Global Economy," *New Left Review*, vol. 204, pp.18–32.

Castells, M. (1996–8). *The Information Age: Economy, Society and Culture*.

Vol. 1: The Rise of the Network Society. Oxford: Blackwell, 1996.

Vol. 2: The Power of Identity. Oxford: Blackwell, 1997.

Vol. 3: End of Millennium. Oxford: Blackwell, 1998.

References

Castells, M. (1997). *La Era de la Información. Economía, Sociedad y Cultura.* Madrid: Alianza.

Castells, M. (2000–4). *The Information Age: Economy, Society and Culture.* 2nd ed.

Vol. 1: The Rise of the Network Society. Oxford: Blackwell, 2000.

Vol. 2: The Power of Identity. Oxford: Blackwell, 2004.

Vol. 3: End of Millennium. Oxford: Blackwell, 2000.

Castells, M. (2000). "Materials for an Exploratory Theory of the Network Society," *British Journal of Sociology* Vol. 51, Issue 1, pp. 5–24.

Castells, M. (2000b). "Information Technology and Global Capitalism," in Hutton and Giddens (eds).

Castells, M. (2001). *The Internet Galaxy: Reflections on the Internet, Business, and Society.* Oxford: Oxford University Press.

Castells, M. (2001a). "Universities Systems of Contradictory Functions," in Muller, J., Cloete, N., and Badat, S. (eds), *Challenges of Globalisation: South African Debates with Manuel Castells.* Cape Town: Maskew Miller Longman.

Castells, M. (2005). *Globalizacion, desarrollo y democracia. Chile en el contexto mundial.* Santiago de Chile: Fondo de Cultura Económica.

Castells, M. (2006). "De la Funcion de Produccion Agregada a la Frontera de Posibilidades de Produccion: Productividad, Tecnologia y Crecimiento Economico en la Era de la Informacion," Acceptance Speech on the Occasion of the Induction to the Real Academia Espanola de Ciencias Economicas y Financieras, Barcelona: Publicaciones de la Real Academia de Ciencias Economicas y Financieras.

Castells, M. (2008). "The New Public Sphere: Global Civil Society, Communication Networks, and Global Governance," in *The Annals of the American Academy of Political and Social Science 2008,* 616, 78, Urbana: Sage Publications.

Castells, M. (2009). *Communication Power.* Oxford: Oxford University Press.

Castells, M. (2012). *Networks of Outrage and Hope: Social Movements in the Internet Age.* Cambridge: Polity Press.

Castells, Manuel (ed.) (2004). *The Network Society: A Cross-Cultural Perspective.* Cheltenham: Edward Elgar.

Castells, Manuel, Caraça, João, and Cardoso, Gustavo (eds). (2012). *Aftermath: The Cultures of the Economic Crisis.* Oxford: Oxford University Press.

Castells, Manuel, Caraça, João, and Cardoso, Gustavo. (2012b). "The Cultures of the Economic Crisis," in Castells et al. (eds), *Aftermath: The Cultures of the Economic Crisis.* Oxford: Oxford University Press.

Castells, Manuel and Himanen, Pekka. (2002). *The Information Society and the Welfare State: The Finnish Model.* Oxford: Oxford University Press.

Castells, Manuel et al. (2007). "e-Health in the Catalan Health System," Project Internet Catalonia. Barcelona: Open University of Catalonia (accessible online).

Castells, Manuel et al. (2007). *La transicio a la societat xarxa a Catalunya.* Barcelona: Ariel.

References

Castells, M. and Cloete, N. (2011). Concept paper prepared for a seminar on *Informational Development and Human Development: South Africa in a Global Context.* Stellenbosch, Institute for Advanced Studies (STIAS), University of Stellenbosch.

CEPAL. (1992). *Educación y conocimiento: eje de la transformación productiva con equidad.* Libros de la CEPAL N° 33. Santiago de Chile: CEPAL.

CERC. (2011). "Barómetro de la política," *Encuesta CERC,* agosto-septiembre 2011 <http://www.cooperativa.cl/noticias/site/artic/20110927/asocfile/20110927120124/1364157_1.pdf>

Chetty, M., Calandro, E. and Feamster, N. (2013). "Measuring Broadband Performance in South Africa," policy paper no. 1. Cape Town: Research ICT Africa (forthcoming).

Chipken, I. (2007). *Do South Africans Exist?* Johannesburg: Wits University Press.

Chiu, Lisa. (2003). "Outbreak of Rumors Has China Reeling," *SFGate.com* (7 May) <http://articles.sfgate.com/2003-05-07/news/17493093_1_sars-cases-beijing-mayor-meng-xuenong-sars-epidemic>

Christensen, Kaare, Doblhammer, Gabriele, Rau, Roland, and Vaupel, James. (2009). "Ageing Populations: The Challenges Ahead," Lancet, Vol. 374, Oct 3.

Citrin, Jack (ed.) (2009). *Proposition 13 at 30.* Berkeley, CA: Berkeley Public Policy Press.

Cloete, N. (ed.) (2009). *Responding to the Educational Needs of Post-School Youth.* Cape Town: Centre for Higher Education Transformation (CHET).

Cloete, N., Bailey, T., Pillay, P., Bunting, I. and Maassen, P. (2011). *Universities and Economic Development in Africa.* Cape Town: Centre for Higher Education Transformation (CHET).

Club of Rome. (1972). *The Limits to Growth* (Meadows, Donatella, Meadows, Dennis, Randers, Jorgen, Behrens, William). London: Earth Island.

Club of Rome. (2012). *2052: A Global Forecast for the Next Forty Years* (Randers, Jorgen). White River Junction, VT: Chelsea Green Publishing.

Cohen, Elie. (2005). *Le Nouvel Age du Capitalisme.* Paris: Fayard.

Collaborative Economics. (2013). "2013 Index of Silicon Valley," Joint Venture: Silicon Valley, 2013 <http://www.siliconvalleyindex.org/>

CONACOM (Consejo Nacional de Competitividad) (2007). *Educación superior y competitividad en Costa Rica.* <http://www.conacom.go.cr>.

Conill, Joana et al. (2013). *Otra Vida es Posible: Practicas Economicas Alternativas Durante la Crisis.* Barcelona: Universitat Oberta de Catalunya (UOC) Press.

Constantini, Valeria and Mazzanti, Massimiliano. (2012). *The Dynamics of Environmental and Economic Systems: Innovation, Environmental Policy and Competitiveness.* Milan: CERIS-CNR.

Contraloría General de la República. (2002*). El sistema tributario costarricense. Contribuciones al debate nacional.* Imprenta Nacional. San José, Costa Rica.

Coriat, Benjamin et al. (eds). (2011). 20 ans d' aveuglement: L' Europe au bord du gouffre, Paris: Editions les liens qui liberent.

References

Credit Suisse Research Institute. (2012). "Global Wealth Report 2012," <https://publi cations.creditsuisse.com/tasks/render/file/index.cfm?fileid=88EE6EC8-83E8-EB92-9D5F39D5F5CD01F4>

Crouch, Colin. (2013). *Post-democracy*. Cambridge: Polity Press.

Csikszentmihalyi, Mihaly. (1990). *Flow: The Psychology of Optimal Experience*. New York: Harper & Row.

Daniels, N. (ed.) (1975). *Reading Rawls: Critical Studies on John Rawls'* A Theory of Justice. New York: Basic Books.

Davies, Anna R. and Mullin, Sue J. (2010). "Greening the Economy: Interrogating Sustainability Innovations Beyond the Mainstream," *Journal of Economic Geography* (2010): 1–24.

Davies, R., Kaplan, D., Morris, M., O'Meara, D. (1976). *Review of African Political Economy*. University of Natal Press.

Department of Higher Education and Training. (2012). *Green Paper for Post-School Education and Training*. Pretoria. <http://www.info.gov.za/view/Down loadFileAction?id=157779> accessed 17 July 2012.

Diener, E., Helliwell, J.F., and Kahneman, D. (eds.). (2010). *International Differences in Well-being*. New York: Oxford University Press.

Dodds, C. (2013). "We CAN Blame Apartheid, says Zuma," *IOL News*, 11 April 2013. <http://www.iol.co.za/news/politics/we-can-blame-apartheid-says-zuma-1.1498541>

Dosi, Giovanni et al. (1998). *Technology, Organization, and Competitiveness*. Oxford: Oxford University Press.

Douglass, John Aubrey. (2000). *The California Idea and American Higher Education: 1850 to the 1960 Master Plan*. Palo Alto, CA: Stanford University Press.

Dube, O., Hausman, R. and Rodrik, D. (2007). *South Africa: Identifying the Binding Constraint on Growth*. Harvard: AGISA Review.

Easterlin, Richard. (1974). "Does Economic Growth Improve the Human Lot?" in Paul David and Melvin Reder (eds), *Nations and Households in Economic Growth: Essays in Honor of Moses Abramovitz*. New York: Academic Press Inc.

Easterlin, Richard. (2004). *Feeding the Illusion of Growth and Happiness: A Reply to Hagerty and Veenhoven*.

Easterlin, Richard, McVey, Laura Angelescu, Switek, Malgorzata, Sawangfa, Onnicha and Smith Zweig, Jacqueline. (2010). "The happiness–income paradox revisited," Proceedings of the National Academy of Sciences of the United States of America, 107 (52).

ECLAC (2012). *La hora de la igualdad*. Santiago de Chile: ECLAC. Global Peace Index 2012. Available online: <http://www.visionofhumanity.org/gpi-data/>

The Economist, "The Giant Cage," *Special report on China and the Internet*, 6–12 April 2013.

Engelen, Edwald et al. (2011). *After the Great Complacence: Financial Crisis and the Politics of Reform*. Oxford: Oxford University Press.

Erasmus, J. (2012). "SA, Australia to share SKA telescope," *South Africa.info*, 25 May 2012. <http://www.southafrica.info/about/science/skashared-250512.htm>

Esping-Andersen, Gösta. (1990). *The Three Worlds of Welfare Capitalism*. Cambridge, UK: Polity Press.

Esselaar, S., Gillwald, A., Moyo, M. and Naidoo, K. (2010). *South African ICT Sector Performance Review 2009/2010, Publication and Presentation*, Vol. 2, Paper 6. Cape Town: Research ICT Africa. <http://www.researchictafrica.net/> accessed 17 July 2012.

ETK. (2011). *Lakisääteiset eläkkeet—pitkän aikavälin laskelmat 2011*. Helsinki: Elakäturvakeskus.

EU Commission. (2011). *Public Procurement Indicators 2010*. Brussels: European Commission.

EU KLEMS (2011). Growth and Productivity Accounts. November 2009 Release, updated March 2011. <http://www.euklems.net>

European Commission. (2008a). "European Satisfaction with Internet Services, 2008," in *Study on User Satisfaction and Impact in EU27*, Directorate General for Information Society and Media. Brussels: European Commission.

European Commission. (2008b). "European Trust in Internet for Public and Private Uses 2008," in *Study on User Satisfaction and Impact in EU27*, Directorate General for Information Society and Media. Brussels: European Commission.

European Commission. (2008c). "European Use of eGovernment by Type, 2008," in *Study on User Satisfaction and Impact in EU27*, Directorate General for Information Society and Media. Brussels: European Commission.

European Commission. (2009a). "2011 EU Digital Agenda Scorecard," in *Better, Faster, Smarter eGovernment*, Directorate General for Information Society and Media. Brussels: European Commission.

European Commission. (2009b). "European Full Online Availability of eGovernance Services for Businesses and Citizens, 2001–2009," in *Better, Faster, Smarter eGovernment*. Directorate General for Information Society and Media. Brussels: European Commission.

European Commission. (2009c). "European Sophistication of eGovernance Services by Country and Governance Type, 2009," in *Better, Faster, Smarter eGovernment*, Directorate General for Information Society and Media. Brussels: European Commission.

European Commission. (2009d). "European Take-up of eGovernance Services, 2008–2009," in *Better, Faster, Smarter eGovernment*, Directorate General for Information Society and Media. Brussels: European Commission.

European Commission. (2009e). "Internet Connection Type in European Hospitals, 2009," in *eHealth Benchmarking III*, Directorate General for Information Society and Media. Brussels: European Commission.

References

European Commission. (2009f). "Penetration of Wireless Communication in European Hospitals by Type, 2009," in *eHealth Benchmarking III*, Directorate General for Information Society and Media. Brussels: European Commission.

European Commission. (2010a). "Digitizing Public Services in Europe: Putting Ambition into Action," 9th Benchmark Measurement, Directorate General for Information Society and Media. Brussels: European Commission.

European Commission. (2010b). "European ICT in Value Added in Percent of GDP, 2010," in *Europe's Digital Competitiveness Report*. Brussels: European Commission.

European Commission. (2010c). "European Individuals Using Internet for Learning, 2007–2010," in *Digital Literacy Benchmarking Report*, Directorate General for Information Society and Media. Brussels: European Commission.

European Commission. (2011). *Digital Agenda Scoreboard, EU eGovernment Benchmark Report*. Brussels: European Commission.

European Commission. (2012a). *Digital Competences in the Digital Agenda, Digital Agenda Scoreboard*. Brussels: European Commission.

European Commission. (2012b). *eGovernment Trends, Digital Agenda Scoreboard*. Brussels: European Commission.

European Council. (2008). *Energy and Climate Change: Elements of the Final Compromise*. Brussels: European Council.

Eurydice. (2011). "Students per Computer in EU Schools, 2007," in IEA TIMSS DATA 2007, cited in *Key Data on Learning and Innovation through ICT at School in Europe*. Brussels: EACEA Eurydice.

EVA. (2012). *EVAn arvo- ja asennetutkimus 2012*. Helsinki: Elinkeinoelämänvaltuuskunta.

Evans, Peter. (1995). *Embedded Autonomy, States and Industrial Transformation*. Princeton University Press.

Eysenck, Michael. (1990). *Happiness: Facts and Myths*. Hove: L. Erlbaum.

Fajnzylber, Fernando. (1983). *La industrializacion trunca de America Latina*. Mexico DF: CET.

Fajnzylber, Fernando. (1989). *Growth and Equity via Austerity and Competitiveness*. Philadelphia: The Annals of the American Academy of Political and Social Science.

Ferrera, Maurizio. (2008). "The European Welfare State: Golden Achievements and Silver Prospects," in *West European Politics*, vol. 31, 1–2, January-March. pp. 82–107.

Ferrera, Maurizio. (ed.) (2005). *Welfare State Reform in Southern Europe*. London: Routledge.

FH [Freedom House]. (2013a). Freedom of the Press 2013. Washington DC: Freedom House. <http://www.freedomhouse.org/sites/default/files/FOTP%202013%20Booklet%20Final%20Complete%20-%20Web.pdf>

FH [Freedom House]. (2013b). Freedom in the World 2013. Washington, DC: Freedom House. <http://www.freedomhouse.org/sites/default/files/FIW%202013%20Booklet%20-%20for%20Web_1.pdf>

Finnish Institute of Occupational Health (2010). Työkyvyttömyyseläkkeistä aiheutuvat työpanosmenetykset (prof. Guy Ahonen).

Finnish Ministry of Finance. (2012). Kansantalousosaston laskelma eri tekijöiden vaikutuksesta kestävyysvajeeseen. [The Public Economy Department's Calculation on the Effect on Alternative Factors on the Sustainability Deficit]. Helsinki: Ministry of Finance.

Fisher, G. and Scott, I. (2011). "The Role of Higher Education in Closing the Skills Gap in South Africa," Background Paper 3 for the World Bank project *Closing the Skills and Technological Gaps in South Africa*. Washington, DC: World Bank.

Fonseca, Elizabeth. (2001). *Centroamérica: su historia*. San José, Costa Rica: Editorial Universitaria Centroamericana EDUCA.

Fraser, Derek. (2009). *The Evolution of the British Welfare State: A History of Social Policy since the Industrial Revolution*. 4th ed. Basingstoke: Palgrave Macmillan.

Fredrickson, Barbara. (2009). *Positivity: Groundbreaking Research Reveals How to Embrace the Hidden Strength of Positive Emotions, Overcome Negativity, and Thrive*. New York: Crown.

Freeman, S. (2007). *Rawls*. London: Routledge.

Frey, Bruno S. (2008). *Happiness: A Revolution in Economics*. Cambridge: MIT Press.

Fu, X., Pietrobelli, C., and Soete, L. (2011). "The Role of Foreign Technology and Indigenous Innovation in the Emerging Economies: Technological Change and Catching-up," *World Development*, 39 (7) 1204–12.

Gali, Jordi (1994). "Keeping up with the Joneses: Consumption Externalities, Portfolio Choice, and Asset Prices, Journal of Money, Credit and Banking," 26 (1).

Gallup (2012). Gallup World Poll database. <https://worldview.gallup.com>

GEM [Global Entrepreneurship Monitor]. (2012). Global Entrepreneurship Monitor. <http://www.gemconsortium.org>

Genesis Analytics. (2009). *The 15-Year Presidential Review of Economic Regulation: Telecommunications*. Author (unpublished).

Genevy, Remy, Pachauri, Rajandra, and Tubiana, Laurence. (2013). *Reducing Inequalities: A Sustainable Development Challenge*. Paris: IDDRI.

Georgescu-Roegen, Nicholas. (1979). *Demain la Décroissance*. Paris.

Giddens, Anthony and Himanen, Pekka. (2006). *Eurooppalainen unelma, Helsingin Sanomat*, 4.6.2006.

Gilbert, Daniel. (2006). *Stumbling on Happiness*. New York: A.A. Knopf.

Gillwald, A. (2009). "Wireless: A Decade of Telecom Reform in South Africa," unpublished PhD dissertation, University of Witwatersrand, Johannesburg.

Global Footprint Network and San Francisco Planning & Urban Research Association. (2011). "Ecological Footprint Analysis: San Francisco, Oakland, Fremont, CA." June 30, 2011. <http://www.footprintnetwork.org/images/uploads/SF_Ecological_Footprint_Analysis.pdf>

References

GFN [Global Footprint Network]. (2012). <http://www.footprintnetwork.org>

Government Communication Information Services. (1997). *The Growth Employment and Redistribution plan (GEAR)*. <http://www.info.gov.za/view/DownloadFileAction?id=70507>

Government Communication Information Services. (2005). *The Accelerated and Shared Growth Initiative (ASGISA)*. <http://www.info.gov.za/asgisa/>

Government Communication Information Services. (2011). *The New Growth Path*. <http://www.info.gov.za/view/DownloadFileAction?id=135748>

Government Communication Information Services. (2012). "Human Rights Day to Evoke the Spirit of the Freedom Charter," <http://www.info.gov.za/speech/DynamicAction?pageid=461&sid=25838&tid=60285> accessed 12 October 2012.

Government Communication Information Services. (2012). "Statement of the Cabinet," <http://www.info.gov.za/speech/DynamicAction?pageid=461&sid=26077&tid=61586>

Gower, P. (2009). "Idle Minds, Social Time Bomb," *Mail & Guardian*. <http://www.mg.co.za/article/2009-07-31-idle-minds-social-time-bomb/> accessed 17 July 2012.

GPI. (2013). Global Peace Index Report 2013. Sydney: Institute for Economics and Peace. <http://www.visionofhumanity.org/pdf/gpi/2013_Global_Peace_Index_Report.pdf>

Grau, Imma. (2011). "Internet, información y salud en un hospital universitario en Barcelona," Tesis de doctorado en sociedad de la información. Barcelona: Universitat Oberta de Catalunya.

Grossman, Gene and Rossi-Hansberg, Esteban. (2008). "Trading Tasks: A Simple Theory of Offshoring," American Economic Review, 98 (5).

Gumede, V. (2010). *A South African Developmental State in the Making*. Development Studies, University of Johannesburg. <http://www.vusigumedethinkers.com/pages/acpapers_log/sadevelop.html> accessed 17 July.

Gurumurthy, Anita. (2010). "From Social Enterprises to Mobiles—Seeking a Peg to Hang a Premeditated ICTD Theory," *Information Technologies and International Development*, volume 6, 2010: 57–63.

Habermas, J. (2010). "El concepto de dignidad humana y la utopía realista de los derechos humanos," in *Dianoia*, vol. LV, No 64 (May).

Hagerty, Michael. (2003). "Was Life Better in the 'Good Old Days'? Intertemporal Judgments of Life Satisfaction," Journal of Happiness Studies, Vol. 4, No. 2.

Hagerty, Michael and Veenhoven, Ruut. (2003). "Wealth and Happiness Revisited: Growing wealth of nations does go with greater happiness, Social Indicators Research," Vol. 64, 2003.

Hämäläinen, Timo. (2013). *Towards a Sustainable Well-being Society*. Helsinki: Sitra.

Han, Rongbin. (2012a). *Challenging the Regime, Defending the Regime: Contesting Cyberspace in China*, unpublished dissertation. Department of Political Science, UC Berkeley.

Han, Rongbin. (2012b). *Power of the Internet and its Limitations: Understanding Online Expression in Chinese Cyberspace*, unpublished PhD dissertation, Department of Political Science, UC Berkeley.

Harlow, Elizabeth and Webb, Stephen A. (eds.) (2003). *Information and Communication Technologies in the Welfare Services*. London: Jessica Kingsley Publishers.

Hart, Stuart. (2005). "Innovation, Creative Destruction and Sustainability," *Research Technology Management*, 48 (5).

Hart, Stuart and Milstein, Mark. (1999). "Global Sustainability and the Creative Destruction of Industries," *Sloan Management Review*, 41 (1).

Hart, Stuart and Milstein, Mark. (2003). "Creating Sustainable Value," *Academy of Management Executive*, 17 (2).

Hartshorn, James, Maher, Michael, Crooks, Jack, Stahl, Richard and Bond, Zoë. (2005). "Creative Destruction: Building Toward Sustainability," *Canadian Journal of Civil Engineering*, 32 (1).

Hay, Colin and Wincott, David. (2012). *The Political Economy of Welfare Capitalism*. Houndmills, Basingstoke: Palgrave-MacMillan.

Heeks, Richard. (2006). "Theorizing ICT4D Research," *Information Technologies and International Development* 3(3): 1–4.

Helliwell, J.F., Layard, R., and Sachs, J. (eds.). (2012). *World Happiness Report*. New York: Columbia University Earth Institute.

Hennock, Ernest. (2007). *The Origin of the Welfare State in England and Germany, 1850–1914: Social Policies Compared*. Cambridge: Cambridge University Press.

Hessel, Stephane. (2010). *Indignez-vous*. Montpellier: Indigène.

Hilbert, Martin, and Lopez, Priscila. (2011). "The World's Technological Capacity to Store, Communicate, and Compute Information," *Science*, 332 (6025), 60–5.

Himanen, Pekka. (2001). *The Hacker Ethic and the Spirit of the Information Age*. New York: Random House.

Himanen, Pekka. (2001b). "A Brief History of Computer Hackerism," <http://linux.omnipotent.net/article.php?article_id=11832>

Himanen, Pekka. (2004a). "The Hacker Ethic as the Culture of the Information Age," in Castells, ed. (2004).

Himanen, Pekka. (2012). "Crisis, Identity, and the Welfare State," in Castells et al. (eds), *Aftermath: The Cultures of the Economic Crisis*. Oxford: Oxford University Press.

Himanen, Pekka. (2012b). "Dignity as human development." Working paper.

Himanen, Pekka and Castells, Manuel. (2004). "Institutional Models of the Network Society: Silicon Valley and Finland," in Castells, ed. (2004).

Hirabayashi. (2012). COMPLETAR

Hirschman, A. (1996). *Tendencias Autosubversivas: Ensayos*. Santiago de Chile: FCE.

Hirschman, Albert O. (1958). *The Strategy of Economic Development*. New Haven, CT: Yale University Press.

References

Horst, Heather A. (2013). "The Infrastructures of Mobile Media: Towards a Future Research Agenda," in *Mobile Media and Communication*, 1:147.

Howard, Philip. (2011). *The Digital Origins of Dictatorship and Democracy: Information Technology and Political Islam*. Oxford: Oxford University Press.

Human Rights Support. (2010). "How the Humans Rights Movement Has Gone Global." Available online: <http://www.cdhrsupport.org/2012/02/20/how-the-humans-rights-movement-has-gone-global/>

Hutton, Will and Giddens, Anthony. (2000). *On the Edge: Living with Global Capitalism*. London: Jonathan Cape. Ministry of Finance.

Hsing, Y. (2010). *The Great Urban Transformation: Politics and Property Development in China*. Oxford: Oxford University Press.

Hsing, You-tien. (2012). "No Crisis in China? The Rise of China's Social Crisis," in Manuel Castells et al. (eds), *Aftermath: The Culture of the Economic Crisis*. Oxford, UK: Oxford University Press. pp. 251–77.

INEC (Instituto Nacional de Estadística y Censos) *Producción de las principales actividades agropecuarias 2003–2009*. San José, Costa Rica: Estadísticas.

Inglehart, Ronald. (1997). *Modernization and Postmodernization: Cultural, Economic, and Political Change in 43 Societies*. Princeton, NJ: Princeton University Press.

Inglehart, Ronald and Welzel, Christian. (2005). *Modernization, Cultural Change, and Democracy: The Human Development Sequence*. New York: Cambridge University Press.

IPCC [Intergovernmental Panel on Climate Change]. (2007). *Climate Change 2007. The Fourth Assessment Report*. 4 vols. Cambridge: Cambridge University Press.

IPU [Inter-Parliamentary Union]. (2012). PARLINE database. <http://www.ipu.org/wmn-e/classif.htm>

ITU [International Telecommunications Union]. (2010a). "European eGovernment Use by Citizens, 2010," in *The World in 2010*. Geneva: ITU.

ITU [International Telecommunications Union]. (2010b). "European Individuals Using Internet for Learning, 2007–2010," in *The World in 2010*. Geneva: ITU.

International Telecommunications Union (ITU) (2012). Measuring the Information Society, Geneva (accessed 10 August 2012). <http://www.itu.int/en/ITU-D/Statistics/Documents/publications/mis2012/MIS2012_without_Annex_4.pdf>

ITU. (2013). *World Telecommunication/ICT Indicators Database*. Geneva: ITU, 2013.

Johnson, Chalmers. (1995). *Japan: Who Governs? The rise of the Developmental State*, New York: W.W. Norton.

Jorgenson, Dale, Ho, Mun and Stiroh, Kevin. (2002). "Projecting Productivity Growth: Lessons from the US Growth Resurgence," *Economic Review (Federal Reserve Bank of Atlanta)*, Vol. 87, No. 3.

Jorgenson, Dale and Stiroh, Kevin. (2000). "Raising the Speed Limit: US Economic Growth in the Information Age," *Brookings Papers on Economic Activity*, Vol. 2. Washington, DC: The Brookings Institution.

Kahneman, Daniel. (2011). *Thinking, Fast and Slow*. New York: Farrar, Straus and Giroux.

Kahneman, Daniel, Diener, Ed and Schwartz, Norbert (eds). (1999). *Well-being: The Foundations of Hedonic Psychology*. New York: Russel Sage Foundation.

Kahneman, Daniel, Krueger, Alan, Schkade, David, Schwarz, Norbert and Stone, Arthur. (2006). "Would You Be Happier If You Were Richer? A Focusing Illusion," *Science,* Vol. 312 No. 5782.

Kahneman, Daniel and Thaler, Richard. (2006). "Anomalies: Utility Maximization and Experienced Utility," Journal of Economic Perspectives, 20 (1).

Katz, R. and Koutroumpis, P. (2012). "The Economic Impact of Telecommunications in Senegal," *Digiworld Economic Journal*, vol. 86, no.2, 2012, pp.1–23. <http://ssrn.com/abstract=2070035>

Katz, R. and Suter, S. (2009). *Estimating the Economic Impact of the Broadband Stimulus Plan*. New York: Columbia Business School. <http://citi25.wordpress.com/raul-katz/articles-2009/2009-impact-of-broadband-stimulus/> accessed 24 July 2012.

Kelly, Kevin. (1998). *New Rules for the New Economy*. New York: Viking Press.

Kemerer, Chris F. (1998/2012). *Information Technology and Industrial Competitiveness: How IT Shapes Competition*. New York: Springer.

Kim, Y., Kelly, T. and Raja, S. (2010). *Building Broadband: Strategies and Policies for the Developing World*. Washington, DC: The World Bank. <http://siteresources.worldbank.org/EXTINFORMATIONANDCOMMUNICATIONANDTECHNOLOGIES/Resources/282822-1208273252769/Building_broadband.pdf>

Klasen, S. (1999). *Social Exclusion, Children and Education: Conceptual and Measurement Issues*. OECD Reports. Available online: <http://www.oecd.org/dataoecd/19/37/1855901.pdf>

Kleine, Dorothea. (2013). *Technologies of Choice? ICTs, Development and the Capabilities Approach*. Cambridge: MIT Press.

Koo, N. (2013). *The Internet and Happiness in the Network Society*, unpublished PhD dissertation, Annenberg School of Communication, University of South California.

Kostzer, D. (2008). "Youth, Work and Human Development: A Scalene Triangle." Paper presented at the Internal Workshop held in Buenos Aires IRDH, June 2008.

Koutroumpis, P. (2009). "The Economic Impact of Broadband on Growth: A Simultaneous Approach," *Telecommunications Policy*, vol. 33, no.9, pp. 471–85.

Kristof, Nicholas. (2005). "Death by a Thousand Blogs," *New York Times*, May 24 2005.

Krugman, P. (2012). *Acabemos ya con esta crisis*. Barcelona: Crítica.

Kuhnle, Stein. (2000). *Survival of the European Welfare State*. London: Routledge.

Kukathas, C. (ed.) (2003). *John Rawls: Critical Assessments of Leading Political Philosophers*, 4 vol., London: Routledge.

Kuusi, Pekka (1961). *60-luvun sosiaalipolitiikka*. Porvoo: WSOY.

Layard, Richard. (2005). *Happiness: Lessons from a New Science*. New York: Penguin Press.

Lechner, N. (2002). *Las sombras del mañana*. Santiago de Chile: Escafandra.

References

Lee, Ching Kwan. (2007). *Against the Law: Labor Protests in China's Rustbelt*. Berkeley: University of California Press.

Lee, Ching Kwan and Zhang, Yong Hong. (2013). "The Power of Instability: Unraveling the Microfoundations of Bargained Authoritarianism in China," *American Journal of Sociology*, 118(6): 1–34.

Legassick, M. (1974). "South Africa: Capital Accumulation and Violence," *Economy and Society*, vol.3, no.3, pp. 253–91.

Leibbrandt, M. and Finn, A. (2012). *Inequality in South Africa and Brazil: Can We Trust the Numbers?* Johannesburg: Centre for Development and Enterprise (CDE). <http://www.cde.org.za/article.php?a_id=425> accessed 24 July 2012.

Leibold, James. (2011). "Blogging Alone: China, the Internet, and the Democratic Illusion?" *The Journal of Asian Studies*, 70(4): 1023–41.

Levitt, P. and Merry, S. (2010). "Law From Below: Women's Human Rights and Social Movements in New York City," in *Law & Society Review*, Volume 44, Nr. 1.

Li, Lianjiang. (2008). "Political Trust and Petitioning in the Chinese Countryside," *Comparative Politics*, Vol. 40, No. 2 (2008), pp. 209–26.

Li, Pei-lin et al. (2008). *Social Harmony and Stability in China Today* (*zhongguo shehui hexie wending baogao*), Beijing: Social Science Press. pp. 32–3 & pp. 66–7.

Liu, Zhong and Whalley, Jason. (2011). "Anti-competitive Behaviors in Managed Competition: The Case of China's Telecommunications Industry," *Communications of the Association for Information System*, Vol. 28 Article 36, pp. 611–28.

Lybeck, Johan A. (2011). *A Global History of the Financial Crash of 2007–2010*. Cambridge: Cambridge University Press.

Lyubomirsky, Sonja. (2008). *The How of Happiness: A Scientific Approach to Getting the Life You Want*. New York: Penguin Press.

MacGregor, K. (2009). "Africa: Call for Higher Education Support Fund," *University World News*. <http://www.universityworldnews.com/article.php?story=20090322082237425> accessed 17 July 2012.

Malecki, Edward. (1997). Technology and Economic Development: The Dynamics of Local, Regional, and National Competitiveness.

Maslow, Abraham. (1954). *Motivation and Personality*. New York: Harper.

Maslow, Abraham. (1962). *Toward a Psychology of Being*. Princeton, NJ: Van Nostrand.

Mason, Roger. (2000). "Conspicuous Consumption and the Positional Economy: Policy and Prescription since 1970," Managerial and Decision Economics, 21 (3/4).

Mbeki, M. (2009). *Architects of Poverty*. Johannesburg: Picador Africa.

McKinsey. (2012). *Urban World: Cities and the Rise of the Consuming Class*. McKinsey Global Institute.

Merry, S. E. et al. (2010). "Law from Below: Women's Human Rights and Social Movements in New York City," Law and Society Review 44 (1):101–28.

Mhenni, L.B. (2011). Tunisian girl. Bloquista por una primavera árabe. Paris: Indigene.

Ministerio Público de Costa Rica. (2007). *Informes y Discursos del Ministerio Público* Informe Final de Labores, 2003–2007. San José, Costa Rica.

Mohamed, S. (2009). *The State of the South African Economy*. Johannesburg: University of the Witwatersrand, Corporate Strategy and Industrial Development (CSID).

Mohamed, S. (2011). "Prospects and Challenges in Building the Trade, Industry, and Financial Sector in South Africa," in Plaatjies, D. (ed), *Future Inheritance: Building State Capacity in Democratic South Africa*. Johannesburg: Jacana Media, pp. 23–45.

Mokyr, Joel. (1990). *The Lever of Riches: Technological Creativity and Economic Progress*. New York: Oxford University Press.

Momino, Josep Maria, Sigales, Carles, et al. (2007). *La escuela en la sociedad red*. Barcelona: Ariel.

Morin, E. (1990). *La pensé ecologicé*. Paris: Editions du Seuil.

Morin, E. (1993). *Madre Tierra Patria*. Buenos Aires: Punto Sur.

Mowery, David and Rosenberg, Nathan. (1989/1995). *Technology and the Pursuit of Economic Growth*. Cambridge: Cambridge University Press.

National Planning Commission (NPC). (2011a). Office of the President of South Africa, *Diagnostic Report*. <http://www.info.gov.za/view/DownloadFileAction?id= 147192> accessed 17 July 2012.

National Planning Commission (NPC). (2011b). Office of the President of South Africa, *National Development Plan: Vision for 2030*. <http://www.npconline.co.za/ medialib/downloads/home/NPC%20National%20Development%20Plan%20Vision %202030%20-lo-res.pdf> accessed 17 July 2012.

Nathan, Andrew. (2003). "Authoritarian Resilience," Journal of Democracy 14 (1): 6–17.

Nederveen Pieterse, Jan. (2009). *Development Theory*. London: Sage.

New Economics Foundation. (2012). *The Happy Planet Index: 2012 Report. A Global Index of Sustainable Well-Being*. London: New Economics Foundation.

Nolan, Peter. (2009). *Crossroads: The End of Wild Capitalism and the Future of Humanity*. London: Marshall Cavendish.

Nussbaum, M. (2000). *Women and Human Development: The Capabilities Approach*. Cambridge: Cambridge University Press.

Nussbaum, M. (2006). *Creating Capabilities: The Human Development Approach*. Cambridge, MA: Harvard University Press.

Nussbaum, M. (2006). *Frontiers of Justice: Disability, Nationality, Species Membership*. Cambridge, MA: Harvard University Press.

Nussbaum, M. (2011). *Creating Capabilities: The Human Development Approach*. Cambridge, MA: Belknap Press of Harvard University Press.

OECD. (2009). *PISA 2009 Results: Students Online, Digital Technologies and Performance*. Paris: OECD.

OECD. (2010). *Green Growth Strategy Interim Report: Implementing Our Commitment for a Sustainable Future*. Paris: OECD.

References

OECD. (2011). "2009 Results: Students Online, Digital Technologies and Performance," *PISA*.

OECD. (2011). *Towards Green Growth*. Paris: OECD.

OECD. (2012). *OECD Health Data*. Paris: OECD.

OECD. (2013a). Paris: OECD. http://www.oecd-ilibrary.org/statistics.

OECD. (2013b). *Better Life Index*. http://www.oecdbetterlifeindex.org.

OECD. (2013c). *Guidelines on Measuring Subjective Well-being*. Paris: OECD. http://www.oecd.org/statistics/guidelines-on-measuring-subjective-well-being.htm

Ohno, I. (1996). *Beyond the East Asian Miracle, an Asian View. UNDP Discussion Paper 5*. New York: UNDP-Oficina de Estudios de Desarrollo.

Oi, Jean C. (1992). "Fiscal Reform and the Economic Foundations of Local State Corporatism in China," *World Politics*, Vol. 45, No. 1, pp. 99–126.

O'Mara, Margaret. (2005). *Cities of Knowledge: Cold War Science and the Search for the Next Silicon Valley*. New Jersey: Princeton University Press.

Organization of American States, 2010. Informe de la misión de observación electoral de la OEA sobre las elecciones generales celebradas en la república de Costa Rica el 7 de febrero de 2010. Observaciones Electorales, Serie Américas, No.55. OEA/Ser. D/XX. SG/DCOE/II.55 ISBN 978-0-8270-5459-2.

Ostrom, Elinor. (2005). *Understanding Institutional Diversity*. Princeton: Princeton University Press.

Ottone, Ernesto. (2012). "The Non-global Global Crisis: Latin America in the Globalization Process," in Manuel Castells et al. (eds), *Aftermath: The Cultures of the Economic Crisis*. Oxford: Oxford University Press.

El Pais, 16 May 2012. San José, Costa Rica.

PAPEP-UNDP. (2012). *Las protestas sociales en América Latina*. Buenos Aires: Siglo XXI.

Patel, V. (2010). "Human Rights Movements in India." Available at: <http://sndtunivsped.academia.edu/VibhutiPatelsndt/Papers/567708/Human_Rights_Movements_in_ India_by_Vibhuti_Patel>

Pestieau, Pierre. (2006). *The Welfare State in the European Union: Economic and Social Perspectives*. Oxford: Oxford University Press.

PIC [Project Internet Catalunya]. (2004a). *The Barcelona II Model: Barcelona City Council in Catalonia's Network Society*. <http://www.uoc.edu/in3/pic/eng/city_council.html>

PIC [Project Internet Catalunya]. (2004b). *e-Government and Public Services: A Case Study of the Internet Administrative Portal CAT365*. <http://www.uoc.edu/in3/pic/eng/egovernment.html>

PIC [Project Internet Catalunya]. (2004c). *Internet and the Catalan University Network*. <http://www.uoc.edu/in3/pic/eng/university_network.html>

PIC [Project Internet Catalunya]. (2006). *e-Governance and Citizen Information: The Generalitat of Catalonia in the International Context*. <http://www.uoc.edu/in3/pic/eng/egovernance.html>

PIC [Project Internet Catalunya]. (2007a). *e-Health and Society: An Empirical Study of Catalonia.* <http://www.uoc.edu/in3/pic/eng/health.html>

PIC [Project Internet Catalunya]. (2007b). *Schooling in the Network Society: The Internet in Primary and Secondary Education.* <http://www.uoc.edu/in3/pic/eng/network_school.html>

PIC [Project Internet Catalunya]. (2008). *University and the Network Society.* <http://www.uoc.edu/in3/pic/eng/university_network_society.html>

Pillay, P. (2010). *Linking Higher Education and Economic Development: Implications for Africa from Three Successful Systems.* Cape Town: Centre for Higher Education Transformation (CHET).

Pizzorno, A. (1984). "Sistema social y clase política," in *Historia de las ideas políticas económicas y sociales.* México: Folios.

Poder Judicial, Departamento de Planificación. (2010). *Compendio de indicadores actualizados.* San José, Costa Rica: Poder Judicial.

Preston, Peter W. (1996). *Development Theory: An Introduction to the Analysis of Complex Change.* Oxford: Blackwell. London: Zed Books.

Programa de las Naciones Unidas para el Desarrollo. (2004). *La democracia en América Latina. Hacia una democracia de ciudadanas y ciudadanos. Compendio estadístico.* 1 UN Plaza, New York, New York, 10017, Estados Unidos de América.

Programa Estado de la Nación en Desarrollo Humano Sostenible. (2009). *Estado de la Nación en Desarrollo Humano Sostenible (Costa Rica).* Decimoquinto Informe Estado de la Nación en Desarrollo Humano Sostenible/ Programa Estado de la Nación. San José, Costa Rica.

Programa Estado de la Nación en Desarrollo Humano Sostenible. (2011). *Estado de la Educación costarricense.* San José, Costa Rica.

PROSIC (Programa de la Sociedad de la información y el Conocimiento) (2011). *Los jóvenes costarricenses en la sociedad de la información.* Universidad de Costa Rica. San José, Costa Rica.

Quesada Camacho, Juan Rafael. (1999). *Costa Rica Contemporánea: Las raíces del Estado de la Nación.* Editorial de la Universidad de Costa Rica. San José, Costa Rica.

Rahkonen, Juho. (2011). Perussuomalaisten ruumiinavaus. *Yhteiskuntapolitiikka* 76 (2011):4.

Rahnema, Majid. (2013). *Quand la pauvrete chasse la misère.* Paris: Fayard/Actes Sud.

Rahnema, Majid and Bawtree, Victoria (eds). (1997). *The Postdevelopment Reader.* London: Zed Books.

Rao, V. and Walton, M. (eds). (2004). *Culture and Public Action.* Stanford University Press.

Rapley, John. (2007). *Understanding Development.* Boulder, Colorado: Lynne Rienner Publishers.

Rawls, J. (1971). *A Theory of Justice.* Cambridge, MA: Harvard University Press.

References

Rawls, J. (2001). *Justice as Fairness: A Restatement.* Erin Kelly, ed. Cambridge, MA: Harvard University Press.

Republic of South Africa. (1996). *The Constitution of the Republic of South Africa.* Pretoria: Government Printers. <http://www.info.gov.za/documents/constitution/1996/a108-96.pdf>

Republic of South Africa. (2007). *Growth Employment and Redistribution Strategy,* available at <http://www.treasury.gov.za/publications/other/gear/chapters.pdf>

Republic of South Africa. (2009). *Accelerated Shared Growth Initiative for South Africa,* available at <http://www.thepresidency.gov.za/pebble.asp?relid=390>

Republic of South Africa, Parliament. (2012). *State of the Nation Address 2012.* Cape Town. <http://www.info.gov.za/speech/DynamicAction?pageid=461&sid=24980&tid=55960> accessed 17 July 2012.

Research ICT Africa. (2012). "Africa Prepaid Mobile Price Index 2012," *Research ICT Africa.* Cape Town. <http://www.researchictafrica.net/fair_mobile.php> accessed 17 July 2012.

Richardson, H., and Weithman, P. (eds.) (1999). *The Philosophy of Rawls: A Collection of Essays,* 5 vol., New York: Garland.

Roberts, A. (2010). *The Logic of Discipline: Global Capitalism and the Architecture of Government.* New York: Oxford University Press.

Rogers, Everett. (1984). *Silicon Valley Fever.* New York: Basic Books.

Rohman, I. and Bohlin, E. (2011). "Towards the Alternative Measurement: Discovering the Relationship Between Technology Adoption and Quality of Life in Indonesia," *Proceedings of 22nd European Regional ITS Conference.* Budapest, 18–21 September 2011.

Rojas, C. (2011). "La multi crisis global," in PAPEP-UNIR, *Los conflictos sociales en América Latina.* La Paz: Plural.

Röller, L.H. and Waverman, L. (2001). "Telecommunications Infrastructure and Economic Development: A Simultaneous Approach," *American Economic Review,* vol. 91, no.4, pp. 909–23.

Román, Isabel. (2009). *Sustentabilidad de los programas de transferencias condicionadas. La experiencia del Instituo Mixto de Ayuda Social y el Programa "Avancemos" en Costa Rica.* Social development division of ECLAC, in the framework of the project "La Sustentabilidad de los programas de transferencias condicionadas" (GER/09/001).

Room, G. (1995). *Beyond the Threshold: The Measurement and Analysis of Social Exclusion.* Bristol: Polity Press.

Sala, Enric. (2008). *El modelo pacifista costarricense.* San José, Costa Rica: Editorial Hidalgo S.A.

SAMDI. (2006). *Strategies, Programmes and Capabilities for building state capacity.* Public Service and Administration Department (Unpublished).

Sapir, Andre. (2005). *Globalisation and the Reform of the Welfare State.* Brussels: Bruegel.

Sauma, Pablo and Marco V Sánchez. (2003). *Exportaciones, crecimiento económico, desigualdad y pobreza. El caso de Costa Rica.* San José, Costa Rica: Editorial Isis.

Sauma Fiatt, Pablo and Isidora Chacón (2006). *Aspectos económicos relacionados con la (in)seguridad ciudadana.* 1st. edn. San José, Costa Rica: Programa de las Naciones Unidas para el Desarrollo, 2006.

Saxenian, AnnaLee. (1983). "The Urban Contradictions of Silicon Valley," *International Journal of Urban and Regional Research* V. 7, n.2.

Saxenian, AnnaLee. (1994). *Regional Advantage: Culture and Competition in Silicon Valley and Route 128.* Cambridge, MA: Harvard University Press.

Saxenian, AnnaLee. (2006). *The New Argonauts: Regional Advantage in a Global Economy.* Cambridge, MA: Harvard University Press.

Schmidt, J.P. and Stork, C. (2008). "E-skills: Towards Evidence-based Policy," Vol.1, Policy Paper no. 3, <http://www.researchictafrica.net/publications/Towards_Evidence-based_ICT_Policy_and_Regulation_-_Volume_1/RIA%20Policy%20Paper%20Vol%201%20Paper%203%20-%20e-skills.pdf>

Schneider, B. R. (1999). "The Desarrollista State in Brazl and Mexico." In M. Woo-Cummings (Ed.), *The Developmental State.* New York: Cornell University Press.

Schor, Juliet. (2010). *Plenitude.* New York: The Penguin Press.

Schumpeter, Joseph. (1942). *Capitalism, Socialism and Democracy.* London: G. Allen & Unwin.

Scopus. (2013). SCImago Journal & Country Rank. http://www.scimagojr.com

Seligman, Martin. (2002). *Authentic Happiness: Using the New Positive Psychology to Realize Your Potential for Lasting Fulfillment.* New York: Free Press.

Seligman, Martin. (2011). *Flourish: A Visionary New Understanding of Happiness and Well-being.* New York: Free Press.

Sen, Amartya (1980). "Equality of What?," in Sterling McMurrin (ed.), *Tanner Lectures on Human Values.* Cambridge: Cambridge University Press.

Sen, Amartya (1981). *Poverty and Famines: An Essay on Entitlements and Deprivation.* Oxford: Clarendon Press, Oxford University Press.

Sen, Amartya (1997). *Choice Welfare and Measurement.* Cambridge, Ma: Harvard University Press.

Sen, Amartya (1997). *La liberta individuale come impegno sociale.* Rome: Editori Laterza.

Sen, Amartya (1998). *Bienestar, justicia y mercado.* Barcelona: Paidós.

Sen, Amartya (1999). *Development as Freedom.* Oxford: Oxford University Press.

Sen, Amartya (2003a). "Development as Capability Expansion," in S. Fakuda-Parr and A. K. Shiva Kumar (eds), *Readings in Human Development.* Oxford: Oxford University Press.

Sen, Amartya (2003b). "Human Rights and Human Development," in S. Fakuda-Parr and A. K. Shiva Kumar (eds), *Readings in Human Development.* Oxford: Oxford University Press.

Sen, Amartya (2009). *The Idea of Justice.* Cambridge, MA: Harvard University Press.

References

Sen, A. and Klisberg, B. (2007). *People First.* Bilbao: Deusto.

Sey, Araba. (2011). "We Use It Different: Making Sense of Trends in Mobile Phone Use in Ghana," *New Media Society,* 13: 375.

Sey, Araba, et al. (2013). "Connecting People for Development: Why Public Access ICTs matter." Seattle: University of Washington, School of Information Science, Technology and Social Change Group.

Shambaugh, David. (2008). *China's Communist Party: Atrophy and Adaptation.* Berkeley and Los Angeles: University of California Press.

Sheppard, C. and Sheppard, R. (2011). "A Statistical Overview of Further Education and Training Colleges," in Perold, H., Cloete, N. and Papier, J. (eds), *Shaping the Future of South Africa's Youth: Rethinking Post-school Education and Skills Training.* Cape Town: Centre for Higher Education Transformation.

Silicon Valley Leadership Group. (2013). "Silicon Valley CEO Survey Business Climate 2013," <http://svlg.org/wp-content/uploads/2013/03/CEO_Survey_2013.pdf>

Social Science Research Council. (2012). *Measure of America: About Human Development.* New York: SSRC (web publication).

Solow, Robert. (1956). "A Contribution to the Theory of Economic Growth," Quarterly Journal of Economics, 70 (1).

Somma, N. (2012). "The Chilean Student Movement of 2011-2012: Challenging the Marketization of Education," *Interface: A Journal for and About Social Movements Event Analysis,* Volume 4 (2): 296–309, November 2012 <http://www.interfacejournal.net/wordpress/wp-content/uploads/2012/11/Interface-4-2-Somma.pdf>

Spector, J.B. (2013). "Crumbling Infrastructure, Red Tape and Fear of Nationalisation Shaft South Africa's Mineral Wealth," *Good Governance Africa.* <http://www.ggaa.org/analysis/crumbling-infrastructure-red-tape-andfear-of-nationalisation-shaft-south-africa2019s-mineral-wealth>

SRI International. (1992). Center for Economic Competitiveness, "An Economy At Risk," Prepared for Joint Venture: Silicon Valley Network. San Jose, CA.

Stamen Design. (2012). "The City from the Valley," <http://stamen.com/zero1/>

Statistics South Africa (Stats SA). (2005). *Income and Expenditure of Households 2005/2006: Analysis of Results.* Pretoria. <http://www.statssa.gov.za/Publications/statsdownload.asp?PPN=Report-01-00-01>

Statistics South Africa (Stats SA). (2010). *General Household Survey 2010.* Pretoria. <http://www.statssa.gov.za/publications/P0318/P0318June2010.pdf> accessed 17 July 2012.

Statistics South Africa (Stat SA). (2011). *Census 2011.* Pretoria. <https://www.statssa.gov.za/census2011/default.asp>

Stern, Nicholas. (2007). *The Economics of Climate Change: The Stern Review.* Cambridge: Cambridge University Press.

Stevenson, Betsey and Wolfers, Justin. (2008). "Economic Growth and Subjective Well-Being: Reassessing the Easterlin Paradox," Brooking's Papers on Economic Activity, Spring 2008.

Stiglitz, J. (2009). "The Great GDP Swindle," *The Guardian*. <http://www.guardian.co.uk/commentisfree/2009/sep/13/economics-economic-growth-and-recession-global-economy>

Stiglitz, Joseph, Sen, Amartya, and Fitoussi, Jean-Paul. (2009). *Report by the Commission on the Measurement of Economic Performance and Social Progress*. (Published as *Mismeasuring Our Lives* by the New Press in 2010.)

STM. (1995). *Sosiaali- ja terveydenhuollon tietoteknologian hyödyntämisstrategia*. Helsinki: Sosiaali- ja terveysministeriön työryhmämuistioita. 1995:27.

Taylor, N. (2011). *Priorities for Addressing South Africa's Education and Training Crisis: A Review Commissioned by the National Planning Commission*. Braamfontein: JET Education Services.

Terplan, Egon. (2013). "Strengthening the Bay Area's Regional Governance," 2013 Special Analysis, *Silicon Valley Index*. San Jose, CA: Silicon Valley Community Foundation.

Terreblanche, S. (2012). *Lost in Transformation*. Johannesburg: KMM Review Publishing Company.

The Mandiant Report. (2013). "APT 1: Exposing one of China's Cyber Espionage Units," (<http://www.mandiant.com>). For the analysis of the controversy, see <http://www.nbcnews.com/technology/technolog/mandiant-goes-viral-after-china-hacking-report-1C8513891>

Times Live. (2012). "Life expectancy in South Africa rises to 60." <http://www.timeslive.co.za/lifestyle/family/2012/11/30/life-expectancy-in-south-africa-rises-to-60-report>

Tocqueville, A. (1969). *Democracy in America*. New York, Doubleday.

Touraine, Alain. (1973). *Production de la société*. Paris: Seuil.

Touraine, Alain. (1984). *Le retour de l'acteur. Essai de sociologie*. Paris: Fayard.

Touraine, Alain. (1988). *La parole et le sang*. Paris: Editions Odile Jacob.

Touraine, Alain. (1997). *Pourrons-nous vivre ensemble? Égaux et différents*. París: Fayard.

Touraine, Alain. (2005). *Un nouveau paradigme*. Paris: Fayard.

Transparency International, 2010. *Informe global de la corrupción Edición 2006: Corrupción y salud*. Primera edición en castellano, julio de 2007. 300 New York Avenue, NW. Washington, DC 20577, Estados Unidos de América, <http://www.iadb.org/pub>

Tuomioja, Erkki. (1996). *Pekka Kuusi: alkoholipoliitikko, sosiaalipoliitikko, ihmiskuntapoliitikko*. Helsinki: Tammi.

Ul-Haq, Mahbub. (1995). "*Desarrollo Humano Sostenible. Nuevo enfoque del desarrollo.*" La Paz: UNDP.

References

Ul-Haq, Mahbub. (1999). *Reflections on Human Development*, 2nd ed. Oxford: Oxford University Press.

Ul-Haque, Irfan and Bell, Martin. (1998). *Trade, Technology and International Competitiveness*. Washington, DC: Institute of Development Studies of the World Bank.

UN. (2012). *Rio+20*. United Nations Conference on Sustainable Development.

UNCTAD (2004) THE DIGITAL DIVIDE: ICT DEVELOPMENT INDICES available at <http://unctad.org/en/docs/iteipc20054_en.pdf>

UNDATA. (2011). United Nations Data. Available online: <http://data.un.org/>

UNDESA. (2011). Intellectual Property Statistics.

UNDP (1993). *Human Development 1993, People's Participation*. New York: Oxford University Press.

UNDP (1999). *Globalization with a Human Face*. HDR 1999.

UNDP (2000). *Human Development Report 2000: Human Rights and Human Development*. New York: Oxford University Press.

UNDP (2001). *Making New Technologies Work With Human Development*. HDR 2001.

UNDP (2002). *Deepening Democracy in a Fragmented World*. HDR 2002.

UNDP (2004). *Human Development Report 2004: Cultural Liberty in Today's Diverse World*. New York: Oxford University Press.

UNDP (2004a). *La democracia en América Latina*. Buenos Aires: Alfaguara.

UNDP (2004b). *Cultural Liberty in Today's Diverse World*. HDR 2004.

UNDP (2007/8). *Fighting Climate Change*. HDR 2007/8.

UNDP (2008). *Ciudadanía y desarrollo humano. Cuaderno I de gobernabilidad democrática*. Buenos Aires: Siglo XXI.

UNDP (2009). *Informe de Desarrollo Humano para el MERCOSUR 2009–2010. Innovar para incluir: jóvenes y desarrollo humano*. Buenos Aires, Zorzal.

UNDP (2010). *Informe Regional sobre Desarrollo Humano para América Latina y el Caribe. Actuar sobre el futuro: romper la transmisión intergeneracional de la desigualdad*.

UNDP (2011). *Sustainability and Equity a Better Future for All*. HDR 2011.

UNDP (2013). *Human Development Report 2013*. <http://hdr.undp.org/en/media/HDR_2013_EN_complete.pdf>

UNDP-Bolivia. (2002). HDR Bolivia 2002. *Political Capabilities for Human Development*. La Paz, UNDP.

UNDP-Bulgaria. (1998). HDR Bulgaria 1998. *The State of Transition and Transition of the State*. Sofia, UNDP.

UNDP-Chile. (1998). HDR Chile 1998. *Paradoxes of Modernity: Human Security*. Santiago de Chile: UNDP.

UNDP-Egypt. (2002). HDR Egypt 2002. El Cairo, UNDP.

UNDP-Egypt. (2010). HDR Egypt 2010. *Youth in Egypt*. El Cairo: UNDP.

UNDP-PAPEP. (2008). *Escenarios políticos en América Latina. Conceptos Métodos y Observatorio Regional*. Buenos Aires: Siglo XXI.

UNDP-Sao Tome and Príncipe. (2004). *Rapport National sur le Development Humain.* Sao Tome and Príncipe: UNDP.

UNESCO [United Nations Educational, Scientific and Cultural Organization]. (2012). Institute for Statistics. <http://stats.uis.unesco.org>

UN General Assembly. (2011). *Happiness: Towards a Holistic Approach to Development.* A/RES/65/309. 19 July 2011.

UNSDSN (United Nations Sustainable Development). (2013). *World Happiness Report 2013,* edited by John Helliwell, Richard Layard, and Jeffrey Sachs. New York: UNSDSN.

US Department of Labor STAN. (2012). Bureau of Labor Statistics Databases. <http://www.bls.gov/data/#productivity>

Varian, Hal. (2010). "Computer Mediated Transactions," *American Economic Review,* v. 100, n. 2.

Veenhoven, Ruut. (2005). "Apparent Quality-of-Life In Nations: How Long and Happy People Live," Social Indicators Research, 71 (1).

Veenhoven, Ruut and Hagerty, Michael. (2006). "Rising Happiness in Nations 1946–2004: A Reply to Easterlin," Social Indicators Research, 79 (3).

Vera, H. (2012). "Epistemologías comunicacionales para comprender el movimiento estudiantil 2011 en Chile," *Razón y palabra.* Número 79, mayo 2012 <http://www.razonypalabra.org.mx/N/N79/V79/24_Vera_V79.pdf>

VM [Valtiovarainministeriö]. (2010). *Julkinen talous tienhaarassa: Finanssipolitiikan suunta 2010-luvulla.* Helsinki: Valtiovarainministeriö.

VM [Valtiovarainministeriö]. (2012). *Kansantalousosaston laskelma eri tekijöiden vaikutuksesta kestävyysvajeeseen.*

VNK [Valtioneuvoston kanslia]. (2011). *Työurat pidemmiksi—työeläkejärjestelmän kehittämisvaihtoehtojen tarkastelua. Työurien pidentämistä selvittävän työryhmän raportti.* Helsinki: Valtioneuvoston kanslia.

VTV. (2012). Valtionavustukset sosiaali- ja terveydenhuollon IT-hankkeissa. Helsinki: Edita.

Wallis, Cara. (2011). "New Media Practices in China: Youth Patterns, Processes, and Politics," *International Journal of Communication,* 5: 406–36.

Walsham, Geoff. (2013). "Development Informatics in a Changing World: Reflections from ICTD 2010/2012," *Information Technologies and International Development* 9(1) (Spring): 49–54.

Walzer, M. (1996). *Las esferas de la justicia.* México: FCE.

Walzer, M. (1998). *Tratado sobre la tolerancia.* Barcelona: Paidós.

Web of Science. (2010). *Thomson Reuters Journal Citation Reports.* <http://thomsonreuters.com/products_services/science/science_products/a-z/journal_citation_reports/> accessed 17 July 2012.

WEF [World Economic Forum]. (2007). *Young Global Leaders Future Mapping for the Global Agenda 2030.* Zurich: Roland Berger.

References

WEF [World Economic Forum]. (2010). *The Global Competitiveness Report 2009–2010.* Geneva: World Economic Forum.

WEF [World Economic Forum]. (2011). *The Global Competitiveness Report 2011–2012.* Geneva: World Economic Forum.

WEF [World Economic Forum]. (2013). *The Global Competitiveness Report 2012–2013.* Geneva: World Economic Forum.

WEF [World Economic Forum]. (2012). *e-readiness Report.* Geneva: World Economic Forum.

WEF [World Economic Forum] with INSEA. (Various years). *Global Technology Report: The Networking Readiness Index.* Geneva: World Economic Forum.

Weiler, H. (1984). "The Political Economy of Education and Development," *Prospects.* vol.19, no.4, pp. 468–77.

Weithman, P. (2011). *Why Political Liberalism? On John Rawls's Political Turn.* Oxford: Oxford University Press.

Wieviorka, M. (2008). *Neuf lecóns de sociology.* Paris: Robert Lafont.

Wilde, G. (2012). "If You're Not Worried About Your Growing Debt, You Don't Understand the Problem!" *Wilde-insights.* <http://blog.wilde-insights.co.za/?p=219>

Wilkinson, Will. (2007). "In Pursuit of Happiness Research: Is It Reliable? What Does It Imply for Policy?," Policy Analysis, No. 590, April 2007.

Willis, Katie. (2011). *Theories and Practices of Development.* London: Routledge.

Wilson, Ernest. (2004). *The Information Revolution and Developing Countries.* Cambridge, MA: MIT Press.

WHO [World Health Organisation]. (1946). "WHO Definition of Health: Preamble to the Constitution of the World Health Organization," as adopted by the International Health Conference, New York, 19–22 June 1946 (signed on 22 July 1946 by the representatives of 61 States and entered into force on 7 April 1948). Geneva: WHO.

WHO [World Health Organisation]. (2008). *The Global Burden of Disease: 2004 Update.* Geneva: WHO.

WIPO (2012). WIPO [World Intellectual Property Organization] (2012). Intellectual Property Statistics. <http://www.wipo.int/ipstats/en/>

Wolpe, H. (1972). "Capitalism and Cheap Labour-Power in South Africa: From Segregation to Apartheid," *Economy and Society,* Vol.1, no.4, pp. 425–56.

Woo-Cumings, Meredith. (1999). *The Developmental State.* Cornell University Press.

Woolard, I. and Leibbrandt, M. (2011). *A Conceptual Framework for Social Security in South Africa.* Paper for the National Planning Commission Office of the President of South Africa.

World Bank Group/MIGA (2006). The impact of Intel in Costa Rica. Nine years after the decision to invest. 1818 H Street, NW Washington, DC 20433.

WB [World Bank]. (2012). *World Development Indicators.* Washington, DC: World Bank. http://data.worldbank.org

World Bank. (2012a). *Closing the Skills and Technological Gaps in South Africa*. Washington, DC.

World Bank. (2012b). *South Africa Economic Update: Focus on Inequality of Opportunity*. Washington, DC.

World Internet Project. (2010). "World Internet and Work Productivity, 2010," in *2010 Report*. World Internet Project.

Xiong, Jianfeng. (2013). Survey of the scale of the government payroll (*zhongguo caizheng gongyang guimo diaocha*). *Phoenix Weekly*, No 10, April 22, 2013. <http://big5. xinhuanet.com/gate/big5/forum.home.news.cn/thread/123108644/1.html>

Xun, Liu. (2010). "Online Posting Anxiety: Impacts of Blogging," *Chinese Journal of Communication,* 3(2): 202–22.

Yang, Chunli. (2013). "The Contribution of Information Consumption to GDP (xinxi xiaofei dui jingjinzengzhanglu gongxian youduoda)," 8-20-2013. *Eastern Morning News* (*dongfang zaobao*).

Yang, Guobin. (2009). *The Power of the Internet in China: Citizen Activism Online*. New York: Columbia University Press.

Yang, Jisheng. (2011). "Analysis of Social Class of Contemporary China (*dongdai zhongguo shehui jieceng fenxi*)," Jiangxi gaoxiao publisher.

Yang, Ruilong, Wang, Yuan, and Nie, Huihua. (2013). "Mechanism of Bureaucrats' promotion: Evidence from National-level State-owned Enterprises (*zhunguanyuan dejinshen jizhi: laizi yangqide zhengju*)," *World of Management* (*guanli shijie*), No 3.

Yangzi, Sima and Pugsley, Peter. (2010). "The Rise of a 'Me Culture' in Postsocialist China: Youth Individualism and Identity Creation in the Chinese Blogosphere," *International Communications Gazette*, 72(3): 287–306.

Yu, Jianrong. (2009). "The Bottom Line of Social Stability (*shouzhu shehui wending de dixian*)," lecture at the Association of Attorney in Beijing, Dec 26, 2009. <http://hkwalker.net/v3/archives/3139>

Yuting, Han. (2011). "A Class in the Chinese Communist Party Academy (*dangxiao yike*)," *The Economic Observer,* 2011-11-26. <http://www.eeo.com.cn/2011/1126/216587.shtml>

Zhong, Wu. (2008). "'Paper Tiger' Tales Shred Credibility," *Asia Times,* April 3, 2008. <http://www.atimes.com/atimes/China/JD03Ad01.html>

Zhou, Feizhou. (2006). "Ten Years of Tax Reforms: The System and its Impact (fenshuizhi shinian: zhidu jiqi yingxiang)," Chinese Social Sciences (zhongguo shehui kexue), No. 5, p.110–15.

Zou, Weiguo. (2013). "The Policy Behind Information Consumption (xinxi xiaofei beihoude jingji shizheng luxiantu)," <http://finance.people.com.cn/n/2013/0815/c1004-22569316.html>

Index

Index

Index

Index

Index